FEMALE FRIENDS AND
TRANSATLANTIC QUAI

Quaker women were unusually active participants in seventeenth- and eighteenth-century cultural and religious exchange, as ministers, missionaries, authors, and spiritual leaders. Drawing upon documentary evidence, with a focus on women's personal writings and correspondence, Naomi Pullin explores the lives and social interactions of Quaker women in the British Atlantic between 1650 and 1750. Through a comparative methodology, focused on Britain and the North American colonies, Pullin examines the experiences of both those women who travelled and preached and those who stayed at home. The book approaches the study of gender and religion from a new perspective by placing women's roles, relationships, and identities at the centre of the analysis. It shows how the movement's transition from 'sect to church' enhanced the authority and influence of women within the movement and uncovers the multifaceted ways in which female Friends at all levels of the Society were active participants in making and sustaining transatlantic Quakerism.

NAOMI PULLIN is a Leverhulme Trust Early Career Fellow at the University of Cambridge and Research Associate at St John's College.

FEMALE FRIENDS AND THE MAKING OF TRANSATLANTIC QUAKERISM, 1650–1750

NAOMI PULLIN
University of Cambridge

CAMBRIDGE
UNIVERSITY PRESS

CAMBRIDGE
UNIVERSITY PRESS

University Printing House, Cambridge CB2 8BS, United Kingdom

One Liberty Plaza, 20th Floor, New York, NY 10006, USA

477 Williamstown Road, Port Melbourne, VIC 3207, Australia

314-321, 3rd Floor, Plot 3, Splendor Forum, Jasola District Centre, New Delhi - 110025, India

79 Anson Road, #06-04/06, Singapore 079906

Cambridge University Press is part of the University of Cambridge.

It furthers the University's mission by disseminating knowledge in the pursuit of education, learning and research at the highest international levels of excellence.

www.cambridge.org
Information on this title: www.cambridge.org/9781316649626
DOI: 10.1017/9781108225069

© Naomi Pullin 2018

First published 2018
First paperback edition 2020

A catalogue record for this publication is available from the British Library

Library of Congress Cataloging in Publication data
Names: Pullin, Naomi, 1987– author.
Title: Female friends and the making of transatlantic quakerism, 1650–1750 /
Naomi Pullin, University of Cambridge.
Description: New York: Cambridge University Press, 2018. |
Series: Cambridge studies in early modern British history |
Includes bibliographical references and index.
Identifiers: LCCN 2017053513 | ISBN 9781316510230 (hardback)
Subjects: LCSH: Quaker women – History. | Female friendship –
Religious aspects – Christianity. | Society of Friends – History.
Classification: LCC BX7748.W64 P85 2018 | DDC 289.6082–dc23
LC record available at https://lccn.loc.gov/2017053513

ISBN 978-1-316-51023-0 Hardback
ISBN 978-1-316-64962-6 Paperback

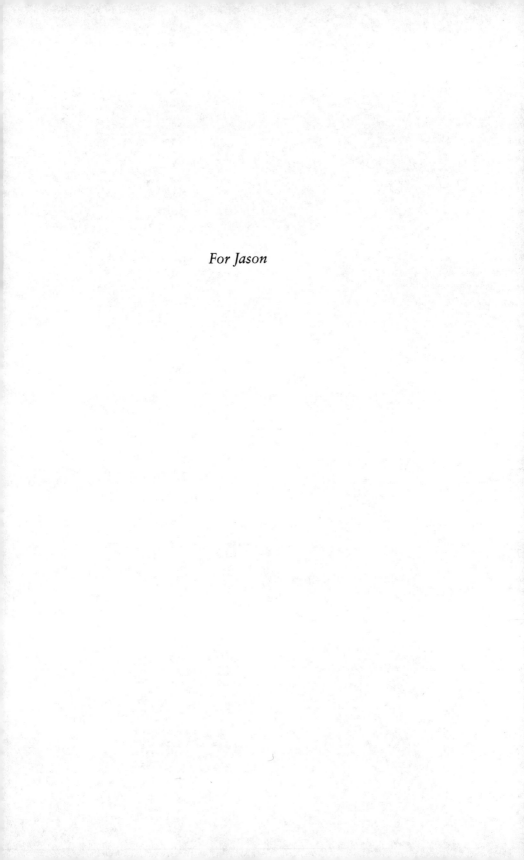

For Jason

CONTENTS

List of Figures and Tables   *page* viii
Acknowledgements   xi
Note to the Reader   xiii
List of Abbreviations   xv

    Introduction   1

1 Spiritual Housewives and Mothers in Israel: Quaker
    Domestic Relationships   33

2 'A Government of Women': Authority and Community
    within the Quaker Women's Meetings   93

3 'United by This Holy Cement': The Constructions,
    Practices, and Experiences of Female Friendship   152

4 'In the World, but Not of It': Quaker Women's
    Interactions with the Non-Quaker World   200

    Conclusion: Quakerism Reconsidered   252

Appendix 1 Male and Female Friends Ministering in Ireland   263
Appendix 2 Tasks Undertaken by the Women's and
  Men's Monthly Meetings   264
Appendix 3 A Recurring Network of Gossips   267
Appendix 4 Ecclesiastical Licensed Midwives at Quaker
  Births, 1680–1690   269
Bibliography   271
Index   293

FIGURES AND TABLES

FIGURES

1.1 Page containing a recipe 'to make a Good salve' from
the almanac Mary Weston carried on her travels in
Pennsylvania in 1751. © Religious Society of Friends
(Quakers) in Britain. LRSF MS Box 6_18   *page 63*

2.1 Chester Meeting House. © Haverford College
Quaker and Special Collections (Haverford, PA).
Identifier HC12-15707   106

4.1 *The Quakers Meeting*, engraved by Marcel Lauron
after Egbert van Heemskerck I, c. 1640–1680.
© Religious Society of Friends (Quakers) in Britain.
LRSF 88_AXL70   209

4.2 *A Quaker*, attributed to Richard Gaywood,
c. 1665–1675. © Religious Society of Friends
(Quakers) in Britain. LRSF Q1   213

4.3 *Thomas Venner*, Anon., c. 1662. © Religious Society
of Friends (Quakers) in Britain. LRSF 80_N128   215

TABLES

2.1 Items of Business in the Women's and Men's Meetings
of Chester, Burlington, Marsden, and Kendal,
1700–1705   109

2.2 Items of Business in the Women's and Men's
Meetings of Chester, Burlington, Fairfax, Marsden,
Kendal, and Tipperary, 1745–1750   111

2.3   Family Connections between Chester, Burlington,
       Fairfax, Marsden, Kendal, and Tipperary Men's and
       Women's Meetings, 1700–1705 and 1745–1750   143
A1.1   Proportion of Male and Female Ministers Who
       Visited Ireland between 1655 and 1750   263
A4.1   Midwives Attendant at Quaker Women's Births
       between 1680 and 1690, as Recorded in the
       London and Middlesex Birth Notes   269

ACKNOWLEDGEMENTS

This book has benefitted from the input of so many people and I am immensely grateful to them all. The initial research for this book was undertaken for my doctorate at the University of Warwick, which was supported by a Warwick Postgraduate Research Scholarship. As a PhD student, I was fortunate to have worked with two inspiring and generous scholars, Mark Knights and Bernard Capp. Both have been constant sources of inspiration and have been fundamental in challenging the direction and scope of my work, which has taken me in directions I would never have anticipated. I could not have wished for two better role models.

The research for this project would not have been possible without financial assistance from various sources. My thanks go to the Royal Historical Society, Economic History Society, Newberry Center for the Renaissance Studies, Andrew W. Mellon Foundation, University of Warwick Humanities Research Fund, University of Warwick American Study and Student Exchange Committee, Higgs and Cooper Educational Charity, and Callum McDonald Memorial. As a postdoctoral researcher, the Queen Mary Centre for Eighteenth Century Studies and British Society for Eighteenth Century Studies awarded me an Early Career Visiting Fellowship and the John Brockway Foundation awarded me a fellowship to conduct research at the Huntington Library, California.

I have been privileged to gain access to some of the most important archival collections of Quaker history and would like to express my special thanks to the hardworking and knowledgeable archivists and librarians at the Library of the Religious Society of Friends, London; Haverford College Quaker and Special Collections; Friends Historical Library, Swarthmore; Historical Society of Pennsylvania and Library Company of Philadelphia; and the Huntington Library.

My research has benefitted greatly from discussions with a number of researchers, and I have been incredibly fortunate to work alongside so many intelligent and thoughtful people on both sides of the Atlantic. I would especially like to thank my thesis examiners Alexandra Walsham and Gabriel Glickman for their helpful suggestions on the revision of the text. Alexandra Walsham in particular encouraged me to publish, and I remain indebted to her generosity, enthusiasm, and support. I am also grateful to a number of other historians and friends who have shown an interest in my work, and have offered helpful comments at various stages: Elizabeth Bouldin, Jennifer Crane, Rebecca Earle, Catie Gill, Kathryn Gleadle, Amanda Herbert, Steve Hindle, David Hitchcock, Grace Huxford, Erin Maglaque, Peter Marshall, John Morgan, Jan Machielsen, Hannah Murphy, Mark Philp, Lyndal Roper, Tessa Whitehouse, and Kathryn Woods.

The preparation of this book for publication was undertaken whilst at the University of Warwick and the University of Oxford. At both institutions, I benefitted from friendship and collegiality at a difficult stage in my career. I was employed on an eighteen-month contract as a Teaching Fellow at the University of Warwick. Had this been a shorter contract, I would not have been in a position to rewrite chapters of this book over the 2016 summer vacation.

During my first research trip to Pennsylvania, I was fortunate to have received the hospitality and support of the International Police Association. I am particularly thankful to Mary Ciacco, and the other members of my American host-family, who made my first research experience abroad so thoroughly enjoyable. The American focus of my thesis is greatly indebted to their kindness, generosity, and good spirits.

I am extremely grateful to my parents, Tim and Andrea Wood, for their loving encouragement. Their kindness, understanding, and belief in me have sustained me through many difficult times. For this and for much more, I am truly thankful. I also extend my gratitude to the rest of my family and my extended family, especially Joe Wood, Sheila and Bernard Pullin, Dave and Sue Hurran, and Andrea, Carol, and Phil Preedy.

I would finally like to thank my husband Jason, who I mention last but is always put first. This monograph would not have been possible without his good humour, love, generosity, and patience. His unwavering support as well as constant encouragement have been much more than I could have asked for, and whilst the gesture by no means repays the debt, this book is dedicated to him.

NOTE TO THE READER

The Quakers were a highly literate community, but their spelling and syntax were often inconsistent. As far as possible, all quotations from contemporary manuscript and printed works retain original punctuation, italicisation, capitalisation, and spelling. Although I have endeavoured to keep all quotations as near as possible to the original manuscript and printed sources, most abbreviations have been silently expanded. This includes the '&' symbol, aside from its function as '&c'. The use of 'u' and 'v', 'i' and 'j', and 'ye' and 'yat' have been replaced with their modern alternatives. Any other alterations to the text have been presented in brackets.

Quakers called March '1st month', April '2[n]d month', and so forth. The Quaker system of dating has therefore been altered to conform to modern practice, whereby 1st month becomes March for all items preceding the change to the Gregorian calendar in 1752. All years have been taken to begin on 1 January, so an item bearing the date '11 12mo 1666', has been transcribed as '11 February 1667'. Any reference made to 1st month after the calendar change in 1752, is presumed to mean January.

'Public Friend' was the formal name given to an individual, whether male or female, who was authorised by the movement to preach in other Meetings and to non-Quaker audiences. I also use the terms 'ministers', 'missionaries', and 'preachers' to denote individuals who travelled to speak about their faith and religious convictions.

Quaker Meetings reserved the title 'Elder' for those appointed to attend the select Meetings for Ministers and Elders, which had monthly, quarterly, and yearly components. However, in this study, the term will be applied more loosely to refer to any Meeting official who provided spiritual and moral guidance to the rest of the congregation.

ABBREVIATIONS

Besse, *Quaker Sufferings*	Joseph Besse, *A Collection of the Sufferings of the People Called Quakers* (2 vols., London, 1753)
FHL	Friends Historical Library, Swarthmore College, PA
FHLD	Friends Historical Library Dublin
fol./fols.	folio/folios
HCQSC	Haverford College Quaker and Special Collections, Haverford, PA
HL	Huntington Library, San Marino, CA
HSP	Historical Society of Pennsylvania, Philadelphia, PA
JFHS	*Journal of the Friends' Historical Society* (66 vols., London, 1903–present)
KAC	Kendal Archive Centre
LA	Lancashire Archives
LRSF	Library of the Religious Society of Friends, London
MM	Monthly Meeting
MS/MSS	Manuscript(s)
NA	The National Archives, Kew, London
sig.	Signature, letters, or figures printed at the foot of the first page of sections to show the correct sequence for binding
UCSC	University of California Santa Barbara Special Collections, Santa Barbara, CA

Introduction

In November 1672, Female Friends meeting together at the Bull and Mouth Meeting House in London addressed an epistle to their 'Deare Friends and Sisters' in Barbados. They described their 'inseparable unity of the heavenly spirit of truth' and communicated how 'with one heart all the faithfull salute you in fellowship of the Gospell'. Despite the vast distances that separated these female correspondents, a sense of unity and spiritual oneness permeated their writing as they described the intimate connection they felt with their distant co-religionists. 'Our hearts open to you as yoars to us', they wrote, 'as drinking togeather in the one spirit of life and endless love, whereby all the faithfull partake of an invisible community to the refreshing and satiating [of] our souls.' Accompanying their letter was a package of books, sent with the Quaker merchant Thomas Hudson for the 'advantage of truth'.[1]

These correspondents were among dozens of Quaker Women's Meetings in the seventeenth- and eighteenth-century British Atlantic, sharing news about the current state of the Society in their regions, with expressions of a spiritually edifying nature. Whilst only two pages in length, this epistle stands as testimony to the powerful bonds shared by female Friends. It was the product of a collaborative endeavour – containing the names of seventeen female signatories who were acting as representatives for the 150 members who comprised the general Women's Meeting in London. Some of these names are known to the scholars of Quaker history. Most are not.[2] But it is the metaphor of the 'invisible community' in which these female writers

---

[1] Library of the Religious Society of Friends (hereafter cited as LRSF), MGR 11a4 London Women's Meeting Epistles, 1671–1753, fol. 25, London Women's Meeting to Women Friends in Barbados, 18 November 1672.

[2] The likely author of the document is Rebecca Travers. The sixteen other names attached to the epistle (as written) are Mary Elsone, Anne Raper, Ruth Grove, Grace James, Susan Yokley, Constance Wing, Ann Travers, Sarah Millman, Isabella Browning, Sara Stewert, Helena Claypole, Liddea Wade, Jane Neore, Sarah Brick, Mary Birkhead, and Ann Whitehead.

imagined themselves that fully encapsulates the sense of female fellowship fostered through their shared religious experiences.

The significance of maintaining contact with distant groups of women on the other side of the Atlantic extended beyond the emotional well-being of the women who subscribed their names to the epistles. It also solidified Quaker testimonies and beliefs and helped to create a uniform international religious movement. Yet the very existence of a transatlantic network of women corresponding with one another and exchanging knowledge, ideas, and material goods raises a multitude of questions for historians. How were these women's lives and social relationships shaped by their religious identity? How did they balance the competing demands of their religious calling with their secular obligations? What opportunities did they have for a public role within the movement? It also raises the more general issue of how far we should view ordinary women, who neither preached nor travelled, as central actors in the developing Quaker movement.

This is a book about the place of women in the transatlantic Quaker community. Quakerism was a movement that spanned the Atlantic world, spreading throughout England, Scotland, Wales, Ireland, continental Europe, the North American colonies, and West Indies during the late seventeenth and eighteenth centuries. Quakerism was the fastest-growing denomination in Restoration England, posing a serious challenge to established religion, with some historians estimating that there were as many as 60,000 Quakers in England by 1660.[3] In the eighteenth century, its dramatic growth in colonies like Pennsylvania, New England, and West Jersey made it one of the most influential religious movements in North America. In this book, I explore the relationships and support structures that evolved within this rapidly growing transatlantic network. I show how being participants in this culture of exchange deepened the public roles open to female Friends at all levels of the movement and enriched their identities in unusual and important ways.

At its centre, this book argues that the process of institutionalisation enhanced rather than diminished women's roles within transatlantic Quakerism. In so doing, it will present a significant challenge to the prevailing feminist and gender scholarship. I show that far from experiencing a decline as the movement transformed from 'sect' to 'church', female Friends' everyday lives and domestic exchanges found an important place within the developing movement.[4] It is nearly twenty years since Natalie Zemon Davis

---

[3] Barry Reay, *The Quakers and the English Revolution* (London, 1985), p. 11.

[4] Max Weber put forward this view about the distinction between churches and sects in his *Protestant Ethic and the Spirit of Capitalism*, trans. by Talcott Parsons with an introduction by Anthony Giddens (London, 2001). This was elaborated by Ernst Troeltsch who created a more clearly formulated thesis about the transformation of loose charismatic sects into bureaucratic churches in *The Social Teachings of the Christian Churches*, vol. 1 (London,

published *Women on the Margins*, which argued that early modern women were particularly adept at managing multiple identities outside of official power structures and were thus able to transform the 'margins of society' into important social and cultural sites.[5] This book will show that Quaker women were no exception. Expanding Davis's thesis on the expectations and experiences of women in different faiths and recognising the complex identity of Quaker women as prophets, elders, worshippers, friends, wives, and mothers, I seek to understand their changing experiences as the movement adapted to different social, economic, and political environments. The approach knits together an assessment of the experiences of both ministers and 'ordinary' members of the Society that allows an investigation of an array of pursuits that have previously been considered as limiting for women.

No major work exists on the lives of Quaker women outside of their public roles as ministers, prophets, and missionaries. Yet within the unusually voluminous archives of Quaker family papers, diaries, spiritual journals, Meeting minutes, and epistles, we can glimpse the extraordinary ways in which otherwise ordinary members of the movement were able to shape international Quakerism. By taking a longer view of the movement's 'origins' and by placing non-itinerant women (those who never received a formal call to preach) alongside their travelling counterparts at the centre of the analysis, we can build a more accurate and comprehensive picture of women's contribution over its first century. As the epistle sent by the London Women's Meeting shows, they were self-conscious actors within a developing and expanding religious community. Reconstructing their experiences and identities provides the inspiration for this book.

FROM SECT TO CHURCH: WOMEN AND THE EVOLUTION OF EARLY QUAKERISM

Quakerism's origins, like those of many of the radical sects, came with the turbulent years of the English Civil Wars, when new and often apocalyptic ideas captured the imaginations of men and women across the sociopolitical spectrum. In the mid-1640s, unsettled by this climate, George Fox, a shoemaker's apprentice from Leicestershire, began a period of restless travel across the Midlands and Northern counties of England speaking with

---

1931). For a good discussion of the church-sect theory, see Richard L. Greaves, *God's Other Children: Protestant Nonconformists and the Emergence of Denominational Churches in Ireland, 1660–1700* (Stanford, CA, 1997), pp. 2–8.
5 Natalie Zemon Davis, *Women on the Margins: Three Seventeenth-Century Lives* (London, 1995).

Baptists and other sectarian groups he encountered. This led him to develop
a radical theology that drew upon the Protestant ideology of the 'priesthood
of all believers' to stress looking inwards for God's guidance and spiritual
truth, and teaching that salvation was possible for all, not only an 'elect'.
Within the space of ten years, a new movement had emerged and rapidly
expanded. Those receptive to the message of Fox and other early leaders
used public preaching, handwritten epistles, and printed texts to spread their
perceived 'Truth' to the widest possible audience, stimulating the conversion
of men and women across the British Isles, Europe, and the Atlantic world.

The question of who made up the rank and file of the first Friends, however, is a subject of considerable historiographical debate. The early Quakers
did not keep membership lists, and one of the difficulties in distinguishing Quakers from other separatists of this period is that this was a movement almost entirely established through the actions and words of itinerant
preachers pursuing their own individual spiritual callings. It was not until
1676 that the first discernible 'Quaker' theology appeared in print, with
Robert Barclay's *An Apology for the True Christian Divinity* (*Theologiæ
Vere Christianæ Apologia*). Barclay had written the text 'to declare and
defend the Truth', but it also provided a systematic statement of Quaker
principles and doctrines that went on to shape the character of the movement for the next three centuries.[6]

Central to both Fox's and Barclay's visions was an insistence that those
who were 'convinced' were to worship as a community of equals 'whether
Jew or Gentile, Turk or Scythian, Indian, or Barbarian'.[7] Quakers united
around the idea of a universal, God-given 'inner light', which they argued
was present in all human beings regardless of their gender, social status,
or race. This provided a significant challenge to conventional Christian
ideals and social customs because it facilitated immediate revelation: God
could speak directly to any individual without a human intermediary. This
removed the office of paid educated ministers and meant that men and
women from all social backgrounds were permitted to preach when they
felt 'moved' to speak. Although the Bible continued to be viewed as a sacred
guide, Quakers argued that the inner light was the only real source of divine
revelation. Group meetings were therefore conducted in silence, as members
waited to channel the word of God. In contrast to most Protestant reformist
groups, Friends denied the church sacraments, denouncing them as distractions from genuine spiritual revelation. The church was not a building or
an institution but a company of true believers. It was also highly mobile,

[6] Robert Barclay, *An Apology for the True Christian Divinity* (London, 1678), sig. B2r.
[7] Ibid., p. 83.

moving with 'enlightened' individuals into fields, marketplaces, shops, barns, and houses.

An unusually cohesive sense of community was forged through this shared experience of joining in spiritual union. From the earliest years, those who shared Fox's vision collectively referred to themselves as 'Friends' and described one another as being part of a shared 'fellowship', 'union', and 'family'.[8] This was encapsulated in a letter Anne Audland wrote to Margaret Fell in September 1655, when she declared: 'Dear sister in the pure Fountaine of eternall Love doe I behold thee; . . . my soul breathes after thee . . . [and] it is Impossible that ever I should bee seperated from thee.'[9] Audland's choice of expression makes clear that adherence to the movement's testimonies opened an expansive sense of identity that was no longer confined to local communities or biological families, but enabled members to imagine themselves as part of a larger world of godly people. What it meant to be both a personal 'friend' and a 'Friend' to the wider body of Quaker believers is a theme that underpins much of this study, but it is important to note that the collective appellation 'Religious Society of Friends', is not thought to enter official use until 1793.[10]

Writing and preaching were essential to the corporate identity of the first Friends, but the imaginary bonds of fellowship forged between believers were strengthened through the experience of suffering. Critics were enraged by almost every aspect of the Quakers' behaviour from their preaching style to their language, customs, and dress. Their emphasis on 'plainness' and 'simplicity', for example, led to a collective renunciation of vain and frivolous excess in outward appearance, language, and social interaction. This included flouting the rituals of social politeness, with male Quakers refusing to remove their hats before social superiors and abandoning honorific titles. They also refused to pay tithes or swear oaths. One of the biggest turning points in the first decade of the movement came with the ill-fated case of the early Quaker leader James Nayler, who took the theology of the indwelling spirit of Christ as literal fact and in 1656 infamously re-enacted Christ's famous Palm Sunday entry into Jerusalem. Nayler was immediately

---

[8] Kate Peters, *Print Culture and the Early Quakers* (Cambridge, 2005), p. 97.

[9] LRSF, MS Vol S 81 Caton MSS vol. 3, pp. 435–436, Anne Audland to Margaret Fell, Banbury Gaol, 23 November 1655.

[10] William C. Braithwaite was able to uncover one dubious reference to 'Society of Friends', dating from 1665, but he argues that this was used in a 'descriptive' rather than a 'customary' sense. William C. Braithwaite, *The Beginnings of Quakerism* (2nd edn, rev. H. J. Cadbury, Cambridge, 1961), pp. 307–308.

The Temporary Subject Catalogue at the LRSF notes that the first official use of the term 'Religious Society of Friends' is thought to be in the 1793 address to George III. It was in common usage by 1800 when Joseph Bevan Gurney published *A Refutation of Some of the More Modern Misrepresentations of the Society of Friends, Commonly Called Quakers.*

arrested, and condemned by Parliament to be flogged, bored through the tongue, and branded with the letter B (for blasphemy).[11] But, above all, Nayler's actions confirmed to critics that the Quakers posed a dangerous threat to religious and social order.

Even the public behaviour of less prominent members was enough to spark widespread criticism. Samuel Pepys's diary entry for 29 July 1667 remarked on 'a man, a Quaker' who had run through Westminster Hall almost naked, 'only very civilly tied about the privates to avoid scandal, and with a chafing-dish of fire and brimstone burning upon his head … crying, "Repent! Repent!"'.[12] Women also boldly challenged authority. A pamphlet in 1656 criticised the blasphemous actions of Susanna Pearson, who insisted that she could raise the Quaker apprentice, William Pool, from the dead.[13] Mary Fisher and Elizabeth Williams were whipped at the market cross in Cambridge after brazenly calling the scholars of Sidney Sussex College 'Antichrists' and 'a Cage of unclean birds' and the College 'a Synagogue of Satan'.[14] Perhaps even more astonishingly, a woman from Appleby was reported to have claimed that she was 'the Eternall Son of God' and when told that she was a woman, claimed 'no, you are women, but I am a man'.[15]

Underlying these dramatic actions was a powerful belief in their status as the persecuted people of God: a spiritual army fighting the Lamb's War. To their critics, however, they posed a dangerous threat. This came to have especial significance during the reign of Charles II, when Friends were fined and imprisoned in large numbers under the terms of the so-called Clarendon Code in the 1660s, which outlawed conventicles (religious assemblies of more than five people). Some estimates suggest that at least 15,000 Quakers were imprisoned or fined in the decades following these acts, with hundreds reportedly dying in prison.[16] Quakers were also punished for various other offences, such as non-payment of tithes, vagrancy, and blasphemy. The persecution experienced by the first Friends illustrates the ways in which they stood out from other dissenting groups as unusual and extreme. It was not until 1689, with the passage of the Act of Toleration and subsequent

---

[11] A good account of the Nayler affair is provided in Leo Damrosch, *The Sorrows of the Quaker Jesus: James Nayler and the Puritan Crackdown on the Free Spirit* (Cambridge, MA, 1996).

[12] Samuel Pepys, *The Shorter Pepys*, ed. Robert Latham (Harmondsworth, 1987), p. 814.

[13] Anon., *A Sad Caveat to All Quakers: Not to Boast Any More That They Have God Almighty by the Hand, When They Have the Devil by the Toe* (London, 1657).

[14] Joseph Besse, *A Collection of the Sufferings of the People Called Quakers* (2 vols., London, 1753), vol. I, pp. 84–85 (hereafter cited as Besse, *Quaker Sufferings*).

[15] Francis Higginson, *A Brief Relation of the Irreligion of the Northern Quakers* (London, 1653), pp. 3–4.

[16] William C. Braithwaite, *The Second Period of Quakerism* (2nd edn, rev. H. J. Cadbury, Cambridge, 1961), p. 115.

Affirmation Act of 1696, that Quaker worship was legally tolerated and members were permitted to hold office without being compelled to swear an oath.

The brutal and widespread experience of suffering made a dramatic mark on the collective memory of the movement. But for those Friends who experienced constant ostracism and political stigmatisation, it had the positive effect of confirming their status as a gathered community of chosen people. This can be observed in the movement's appropriation of the name 'Quaker' in their printed writings, despite the fact that it was a highly pejorative label employed by their enemies to describe the physical shaking and trembling members experienced during worship.[17] One critic, for instance, likened 'quaking Fits' to 'Diabolical Raptures'.[18]

Moreover, it was through this profound experience of persecution that Friends were forced to reconsider their public presentation to wider society. In the late 1660s, George Fox, with the assistance of his wife Margaret Fell, began to establish a basic organisational structure for the Society. This came in the form of a hierarchical order of Meetings in those areas where Quaker members resided. The nature of the Quaker inner light meant that there was not a uniform set agenda for Meetings and no formal bureaucracy overseeing the direction they took. Each community of Friends, however, was overseen by a local Monthly Meeting, regional Quarterly Meeting, and national Yearly Meeting for business. The Yearly Meetings were held in London and the major cities of the American colonies. A Half-Year Meeting also existed in Dublin until it started meeting annually from 1798.[19] London Yearly Meeting was to become the chief source of authority in matters of faith and practice across the international Quaker community, and its widely circulated annual epistles set the tone for much of the Society's culture.

This structural transformation marks the movement's evolution from its first to second generation, as the efforts of its leaders moved from the creation of an 'invisible Church' to establishing a faith system that ensured the preservation of its customs and sustained its converts.[20] In many ways, it was a pragmatic response to a savagely hostile political environment, whereby Meetings became a means of obtaining relief and providing material, financial, and legal support for suffering Friends and their families. In addition, these institutional reforms also provided mechanisms to ensure the 'respectability' of the movement. The emergence of bodies like the Meeting for

---

[17] See Peters, *Print Culture and the Early Quakers*, pp. 91–123.
[18] Higginson, *A Brief Relation of the Irreligion of the Northern Quakers*, p. 16.
[19] The last Half-Year Meeting in Dublin was held on 1 May 1797. At this Meeting, it was agreed that the biennial national Meeting would be discontinued and that the Yearly Meeting of Friends in Ireland would be held at the end of April each year.
[20] Greaves, *God's Other Children*, p. 5.

Sufferings and Second Day Morning Meeting, for example, carefully controlled the Quaker message by censoring what was published and requiring
ministers to be approved for travel by issuing certificates.[21]

There are, therefore, a range of possible ways of thinking about the
gendered experiences and relationships that evolved within Quakerism.
Historians are generally in agreement that the numerical significance of
women within Quakerism, combined with the leading roles they played in
the organisation's structure and in evangelising and missionary service, was
unrivalled by any other movement or group in the revolutionary years. Long
before other Christian denominations provided official roles for women as
ministers, Quaker women were establishing themselves as preachers, some
leaving their children in the care of their husbands and travelling as far as
Rome, the West Indies, the Ottoman Empire, and the American colonies to
spread the faith abroad.

Those women who converted to the movement, wrote, preached, and
undertook missionary work have entered history as radical zealots and
enthusiasts who stood apart in their social attitudes and defied patriarchal
norms. A number of scholars have praised these public women for achieving social identities that were distinct from their position within families.[22]
Their travels were characterised as a craving for freedom from their household cares. Called to deliver a written testimony to King Charles II in 1670,
urging him to halt the persecution of Quakers, Elizabeth Stirredge spoke
for many of her female co-religionists when she explained that her personal
calling to ministry was to be placed before her domestic responsibilities. She
noted that 'when I looked upon my children, my Bowels yerned towards
them'. However, as she explained, she could 'get no rest, but in giving up to
obey the Lord in all things that he required of me'.[23]

Stirredge's statement suggests that Quaker women's public roles were seen
as incompatible with their expected duties as wives and mothers. Ordinary
domestic concerns, as Hilary Hinds notes, were 'marginalised' within their
writings, with family matters only being considered 'in an unfavourable
comparison with the importance of their spiritual obligations'.[24] However,

---

[21] See Jordan Landes, *London Quakers in the Trans-Atlantic World: The Creation of an Early Modern Community* (Houndmills, 2015), pp. 4–21.
[22] Mabel Richmond Brailsford argued that Quaker women's public roles were not compatible with their duties as wives and mothers and should therefore be viewed as evidence of them craving freedom from household cares. Mabel Richmond Brailsford, *Quaker Women, 1650–1690* (London, 1915), pp. 223–225.
[23] Elizabeth Stirredge, *Strength in Weakness Manifest: In the Life, Various Trials, and Christian Testimony of That Faithful Servant and Handmaid of the Lord, Elizabeth Stirredge* (London, 1711), pp. 36–37.
[24] Hilary Hinds, *God's Englishwomen: Seventeenth-Century Radical Sectarian Writing and Feminist Criticism* (Manchester, 1996), pp. 176–177.

despite their seeming incompatibility, Stirredge's motherly responsibilities now extended to caring for a broader spiritual family. Her published account was addressed to 'my Children, that are coming up after me', but her experiences and counsel were intended for the universal edification of all young Friends.[25] The activities of many of the first early Quaker prophets challenged the patriarchal conventions of their age and could be viewed as protests against male power. Feminist scholars of the 1970s often admired the radicalism of the first Quaker women, whose struggles, they argued, marked the origins of the nineteenth-century campaigns for women's rights. Margaret Hope Bacon in *Mothers of Feminism* cited the struggles and actions of early Quaker women in America as 'a microcosm of the long struggle for gender equality in society at large'.[26]

Much of the existing scholarship on Quaker women tends to focus on this body of rather exceptional 'visionary' women, whose actions as travelling prophets and polemical authors sparked controversy and debate about the place of women in the evolving organisation. Women such as Margaret Fell, Elizabeth Hooton, Jane Holmes, Martha Simmonds, Mary Fisher, Katharine Evans, and Sarah Cheevers are now very familiar in the history of early Quakerism and to scholars of the seventeenth century more widely. Yet, as Christine Trevett acknowledges, such activities were beyond many female Quakers because of their familial and financial circumstances.[27] Phyllis Mack's seminal *Visionary Women* provides the fullest and most complex reading of the changing status of women within early Quakerism. She recognises that travelling ministry was a 'transient' experience that was integrated into other areas of women's everyday existences.[28] However, it is necessary to consider how we can reconcile the extravagant and public facets of Quaker women's experiences with the more private and personal aspects of their lives. Although Friends kept no formal membership records during this period, it is evident from the surviving data that women missionaries formed only a tiny minority of the female Quaker population at any particular time and it was only on exceptional occasions that they were inspired to write and preach on behalf of the Society.

The Quakers' desire to set themselves apart as a godly people and 'true church', eventually led to a more systematised, centralised, and conservative organisation. The period between 1692 and circa 1805 has been commonly defined as the 'Quietist' period in Quaker history, where persecution

---

[25] Stirredge, *Strength in Weakness*, pp. 1–2.
[26] Margaret Hope Bacon, *Mothers of Feminism: The Story of Quaker Women in America* (San Francisco, 1986), p. 3.
[27] Christine Trevett, *Women and Quakerism in the 17th Century* (York, 1991), p. 70.
[28] Phyllis Mack, *Visionary Women: Ecstatic Prophecy in Seventeenth-Century England* (Berkeley, CA, 1994), p. 214.

had largely ended and leaders were more concerned with retaining members than with expansion. This inward focus and isolationism was also encouraged by the introduction of the multi-tiered system of Monthly, Quarterly, and Yearly Meetings for business from the 1670s, in which women had a special place. Informal Women's Meetings had existed in London from the late 1650s as a means of relieving Friends in the face of overwhelming suffering and hardship.[29] Inspired by the efforts of these women, it was whilst undertaking ministerial work in the American colonies in 1671 that George Fox proposed the creation of a nationwide system of separate Meetings for female Friends that recognised their special duties and roles as overseers of female members. He noted:

there is many things that is proper for women to look into both in their families, and concerning of women which is not so proper for the men, which modesty in women cannot so well speak of before men as they can do among their sex ... And many women are of more capacity than others are, and so they must instruct and inform the rest.[30]

Separate Women's Meetings for business were subsequently established across the British Isles and American colonies at Monthly, Quarterly, and, in some American colonies, Yearly levels. Whilst subject to geographical variation, the Women's Meetings were mainly accountable for overseeing the behaviour of female members; granting financial relief and material assistance to poor Friends; and overseeing the complex Quaker marriage discipline procedure.

The institution of this bureaucratic administrative structure has long been regarded as a particular development of second-generation Quakerism that brought a decline in women's significance and visibility.[31] The structure of the Meetings was patriarchal and facilitated the rise of a hierarchy of male leadership, with male elders dominating the national Meetings and the Men's Meetings holding the notional right to define the power of the female members of their districts. Moreover, the establishment of these female Meetings heralded a change in the role of women within the Society, as they channelled the sometimes publicly extravagant behaviour of the movement's female converts into more acceptable and conventional spheres. Some scholars

---

[29] See Landes, *London Quakers in the Trans-Atlantic World*, pp. 33–34; and Michele Denise Ryan, '"In my hand for lending": Quaker Women's Meetings in London, 1659–1700', University of California, Santa Cruz, PhD thesis (2003). I am grateful to Simon Dixon for this reference.

[30] George Fox, 'Friends Fellowship Must Be in the Spirit; and All Friends Must Know One Another in the Spirit and Power of God', undated, 'Book of Epistles of George Fox, 1666–1682', cited in Mack, *Visionary Women*, p. 286.

[31] 'With organisation', writes Patricia Crawford, 'female participation lessened.' Patricia Crawford, *Women and Religion in England 1500–1720* (London, 1993), p. 160.

have suggested that the measure of introducing certificates for travel limited the opportunities available to women because they now had to request permission from the male-dominated Second Day Morning Meeting and were evaluated, among other criteria, on the basis of their familial obligations. A woman's responsibilities to her family could be judged by the movement as more important than her divine calling.[32]

This sense that the loss of women's work as prophets equated to a real decline in their public status is best expressed by Mack, when she writes that:

Tracking the movement's evolution from sect to church, one watched prophetic women, once the bearers of considerable charismatic authority, slowly disappear behind the rising edifice of the new structure, their voices muffled by the clearer discourse of the proponents of new rules and values.[33]

Whilst she consciously avoids the language of 'advance' and 'decline', this passage nonetheless echoes gendered histories of Quakerism, which suggest that once the charismatic movement of the 1650s became subject to bureaucratisation and regulation, the opportunities available to women were progressively more restricted.[34] The accountability that female leaders owed to men within this system has led historians to conclude that the most remarkable feature of the Women's Meetings was 'the lack of power associated with them'.[35] Even relatively recent assessments, like Catie Gill's 2005 study of Quaker women's writings, have lamented the fact that compared to its early activism 'later Quakerism seems far more limiting in the roles it provided' for women.[36]

By the time of George Fox's death in 1691, Quakerism had metamorphosed from an unruly radical sect to a settled church. In the words of Rebecca Travers, an influential figure in the London Women's Meeting, and likely author of the letter sent to Barbados in 1672, 'Prophecy has and must cease.'[37] This statement encapsulates the impact that changing expectations could have on women's public roles within the movement, as Friends turned away from the radical sense of the indwelling light towards other forms of spiritual and religious expression. For historians of Quaker women, this

---

[32] Ibid., p. 193; Amanda E. Herbert, 'Companions in Preaching and Suffering: Itinerant Female Quakers in the Seventeenth- and Eighteenth-Century British Atlantic World', *Early American Studies: An Interdisciplinary Journal*, vol. 9, no. 1 (2011), p. 93.

[33] Mack, *Visionary Women*, pp. 274–275.

[34] Ibid., p. 412.

[35] Trevett, *Women and Quakerism*, p. 81.

[36] Catie Gill, *Women in the Seventeenth-Century Quaker Community: A Literary Study of Political Identities, 1650–1700* (Aldershot, 2005), p. 186.

[37] Anne Martindell et al., *A Relation of the Labour, Travail and Suffering of That Faithful Servant of the Lord, Alice Curwen* (1680), sig. A4v [pagination confused], Rebecca Travers's 'A Testimony Concerning Alice Curwen'.

raises the issue of female autonomy in the face of a declining visionary outlook, especially when scholars like Mack have asserted that it was only in
their roles as prophets that women were able to enjoy a 'taste of public
authority'.[38]

The question of how far and in what ways women's roles were restricted
after they experienced institutionalisation and separation of spheres of
authority forms the central focus of this book. Certainly, the movement
underwent an important cultural, political, and structural shift as it entered
its second and third generations.[39] But a decline in status was not an experience common to the majority of women who make up the history of early
Quakerism.

An investigation of the lives of Quaker women intersects with several
wider debates in early modern social and cultural history. These include the
relationship between church and polity in religious women's history; the
intersection of the household with the wider realm of politics; approaches
to gender and religion in Atlantic history; and the place of sectarian movements within studies of the early modern community. It offers the opportunity to compare their experiences with those of other religious women
at a time when official toleration and increasing institutionalisation of
worship transformed the relationship that dissenters had with each other
and with wider society. Similarly, the culture of Christianity was being
modified by Enlightenment discourses about the ways in which women's
spiritual capacities could be equated with their intellectual potential. The
late-Stuart period was an era in which arguments about woman's nature
increased in intensity and 'unprecedented numbers of women' were moved
'to intervene in debates about religion, marriage and education'.[40] One
central aim of this book is to show how the movement's increasing emphasis on the home did not limit women's functions. It builds upon a number
of recent developments in the scholarship on women, gender, and religion,
which have highlighted how a female-dominated separate sphere provided

[38] Mack, *Visionary Women*, p. 5.
[39] For the purposes of this book, first-generation Quakerism is given to mean the period
between 1650 and the period roughly beginning with the institution of the Meeting system
from c. 1668. The second and third generations are characterised as beginning in the late
1660s until Friends started to lose their status in Pennsylvanian politics in the mid-eighteenth century (roughly 1755).
[40] Sarah Apetrei, *Women, Feminism and Religion in Early Enlightenment England* (Cambridge,
2010), p. 9.

women with a diverse range of opportunities within specific religious communities.[41]

As Su Fang Ng has argued, women could gain authority and participate in public life within 'the organization of a quietist sect'.[42] Despite the evolving organisational structure, female Quaker ministers continued to function in public roles throughout the eighteenth century. Indeed, they remained an accepted and important component of the religious life of the eighteenth-century movement. It is almost impossible to calculate with any certainty the number of ministers (male or female) active in transatlantic Quakerism over the seventeenth and eighteenth centuries. This is partly because the identity of a 'Public Friend' (as both male and female ministers came to be known) was highly fluid and could include both individuals who only ever experienced one call to preach over their lifetime, and others whose entire lives were dedicated to delivering their spiritual testimonies to Quaker communities across the British Atlantic. Moreover, no formal records were kept about those who travelled on 'gospel service', and those that do survive were dependent on an individual declaring their 'calling' to travel to their local Monthly or Quarterly Meeting. An indication of the number of active ministers within Britain can nevertheless be inferred from the number of deaths of Quaker ministers as recorded by the London Yearly Meeting, which reported the deaths of 144 male and 43 female ministers between 1700 and 1709, and 93 male and 95 female ministers in the period from 1770 to 1779. These records also report the deaths of 611 female ministers who had undertaken transatlantic travel at some point between 1700 and 1769.[43] This indicates that the number of Public Friends undertaking transatlantic missionary work declined sharply after the Society's first few decades.

Despite a lessening number of ministers, however, the surviving evidence from the London Yearly Meeting suggests that the proportion of female to male ministers actually increased: from 23 per cent in 1700 to 51 per cent in 1779. Rebecca Larson has estimated that there were 1,300 to 1,500 active female ministers in the American colonies over this period.[44] This is supported by a catalogue kept by Irish Friends documenting those Friends 'in the Ministry' who visited Ireland between 1655 and 1781. The data collated shows that the proportion of itinerant female ministers dramatically

---

[41] See Sarah Apetrei and Hannah Smith, 'Introduction' in Sarah Apetrei and Hannah Smith (eds.), *Religion and Women in Britain, c. 1660–1760* (Farnham, 2015), pp. 1–22.

[42] Su Fang Ng, *Literature and the Politics of Family in Seventeenth-Century England* (Cambridge, 2007), p. 221.

[43] John S. Rowntree, *Life and Work* (London, 1908), p. 252, cited in Rebecca Larson, *Daughters of Light: Quaker Women Preaching and Prophesying in the Colonies and Abroad, 1700–1775* (New York, 1999), p. 334.

[44] Ibid., p. 63.

increased by the end of our period. By 1750, women formed the majority (57 per cent) of ministering Friends.[45] This stands in contrast to the number of Friends first visiting Ireland between 1655 and 1670, where visits by women ministers constituted only 21 per cent (see Appendix 1 for a full numerical breakdown).

In addition to their public responsibilities, the family and household were also central to the early Quaker mission, providing women with opportunities for roles within the developing organisation. Although the Quakers' emphasis on the Women's Meetings and their domestic responsibilities stood in marked contrast to the early enthusiasm of female preachers, as we shall see, Friends succeeded in projecting domestic values into the public life of the organisation. Richard T. Vann has estimated that by the end of the first century, as many as 90 per cent of Quakers were children of Quakers, highlighting the potential influence of the wife or mother in the development of the faith.[46] The place of the family and an emergent concept of 'birthright' Quakerism had important benefits for the movement's female members and in strengthening their authority.[47] The Quakers, as Barry Levy argues, 'were the first to develop a form of domesticity as part of their religion' and therefore offered a consistent social role for women within the organisational life of the Society.[48]

In Quakerism, Meetings for worship could take place in a range of spaces from the intimate setting of Friends' houses to mass public gatherings. Moreover, their segregated Meetings for business enabled those women who did not travel to learn and use their domestic skills in a space that 'would otherwise have been denied them'.[49] The Meetings had their own clerks, treasurers, and overseers, who were appointed by their female members. Many of these women had never been active as travellers or prophets. Ensuring conformity and adherence to church testimonies within their Meetings therefore gave them the opportunity to be accountable and active members of their religious community. These elders were self-sufficient: able to control their own agendas, allocate their own funds, and exercise disciplinary authority over errant members. As Mary Maples Dunn observes, American Quaker women even had control over their physical space through the use of sliding

---

[45] Friends Historical Library Dublin (hereafter cited as FHLD), YM C3 Names of Friends in the Ministry in Ireland, 1655–1781. The collection relates to those Friends who 'visited the meetings of Friends in Ireland, but more particularly Corke, Bandon and the parts westward of Bandon', fol. 1 [unpaginated].

[46] Richard T. Vann, *The Social Development of English Quakerism 1655–1755* (Cambridge, MA, 1969), p. 167.

[47] See Barry Levy, *Quakers and the American Family: British Settlement in the Delaware Valley* (Oxford, 1988), pp. 1–21.

[48] Ibid., p. 25.

[49] Trevett, *Women and Quakerism*, p. 115.

partitions in the centre of their purpose-built Meeting Houses. This provided female Friends with a separate space to conduct their business, serving as a reminder of their own autonomy within their local Quaker community.[50]

The household holds an ambiguous and, at times, inconsistent place in Reformation and Counter-Reformation histories. Some accounts of the shift from public worship to domestic devotion, in its various forms, emphasise the marginalisation of religion and of women from the public realm, while others stress the importance of the 'domestication' of religion for women's social and political development. Lyndal Roper argues that the Protestant Reformation was largely a force for conservatism and patriarchy that aspired to constrain women within the domestic sphere and inhibited their independence by 'reinscribing' them within the family.[51] At the same time, women's roles within conventional spheres have been regarded as a positive development for determining their identity and status within both the household and in religious movements. Research into the general 'domestication' of religion brought about by the Reformation has stressed the ways in which the private space of the household gained increasing prominence in the practice of piety and also facilitated women's engagement with the public realm of politics.[52] This intersection of private devotion and public duty is perfectly encapsulated in the Presbyterian Thomas Jacombe's *A Treatise of Holy Dedication* (1668), which offered counsel and guidance to London householders rebuilding their homes in the aftermath of the Great Fire. In his instructions about the different realms of prayer, Jacombe discussed the hybrid nature of 'Family prayer': "tis *private*, and yet (in *part*) 'tis *publick*; 'tis *publick*, and yet (in *part*) 'tis *private*'.[53]

The Quakers' unusual willingness to promote women's spiritual authority and permit them to preach, minister, travel, and oversee their own organisational procedures often put them at odds with their contemporaries. The nineteenth-century abolitionist Thomas Clarkson aptly described the Quakers as a 'peculiar' people, who 'differ more than even many foreigners

---

[50] Mary Maples Dunn, 'Saints and Sisters: Congregational and Quaker Women in the Early Colonial Period', *American Quarterly*, vol. 30, no. 5, Special Issue: Women and Religion (1978), p. 600.

[51] Lyndal Roper, *The Holy Household: Women and Morals in Reformation Augsburg* (Oxford, 1989), pp. 1–5.

[52] See Crawford, *Women and Religion*, pp. 38–52; Anthony Fletcher, *Gender, Sex, and Subordination in England, 1500–1800* (New Haven, CT, 1995), pp. 347–363; Alison Searle, 'Women, Marriage and Agency in Restoration Dissent', in Apetrei and Smith, *Religion and Women in Britain*, pp. 23–40; and Alasdair Raffe, 'Female Authority and Lay Activism in Scottish Presbyterianism, 1660–1740', in Apetrei and Smith, *Religion and Women in Britain*, pp. 61–78.

[53] Thomas Jacombe, *Hooinh Egzainiomnh, or, A Treatise of Holy Dedication Both Personal and Domestick the Latter of Which Is (in Special) Recommended to the Citizens of London* (1668), part 2, pp. 88–89.

do, from their own countrymen'.[54] One way to understand more fully the distinctiveness of women's roles within the early Quaker movement is to compare their experiences with those of other religious women in this period. Contrasting female Friends' experiences and those of contemporary Baptists, Methodists, and other nonconformists reveals how Quakerism shaped women's identities in unusual ways. This comparative approach, I hope, will encourage research into the less well-known and private experiences of the female (and indeed male) members of other transatlantic religious movements. It foregrounds the distinctive opportunities that were open to Quaker women from a range of backgrounds to contribute to the political, economic, and cultural life of their religious community.

The English Baptists and other nonconformist groups of the seventeenth century that form part of this analysis were much fewer in number than their Quaker contemporaries, and women never had the same structural role within their respective organisations. Baptists emerged as a dissenting group from the early 1600s and gained much popular support in the millenarian climate of the Civil Wars, when they sought to prepare the world for the Second Coming of Christ. Particular (or Calvinistic) Baptists believed that Christ had died to save only the predestined elect. Within this framework, women were permitted to speak at Baptist meetings, vote to admit members, become female deacons, and join the movement without the consent of their husbands, 'but their authority to preach or to lead meetings was contested'.[55] Baptists arrived into the American colonies in large numbers in the late seventeenth century, following the first settlements in Pennsylvania in the 1680s. Virginia also became an important site of Baptist church polity in the eighteenth century, and the movement experienced a surge in numbers during the evangelical revivalism of the 'Great Awakening'.[56] Similar parallels are found in the reform movements known as Pietism, Behmenism, Moravianism, and the Philadelphian Society, which flourished in England and the Americas in the late seventeenth and eighteenth centuries. Originating first in northern and central Europe, these Pietist communities drew extensively on the 'spiritualist-theosophical tradition' embodied in the thinker Jacob Boehme. Like the Quakers, they believed in direct divine inspiration, and emphasised the perfectibility of the pious. They also stressed repentance, virtue, devotion to scripture, and insisted on the return

---

[54] Thomas Clarkson, *A Portraiture of Quakerism* (3 vols., New York, 1806), vol. 1, p. ii.
[55] Mack, *Visionary Women*, p. 123. See also Rachel Adcock, *Baptist Women's Writings in Revolutionary Culture, 1640–1680* (London, 2015), pp. 117–145.
[56] Janet Moore Lindman, *Bodies of Belief: Baptist Community in Early America* (Philadelphia, 2008), pp. 71–89.

of Christ's kingdom on earth.[57] Although distinguishing these movements from other radical dissenting congregations has remained a difficult task for historians, recent work by Elizabeth Bouldin has shown the important role of female prophets such as Jane Lead, Ann Bathurst, and Antoinette Bourginon within these communities. Particular stress has been placed on the conventicle in enabling these radical communities to flourish.[58]

Evangelicalism was a prominent strand in several periods of seventeenth- and eighteenth-century religious culture. It has been argued that its highly evocative and emotional nature brought 'a new sensibility' to domestic and family life.[59] Of particular significance was the emergence of Methodism in Britain and the American colonies from the 1730s. Although it did not formally secede from the Church of England until 1795, it was a controversial movement from its inception. Like Quakerism, the momentum by which it gathered converts on both sides of the Atlantic posed a serious threat to the established Church, demonstrating that eighteenth-century religious culture was still resistant to dissenting religion. Its charismatic preachers were notorious for attracting large mixed crowds. Women were part of this expansive network of leaders, and were permitted to speak publicly to lead prayer, tend to the sick, and assumed lay leadership of classes and bands, the two basic units of Methodist organisation, which divided the congregation according to sex, marital status, and age. The popular understanding of Methodism as particularly attractive to women meant that Methodist women were often the targets of criticism and public ridicule.[60] Like Quakers, some Methodist woman were authorised to preach by virtue of what became known as an 'extraordinary call', a belief that God could occasionally inspire women to speak. But female preaching was never permitted as a general practice within Methodism as it was within Quakerism and, by 1803, it was forbidden by the mainstream Wesleyan movement altogether.[61]

The flourishing of these dissenting communities is revelatory of how the makeup of religious culture in the British Atlantic underwent a notable 'feminisation'. This complemented broader debates about women's involvement in public life, as religious women became 'the lifeblood of the churches'.[62] This development in both England and the American colonies was linked to

[57] Kaspar von Greyerz, *Religion and Culture in Early Modern Europe, 1500–1800* (Oxford, 2008), pp. 176–181.
[58] Elizabeth Bouldin, *Women Prophets and Radical Protestantism in the British Atlantic World, 1640–1730* (Cambridge, 2015), pp. 89–118.
[59] Anna M. Lawrence, *One Family under God: Love, Belonging, and Authority in Early Transatlantic Methodism* (Philadelphia, 2011), p. 4.
[60] See ibid., pp. 1–16.
[61] Paul Wesley Chilcote, *John Wesley and the Women Preachers of Early Methodism* (London, 1991), pp. 253–256.
[62] Apetrei, *Women, Feminism and Religion*, p. 14.

changing patterns of worship, where the church was becoming an observably more feminine institution and the number of women in nonconformist congregations increasingly outnumbered men. It has been observed that the numerical preponderance of Baptist women in England, Pennsylvania, and Virginia enabled them to pursue their own devotional culture based in the family and local community.[63] Even though women were denied authority within the wider organisation of the Baptist church, as Janet Moore Lindman has shown, the household, as a site of female piety, could confer spiritual authority upon them.[64] The stress on lay leadership in both eighteenth-century England and America, similarly provided significant opportunities for women within the early Methodist societies. Women outnumbered men by three to two in some Wesleyan Methodist congregations during its first decades in America.[65]

A number of influential discussions about the eighteenth-century household have shown how women could accrue status through their domestic roles. It was through domesticity, argues Karen Harvey, that 'women gained power'.[66] Their 'separate sphere' was socially constructed *for* and *by* them. It also influenced how men behaved and was affected by what 'men did'.[67] Research into the lives of women in the early modern cloister, for example, has highlighted the multifarious ways in which nuns were able to negotiate the barriers restricting active female participation in early modern Catholic affairs.[68] One aim of this book is to show how histories of Quaker women can be enriched by observing the interaction of women and men in public and private spaces, and to show how men's lives were changed by adhering to Quaker values and beliefs. Some scholars have acknowledged that the promotion of women to public roles did not necessarily predispose men to recognise their authority.[69] But by examining the writings, correspondence,

[63] See Lindman, *Bodies of Belief*, pp. 71–89.
[64] Ibid., pp. 112–130.
[65] Lawrence, *One Family under God*, p. 38.
[66] Karen Harvey, *The Little Republic: Masculinity and Domestic Authority in Eighteenth-Century Britain* (Oxford, 2012), p. 9.
[67] Linda Kerber, 'Separate Spheres, Female Worlds, Woman's Place: The Rhetoric of Women's History', *Journal of American History*, vol. 75, no. 1 (1988), p. 18.
[68] See Emily Clark and Mary Laven (eds.), *Women and Religion in the Atlantic Age, 1550–1900* (Farnham, 2013); Claire Walker, ' "When God Shall Restore Them to Their Kingdoms": Nuns, Exiled Stuarts and English Catholic Identity, 1688–1745', in Apetrei and Smith, *Religion and Women in Britain*, pp. 79–97; and Claire Walker, *Gender and Politics in Early Modern Europe: English Convents in France and the Low Countries* (Basingstoke, 2003). I am grateful to Amanda Herbert for this reference.
[69] Catherine M. Wilcox, *Theology and Women's Ministry in Seventeenth-Century English Quakerism* (Lampeter, 1961), pp. 253–254. This is also discussed in Margaret Hope Bacon, 'The Establishment of London Women's Yearly Meeting: A Transatlantic Concern', *Journal of the Friends' Historical Society*, vol. 57, no. 2 (1995), pp. 151–165 (hereafter cited as JFHS).

and journals of both the male and female members of early Quakerism, this book explores whether redefining roles for women also reshaped masculinity in the process. After all, granting women their own Meetings and separate space to conduct business implies that male Friends, for the most part, accepted their decisions and counsel. The correspondence of the London Women's Meeting to female Friends in Barbados, for example, stood apart from the centralised message that the male-dominated Meetings for discipline were conveying. Their advice and spiritual directions had the potential to separately shape the transatlantic message of the movement.

Quakerism must also have had an important impact on domestic relations, which raises the question of whether marriage to a female minister or elder affected men's roles and identities. Fathers became the primary carers of their children whilst their wives travelled on gospel service. James Stirredge was left to care for his children whilst his wife Elizabeth delivered her message to the King in 1670.[70] In some cases, this role-reversal could last several years. John Evans and Henry Cheevers took over household responsibilities for nearly four and a half years between 1658 and 1663 whilst their wives, Katharine and Sarah, were held captive by the Maltese Inquisition.[71] The relationships formed between men and women in the Quaker household are therefore an important focus of this study. Evidence will also be drawn from the writings of male and female Friends to compare the ways in which gender could shape their experiences and self-definition.

THE TRANSATLANTIC COMMUNITY AND 'HOUSEHOLD' OF FAITH

The 'Quaker community' at the heart of this book encompassed seventeenth- and eighteenth-century England and Wales, Scotland, Ireland, and the British colonies in mainland North America and the West Indies. It adopts such a broad geographical focus for two reasons. First, Quakerism was an itinerant movement and many of the women I examine were mobile. Female Quaker ministers spent years travelling across the British Isles and American colonies. In the process, they connected with different groups of Friends and entered into new social alliances with individuals within and outside their religious community. Second, even those women who did not undertake ministerial service were connected with their distant co-religionists

---

[70] Stirredge, *Strength in Weakness*, pp. 37–41.

[71] This can be observed in the correspondence published at the end of their account of captivity in Malta: Katharine Evans and Sarah Cheevers, *This Is a Short Relation of Some of the Cruel Sufferings (for the Truths Sake) of Katharine Evans and Sarah Chevers in the Inquisition in the Isle of Malta* (London, 1662), pp. 51–63. The two women set sail for Alexandria in the Autumn of 1658 and did not return to England until the beginning of 1663.

through kinship networks and long-distance communication. This was an age of 'Atlantic families', to borrow Sarah M. Pearsall's terminology. Britons found themselves increasingly displaced and dispersed across the Atlantic world and were sustained and connected through intricate webs of correspondence and communication.[72] Ian K. Steele has shown how the frequency of Atlantic voyages between 1675 and 1740 magnified the speed at which news and correspondence could travel across the Atlantic.[73] Quakerism matured within this culture of transatlantic exchange.

Since Quakers were not bound to a single location, it is important to note that their experiences were also not circumscribed to a single national historiography. A strong tradition of ministering in Ireland and the American colonies had existed from the movement's beginnings and Fox's system of Monthly, Quarterly, and Yearly Meetings were quickly established in New England (1661), Virginia (1673), and Maryland (1672), as well as the major Quaker settlements in Ireland, such as Dublin, Cork, Waterford, and Limerick (1669). The real catalyst in the development of North American Quakerism, however, came in 1681 when William Penn was granted a charter for a new colony that became Pennsylvania. Penn viewed his colonial commission as an opportunity to create a haven for both his persecuted co-religionists and those suffering religious oppression elsewhere in the world. This so-called 'Holy Experiment' was theorised as a 'civil union' that transcended religious difference and its governance was based upon Quaker principles of universalism, aspiring for prosperity, piety and peaceful relations with Native American populations.[74] Penn's vision for Pennsylvania, which replicated many of the ways of life and worship patterns practised by English Friends, was not for the improvement of individual fortunes, or simply as a means of escaping persecution, but to pursue a godly lifestyle, in a society where religious values firmly penetrated the colony's government. The choice of name for its capital, Philadelphia, was derived from the Greek for 'City of Brotherly Love', encapsulating the peaceful and collaborative community envisaged by Penn.

The chronology of Quakerism's rise on both sides of the Atlantic therefore makes this a complex story to tell. More than 3,000 English Quakers are estimated to have settled in Pennsylvania between 1681 and 1683, and by 1775 it has been calculated that there were 100,000 Quaker

---

[72] Sarah M. Pearsall, *Atlantic Families: Lives and Letters in the Later Eighteenth Century* (Oxford, 2008).

[73] Ian K. Steele, *The English Atlantic 1675–1740: An Exploration of Communication and Community* (New York, 1986), pp. 275–276.

[74] William Penn, *One Project for the Good of England: That Is, Our Civil Union Is Our Civil Safety, Humbly Dedicated to the Great Council, the Parliament of England* (London, c. 1679).

inhabitants residing in North America out of a population of three million.[75] Paradoxically, despite the initial numerical strength of Quakerism in the British Isles, by the eighteenth century the movement was declining. It has been estimated, for example, that Friends in England numbered one third of their former strength when William III and Mary II ascended the throne in 1689, and by 1800, the size of the English Quaker community had fallen to 19,800.[76] The enduring persecution of Friends in Britain and the mass migration of families to the Americas, combined with the widespread appeal of eighteenth-century evangelical movements like the Methodists, largely explain this decline. Quakerism never gained much of a foothold in Scotland, with many converts preferring to settle in America than to become the targets of persecution in the bitter conflict between the Episcopalian and Presbyterian churches. There was nevertheless a thriving Quaker movement in Ireland, especially around English Protestant settler communities in Leinster and Ulster. Irish Quaker communities were relatively small in comparison to those in England or the Americas, with an estimated 5,000 Friends resident in Ireland when Quakerism was at its peak in the late seventeenth century, and falling sharply from about 1720 onwards.[77]

Penn's 'Holy Experiment' has long been regarded as providing a model of social organisation where domesticity was placed at the very centre. Even contemporary observers came to admire the distinctive familial ideology propounded by the Quaker inhabitants of Pennsylvania, repeatedly praised for their orderly domestic habits and their rejection of worldly cultural customs. Visiting Pennsylvania in 1754, the German traveller Gottlieb Mittelberger described the conditions that he found as 'a paradise of women'.[78] As we shall see, the peculiar brand of domesticity that characterised eighteenth-century Pennsylvania made the colony the most studied and certainly the most appreciated of all the British North American colonies during the early Enlightenment. Indeed, thinkers including Locke, Voltaire, Crèvecoeur, Brissot, and Rousseau viewed the 'Holy Experiment' in Pennsylvania as compatible with Enlightenment values and devoted some attention to the arrangement of family life and religious practices in their

---

[75] Thomas D. Hamm, *The Quakers in America* (New York, 2003), p. 33.

[76] S. J. Rowntree, *Quakerism Past and Present: Being an Inquiry into the Causes of Its Decline* (London, 1859), p. 88.

[77] Richard T. Vann and David Eversley, *Friends in Life and Death: The British and Irish Quakers in the Demographic Transition, 1650–1900* (Cambridge, 1992), p. 39.

[78] Gottlieb Mittelberger, *Gottlieb Mittelberger's Journey to Pennsylvania in the Year 1750 and Return to Germany in the Year 1754*, transl. Carl Theo. Eben (Philadelphia, 1898), pp. 122–123.

writings.[79] Of particular value was the fact that the settlers were able to live in harmony under the principle of mutual toleration without any ecclesiastical hierarchy or institutionalised authority imposed from above.

In such a pluralistic society, the household was to occupy a central place in the reproduction of religious values and beliefs. Levy suggests that it was in placing the domestic sphere at the heart of their faith that Friends were able to continue to maintain strong communities while tolerating the influx of a wide array of settlers into the colony.[80] This unusual blend of domesticity and religious authority provided 'the animus' for Quaker dominance over all aspects of Pennsylvanian life during this period.[81] It is striking, however, that women's position within colonial Quakerism remains a largely neglected subject in the history of the movement. In part this can be attributed to the general lack of interest that scholars have shown in those generations of Friends that followed the institution of the Quaker Meeting system more generally.[82] It is also symptomatic of a wider gap within the scholarship on the American colonies and the British Atlantic in discussions of religious and gendered experience. Daniella Kostroun and Lisa Vollendorf realised in their 2009 study of *Women, Religion, and the Atlantic World* that little sustained effort had been made to ask what could be learnt about the Atlantic world 'through the lens of women, gender and religion'.[83]

Quakerism was certainly not the only religious movement at this time with a transatlantic outlook. It was, however, distinct in a few important ways. It is by breaking down fixed geographical boundaries and placing women, domesticity, and religion at the centre of the discussion, that this book shows how less-known women who did not travel could nonetheless also actively contribute towards their religious community and thus

---

[79] See Chapter 4 for a more thorough investigation of their views. See also Levy, *Quakers and the American Family*, pp. 3–22; and James Emmett Ryan, *Imaginary Friends: Representing Quakers in American Culture, 1650–1950* (London, 2009), pp. 63–91.

[80] Levy, *Quakers and the American Family*, p. 16.

[81] Ibid., p. 5.

[82] Many of the first historians of the movement viewed the inward focus of the eighteenth-century movement and significant decline in numbers as developments unworthy of attention. Brailsford, for example, described the eighteenth century as the movement's 'dark ages' and lamented its 'drab uniformity' in the years following the death of the Quaker leader, George Fox, in 1691. Brailsford, *Quaker Women*, pp. 328–329.

J. Punshon pronounced eighteenth-century Quaker Meetings as 'lifeless' and Friends' ministry 'uninspiring', and described the separation of Quakers from the world as 'one of the tragedies of English religious history'.

Quoted in Robynne Rogers Healey, 'Quietist Quakerism, 1692–c. 1805', in Stephen W. Angell and Pink Dandelion (eds.), *The Oxford Handbook of Quaker Studies* (Oxford, 2013), pp. 47–48.

[83] Daniella Kostroun and Lisa Vollendorf, 'Introduction', in Daniella Kostroun and Lisa Vollendorf (eds.), *Women, Religion, and the Atlantic World (1600–1800)* (Toronto, 2009), p. 6.

influence group identity. Comparisons will therefore be drawn between the experiences of British and American Friends, investigating the extent to which settlement in the Americas impacted upon women's lives and exchanges in different contexts. Quaker ministers often commented on the very different nature of the groups they visited in other nations. The Irish Friend Elizabeth Shackleton, in March 1755 reflected on the challenges of ministering in different places, observing that 'the custome of one country differ[s] much from those of another' and 'what might do vary well in one, wou'd not at all as well in another'.[84] This transatlantic approach draws attention to the broader social, cultural, and political developments taking place in the Atlantic, as well as distinct geographical variations between different groups of Friends residing in Britain and North America.

The 'Atlantic' therefore becomes both a category of analysis as well as a method of approach. This has been advocated by David Armitage as particularly useful for historians to view developments from a broadly international perspective, whilst enabling them to draw meaningful comparisons between specific locations within the Atlantic world.[85] Unified states and nations had not yet fully developed and continued to rely upon other influences to guide political and social development. Settlers in Britain's North American colonies did not live isolated, secluded lives independent of the concerns of their native land. A rich historiography is now showing how colonists' writings, stories, and news shaped ideas, politics, and society in England and in the process, 'England's Atlantic identity and imperial destiny'.[86] *Female Friends* continues this line of argument by integrating the history of seventeenth- and eighteenth-century Quakerism in England and America into one connecting story.

This book highlights how women were both respected and central figures in shaping transatlantic Quakerism. In doing so, it engages with an important theme in social history: the early modern community. The concept of 'community' is contentious in academic scholarship, although recent work has done much to celebrate its continued validity as a lens for studying the past.[87] The imagined bonds shared between Quaker believers scattered throughout the Atlantic world created the communicative, economic, and organisational frameworks necessary to bring a fragmented and culturally

---

[84] Huntington Library, San Marino, CA (hereafter cited as HL), mssSHA Shackleton Family Correspondence Box 1, 1658–1752, fol. 171, Elizabeth Shackleton to Joshua Carleton, Dublin, 25 March 1755.

[85] David Armitage, 'Three Concepts of Atlantic History', in David Armitage and Michael J. Braddick (eds.), *The British Atlantic World, 1500–1800* (Basingstoke, 2002), p. 18.

[86] Malcolm Gaskill, *Between Two Worlds: How the English Became Americans* (Oxford, 2014), p. v. See also Pearsall, *Atlantic Families*.

[87] See Phil Withington and Alexandra Shepard, 'Introduction: Communities in Early Modern England', in Alexandra Shepard and Phil Withington (eds.), *Communities in Early Modern England: Networks, Place, Rhetoric* (Manchester, 2000), pp. 1–15.

diverse group of believers together through a shared spiritual experience. Early Quakers, as Larson has suggested, identified themselves globally 'as members of one community linked by shared beliefs, instead of geographical boundaries'.[88] This book argues that the 'imaginary' dimension of Quaker community enabled the formation of strong connections across great distances, as Friends remained emotionally invested in developments taking place on both sides of the Atlantic. The aforementioned female correspondents of London Women's Meeting, for example, spoke of 'an invisible community'; others described their sense of belonging to 'the household of faith and family of God'.[89] In one reply to the Women's Meeting in London dated April 1676, Quaker women in Barbados addressed their co-religionists as 'Deare friends: sisters: and mothers', a choice of language that demonstrates the intense emotional bond experienced between these two geographically separated groups of women.[90]

Friends saw the scope of their mission as spreading across the Atlantic, where the metaphorical family encompassed a shared sense of intimacy, obligation, and cohesion, despite the highly dispersed nature of Quaker settlements. As we shall see, such expressions of community were vital in conferring public significance upon the domestic sphere and women's roles within the broader 'household of faith'. Some challenges do, of course, surround using the Atlantic as a model for understanding women's identities and experiences.[91] But we are now entering a period where the place of women, religion, the family, and household are being re-examined through an Atlantic lens to show the places of divergence and continuity in women's experiences. Recent studies have shown the dynamic place of women within the Atlantic world by mapping how confessional difference shaped gender roles, whilst also acknowledging that the ways women 'acted out their faith influenced the ways in which societies developed'.[92] Pearsall

---

[88] Larson, *Daughters of Light*, p. 40.

[89] LRSF, MGR 11a4, London Women's Meeting Epistles, 1671–1753, fol. 25, from the Women's Meeting in London to the Women's Meeting in Barbados, 18 November 1672; 'An Epistle from the Women Friends in London to the Women Friends in the Country, also Elsewhere, About the Service of a Women's Meeting, 4 January 1674', in A. R. Barclay (ed.), *Letters, &c., of Early Friends; Illustrative of the History of the Society, from Nearly Its Origin, to About the Period of George Fox's Decease* (London, 1841), p. 345.

[90] LRSF, MGR 11a4 London Women's Meeting Epistles, 1671–1753, fol. 30, from the Women's Meeting in Barbados to the Women's Meeting in London, 30 April 1676.

[91] See, e.g., Karin Wulf, 'Women and Families in Early (North) America and the Wider (Atlantic) World', *History Compass*, vol. 8, no. 3 (2010), p. 238. This was part of a series of essays published 'to inspire debate about the conceptual utility of the Atlantic as a paradigm for understanding issues of gender, family and sexuality, as well as its ramifications for feminist scholarship everywhere'.

[92] Emily Clark and Mary Laven, 'Introduction', in Clark and Laven (eds.), *Women and Religion*, p. 2. Other studies include Nora E. Jaffary (ed.), *Gender, Race and Religion in the Colonization of the Americas* (Aldershot, 2007); Susan E. Dinan and Debra Meyers

has been particularly influential in showing the key role of families in the eighteenth century, emphasising their agency (as glimpsed through their letters) in shaping the political and economic language of the Atlantic.[93] An Atlantic perspective 'allows the telling of more complex stories about the variety of ways in which people experienced the early modern period's transformative process of nation-building and state formation'.[94] Based on this emerging scholarship, this book emphasises the need to view the lives and experiences of Quaker women in relation to the wider social and political developments within and without their spiritual community that took shape across the Atlantic.

THE FRAMEWORK OF DISCUSSION: SOURCES AND STRUCTURE

The experiences of female Friends in seventeenth- and eighteenth-century Britain and North America were vibrant, diverse, and often progressive. This book advances the scholarship on Quaker women in three important ways: firstly, by adopting a dual focus that contemplates the experience of both ministers and non-itinerant Quakers; secondly, through extending the geographical and chronological scope through which the experiences of female Friends are assessed; and finally, by focusing on the relationships, identities, and roles common to all Quaker women in this period rather than just the activities of those exceptional female ministers, prophets, writers, and sufferers. In adopting this framework, *Female Friends* develops a more nuanced account of Quaker women's identities and personal relationships. In the process, it restores the archetypal second- and third-generation woman – the non-itinerant homemaker – as a subject of analysis. This was the woman who Levy argues 'indirectly but intimately affected' the developments within colonial Quakerism and came to characterise the evolving movement, when Quaker activity became focused on the home and the spiritual maintenance of the community.[95]

To achieve a more comprehensive understanding of female Friends' experiences, the book engages with a range of printed and manuscript materials by both Quaker and non-Quaker writers, and by writers of both sexes. Records of the early itinerant ministers are easily available in the spiritual

---

(eds.), *Women and Religion in Old and New Worlds* (London, 2001); and Kostroun and Vollendorf, *Women, Religion, and the Atlantic World.*

[93] Pearsall, *Atlantic Families*, esp. pp. 12–13.

[94] Kate Chedgzoy, *Women's Writing in the British Atlantic World: Memory, Place and History, 1550–1700* (Cambridge, 2007), pp. 7–8.

[95] Levy, *Quakers and the American Family*, p. 221.

autobiographies, journals, and life accounts they penned. Many of these were posthumously published during the late seventeenth and eighteenth centuries and continue to hold an important place in the movement's history. We can also glimpse the experiences of female Friends through the diaries of non-itinerant women, published tracts, testimonials recorded by local Meetings after the death of a Friend, and in the correspondence and diaries of male ministers. Non-Quaker writings will also be used to show how Quaker women's experiences were shaped in part by developments outside the Society.

Valuable evidence also comes from the extant Women's Meeting minutes. Unlike any other religious denomination of the period, early Friends expected their female-led Meetings to keep a permanent record of their proceedings. This means that where historians of other sectarian movements have been forced to rely upon institutional records kept by and about men, the information contained within the Quaker Women's minutes provides us with a unique insight into women's roles within the institutional life of a religious community, as recorded by women. Not all of these Meeting records have survived, and the content of the minutes was never uniform, with some gaps and omissions. They nevertheless enable us to glimpse the shared concerns and experiences of the movement's female leaders at the various levels of the Meeting structure.

To capture the essence of the private experiences and social interactions of female Friends, this study also makes extensive use of letters, memoirs, and memorials. The information contained within personal and familial correspondence offers an important insight into female Friends' everyday lives and interactions, an issue that has largely been overlooked in the historiography. Indeed, much of the research that has been undertaken on Quaker women to date has relied upon their spiritual autobiographies and life accounts, especially those that were printed, which include very little information about their domestic relationships. These personal histories, which document travels, Meetings attended during visits, and the various spiritual trials they encountered during their lives, prioritise this kind of information over that of families or personal relationships.[96] As Hinds argues, it is only when these women compare God's demands with those of the temporal concerns of household and family that family is mentioned at all.[97] Whilst these accounts can still shed some new light on the effects of religious affiliation on household relationships, existing studies on Quaker women have depended heavily on such sources. This is especially the case when the focus is turned towards colonial Quaker women, for the printed output of Pennsylvanian

[96] Bacon, *Mothers of Feminism*, p. 66.
[97] Hinds, *God's Englishwomen*, p. 172.

Friends remained very small.[98] Undeveloped printing processes and a fledgling colonial book trade meant that printed artefacts authored by American women were the exception rather than the rule.[99]

This study will also make extensive use of correspondence exchanged between Quaker families and Meetings across the British Atlantic. The writing, reading, and dissemination of letters has been recognised as forming part of a broader cultural process, an idea pursued by Susan E. Whyman in her study of English letter writers in the long-eighteenth century.[100] There are naturally a number of limitations in using letters as a source for accessing early modern mentalities. One issue of note is that of intended audience. Many of the writers studied in this book were conscious that the contents of their letters would be retold and perhaps even distributed to readers beyond the recipient. This raises questions about the degree to which they can be considered 'personal' or self-reflective, particularly when the writer may have had a broader audience in mind or consciously chose to imitate appropriate convention rather than express genuine sentiments. The preacher Joan Vokins, for instance, frequently left instructions about how she expected her epistles to be distributed. In one 1680 missive to Friends in Long Island, Vokins expresses her desire for 'this Epistle to be Copied and sent to *Mattincoke*, to *M. Fryer* and Friends thereaway, to be read among them'.[101] Another female elder, Mercy Bell, described the collaborative nature of her writing process to her close friend Priscilla Farmer. One letter caused her particular anxiety. 'After it was done', she wrote, 'I show'd it to three or four Friends being realy distress'd for fear of doing wrong.' She explained that after they had approved it, she then showed a copy to her husband who 'found no other fault with it, but being long'.[102]

---

[98] Betty Hagglund, 'Quakers and Print Culture', in Angell and Dandelion, *Oxford Handbook of Quaker Studies*, p. 482.

[99] Michael Warner, *The Letters of the Republic: Publication and the Public Sphere in Eighteenth-Century America* (London, 1990), pp. 15–16; James N. Green, 'The Book Trade in the Middle Colonies, 1680–1720', in Hugh Amory and David D. Hall (eds.), *The Colonial Book in the Atlantic World* (Chapel Hill, NC, 2007), pp. 199–223.

[100] Susan E. Whyman, *The Pen and the People: English Letter Writers, 1660–1800* (Oxford, 2009). For other studies on letter writing, see Pearsall, *Atlantic Families*; James Daybell (ed.), *Early Modern Women's Letter Writing, 1450–1700* (Basingstoke, 2001); Rebecca Earle, 'Introduction: Letters, Writers and the Historian', in Rebecca Earle (ed.), *Epistolary Selves: Letters and Letter-Writers 1600–1945* (Aldershot, 1999), pp. 1–12; and David Cressy, *Coming Over: Migration and Communication between England and New England in the Seventeenth Century* (Cambridge, 1987).

[101] Joan Vokins, *God's Mighty Power Magnified: As Manifested and Revealed in His Faithful Handmaid Joan Vokins* (London, 1691), p. 58, undated, c. 1680, to 'Friends at Gravesend in Long-Island, and Elsewhere'.

[102] LRSF, Temp MSS 403/1/2/3/22 Arthur B. Braithwaite Family Papers, Mercy Bell to Priscilla Farmer, London, undated, c. 1760.

Mercy Bell was a witty and humorous correspondent, as well as a prominent member of the London Quaker Women's Meeting. However, it is difficult to make broader generalisations about women's everyday lives and experiences from those letters that have survived. This is especially true of published collections of women's correspondence and posthumous memorials, which were often edited by men and may have lost their more 'personal' qualities in the transition from manuscript to print. John Whiting's comments following the death of his sister Mary exemplify the way in which Friends consciously sought to preserve documents deemed to have a 'public value'. He states that during her life she wrote 'several Letters to Particular Friends ... but they being more Private, and not of so General a Concern, are here omitted'.[103] This shows how certain documents were selected to present a particular image of Quaker womanhood that would then go on to shape the collective memory of the Society as it evolved. Certain aspects of women's lives and writings that were deemed more 'trivial' or of less importance were therefore not necessarily preserved by the developing movement.

This study will show, however, that the benefits of using personal letters, memorials, and published letter collections as a means of accessing Quaker women's experiences far outweigh their limitations. Letters contain a much freer flow of emotion, information, ideas, and dialogue than printed texts.[104] They can give us a sense of women's shared concerns and experiences and a more nuanced reading into hitherto uncharted aspects of their lives. It is through these personal writings that we are able to access the 'unpredictable variety of private experience' and observe how non-ministering women could become participants in national and international cultural exchanges.[105] Memorials commemorated the lives of pious Friends and were often compiled by local Meetings or close family members. The subjects of these accounts were held up as models for achieving a perfect Quaker life. Despite the idealised and, at times, problematic image of Quaker femininity presented in these published testimonies, which were often penned after the death of a member, these sources are often the only record we have of many women's lives. As we shall see, they offer glimpses into the extraordinary ways in which their adherence to the movement shaped the identities of women from different social backgrounds and at different levels within the movement's hierarchy.

---

[103] John Whiting, *Early Piety Exemplified, in the Life and Death of Mary Whiting: A Faithful Handmaid of the Lord* (London, 1681), p. 16.

[104] Clare Brant, *Eighteenth-Century Letters and British Culture* (Basingstoke, 2006), p. 229.

[105] Amanda Vickery, 'Golden Age to Separate Spheres? A Review of the Categories and Chronology of English Women's History', *Historical Journal*, vol. 36, no. 2 (1993), pp. 390–391.

Rather than adopting a spatial or chronological framework, the book is organised around the more flexible category of women's relationships, which facilitates discussion of women whose religious vocations were situated both within and without the physical space of the household. This also enables attention to be directed towards their interactions with men in a variety of different social contexts and settings. The chapters are structured around the relationships that female Friends developed both within and without the Quaker community, with the focus shifting outwards from the family to the local Meeting system, then to the connections and friendships they formed with other members of the Society, and finally, to their relationship with the non-Quaker world. These sites were not, of course, mutually exclusive and female Friends moved seamlessly between them in their daily lives. By viewing women's experiences from the perspective of their social interactions it becomes possible to observe women contributing in both public spaces, like the marketplace or their published writings, and in less obvious places including the home, birthing chamber, Men's and Women's Meetings, and as entrepreneurs.

Chapter 1 begins this work by considering the home and family as key sites in the formation of Quaker women's public identities. The strong domestic outlook of the movement has been frequently acknowledged, yet little has been done to uncover the model of household order that evolved. Challenging the view that this more overtly domestic focus led to a decline in women's status, the chapter demonstrates the multiplicity of ways in which the private domain of the household could become entwined in the public concerns of the movement. Central to the discussion is the figure of the non-itinerant Quaker wife, whose fixed position within the household and local community provided a powerful supportive accompaniment to the national and transatlantic missions. This included raising the next generation of members and ministers, as well as supporting the ministerial careers of their husbands.

In the case of women who did undertake public ministerial work, their private correspondence reveals that this religious contribution was carefully balanced by the obligations, duties, and responsibilities they felt for their families. Even the most radical of Quaker prophets were exhorted to serve God in ordinary ways, as ordinary people. George Fox declared in 1658 that whilst prophets 'may have openings when [they are] abroad to minister to others', their own spiritual or 'particular growth' would only occur by 'dwell[ing] in the life which doth open'.[106] Far from pursuing their own

---

[106] George Fox, *The Journal of George Fox*, ed. John L. Nickalls (Cambridge, 1952), pp. 340–341, George Fox's Address to Friends in the Ministry, given at John Crook's house, 31 May 1658.

personal agendas, many women believed that they were undertaking such work for the spiritual benefit of their families. Assessing their printed and private correspondence, the chapter shows how the domestic sphere influenced the public character of the movement and in turn, shaped female Friends' relationships with the wider Quaker community.

The extensive overlap between women's domestic and public roles is well demonstrated through their involvement in their separate Women's Meetings. Whilst their minutes do not, at first glance, appear to offer much insight into their everyday experiences or relationships, Chapter 2 shows how detailed case studies of particular Meetings can enrich our understanding of the position of female Friends in their local communities and the effect that settlement in the colonies had on their personal relationships. For practical reasons, the women who occupied the highest positions in their local Meetings could not undertake extensive missionary service, and their lives offer us a valuable glimpse of the public work of non-itinerant women in the movement. Through a comparison of the minutes of six Women's Monthly Meetings, two in the northwestern counties of England, one in Ireland, and three in the rural hinterlands of Pennsylvania, West Jersey, and Virginia, the chapter assesses the extent to which settlement in the colonies shaped Quaker women's experiences. In contrast to existing histories of the Women's Meetings, which suggest that their introduction was linked to the decline of women's visibility and roles in the movement, it will show the positive ways in which family life and domestic harmony could confer authority upon women.

The pyramid-like structure of local, district, regional, and national Meetings provided female Friends with unparalleled opportunities in the organisational structure and governance of the Society at all levels. They also offer us further insight into women's relationships with other members of their religious community. The opportunities provided by the Women's Meetings for regular contact with like-minded pious women should not be underestimated. They provided a sense of purpose and identity within communities where Quaker women often continued to be shunned and isolated for their beliefs. They also gave access to a wider community of Friends. By encounters with visiting ministers and trans-oceanic epistolary exchanges, women could enjoy contact with fellow members they would often never meet in person. Chapter 3 takes this further by exploring the friendships and personal connections that women developed in the 'real' and 'imagined' community of Friends. This chapter charts new territory in the history of Quaker women by arguing that friendship was at once a personal and spiritual relationship, and thus intrinsic to how the community was theorised and constructed. Building upon the recent scholarly interest in female friendships, the chapter explores both the unique definition that early Quakers (men and women) attached to their personal relationships and how connections within a 'Society of Friends' specifically shaped female alliance formation. Rather than developing close alliances with their neighbours, they engaged in a shared spiritual mission with their co-religionists, guarding one another against the dangers of the material world. The most distinctive feature of Quaker women's alliances was the vast distances over which they were often initiated and maintained. The spiritual connections between female Friends enabled an 'imagined' community of intimate friendships and close personal networks to emerge, with little physical contact, as the epistles sent between the Women's Meetings in Barbados and London signify. This, I suggest, played an important role in defining the transatlantic mission.

It is also necessary to expand the analysis to include interactions between Quaker women and individuals outside their religious community. The story of Quaker suffering and persecution is a familiar one to historians of the seventeenth century, as are the seemingly outrageous actions of many early Friends, which served to inflame these tensions further. The 'identity' of the Quakers, as Mark Knights has astutely noted, is almost impossible 'to disentangle' from the opinions of their opponents.[107] Studies of printed and visual satire have proved especially productive in recent years, drawing particular attention to the character of anti-Quaker sentiment, the strength of animosity felt towards the movement's adherents, and the pejorative ways in which the beliefs of Dissenters were understood.[108] Such accounts form an important source base for Chapter 4, which explores two distinct facets of Quaker women's relationships with the rest of society over this period, firstly focusing on negative reactions to Quaker women's status at an intellectual and communal level, especially in anti-Quaker printed works; and secondly, on their gradual acceptance and integration into local communities and early Enlightenment culture. Numerous studies have stressed that Friends did not live in a social or cultural vacuum, and have been influential in highlighting Quaker engagement with their local parish communities.[109] Indeed, they tell us that far from being isolated from the rest of society,

---

[107] Mark Knights, *The Devil in Disguise: Deception, Delusion, and Fanaticism in the Early English Enlightenment* (Oxford, 2011), p. 77.

[108] Knights, *The Devil in Disguise*, pp. 82–88. See also Emma Major, *Madam Britannia: Women, Church, and Nation 1712–1812* (Oxford, 2011), pp. 135–151.

[109] Adrian Davies, *The Quakers in English Society, 1655–1725* (Oxford, 2000); Simon Dixon, 'Quaker Communities in London, 1667–c. 1714', Royal Holloway, University of London, PhD thesis (2005); Carla Gardina Pestana, *Quakers and Baptists in Colonial Massachusetts* (Cambridge, 1991); David Scott, *Quakerism in York, 1650–1720* (York, 1991); Bill Stevenson, 'The Social Integration of Post-Restoration Dissenters, 1660–1725', in Margaret Spufford (ed.), *The World of Rural Dissenters, 1520–1725* (Cambridge, 1995), pp. 360–387; and Alexandra Walsham, *Charitable Hatred: Tolerance and Intolerance in England, 1500–1700* (Manchester, 2006), pp. 228–322.

Friends were much more integrated into their communities than has previously been imagined.[110] Pursuing these developments further, this chapter seeks to reassess the position of Quaker women within the wider community. It questions the ways in which Quaker women's particular denominational traits shaped their interactions with non-Quakers. Rather than viewing the 1689 Toleration Act as a turning point in terms of the relationship between Quakers and their neighbours, the chapter argues that it was developments within the movement, including the introduction of the Women's Meetings in the 1670s, which brought about a change in how they were perceived by the non-Quaker public.

This study aspires to offer a more comprehensive history of early female Friends than has previously been attempted, whilst recognising that some of their other experiences still remain to be charted. Collectively, the following chapters show us how female Friends' everyday lives were inextricably bound to a dynamic web of transatlantic interaction and cultural exchange. In arguing that Quaker women's domestic identities helped shape both their ministerial careers and the wider outlook of the movement, the book will show how their social identities within the 'whole family and Household of faith' shaped both their spiritual and everyday encounters.[111] After all, Quakerism would not have survived without the interaction of the family, the Meeting, and more distant fellow members. The shape of these exchanges, in the home, Meeting House, neighbourhood, and the wider Atlantic community, is the subject of what follows.

---

[110] Dixon has effectively demonstrated how individual Quakers residing in London did not confine themselves to their own separate religious community, but instead negotiated a role for themselves within wider London society, for example through obtaining entry into City guilds. See Dixon, 'Quaker Communities in London', esp. pp. 248–272; and Simon Dixon, 'The Life and Times of Peter Briggins', *Quaker Studies*, vol. 10, no. 2 (2006), p. 198.
    Adrian Davies's study of Quakers in Essex has also seriously qualified the traditional picture of Quakers living in self-imposed and embattled isolation from the wider world. Davies, *The Quakers in English Society*, pp. 191–215.
[111] LRSF, MS Vol 335 Gibson MSS, fol. 3, Samuel Neale to Ann and Sally Kendal, Amsterdam, 10 September 1752.

– I –

Spiritual Housewives and Mothers in Israel: Quaker Domestic Relationships

> A wife I have but not at home
> She's gone abroad and I'm alone
> O that I had it in my power
> To enjoy her company for one hour
> But alas that's not to be had
> The thought, it makes me feel quite sad.
>
> HCQSC, MS Coll 1100 Scattergood
> Family Papers, 1681–1903, vol. 9,
> undated, c. 1764–1794

In 1755 the Irish Friend Richard Shackleton proposed marriage to Elizabeth Carleton, an esteemed minister of Dublin Monthly Meeting. The recently widowed Shackleton, who ran a boarding school in Ballitore, County Kildare, had long been acquainted with Carleton, who was a gifted minister and regularly undertook gospel service in Ireland. When presented with the prospect of marriage, however, Carleton questioned whether married life would be compatible with her vocation as a Quaker minister. As the posthumous memoirs compiled by her daughter Mary Leadbeater recount, 'the two situations which she most wished to avoid, that of a step-mother and mistress of a boarding-school were involved in the serious subject for consideration laid before her'. Despite her reservations, Carleton agreed to marry Shackleton after patiently seeking divine counsel.[1]

Elizabeth Shackleton's newfound domestic obligations, however, did not hinder her spiritual labours. Her status was enhanced and 'sphere of usefulness was enlarged' as she 'became one of the best of step-mothers, and one of the best of matrons to a public school'. As her daughter recorded, 'many remembered, and … profited by the tender admonitions which she was wont to impart'. The work of Elizabeth and Richard Shackleton had an important impact on the wider community, for it was remembered that

[1] Mary Leadbeater (ed.), *Memoirs and Letters of Richard and Elizabeth Shackleton, Late of Ballitore, Ireland* (London, 1849), p. 17.

'the advantage of their example extending beyond their sphere in life, was felt throughout the neighbourhood'. Their influence was so extensive that 'many of the higher ranks desired to cultivate a familiar intercourse with a man distinguished by his talents and learning, and a woman of so benevolent a character'.[2]

For several decades, historians of early Quakerism have regarded the ability of women to undertake ministerial service as providing them with radical opportunities to liberate themselves from domestic concerns.[3] The spiritual democratisation of the Quaker inner light gave rise to a culture where all members, whether male or female, were permitted to follow their individual spiritual callings. This meant that women like Elizabeth Shackleton were extremely active in spreading the Quaker message and were permitted to undertake vast itinerant missions, even if they were married or had children or relatives to care for. Like some of the other radical sects of this period, they threatened to 'shake patriarchy's foundations' by joining the movement independently of their husbands or other male relatives.[4] Much research into the transient lives of female ministers has maintained that one of the most significant ways in which Quakerism departed from contemporary norms, was through women's abilities to transcend their gender, 'casting-off' their domestic and social identities.[5]

Less attention, however, has been paid to their labour within the home. Elizabeth Shackleton's experiences reveal the complex and rich ways in which the household exerted a strong and positive influence on her public career. She was one of many gifted female ministers who came to dedicate their spiritual careers to their families and households. Quaker theology stressed direct divine revelation, which meant that women, whether preachers or not, achieved a more authoritative role within the household than their contemporaries. This was because the emphasis on spiritual equality and absence of ordained ministers from the Society's hierarchy meant that a woman, regardless of her status within the movement, could take the lead in directing the spiritual life of the family. More than this, Shackleton's memorial also tells us much about the esteem and veneration with which the movement held the domestic identities of its most acclaimed female ministers. It

---

[2] Ibid., pp. 2, 17–20.
[3] Scholars like Mabel Richmond Brailsford have argued that Quaker women's public roles were not compatible with their duties as wives and mothers and should therefore be viewed as evidence of them craving freedom from household cares. Mabel Richmond Brailsford, *Quaker Women, 1650–1690* (London, 1915), pp. 223–225.
[4] Dorothy Ludlow, 'Shaking Patriarchy's Foundations: Sectarian Women in England, 1641–1700', in Richard L. Greaves (ed.), *Triumph over Silence* (London, 1985), pp. 93–124.
[5] Phyllis Mack, *Visionary Women: Ecstatic Prophecy in Seventeenth-Century England* (Berkeley, CA, 1994), p. 407.

was noted, for example, that she and her husband were 'the more respected' for devoting 'their time and thoughts' to their domestic duties.[6]

In many respects, Shackleton is representative of the women character-ised by Christine Trevett as 'remarkable not for their travels, their public confrontations, their prophetic gestures or their publications, but as quieter, though no less intransigent, souls'.[7] Their faithful obedience to the cause, loyalty to their husbands, and contribution to Quakerism in their families and communities made them extraordinary. No history of the movement, however, has explored the place of the household in the experiences of those women who were attracted to Quakerism, but did not travel or document their spiritual exercises in print. Maintaining the household as a site of order and harmony formed a crucial aspect of female Friends' experiences and, as we shall see, offered a space for them to contribute to the movement. They managed their daily lives, marriages, and families around its testimonies. Moreover, after Quakerism entered its more conservative second genera-tion in the late 1660s, the household was increasingly placed at the heart of the transatlantic Quaker mission and became the chief instrument for the propagation of the faith. The 'radical child-centredness' of the early Quaker movement, as Barry Levy has argued, facilitated the growth of a strong reli-gious community.[8]

This chapter explores the nuances of this relationship between Quaker women's daily lives, domestic labours, and public religious identities. It will argue that the religious life of early Quakerism was inextricably linked to the domestic sphere, where Quaker ideals were constructed, nurtured, and developed. The correspondence, memorials, and epistles exchanged by fami-lies and Meetings across the Atlantic world of Quakerism illuminate the rich and complex interactions of female Friends and encapsulate the experiences of both those who travelled and those who remained at home. Looking at the ways families endured transatlantic distance and how this was pre-sented in their letters and personal writings, offers an interesting insight into how Quaker values, beliefs, and ideas were perpetuated across Britain and the North American colonies. Such sources reveal the disorder, emotional hardship, and vulnerability of the movement's male and female members who were separated because of their spiritual callings, or faced abuse from unconverted relatives. Analysis of the lives of itinerant and non-minister-ing female Friends will show that the early Quakers' emphasis on domestic relationships was empowering rather than constraining.

---

[6] Leadbeater, *Memoirs and Letters of Richard and Elizabeth Shackleton*, p. 20.
[7] Christine Trevett, *Women and Quakerism in the 17th Century* (York, 1991), p. 41.
[8] Barry Levy, *Quakers and the American Family: British Settlement in the Delaware Valley* (Oxford, 1988), p. 127.

However, 'family' and 'household' are terms that do not have a static meaning throughout history and cannot be reduced to simple economic units of production, reproduction, and consumption with a male head at their centre. Naomi Tadmor has shown that the historical construction of the 'family' incorporated a variety of relationships that extended beyond the ties of blood and marriage. When 'English people spoke or wrote about "families"', she notes, it was very often 'not the nuclear unit that they had in mind'.[9] In the Quaker case, the blood family was often overshadowed by the metaphorical religious family, a broad association of unrelated people. The Meeting, in particular, gave Friends a sense of belonging to a family much larger than their immediate kinship network. Early converts were often at pains to separate themselves from their natal relations, becoming 'brothers', 'sisters', 'fathers', and 'mothers' in their new spiritualised household. Many of the women under investigation were labelled 'mothers in Israel', a term not only used to describe female prophets, but any venerable woman within the community who was renowned for nurturing and caring for others, whether in her own household or within the wider spiritual family.[10] This underscores the necessity of studying the Quaker family from both the perspective of conjugal families and the wider body of believers. The spiritual, emotional, and economic support structures that evolved within the wider 'household of faith' will therefore also be explored in Chapters 2 and 3.

QUAKER CONSCIENCE AND FAMILY LIFE

One of the most notable challenges posed by early Quakerism was the freedom for women to join the movement without the approval of their fathers or husbands. The husband was normally the dominant partner in the religious life of the household; he was a 'Bishop' over his 'little Church' and 'little commonwealth'.[11] Conduct-book writers like William Gouge, whose *Of Domesticall Duties* went through multiple editions throughout the seventeenth century, presented the agreed view that a woman 'must yeeld a chaste, faithfull, matrimoniall subjection to her husband'.[12] It is now generally accepted that the social changes brought about by the Reformation gave women increased opportunities to exercise agency in the religious life

---

[9] Naomi Tadmor, *Family and Friends in Eighteenth-Century England: Household, Kinship, and Patronage* (Cambridge, 2001), p. 19.

[10] Hugh Barbour, 'Quaker Prophetesses and Mothers in Israel', in J. William Frost and John M. Moore (eds.), *Seeking the Light: Essays in Quaker History in Honor of Edwin B. Bronner* (Wallingford, PA, 1986), pp. 41–60.

[11] William Gouge, *Of Domesticall Duties* (London, 1622), p. 18.

[12] Ibid., p. 28.

of their families.[13] This is most persuasively demonstrated through their notional right to disobey their husbands' commands if they conflicted with the Church's teachings, since service to God was to be placed before any worldly authority. But, as Bernard Capp has shown, there was a clear lack of guidance in Puritan texts on 'the practical implications, or the difficulties of a conscientious woman facing a moral dilemma'.[14] How far the duty of wifely obedience extended was an ambiguous issue. 'If the husband were an unbeliever, or of a different faith', asks Patricia Crawford, 'whom was the wife to obey?'[15]

The calling of the Quaker inner light naturally created the conditions for a direct affront to the patriarchal order, as personal convincement and inward revelation made salvation possible. It also heightened the conditions for conflict and, at times, violence between a Quaker woman and her unconverted husband. The strong focus on individual conscience is encapsulated in the life account of the minister Alice Hayes, who joined the movement in 1680. She described the theological tensions in her marriage to have been so great that she was forced to decide 'Whether I loved Christ Jesus best or my Husband; for now One of the Two must have the Preheminence in my Heart'. Alice's husband, Daniel, who had forbidden her to join the movement and had threatened to leave her, allegedly went to the extremes of hiding her clothes before she went to Meeting.[16] However, in true Quakerly manner she was not deterred, and recalled how she 'would go with such as I had, so that he soon left off that'.[17] Women's potential disavowal of patriarchal authority certainly did not extend to joining religious sects independently without their husbands' consent, which Keith Thomas describes as being viewed as 'monstrous and unnatural'.[18] 'A wife', as Gouge advised,

---

[13] See Emily Clark and Mary Laven, 'Introduction', in Emily Clark and Mary Laven (eds.), *Women and Religion in the Atlantic Age, 1550–1900* (Farnham, 2013), pp. 1–11. For more on the opportunities of women to exercise agency in the religious life of the household see Patricia Crawford, *Women and Religion in England 1500–1720* (London, 1993), pp. 38–52; and Christine Peters, *Patterns of Piety: Women, Gender and Religion in Late Medieval and Reformation England* (Cambridge, 2003), pp. 314–342.

[14] Bernard Capp, 'Gender, Conscience and Casuistry: Women and Conflicting Obligations in Early Modern England', in Harald E. Braun and Edward Vallance (eds.), *Contexts of Conscience in Early Modern Europe, 1500–1700* (Basingstoke, 2004), pp. 117–118.

[15] Crawford, *Women and Religion*, p. 52. See also Patricia Crawford, 'Public Duty, Conscience, and Women in Early Modern England', in John Morrill, Paul Slack, and Daniel Woolf (eds.), *Public Duty and Private Conscience in Seventeenth-Century England* (Oxford, 1993), pp. 57–76.

[16] Although not explicitly stated in the account, it is possible that Hayes was intending to wear something to the Meeting for worship that was in keeping with the Quaker testimonies on modesty and 'plainness'.

[17] Alice Hayes, *A Legacy, or Widow's Mite; Left by Alice Hayes, to Her Children and Others* (London, 1723), pp. 39–41.

[18] Keith V. Thomas, 'Women and the Civil War Sects', *Past and Present*, vol. 13 (1958), p. 52.

'must doe nothing which appertaineth to her husband['s] authoritie simply without, or directly against his consent.'[19] Alice Hayes made express mention of this in her account, when her mother-in-law declared that Alice's disobedience would crush her husband. Although the bitter marital feud between Daniel and Alice went on for some time, she tells us that he eventually came to respect her beliefs. His 'love returned again' and he 'was convinced that it was the Truth I suffered for'.[20]

In similarity to any woman who defied a family member to join a radical sect, conversion to Quakerism altered women's perception of their position within the household and the obedience they owed as dutiful wives. Numerous accounts of Quaker suffering include scenarios of female Friends who endured the wrath of unsympathetic husbands. Mary Akehurst was beaten by her husband and bound 'with a great Iron Chaine ... night and day for a month' after she felt moved to reprove an Independent priest at Lewes and refused to 'deny the Truth'.[21] The conflict between female converts and their unconvinced husbands was demonstrated in dramatic style in 1670, when Anne Wright felt a 'command from God' to run through St Patrick's Cathedral in Dublin dressed only in ashes and sackcloth. Her husband, on hearing of her actions and intended journey to deliver a message to the King in England, disapproved, explaining that he was 'not willing to part with her upon any such conceits or strong fancy as she was daily conceiving in her melancholy mind'. Refusing to provide her with a horse and money for her journey, he questioned 'how she could make it out to be lawful, by any law of God or man, for a wife to leave her husband and family, against his will and without his consent'. After anguished deliberation, Anne realised that she could not ignore her spiritual calling and continued to make plans for the journey. She also started daily negotiations with her husband to gain his consent, telling him that if he 'let her go to do this work God had commanded her, she would be willing to do any thing for me all her days, that would not offend God'. William reluctantly agreed to her supplications, but never joined the movement.[22]

Religious teachings buttressed the conventional belief in wifely subjection. Ephesians 5:23 taught women to submit to their husbands as unto the Lord, for the husband was the wife's head, as Christ was the head of the

[19] Gouge, *Of Domesticall Duties*, p. 290.
[20] Hayes, *A Legacy, or Widow's Mite*, pp. 45–49.
[21] LRSF, YM/Mfs/GBS/2 Great Book of Sufferings, London and Middlesex to Yorkshire, Ireland and New England, Sussex, p. 8.
[22] William Wright, 'A Brief and True Relation of Anne, the Wife of William Wright, of Castledermot, in the County of Kildare in Ireland, Who Deceased the 1st Day of December, 1670', in Mary Leadbeater (ed.), *Biographical Notices of Members of the Society of Friends Who Were Resident in Ireland* (London, 1823), pp. 60–61.

Church.[23] Disobedient women guided by their perceived false consciences therefore posed a threat not only to the stability of the family but also to the wider social and religious order. After Anne Wright ran through the streets of Cork and reproved the mayor for persecuting Quakers, she was imprisoned as a vagabond. Her captors then interrogated her and asked whether she travelled with her husband's consent, advising that she would not be released until he certified before the local justices that he had approved her journey.[24] The non-Quaker reaction to female Friends is explored in detail in Chapter 4, but it is clear that these women were seen as departing from prevailing gender ideologies.[25] Hostile propaganda repeatedly connected female converts with other women beyond male control. Dorothy Waugh was symbolically forced to wear the scold's bridle after preaching in the Carlisle marketplace in 1656.[26]

Naturally, the number of accounts delineating conflict between spouses reduced as Quakerism moved into its second and third generations, when most adherents were born into the faith and were expected to respect one another's divine calling. However, some stigma still seems to have been attached to women independently joining religious groups without the consent of their male relations in the eighteenth century. Elizabeth Ashbridge described in detail the estrangement she experienced from her husband shortly after she migrated to the American colonies in the late 1730s. Following one dispute, Ashbridge asserted 'that, as a dutiful wife, I was ready to obey all lawful commands; but, when they imposed upon my conscience, I could not obey him'.[27] Her decision to become a Quaker preacher had violent consequences. She recorded one occasion when her husband attacked her with a penknife saying: 'If you offer to go to meeting to-morrow, with this knife I'll cripple you, for you shall not be a Quaker.' Undeterred, Ashbridge describes how she 'set out as usual' the following morning.[28] In 1720, Margaret Lucas, a Staffordshire Friend, similarly described how her conversion to the movement had occasioned family conflict after her uncle threatened violence: '[I]f I ever went to the meeting again, he would bereave me of my life.'[29] Both women were eventually able to reconcile with their

---

23 Gouge, *Of Domesticall Duties*, p. 29.
24 Wright, 'A Brief and True Relation of Anne, the Wife of William Wright', pp. 58–59.
25 See David Underdown, 'The Taming of the Scold: The Enforcement of Patriarchal Authority in Early Modern England', in Anthony Fletcher and John Stevenson (eds.), *Order and Disorder in Early Modern England* (Cambridge, 1985), pp. 116–136.
26 'A Relation Concerning Dorothy Waughs Cruell Usage by the Mayor of Carlile' in James Parnell, *The Lambs Defence Against Lyes* (London, 1656), pp. 29–30.
27 At this time, Ashbridge was married to a man by the name of Sullivan (further details are unknown). Elizabeth Ashbridge, *Some Account of the Early Part of the Life of Elizabeth Ashbridge* (Philadelphia, 1807), p. 43.
28 Ibid., p. 44.
29 Margaret Lucas, *An Account of the Convincement and Call to the Ministry of Margaret Lucas* (London, 1797), p. 37.

male relatives, but their actions and threats show the persistence of hostile attitudes towards the movement in both England and the American colonies long after the introduction of formal toleration.

This was a pattern glimpsed not only in eighteenth-century Quakerism, but also in other religious movements where individual conscience was emphasised above duty to a spouse. Methodism was frequently accused of being 'the old Puritan fanaticism revived', and many criticised its incompatibility with Anglican domestic values.[30] The Methodist convert, Catherine Exley, for instance, described how her husband 'was rather severe with me, and sometimes said he feared I was going out of my mind'. Another instance she recounted was his wish that she would pray in silence and not speak so loudly that the neighbours would hear.[31] Similarly, Grace Murray's husband felt so alienated by his wife's conversion to Methodism in the 1740s that 'he threatened to put her away in a madhouse'.[32] Their experiences, along with those of their Quaker contemporaries, encapsulate the destabilising effect that women's independent conversion to religious sects had on domestic harmony.

'TRULY UNITED IN SPIRIT': QUAKER MARRIAGE AND MOTHERHOOD

But how unique was the Quaker ideal of domesticity, and how did female Friends challenge contemporary patriarchal attitudes? Historians of the early modern period agree that there was no single Protestant or even Puritan view of marriage and family life, a fact expressed by Karen Harvey, who states that patriarchy was not 'a rigid system of male governance, but a flexible "grid of power" in which several different groups attained status and authority'.[33] Similarly, early Quakers did not develop a systematic theology or provide members with a singular manual about their expectations of

[30] Emma Major, *Madam Britannia: Women, Church, and Nation 1712–1812* (Oxford, 2011), pp. 125–133.
[31] See Naomi Pullin, 'In Pursuit of Heavenly Guidance: The Religious Context of Catherine Exley's Life and Writings', in Rebecca Probert (ed.), *Catherine Exley's Diary: The Life and Times of an Army Wife in the Peninsular War* (Kenilworth, 2014), pp. 88–89.
[32] Phyllis Mack, *Heart Religion in the British Enlightenment: Gender and Emotion in Early Methodism* (Cambridge, 2008), pp. 75–76. I am grateful to Thomas Dixon for this reference.
[33] Karen Harvey, *The Little Republic: Masculinity and Domestic Authority in Eighteenth-Century Britain* (Oxford, 2012), p. 4. For studies on women and the early modern household see Margaret J. M. Ezell, *The Patriarch's Wife: Literary Evidence and the History of the Family* (London, 1987); Anthony Fletcher, *Gender, Sex, and Subordination in England, 1500–1800* (New Haven, CT, 1995); Ralph A. Houlbrooke, *The English Family 1450–1700* (London, 1984); Rosemary O'Day, *The Family and Family Relationships, 1500–1900* (Basingstoke, 1994); Sarah M. Pearsall, *Atlantic Families: Lives and Letters in the Later Eighteenth Century* (Oxford, 2008); and Robert B. Shoemaker, *Gender in English Society, 1650–1850: The Emergence of Separate Spheres?* (London, 1998).

an orderly 'idealised' household.[34] The guidance they did offer was adapted as the movement evolved, and it wasn't until the eighteenth century that detailed advice about the nurture and education of the Quaker family was written. This makes it hard to decipher how far the movement's conception of family relations differed from that of their contemporaries. However, to be a Quaker meant to share certain values concerning the family and women's place within the home that were perpetuated in Meeting minutes, epistles, life accounts, and testimonies of deceased Friends.

Although the religious commitment of female Friends could involve a serious challenge to domestic arrangements, the family could also be an empowering and supportive institution in their daily lives. As the movement developed from an evangelic sect into a more settled church, the household became integral to its construction. Early Friends believed in the all-encompassing power of the inner light, which meant that it was necessary for Quaker children to experience their own spiritual convincement. Stimulating a conversion within the family was therefore just as important as making their message accessible to individuals outside their faith. In comparison to many of their Puritan and Protestant contemporaries, Quakers believed in the inherent perfectibility rather than sinfulness of children. The culpability for the transgression of young members therefore came to be firmly associated with parents for failing to fulfil their duties.[35] Thus when Elizabeth Hutchinson's daughter married a non-Quaker, she was forced to condemn (apologise for) her role in the clandestine marriage. As one elder explained to Hutchinson, she was expected to give 'an open and free confession of faults', for letting 'that worldly spirit which entered thy heart on account of the marriage (yea wrong marriage) of an otherwise innocent promising youth (a young woman)'.[36]

In the years following the Restoration, and during the settlement of the hierarchical Meeting structure from the late 1660s, the question of ensuring continuity of the faith came to be firmly focused on perpetuating Quaker beliefs and values within the family. It became 'the key to any future progress'.[37] Epistles that addressed the education and correct upbringing of Quaker youth were regularly exchanged by Meetings in London, the American colonies, and the rest of the British Isles. One 1688 epistle issued

---

[34] Despite their strong focus on the family, Richard Vann has commented that 'scarcely anything was written about the proper kind of domestic life or the upbringing of children during the first two decades of Quakerism'. Richard T. Vann, *The Social Development of English Quakerism: 1655–1755* (Cambridge, MA, 1969), p. 167.

[35] This is discussed by Levy, *Quakers and the American Family*, pp. 75–77.

[36] HL, mssSHA Shackleton Family Correspondence, Box 3, fol. 120, Robert Lecky to Elizabeth Hutchinson, Durham, 15 February 1773.

[37] Vann, *The Social Development of English Quakerism*, p. 205.

by the London Yearly Meeting counselled parents that they were appointed in their families 'as judges for God'.[38] Eight years later, the same Meeting advised that the only way for Friends to retain their status as 'a peculiar people' was through the work of parents in 'diligently improving that good understanding, and those heavenly gifts the Lord hath endued you with' and to ensure their children were brought up in plainness and the discipline of the truth.[39] The circulation of such advice ensured the continuity of Quaker values and ideas across the transatlantic community of Friends.[40] A surviving collection of epistles received by Philadelphia Quarterly Meeting shows that the spiritual upbringing of Quaker children was one of the most pressing issues the Society was facing by the mid-eighteenth century. In their epistle dated May 1751, London Friends expressed concerns about the few opportunities available to Quaker children to be educated at Quaker schools, and counselled parents 'to be properly engaged for their due education, and the forming their tender Minds to the exercise of Piety'.[41]

The household therefore became integral to the construction and development of Quakerism and provides an important example of how women's domestic authority indirectly but closely affected the experiences of men and children. Numerous spiritual autobiographies written by ministering Friends informed readers about their childhood experiences and showed the influence of their mothers on their spiritual service. The eighteenth-century minister Samuel Bownas, for instance, was continually reminded of his mother's counsel throughout his career as a public minister. In his life account, he described how she:

had kept me very strict while I was under her Care, and would frequently in Winter Evenings take Opportunities to tell me sundry Passages of my dear Father's Sufferings, admonishing me so to live ... also frequently putting me in mind, that if she should be taken away, I should greatly miss her, both for Advice and other Ways to assist me; and advised me to fear the Lord now in my Youth, that I might be favoured with his Blessing.[42]

---

[38] London Yearly Meeting 'To the Quarterly and Monthly Meetings in England and Wales, and Elsewhere', *Extracts from the Minutes and Advices of the Yearly Meeting of Friends Held in London, from Its First Institution* (1783), p. 175.

[39] London Yearly Meeting, 'Epistle 1696', in *Epistles from the Yearly Meeting of Friends, Held in London to the Quarterly and Monthly Meetings in Great Britain, Ireland, and Elsewhere, from 1681 to 1817* (London, 1818), p. 94.

[40] See Jordan Landes, *London Quakers in the Trans-Atlantic World: The Creation of an Early Modern Community* (Houndmills, 2015), pp. 50–62.

[41] Haverford College Quaker and Special Collection (hereafter cited as HCQSC), MS Coll 971 Yearly Meeting Epistles and Extracts, 1698–1842, London Yearly Meeting to Friends at their Quarterly and Monthly Meetings in Great Britain, Ireland &c, 27–31 May 1751.

[42] Samuel Bownas, *An Account of the Life, Travels, and Christian Experiences in the Work of the Ministry of Samuel Bownas* (London, 1756), p. 4.

Moreover, on first experiencing a call to minister, Bownas was reminded of 'what my mother told me some years before, that when I grew up more to Man's Estate, I should know the Reason of that Tenderness and Weeping, and so I now did to purpose'.[43] The eighteenth-century Friend Joseph Pike also recalled his mother's influence on his ministerial career. Her death in 1688 prompted him to reflect on the example she had set, noting that 'if parents rightly discharged their duty towards their children, it might go a great way, (together with their own good examples,) in making religious impressions upon them'.[44] Although these accounts are somewhat problematic in their idealised representation of family life, the fact that these ministers draw attention to their childhood upbringing is nevertheless significant. As I will discuss later in this chapter, in comparison to their female counterparts, Quaker male ministers did not provide a significant commentary on their domestic circumstances in their spiritual journals. As these testimonies make clear, however, their upbringing held an important place in their self-identity and was central to how they viewed the world and understood their own roles within it.

Friends' belief in spiritual equality also challenged the conventional status of the mother as subordinate to her husband in the domestic hierarchy. Su Fang Ng has argued that the Quakers' emphasis on obedience to God rather than an earthly authority had significant implications for both the family and the commonwealth, as Friends 'deemphasized the authority of both the king and father'.[45] The inner spiritual light dissolved the sexual inequality of marriage introduced by the Fall. 'Love between Quaker husbands and wives', writes Jacques Tual, 'had been cleansed of all guilt thanks to the new covenant of the second birth.'[46] As a consequence, female Friends could attain theoretical equality in the marriage partnership. The eighteenth-century Quaker minister Deborah Bell was described by her husband as 'the gift of God to me', prized as 'a help-meet ... and a true and faithful yoke-fellow in all our services in the church: for being ever one in spirit, we became one in faith and practice, in discerning and judgment ... which nearly united us'.[47] Although testimonies of Quaker wives almost always stressed the positive

---

[43] Ibid., p. 5.

[44] Joseph Pike, *Some Account of the Life of Joseph Pike, of Cork, in Ireland, Who Died in the Year 1729*, John Barclay ed. (London, 1837), p. 14.

[45] Su Fang Ng, *Literature and the Politics of Family in Seventeenth-Century England* (Cambridge, 2007), p. 199.

[46] Jacques Tual, 'Sexual Equality and Conjugal Harmony: The Way to Celestial Bliss– A View of Early Quaker Matrimony', *JFHS*, vol. 55, no. 6 (1988), p. 166.

[47] Deborah Bell, *A Short Journal of the Labours and Travels in the Work in the Ministry, of That Faithful Servant of Christ, Deborah Bell* (London, 1776), p. xxvi, 'The Testimony of John Bell, Concerning His Wife Deborah Bell'.

aspects of their family life over marital tension, the emphasis was on unity and oneness with their husbands rather than obedience and loyalty.

The Quakers thought that the illuminating presence of the inner light within every individual was the primary source of revelation. This meant that the Quaker faith did not rely upon the patriarch's ability to interpret the scriptures and lead family prayers. After all, the Bible was understood as a useful sacred guide, but not as literal truth. In enabling men and women to balance earthly and spiritual ties, Quaker experientialism thus encouraged marital partnership whilst permitting women to take a leading role in the religious life of the household. The Quaker minister Alice Curwen was even described by her husband as being 'tender over me'.[48] This expression, as Catie Gill has argued, carried startling connotations of hierarchy and implied supremacy.[49]

Quaker domestic arrangements came to be praised by many eighteenth-century non-Quaker writers as superior to those of any other group. The abolitionist, Thomas Clarkson, for instance, who worked extensively with Quakers, wrote that 'domestic happiness' was their chief source of enjoyment and 'only bliss'.[50] The transmission of the Holy Spirit thus became an intimate and increasingly domestic concern for Quaker leaders, moving beyond rituals and public exhortations. As we shall see, the language of love and courtship within Quaker culture was unusual, since prospective partners were directed to the spiritual 'light' within one another, rather than their physical characters.[51] Pietist and Behmenist communities also stressed women's equal ability to access Divine Wisdom. However, in contrast to the Quakers, emphasis was placed on the soul's marriage to Christ, which meant that the believer had to become 'disassociated from all external things'.[52] Thus, although attending to spiritual concerns was central to early Quaker values, the physical union of marriage, as a manifestation of kindred souls joining together, meant that it remained a central component of women's identities.

The Quaker household was regarded as a union of individuals in the sight of God, and Friends believed that marriage was a bond of equals based on love. This was reinforced through their choice of language, which emphasised harmony and companionship. During a business visit to London, the

---

[48] Anne Martindell et al., *A Relation of the Labour, Travail and Suffering of That Faithful Servant of the Lord, Alice Curwen* (London, 1680), sig. B1r [pagination confused], 'Thomas Curwen His Testimony'.

[49] Catie Gill, *Women in the Seventeenth-Century Quaker Community: A Literary Study of Political Identities, 1650–1700* (Aldershot, 2005), p. 157.

[50] Thomas Clarkson, *A Portraiture of Quakerism* (3 vols., New York, 1806), vol. 1, p. 101.

[51] Jacques Tual, 'Sexual Equality and Conjugal Harmony', p. 167.

[52] Elizabeth Bouldin, *Women Prophets and Radical Protestantism in the British Atlantic World, 1640–1730* (Cambridge, 2015), pp. 89–93.

Quaker minister Samuel Sansom told his wife that 'my greatest pleasure in this life, is the hopes of the Enjoyment of thy Company, my Dearest (bosom friend) which I pray God grant to our Mutuall Comfort'.[53] Scholars frequently comment on the 'unusual sociability' of Quaker spouses, and it is unsurprising that Quaker writers often described the marital bond as the highest form of friendship.[54] William Penn, for example, proclaimed a wife is 'a Friend, a Companion, a *Second Self*', owing to the sexless nature of the souls.[55] The Quaker understanding of friendship in both a physical and spiritual sense will be further explored in Chapter 3. It is clear, however, that love and friendship for early Friends were intimately linked. It also underscores the theoretical equality of husband and wife in the Quaker household, for writers like Michel de Montaigne and Francis Bacon theorised friendship as a flow of affection between two equals.[56] Whilst marriage was often considered a form of friendship, and writers like John Milton argued for a more equitable relationship between husband and wife, it was generally accepted they could not be true friends because of the natural inequality of the relationship.[57] This contemporary attitude was encapsulated by the seventeenth-century religious writer Jeremy Taylor. In his acclaimed essays on friendship, he explained that domestic friendship 'is not equall, and there is too much authority on one side and too much fear on the other to make equal friendships'.[58]

The equality of Quaker marital arrangements is accentuated by the emphasis Friends placed on loving and free relations between husband and wife. Whilst early modern writers continually stressed loving matches free from parental pressure and financial inducements, Quakerism placed an unusual amount of emphasis on marital relationships based primarily on a principle of reciprocal love.[59] The Puritan writer William Gouge,

53 HCQSC, MS Coll 1008 Morris-Sansom Collection, c. 1715–1925, Box 18, Samuel Sansom folder, Samuel Sansom to 'My Dear and Loving Wife', London, 10 February 1739.

54 Richard T. Vann and David Eversley, *Friends in Life and Death: The British and Irish Quakers in the Demographic Transition, 1650–1900* (Cambridge, 1992), pp. 243–244.

55 William Penn, *Some Fruits of Solitude: In Reflections and Maxims Relating to the Conduct of Human Life* (London, 1693), p. 32.

56 Laura Gowing, Michael Hunter, and Miri Rubin, 'Introduction' in Laura Gowing, Michael Hunter, and Miri Rubin (eds.), *Love, Friendship and Faith in Europe, 1300–1800* (Basingstoke, 2005), p. 4.

57 Sheila Wright, '"Truly Dear Hearts": Family and Spirituality in Quaker Women's Writings, 1680–1750', in Sylvia Brown (ed.), *Women, Gender and Radical Religion in Early Modern Europe* (Leiden, The Netherlands, 2007), p. 101.

58 Jeremy Taylor, *The Measures and Offices of Friendship: With Rules of Conducting It* (London, 1657), p. 68.

59 The emphasis that early modern courtship culture placed on 'Mutual Love and Good Liking' is explored by David Cressy, *Birth, Marriage, and Death: Ritual, Religion, and the Life-Cycle in Tudor and Stuart England* (Oxford, 1997), pp. 260–263.

for instance, insisted that 'the nearest bond of all is betwixt man and wife' and that a prospective couple must always put their 'mutuall liking of one another' before any other considerations. However, he also recognised the necessity of children to consult with their parents before marriage, acknowledging that 'the authority of parents' was 'inviolable'.[60] William Penn, like many of his Quaker contemporaries, took a different approach and advised Friends to 'Never marry but for Love; but see that thou lov'st what is *lovely*' and emphasised that 'between a Man and his Wife nothing ought to rule but *Love*'.[61] There were some Quaker matches motivated by considerations beyond the mutual affection of husband and wife, but a strongly platonic vision of matrimony nevertheless emerges from early Quaker writings.

These were matches surpassing the bounds of physical and material considerations, where a love of others became a symbolic expression for love of Christ. The spiritual seeking expected of prospective couples was articulated in a number of testimonies and spiritual autobiographies. John Bowne claimed that 'a true Love was begotten in my heart' towards his wife Hannah 'before I knew her Face', which he attributed to 'the Love of God, that lived in her'.[62] Similarly, Richard Davies of Southwark recorded in his journal his first encounter with his future wife: 'It was not yet manifest to me where she was, or who she was. But one time, as I was at Horselydown meeting in Southward [*sic*], I heard a woman Friend open her mouth ... [and] it came to me from the Lord that the woman was to be my wife, and to go with me to the country, and to be an helpmeet for me.'[63] Although somewhat idealised, these accounts nonetheless reveal how the Quaker culture of waiting for divine guidance permeated Quaker marital relations. The love these Quaker couples felt towards one another provided a strong indication that their match was divinely ordained.

In wider society too, seventeenth- and eighteenth-century writers invoked the ideal of women as helpers and supporters to their husbands, and both sexes were advised to be careful in choosing a spouse who would be 'an helpe meet for them'.[64] Husband and wife were expected to 'conferre, read, pray, confesse, and give thanks together' and look to one another for spiritual counsel and admonition.[65] The wife was nevertheless a subordinate within this relationship, expected to submit to her husband's government.

---

[60] Gouge, *Of Domesticall Duties*, pp. 564.
[61] Penn, *Some Fruits of Solitude*, pp. 27, 36.
[62] LRSF, MS Vol 150 Luke Howard Collection, fol. 15, 'The Testimony of John Bowne Concerning His Innocent Wife and Faithful Yoke-Fellow Hannah Bowne', undated, c. 1677.
[63] Quoted in Kristianna Polder, *Matrimony in the True Church: The Seventeenth-Century Quaker Marriage Approbation Discipline* (London, 2015), p. 61.
[64] Gouge, *Of Domesticall Duties*, p. 185.
[65] Houlbrooke, *The English Family*, pp. 111–112.

Affection was often expressed in written testimonies through a wife's willingness to subject herself to her husband. Writers like Gouge, for example, dwelt on women's subordination within the marital relationship, affirming that 'every dutie which they [wives] performe to their husband, their very opinion, affection, speech, action, and all that concerneth the husband, must savour of *subjection*'.[66] Quakers, by contrast, believed husband and wife should contribute to each other's happiness and comfort as spiritual helpmates. It has been argued that the sexual equality promoted by Friends extended to dispensing the vow of obedience in their marriage ceremony, which released women from 'the restraints of subservience' and placed them in a more equal position within the household.[67] This was eloquently demonstrated in the testimony the English Friend Eleanor Haydock wrote after the death of her husband, Roger, in 1696. In her account, she described their fourteen years of marriage as one of conjugal harmony:

> we laboured in our respective Gifts in the Work of the *Ministry*, being truly united in Spirit … so that we lived in great Love and Peace … in which time we were never straitned [*sic*] one towards another, always one Heart, and of one Mind, purely knit together in the Covenant of Life.[68]

This ideal was particularly well suited to the Quaker marital partnership, where husband and wife were deemed spiritual equals and perceived as labouring together to fulfil the Lord's work at home and abroad.

Whilst love was widely held to be an essential element in marriage throughout this period, it was not considered a necessity before the match was made. Ralph A. Houlbrooke notes that, in seventeenth-century courtship culture, it was believed mutual affection was the natural product of a well-matched marriage.[69] Love alone was not the key to a happy marriage, but depended upon other considerations, including parity of piety, wealth, status, and age. Moreover, Puritan and other nonconformist writers often worried that too much love might distract a husband and wife from their love of God. This was a view that was advanced by Methodists who, according to Phyllis Mack, believed that family relationships could pose a threat to salvation if they 'loved too much'.[70] Kristianna Polder has argued that Quakers also rarely mentioned love as a motivating factor in bringing a couple together, as it could be construed as following a personal leading,

---

[66] Quoted in Sara Mendelson and Patricia Crawford, *Women in Early Modern England, 1550–1720* (Oxford, 1998), p. 135.

[67] Wright, '"Truly Dear Hearts"', pp. 104–105.

[68] Roger Haydock et al., *A Collection of the Christian Writings, Labours, Travels and Sufferings of That Faithful and Approved Minister of Jesus Christ, Roger Haydock* (London, 1700), sig. B3r, B4r–B4v, 'Eleanor Haydock's Testimony Concerning Her Husband Roger Haydock'.

[69] Houlbrooke, *The English Family*, p. 76.

[70] Mack, *Heart Religion*, p. 97.

based on sexual attraction, rather than being ordained by God.[71] Quaker marriage, however, was regarded as being grounded in mutual spiritual improvement, where husband and wife sought in one another a loving help-mate. This was reflected in the marriage proposal the Quaker theologian Robert Barclay wrote to his future wife Christian Mollison in 1669:

> Many things in the natural [world] concurs together to strengthen and increase my affections towards thee, and to endear thee unto me, but that which is before all and beyond all, is, that I can say in the fear and presence of the Lord, that I have received a charge from him to love thee, for I know his love is towards thee.[72]

Clearly, Quakers like Barclay found in God their reasons for loving a spouse. Many of the surviving letters of Quaker courtship shift easily from these overt terms of endearment and spiritual expressions. Because the inner light directed their matches, the godly virtues of potential spouses were accepted as providentially ordained.[73] Such language is indicative of one way that Quaker couples overcame the tension inherent in the Quaker theology of pleasure between husband and wife. Indeed, too much sexual passion could weaken the spiritual foundation of their marriage. This is a theme to which I shall return in the next section, but in many ways, the language surrounding marital friendship and spiritual longing stands at odds with the highly sexualised corporeal dimension of friendship discussed by Alan Bray. As I will show in Chapter 3, the bodily intimacy so fundamental to Bray's thesis on the making of friendship was replaced in Quaker writings with a highly somatic, spiritual intimacy that transcended physical encounter.[74]

Even in the American context of Quakerism, where many belonged to the wealthy merchant class, Friends frequently put the independent judgements of members before all other temporal concerns. Richard Hill of Pennsylvania told his daughter Rachel in 1758 that he believed the happiness of a marriage depended 'principally on a mutual and well-grounded affection'. As he explained, he would never press his children to marry anyone without such mutual affection.[75] It was quite common for women to reject marriage proposals if they did not feel sufficient affection for their suitor. This is demonstrated in the 1705 minutes of Chester Monthly Meeting in Pennsylvania,

[71] Polder, *Matrimony in the True Church*, p. 52.
[72] LRSF, Temp MS 745 Robson Papers, Vol. 37, Box 1, pp. 11–12, Robert Barclay to Christian Mollison, Urie (copy), 29 October 1669.
[73] Penn wrote in another treatise that 'They that love *beyond* the world, cannot be *separated* by it ... Nor can spirits ever be *divided*, that love and live in the same divine principle'. William Penn, *The Select Works of William Penn* (3rd edn, 5 vols., London, 1782), vol. 5, p. 183.
[74] Alan Bray, *The Friend* (London, 2003), pp. 156–158.
[75] Richard Hill to Rachel Hill, Madeira, 28 July 1758, in John Jay Smith (ed.), *Letters of Doctor Richard Hill and His Children: Or, The History of a Family, as Told by Themselves* (Philadelphia, 1854), p. 156.

where a committee of female Friends was appointed to investigate why John Martin and Jane Hunt's marriage had not taken place. Hunt's answer was telling: she reported that 'she could not love him well enough to take him to be her husband'.[76] Matches determined by love gave female Friends a high level of autonomy in entering into marriages and deciding on suitors. Other women also made the decision to turn down suitors they did not love, but the Quaker model of marital arrangements made an equal match grounded in love for God the overriding factor in their decision. This view has been widely supported in the secondary literature on the unusually large numbers of Quaker women, especially those inhabiting the American colonies, who chose to remain single rather than marry a husband with whom they did not share spiritual affinity.[77]

Those female Friends who failed to follow divine guidance and entered into unequal or 'mixed' marriages, often commented on the trials of balancing their temporal and spiritual concerns. Elizabeth Dale, for example, poignantly expressed that 'I am obliged frequently to appear serene and cheerful, when my poor heart is torn with conflicting passions'.[78] She was born into a notable Quaker family from North Yorkshire, but married her non-Quaker neighbour in 1757. Six years later, she corresponded with Friends and relatives in Ballitore, Ireland, describing the anguish she faced. 'I seldom get to meeting', she wrote, 'my husband being unwilling that any business, though ever so trifling should be neglected on that account.'[79] In another letter, she told her Irish acquaintances that her husband was a 'sober and industrious man' and having 'no aversion to Friends', but noted that he was unhappy with her attending Quaker Meetings 'when I am likely to be wanted at home, which on week days especially is frequently the case'.[80] A similar situation was recounted by Abigail Trindale, a young servant from Lancashire, who had worked in the home of Rachel Abraham, the daughter of the Quaker leader Margaret Fell. Trindale had forsaken the guidance and counsel of her mistress and local Women's Meeting and married a non-Quaker. Like Dale, she commented on the honesty and integrity of her

---

[76] Friends Historical Library, Swarthmore College, PA (hereafter cited as FHL), MR-Ph 98 Chester Women's Monthly Meeting (hereafter cited as MM), 1695–1733, minutes for 29 October 1705.

[77] See, especially, Karin Wulf, *Not All Wives: Women of Colonial Philadelphia* (London, 2000), pp. 31–52.

[78] University of California Santa Barbara Special Collections (hereafter cited as UCSC), Mss4 Ballitore Collection, Box 1, folder 3, p. 56, copied in a letter Richard Shackleton sent to his father Abraham Shackleton, Ballitore, 20 February 1763.

[79] UCSC, MSS 4 Ballitore Collection, Box 1, folder 3, pp. 55–56, copied in a letter Richard Shackleton sent to his father Abraham Shackleton, Ballitore 20, February 1763.

[80] HCQSC, MS Coll 859 Shackleton Family Papers, 1707–1785, Elizabeth Dale folder, Elizabeth Dale to Elizabeth Raynor, Skipton, 26 August 1762.

husband, 'who never debars me off [*sic*] going to the meetings of Friends as oft as I please'. She nevertheless lamented the 'great loss' of not having a husband with 'my own Principles'.[81] Without spouses who supported their attendance at Quaker Meetings, both Dale and Trindale failed to balance their Quaker beliefs with their domestic relationships. Dale's husband denied her a role in the spiritual instruction of her eldest daughter, who was forcibly taken from her to be brought up by her non-Quaker mother-in-law.[82] Well-matched and loving relationships between Quaker spouses thus provided the emotional and domestic security necessary to thrive within their spiritual community.

RECONCILING SPIRITUAL AND DOMESTIC DUTIES

Allegiance to Quakerism brought about a significant redefinition of roles within the household. Whilst historians like Thomas have emphasised the traditional and patriarchal nature of Quakerism once it took on an 'institutional form', the emphasis placed upon spiritual equality granted women an unusual level of freedom and authority.[83] One of the clearest and most direct challenges posed to traditional domestic relationships was the capacity of a woman to feel 'drawings' to undertake religious service. Members throughout our period accepted women's absences from the family home as a necessary aspect of their ministerial obligations. In 1701, Richard Jacob confessed to his wife Elizabeth, that 'Thy company is so desirable to me that I think no not [*sic*] all the wealth of this world if it might be had should not purchase thy absence.' Nonetheless, he supported her ministerial vocation: 'I am sensible that the Lord concerned thee and is with thee, [and] I am willing to brook thy absence and shall wait the Lord's time for thy return.'[84] The itinerancy of women like Elizabeth Jacob contrasted with the Puritan aphorism that the faithful wife should not 'be too much *from Home*'.[85]

Perhaps more remarkably, however, Quaker husbands not only had to accept their wives' absences when they felt a calling to travel abroad, but

---

[81] LRSF, MS Vol 364 Abraham MSS, fol. 45, Abigail Trindale (alias Curtis) to Rachel Abraham, Dublin, 29 October 1709.

[82] She recounts this scenario in HCQSC, MS Coll 859, 1707–1785, Shackleton Family Papers, Elizabeth Dale folder, Elizabeth Dale to Elizabeth Raynor, Skipton, 26 August 1762.

[83] Thomas, 'Women and the Civil War Sects', p. 53.

[84] FHLD, *Grubb Collection S*, folder 10, Limerick, 10 July 1701, Richard Jacob to Elizabeth Jacob, quoted in Phil Kilroy, 'Quaker Women in Ireland, 1660–1740', *Irish Journal of Feminist Studies*, vol. 2, no. 2 (1997), p. 13.

[85] The Puritan colonist Cotton Mather expected women to provide the necessary housekeeping services for their families, so that if her husband was asked where she was, he could answer 'as once *Abraham* did, *My wife is in the Tent*'. Cotton Mather, *Ornaments for the Daughters of Zion, on the Character and Happiness of a Woman* (London, 1694), p. 112.

were also expected to care for their children and provide their wives with financial and material support. Whilst his wife Mary was undertaking ministerial work in the colonies in 1750, the London Friend Daniel Weston admitted that 'It was a very near tryall to be so depriv'd of One of the most affectionate and best of wifes and a true help Meet'. But as he went on to declare, 'as it was a Duty requir'd by her great Lord and Master, [I] could do no other than resign her to his work and service.'[86] John Bowne made a similar declaration in his wife's memorial. He could have 'freely' accompanied her after she first felt a calling to travel, 'but not daring to stir without the Leading of the Lord, I was made freely willing to part with her, and remain at home with my Little ones.'[87] The great level of support provided by Quaker husbands is also detailed in the correspondence between the Lancashire minister Ruth Follows and her husband George. In 1748 she explained the comfort that 'thy Care over our Dear Babes' brought her, confessing that she thought 'it a great mercy that I had such a Loveing husband and a tender Father to Leave them with'.[88]

Such declarations of love and support stand as testament to the elevated place of the Quaker ministering wife within the domestic hierarchy. They also offer a striking challenge to traditional notions of masculinity. As scholars like Elizabeth Foyster and Alexandra Shepard have argued in their studies on early modern manhood, the gendered division of labour and sexual honour were two of the most fiercely contested aspects of male identity in the seventeenth century.[89] Having a wife leave the family home for long stretches of time, without any guarantees of when she might return, must have placed Quaker men's honour and reputations in a precarious position, for it was essential that they were able to safeguard their wives' sexuality. This can be glimpsed in the continual criticism of the movement in the anti-Quaker press. One anonymous writer contended in 1653 that Friends' self-imposed itinerancy was simply an excuse for fulfilling 'the sinfull ways of the flesh'. They questioned 'Whether they have not the Word of God as a shadow, when they make it stand by at their pleasure?'[90] We

---

[86] Historical Society of Pennsylvania (hereafter cited as HSP), MS Coll 484A Pemberton Family Papers, vol. 6, p. 90, Daniel Weston to Israel Pemberton Jr, London, 22 August 1750.
[87] LRSF, MS Vol 150 Luke Howard Collection, fol. 15, 'The Testimony of John Bowne Concerning His Innocent Wife and Faithful Yoke-Fellow Hannah Bowne', 2 February 1678.
[88] LRSF, Temp MSS 127/2/2 Ruth Follows Papers, Ruth Follows to George Follows, Isle of Ely, Cambridgeshire, 21 May 1748. I am grateful to Susan Whyman for this manuscript reference.
[89] Elizabeth A. Foyster, *Manhood in Early Modern England: Honour, Sex and Marriage* (London, 1999), pp. 103–146; and Alexandra Shepard, *Meanings of Manhood in Early Modern England* (Oxford, 2003), pp. 152–185.
[90] Anon., *Certain Quæries and Anti-Quæries, Concerning the Quakers, (So Called) In and About Yorkshire* (London, 1653), pp. 5, 2.

will return to the slurs levelled against Quaker ministry in Chapter 4, but such statements make clear that it was extraordinary for women to absent themselves from their families to follow such callings. Separation from the household meant a renunciation of wifely duties.

Quaker leaders recognised that family divisions and even separation might be necessary to pursue God's work in the world. 'Opinions do tend to break the relation of Subjects to their Magistrates, Wives to their Husbands, Children to their Parents', wrote George Fox in 1653.[91] A vision of spiritual community extended back to the primitive church when the first apostles left behind family and friends to pursue their spiritual fellowship. Yet the hardships associated with separation from families in service to God were not unique to Quakerism and form a common trope in sectarian writings. An interesting parallel is found at the start of John Bunyan's *Pilgrim's Progress*, when Pilgrim first commences his journey. His family stood at the door of their house 'cry[ing] after him to return', but Pilgrim, refusing to be deterred from his mission, 'put his fingers in his Ears, and ran on, crying, Life, Life, Eternal Life'.[92] Whilst Pilgrim later made his journey with his family, his early experience of conversion, like those of many Quaker preachers, led him to believe separation from his family was one of many necessary trials on his religious journey.

A Quaker woman, however, was not expected to withdraw from the world, remain celibate, or neglect her domestic obligations. Unlike most over movements of this period, Quakers considered spiritual and domestic work to be intrinsically linked.[93] The comparisons between Quakerism and Methodism in this sense will be returned to shortly. It is nevertheless worth emphasising here that women in other dissenting congregations like the Baptists, Methodists, Pietists, Moravians, or Behmenists who experienced visions or a call to minister or prophecy not only were recognised for their spiritual gifts, but also adopted positions within their communities almost entirely divorced from traditional female roles. The Philadelphian visionary Ann Bathurst, for example, set herself apart from temporal relationships to show that she was 'one chosen to receive tremendous spiritual favour'. Family, as Elizabeth Bouldin has discussed, was central to her writing and self-identity, but only in a metaphorical sense to confirm her status as a mother figure and prophet within the community.[94] Quakerism, by contrast,

---

[91] George Fox, *Saul's Errand to Damascus with His Packet of Letters from the High-Priests, against the Disciples of the Lord* (London, 1653), p. 4.

[92] John Bunyan, *The Pilgrim's Progress: From This World to That Which Is to Come Delivered under the Similitude of a Dream* (London, 1678), p. 3.

[93] Rebecca Larson, *Daughters of Light: Quaker Women Preaching and Prophesying in the Colonies and Abroad, 1700–1775* (New York, 1999), p. 134.

[94] Bouldin, *Women Prophets and Radical Protestantism*, pp. 109–110.

seems to have found a balance between recognising the necessity of the family and the needs of the individual in undertaking God's work.

George Fox counselled Friends in 1657 not to travel and preach as a continuous way of life, and advised that 'if any have been moved to speak' and had 'quenched that which moved them', they should return home to their family and 'not go forth afterwards into words, until they feel the power arise and move them thereto again'.[95] Even those Friends who undertook evangelical service beyond the household continued to place an extraordinary emphasis on their efforts in their families. Following the death of Elizabeth Dennis in 1748, Colchester Meeting carefully balanced recognition of her spiritual and domestic labours in their memorial. The Friends recounted how she was a pattern of exemplarity 'when at home in her Business' where she 'work[ed] of her own hands to administer to her necessities' and 'could not be free to leave her home, unless necessity, either to visit the Churches, or upon the account of her Business, called her to it'.[96] Archetypal women like Dennis, whose eulogies gave equal weighting to their domestic duties and spiritual service, could act as encouragement for female Friends wishing to pursue ministerial careers without having to relinquish all ties to their families.

This pattern had interesting gendered implications for Quaker men too. Many were memorialised for their dedication and devotion to their outward labours and commitment to their families. John Banks, for instance, described in detail life outside of his ministerial work, noting how 'I laboured with my hands, with honest endeavours, in lawful employments, for the maintenance of my family'.[97] Leinster Province Meeting in Ireland in 1754 described how Thomas Wilson was not only an 'able Minister of the Gospel', but would also return *speedily* to his outward Abode', after he delivered his spiritual testimony and 'found himself clear'. He 'was *Diligent* in his lawful Vocation of Husbandry, for the good of his Family, wherein the Lord blessed his Endeavours with Prosperity and Plenty'.[98] Outward assiduousness and labour towards the family became symbolic of spiritual integrity and had important implications for masculinity. Indeed, those who

[95] George Fox, *The Journal of George Fox*, ed. John L. Nickalls (Cambridge, 1952), p. 341, George Fox's Address to Friends in the Ministry, given at John Crook's house, 31 May 1658.
[96] LRSF, YM/TCDM Testimonies Concerning Ministers Deceased, vol. 1 1728–1758, p. 286, 'A Testimony Concerning Our Deceased Friend Elizabeth Dennis', 3 March 1749.
[97] John Banks, *A Journal of the Labours, Travels, and Sufferings of That Faithful Minister of Jesus Christ, John Banks* (2nd edn, London, 1798), p. 72.
[98] Leinster Province Meeting 'A Brief Abstract of the Testimonies of Friends of the Three Provinces, Concerning Our Deceased Friend, Thomas Wilson', in Thomas Wilson, *A Brief Journal of the Life, Travels and Labours of Love … Of That Eminent and Faithful Servant of Jesus Christ, Thomas Wilson* (Dublin, 1728), p. xvii.

failed in upholding the order of their household, were subject to intense scrutiny by their local Monthly Meetings, as I will discuss in Chapter 2.

The Quaker focus on the domestic aspects of men's and women's identities stood in contrast to the roles provided for ministers in other dissenting congregations, which consistently held up single and unattached lifestyles as ideals of religiosity. The Presbyterian minister Christopher Love, for instance, was allegedly so desirous to avoid becoming 'entangled with the business of the world', that he rented a separate home from his wife and children so he could work undisturbed.[99] Many Methodist converts viewed their families as hindrances to attaining spiritual perfection and, as Anna M. Lawrence has shown, many freed themselves from bad marriages.[100] Whilst Methodists did not prevent preachers from marrying, they believed a celibate life was superior for religious teachers, as family and secular concerns could interfere with spiritual service. Drawing upon St Paul's words, the Methodist leader John Wesley explained that 'the unmarried woman careth for the things of the Lord, that she may be held both in body and spirit, but she that is married careth for the things of the world, how she may please her husband'.[101] This was echoed by the Methodist writer Mary Fletcher, who in one 1766 devotional pamphlet entitled *Jesus, Altogether Lovely: Or a Letter to Some of the Single Women in the Methodist Society*, counselled her 'dear Sisters' on the necessity of self-denial. She urged them to maintain strict chastity over their minds and bodies.[102]

In contrast to the Quaker inner light, which constituted sporadic ministerial service based on individual conscience, the demands of ministerial life compelled Methodist preachers to move around their circuits on a daily basis, preaching in different houses and chapels. Continuous and unpaid service in this form was almost incompatible with a normal family life. Such a policy, Russell Richey has argued, promoted a celibate class of single men and women and threatened prevailing domestic structures. Some used conversion to Methodism as a means of delaying marriage or avoiding it altogether.[103] Leaders like Wesley stressed that itinerant preachers should identify with the communities they served rather than their biological families. Thus when John Nelson's daughter died during his travels and his

[99] Mendelson and Crawford, *Women in Early Modern England*, p. 311.
[100] Anna M. Lawrence, *One Family under God: Love, Belonging, and Authority in Early Transatlantic Methodism* (Philadelphia, 2011), pp. 139–155.
[101] Cited in ibid., p. 137.
[102] Mary Fletcher (later Bosanquet), *Jesus, Altogether Lovely: Or a Letter to Some of the Single Women in the Methodist Society* (London, 1766), pp. 3–6.
[103] Russell Richey, *Early American Methodism* (Bloomington, IN, 1991), pp. 1–20; and Gail Malmgreen, 'Domestic Discords: Women and the Family in East Cheshire Methodism, 1750–1830', in Jim Obelkevich, Lyndal Roper, and Raphael Samuel (eds.), *Disciplines of Faith: Studies in Religion, Politics and Patriarchy* (London, 1987), pp. 60–61.

pregnant wife was attacked by 'a group of angry women and lost the baby', he did not seem to lament the circumstances. Instead, he responded that 'God had more than made it up to her by filling her with peace and love'.[104]

For many nonconformist religious groups, family relationships were often viewed as hindrances to attaining spiritual perfection. The Philadelphian Society and German Pietists provide another interesting point of comparison in this respect. Like the Quakers, Pietists advocated divine revelation and ignored social boundaries, permitting women to travel and preach as part of their godly responsibilities. However, many leading Pietists strongly advocated celibacy out of the belief that sexual relations would distract ministers from their '"true" or "spiritual" marriage in heaven'. One of their leading female figures, Jane Lead, experienced a happy marriage before her conversion, but later commented that it had delayed her 'true marriage of the soul with the Heavenly Sophia'.[105]

It is certainly true that pursuing a ministerial career was easier for those male or female Friends who were not responsible for managing a household. Unmarried women and mature widows had the most freedom to travel and their limited family commitments enabled them to submit themselves entirely to God's will.[106] The eighteenth-century minister Catherine Payton, for example, waited twenty-three years to marry William Phillips, who she first met in 1749 during a ministerial visit to Swansea. She rationalised her decision to defer the marriage because she 'feared to indulge thoughts of forming a connection, which, from its incumbrances, might tend to frustrate the intention of Divine wisdom respecting me'.[107] Communal structures were also in place to support single women with a spiritual calling who did not have the financial resources to undertake ministerial work on their own.[108]

However, the ideal of a single, celibate lifestyle for ministers was never formulated or encouraged by early Quakerism. Where incidents of celibacy are recorded, they tend to be from the earliest and most extreme years of the movement, when no coherent testimony had been established in England

---

[104] Quoted in Mack, *Heart Religion*, pp. 84–85.

[105] Lucinda Martin, 'Jacob Boehme and the Anthropology of German Pietism', in Ariel Hessayon and Sarah Apetrei (eds.), *An Introduction to Jacob Boehme* (Abingdon, 2014), p. 133. See also Sarah Apetrei, 'Masculine Virgins: Celibacy and Gender in Later Stuart London', in Apetrei and Smith, *Religion and Women in Britain*, pp. 41–59.

[106] See Amy M. Froide, 'The Religious Lives of Singlewomen in the Anglo-Atlantic World: Quaker Missionaries, Protestant Nuns, and Covert Catholics', in Daniella Kostroun and Lisa Vollendorf (eds.), *Women, Religion, and the Atlantic World (1600–1800)* (Toronto, 2009), pp. 60–78.

[107] Catherine Phillips (née Payton), *Memoirs of the Life of Catherine Phillips* (London, 1797), pp. 207–208.

[108] Wulf, *Not All Wives*, pp. 56–70.

or the colonies. A Quaker woman might legitimately remain single or defer marriage, but unlike Methodist female preachers or Catholic nuns, this was the exception rather than the rule. Rebecca Larson's study of eighteenth-century transatlantic female Quaker ministers, for instance, reveals that 70 per cent of female preachers were married at the time of their religious service, and 'nearly all' of those undertaking transatlantic work married at some point during their lives.[109] Female Friends were able to combine marriage and ministry without one set of obligations conflicting with the other.

The Quakers' advocation of an austere lifestyle, devoid of pleasure, has often been misunderstood as promoting an ideal of celibacy. A frequently cited example surrounds the life of Elizabeth Holme, who was reprimanded by the Quaker leader Margaret Fell in 1654 on hearing she was pregnant.[110] Trevett has characterised Fell's response to have been guided by her belief that the pregnancy would mark the end of a successful preaching career. However, it is more probable that Fell's concerns stemmed not from Holme living a celibate life, but by the belief the baby would be an unnecessary burden on Friends in the region she was visiting. Indeed, Holme left the newborn in the care of a Cardiff Quaker to continue her ministry.[111] Such concerns were echoed in an undated epistle sent by the women Friends of London to Women's Meetings across the country. They advised that 'it is desired that young Women would for bear to Travell when they are with Child, [for] there is a considerable danger attends it and it is looked upon not to be commendable nor honourable'.[112] In the American colonies, Levy has shown that George Fox's warnings about lust in marriage and living chaste lives were taken to the extreme when a group of Quakers in Salem advocated a lifestyle 'literally above lust', where husband and wife were to live celibately.[113] The extreme asceticism of these New England Friends was recounted in a letter Joseph Nicholson sent to Margaret Fell in April 1660, when he complained that his co-religionists refused to share a prison cell with him 'because my wife was with chilld'.[114]

In post-Restoration Quakerism, neither marriage nor childrearing was considered an obstacle to male or female ministers carrying on their spiritual

---

[109] This analysis of marital status has been taken from the list of transatlantic ministers provided by Larson in the appendices to *Daughters of Light*, which provides short biographies of fifty-six female ministers in the transatlantic community during the period 1700–1775, pp. 135–137, 305–319.

[110] The short career of Elizabeth Holme is explored in Brailsford, *Quaker Women*, pp. 148–156.

[111] Trevett, *Women and Quakerism*, 98–99.

[112] LRSF, MGR 1114 London Women's Meeting Epistles, 1671–1753, fol. 15, Epistle sent from the Women's Meeting in London to 'Dear Friends & Sisters in the Lord', undated, c. 1671–1675.

[113] Levy, *Quakers and the American Family*, pp. 71–72.

[114] Mack, *Visionary Women*, p. 182.

work. It was not until the Philadelphian missionary Margaret Lewis arrived in England with her companion Margaret Ellis in October 1752 that she realised she was about '4 months gone with Child'. Nevertheless, as the correspondence sent from English Quakers back to her friends and family in Philadelphia reveals, the ministerial work of the pregnant Margaret was not hindered by her 'unpleasant condition' and both she and her companion continued their journey across England, eventually settling in Bristol for her lying-in.[115] Margaret continued to labour in England for another two years until she was 'Clear of … religious service'.[116] The ability of Quaker women like Margaret Lewis to pursue a ministerial career without renouncing marriage or motherhood was an element of their 'calling' substantively different from that of women in other sects, which tended to adopt a more ascetic stance towards female prophecy and dissociate women's spiritual and temporal roles. This supports Mack's contention that the most creative feature of early Quaker life was the synthesis of 'the fluid elements of an ecstatic movement with social identities that were stable and also surprisingly traditional'.[117] One of the most distinctive and surprising features of Quakerism was the integration and compatibility of ecstatic preaching with their expected social roles.

'SUPPLYING MY PLACE IN MY ABSENCE': MINISTERING WIVES AND MOTHERS

An active and visible body of married female preachers, guided not by their domestic responsibilities but by their own spiritual callings, served to destabilise the patriarchal household. Historians of Quakerism have acknowledged the readiness of early proselytes to follow their calls to ministry and leave their temporal affairs behind.[118] Feminist scholars have often viewed female converts as being attracted to Quakerism because of the opportunities it offered them to escape from household concerns. Their status as wives and mothers often become tangential when compared to their wider roles within the movement. Rachel Labouchere, for instance, has hinted that the

---

[115] HSP, MS Coll 484A Pemberton Family Papers, vol. 8, p. 70, Mary Weston, Wapping, Surrey to Israel Pemberton Jn., Philadelphia, 25 October 1752.
[116] HSP, MS Coll 484A Pemberton Family Papers, vol. 10, p. 25, Mary Weston, London to John Pemberton, Philadelphia, 6 October 1754.
[117] Mack, *Visionary Women*, p. 239.
[118] Barry Reay has suggested that of the first ministers who arrived in America during the period 1656 to 1663, 45 per cent were women. Barry Reay, *The Quakers and the English Revolution* (London, 1985), p. 26. Larson, in her survey of eighteenth-century female preachers, has estimated that there were 1,300–1,500 active female ministers in the transatlantic Quaker community over the first three-quarters of the eighteenth century. Larson, *Daughters of Light*, p. 63.

Quaker minister Deborah Darby used her ministry to take extended leave from the demands of family life. This included coping with her husband's recurring mental illness.[119] Hilary Hinds praises Quaker women for refusing 'to be bridled and constrained' by contemporary ideals. Family matters, she argues, become only marginal concerns in their writings, with their spiritual obligations surpassing all domestic concerns.[120] Moreover, Amy Froide's recent study of single women in the Anglo-Atlantic world regards female Friends as making a conscious decision to pursue a ministering career to bypass childbirth.[121]

The unusual role of the itinerant female preacher undoubtedly affected her life in significant ways, impacting upon her domestic status. However, as I have established, Quakers saw everyday tasks as much as preaching as a calling from God. This meant that the household was far from a peripheral concern in ministerial women's lives and shaped their public personas as preachers and as members of communities. Their extant spiritual autobiographies and correspondence underscore the ways in which their household work defined their ministerial experiences and, conversely, how their status as ministers enhanced, rather than undermined, their position in the family.

Female Quakers understood that their religious calling posed a potential threat to the welfare of their own families and many chose to present their familial sacrifices as part of the trials they faced for their faith. Joan Brooksop spoke for many of her Quaker contemporaries when she declared: '[I have] forsaken all my Relations, Husband and Children, and whatsoever was near and dear unto me, yea and my own Life too, for his own Names sake.'[122] Juxtaposing the obligations of the family and their divine 'leadings', women like Brooksop used their domestic relationships to define their public identities as preachers. Numerous Quaker women justified their decision to travel by explaining that their divine calling would ultimately secure the spiritual welfare of their families. Like the early apostles, they believed eternal glory would come to the families of those who sacrificed everything to follow Jesus, preach the gospel, and suffer persecution in His name.[123] The

---

[119] Rachel Labouchere, *Deborah Darby of Coalbrookdale, 1754–1810: Her Visits to America, Ireland, Scotland, Wales, England and the Channel Isles* (York, 1993), pp. 34, 38–39.

[120] Hilary Hinds, *God's Englishwomen: Seventeenth-Century Radical Sectarian Writing and Feminist Criticism* (Manchester, 1996), pp. 176–177.

[121] Froide, 'The Religious Lives of Singlewomen', p. 64.

[122] Joan Brooksop, *An Invitation of Love Unto the Seed of God, Throughout the World, with a Word to the Wise in Heart, and a Lamentation for New England* (London, 1662), p. 12.

[123] Mark 10:28–30: 'Then Peter began to say to him, Lo, we have left all, and have followed thee. And Jesus answered and said, Verily, I say unto you, There is no man that hath left house, or brethren, or sisters, or father, or mother, or wife, or children, or lands, for My sake and the gospel's, But he shall receive an hundredfold now in this time, . . . and in the world to come eternal life' (King James version).

'Faithful handmaid' Joan Vokins admitted in her published spiritual autobiography that despite her love for her husband and seven young children,
disobedience to her spiritual calling would have provoked the Lord 'to have
witholden his Mercies from us all, and to bring his Judgements upon us ...
in the Day of Acco[un]t'.[124]

Whilst the primary emphasis in the published writings of public female
Friends was on their spiritual labours, a continued emphasis on their domestic relationships was significant on two accounts. In the first place, it adds
weight to the argument that Quakerism was unique in balancing women's
spiritual and outward identities by encouraging gifted married women to
take on positions of spiritual authority. It also underlines the gendered
nature of these female ministers' testimonies. They stand in contrast to the
spiritual autobiographies and life accounts published by their male brethren, who rarely made reference to their families or domestic ties. The edi-
tors of Thomas Story's life account offered an apology to the reader for the
omission of particular details and 'private Persons', noting that the author
'esteem'd them as Subjects of too light and insignificant a Nature to bear
any Part or Mixture with Things appertaining to Religion'. They went on to
recount that it 'is not a little remarkable, that he has not once mentioned his
ever having been in the conjugal State, though 'tis certain that he was married in 1706 to *Anne* Daughter of *Edward Shippen*, with whom he lived in
great Harmony and Affection several Years'.[125]

The published accounts of female Friends, by contrast, consistently drew
attention to their identities as wives and mothers. Gill comments on the
strong familial context featured in the life accounts of many ministering
women's writings published after the Restoration, which was evidenced
by framing the minister's narrative around the testimonies of the husband
and children.[126] This trope was much less common in the accounts of male
Friends and suggests that the value of Quaker women's spiritual accounts
lay in the continued presence of the household and family in their writings. It also served to anticipate and rebut the charge that female ministers
were abandoning their family responsibilities. As the mothers of young children, these women's absences from the home were radical. Nevertheless,
in drawing attention to their families and openly acknowledging that they
were breaking with convention, these women were able to use their stories

---

[124] Joan Vokins, *God's Mighty Power Magnified: As Manifested and Revealed in His Faithful Handmaid Joan Vokins* (London, 1691), p. 23.

[125] Thomas Story, *A Journal of the Life of Thomas Story: Containing an Account of His Remarkable Convincement of, and Embracing the Principles of Truth* (Newcastle, 1747), pp. ii–iii, 'To the Reader', written by James Wilson and John Wilson, Kendal, 24 July 1747.

[126] Gill, *Women in the Seventeenth-Century Quaker Community*, p. 153.

of familial sacrifice to enhance the spiritual authority of their published testimonies.

A common theme in itinerant women's private writings was therefore the conviction that the sacrifices they were making for their families was on behalf of a far greater cause. During her travels to America in October 1750, the English Friend Mary Weston communicated how she hoped both her husband and daughter 'may still with me be sharers of Divine Bounty' in both 'health of body' and 'the influences of the blessed spirit' in which, as she explained, they were all participants.[127] Similarly, the Lancashire minister Ruth Follows cited the scriptural example of 'strength in weakness' to accentuate her trials when leaving her husband and small children 'to his divine protection'.[128] Her travels took on providential significance when she declared that the Lord preserved her family in her absence. 'Although it is a pinching trial to leave dear husband and children', she took reassurance from the fact that 'great peace' came to those 'who are obedient to the Lord's requirings'.[129] This was encapsulated in a letter she penned to her husband, George, in August 1760 during her travels in East Anglia. She informed him that it was not an 'omition of Duty that Detains me', but asked him to consider 'how afflicting would it be to us both for me to bring a burden home with mee'.[130]

Another feature of ministering Quaker women's published writings rarely glimpsed in those of their male contemporaries is evidence of them postponing missionary service on account of particular family circumstances. Alice Curwen, for example, revealed in her spiritual autobiography that she felt a calling to go to Boston and New England, 'at which', she confessed, 'my Heart was exceedingly broken, and I cryed unto the Lord with many Tears, and said, *O Lord, what shall become of my little Children, and of my poor Husband?*'[131] She was troubled because, at the time of her calling, her husband Thomas was incarcerated for his testimony against tithes. Alice, the mother of a large family, was consequently the sole provider and caregiver and could not easily justify her absence. Alice's self-interrogation lasted many years, and it was not until her family obligations lessened and her husband was released from prison that she took up the call to travel abroad at God's command. Adopting an itinerant lifestyle, as Cristine M. Levenduski

---

[127] LRSF, MS Vol 312 Journal of Mary Weston, insert before p. 71, Mary Weston to Daniel Weston, New York, 9 December 1750.

[128] The idea of 'strength' being 'made perfect in weakness' was described in 2 Corinthians 12:9.

[129] Ruth Follows, *Memoirs of Ruth Follows, Late of Castle Donnington, Leicestershire*, ed. Samuel Stansfield (London, 1829), p. 20.

[130] LRSF, Temp MSS 127/2/3 Ruth Follows Papers, Ruth Follows to George Follows, Norwich, 18 August 1760.

[131] Martindell et al., *A Relation of the Labour, Travail and Suffering of ... Alice Curwen*, p. 2.

has stressed, was 'problematic in a culture emphasizing family stability as the basis for communal solidity'.[132] In showing that their family obligations were carefully balanced and there were occasions when the family could be placed above spiritual concerns, these women represented a model of domesticity much more in line with contemporary expectations.

Male Friends, by contrast, often recounted their decision to travel and undertake ministerial work with the knowledge that it could have an impact on family life. The Nottingham Friend John Gratton left his heavily pregnant wife to undertake ministerial work in London. Whilst he was away, Anne had a traumatic birth, 'the child was Buried' and he came home to find her 'very weak'. The reaction of his father, who was not a Quaker, made clear the potential harm that such a decision to travel abroad could do. He came to visit Gratton after he returned home and chided him 'for leaving my Wife in her Condition', making it clear that he should not have travelled when he knew 'how things were at home'.[133] Like female Friends, male Quakers presented such details to foreground the sacrifice they were making for their faith.

However, no female minister recounts making a conscious decision to leave the family home when her husband, children, or relatives would be endangered by her absence. When Catherine Payton's brother was taken ill on their return from the London Yearly Meeting in 1759, she was torn between her calling to preach, which she described as 'the relief of my own mind', and 'the discharge of that duty which I owed to an affectionate brother'. She stayed by his bedside until her sister could take him to Bath to recover. Payton thanked God, 'who, in this critical juncture, directed me to act for the help of my dear brother'.[134] Perhaps more strikingly, the eighteenth-century Carlisle minister Jane Pearson instructed her readers to return home if they felt under a burden to do so. Whilst travelling in Lancashire, she described having a strong drawing towards her home after receiving news of her mother's illness and imminent death. 'I mention this', she wrote, 'that friends may attend to their feelings and drawings as to returning home, for had she departed in my absence, I should have been in danger of letting in the reasoner.'[135]

---

[132] Cristine M. Levenduski, *Peculiar Power: A Quaker Woman Preacher in Eighteenth-Century America* (London, 1996), p. 31.

[133] John Gratton, *A Journal of the Life of That Ancient Servant of Christ, John Gratton* (London, 1720), pp. 55–56.

[134] Phillips, *Memoirs of the Life of Catherine Phillips*, pp. 184–185.

[135] Jane Pearson, *Sketches of Piety: In the Life and Religious Experiences of Jane Pearson* (York, 1817), p. 37. It is almost certain that 'the reasoner' in this context was the devil, see esp. pp. 19–26.

Even for those women who undertook prolonged ministerial service, there was no question of them abandoning their long-term domestic responsibilities. Itinerant women's personal letters reveal the conflict they could face, as mothers whose natural urge was to be present when the family was in need. In a letter of 1751, the Philadelphian Quaker Mary Pemberton spoke for many of her contemporaries when she assured her husband she took 'no Pleasure' in being 'absent from thee and our Dear Children Who I sincerely Esteem'.[136] The Bristol Friend Edith Lovel, who died in a shipwreck in 1781, confessed to her husband the frustration of not knowing where or when she would be 'called' to travel. She often stated how she imagined her family accompanying her on her journey, and described in detail the conflict of such duties. On feeling a calling to visit Quaker families in Cork, rather than return home, she recounted how she 'lay most part of the night watering my pillow with tears', for she 'could not think of giving up to go'. She then went on to divulge how she hoped her husband would 'be enabled to bear this trial for me', for it was one she could not bear alone.[137] The careful balance female preachers attained between their prophetic and domestic identities is visibly demonstrated in a pocket almanac from 1751, carried by the English preacher Mary Weston during her visit to Pennsylvania (Figure 1.1). In her small handbook, no more than four inches tall, Weston recorded details of the Friends and Meetings she encountered on her travels along with recipes she had learned, including one 'to make Good salves'.[138] This may have been useful for her to know during dangerous travels, but it also provides tangible evidence of how female missionaries acquired knowledge for the benefit of their households during their service abroad.

The ministry of some women Friends may even have suffered because of their deep attachment to their domestic concerns. Jane Pearson presented a striking providential scenario about the consequences of failing to follow a divine leading. She confessed in her spiritual autobiography that divine disappointment may have brought about the premature death of her husband because 'I had not faithfully discharged myself in the ministry'.[139] A letter sent from Henry Gouldney to Abigail Boles's husband in September 1722 similarly recounted how Boles's ministry seemed to suffer because of her thoughts of home. 'Thy wife', Gouldney wrote, 'would sometimes be chearfull, but then againe would reflect upon the long absence from thee,

---

[136] HSP, MS Coll 484A Pemberton Family Papers, vol. 7, p. 123, Mary Pemberton to Israel Pemberton Jr, Shrewsbury, MA, 29 October 1751.

[137] HCQSC, MS Coll 955 Edward Wanton Smith Papers, 1681–1971, Box 5, Edith Lovel folder, 'Extracts of Letters from Edith Lovel to Her Husband', Dublin, 8 November 1781.

[138] LRSF, MS Box 6.18 Pocket Almanac for 1751 carried by Mary Weston on her travels to the Americas.

[139] Jane Pearson, *Sketches of Piety*, p. 40.

Figure 1.1. Page containing a recipe 'to make a Good salve' from the almanac Mary Weston carried on her travels in Pennsylvania in 1751. (© Religious Society of Friends (Quakers) in Britain. LRSF MS Box 6_18).

which I thinck was some disadvantage to us, hastening away at least a week before her time.'[140] The experiences of these women underscore the trying and often highly emotional circumstances they faced as wives and mothers who wanted to return home to their families.

Many itinerant women's written testimonies also reveal the tension between their identities as spiritual prophets who owed obedience to God and their duties as wives, who were expected to remain loyal to their husbands.[141] The New England Friend Hannah Bowne undertook ministerial travel in England and the Low Countries in the 1670s, leaving her husband

---

[140] LRSF, MS Vol 296 Watson MSS, fol. 2, Henry Gouldney to John Boles, London, 15 September 1722. Abigail Boles married Samuel Watson in 1731.

[141] Only on rare occasions did an outright renunciation of spousal responsibility occur. These include the accounts published in Katharine Evans and Sarah Cheevers, *This Is a Short Relation of Some of the Cruel Sufferings (for the Truths Sake) of Katharine Evans and Sarah Chevers in the Inquisition in the Isle of Malta* (London, 1662); Rebecca Travers et al., *The Work of God in a Dying Maid Being a Short Account of the Dealings of the Lord with One Susannah Whitrow* (London, 1677); Hayes, *A Legacy, or Widow's Mite*; and Ashbridge, *Some Account of the Early Part of the Life of Elizabeth Ashbridge*.

to care for their children. Yet in the testimony her husband, John, wrote after her death in 1678, he was at pains to emphasise her wifely responsibilities. 'The resolution of her heart and the Bent of her Spirit', he wrote, 'was altogether to be Subject unto me in all things, which for conscience sake she could do.' His language reinforces the idea of wifely obedience. During her travels, he continued to exert his influence and at one point decided to accompany her, so he could 'press her ... to haste away to her Children'.[142] To some degree, such evidence throws into question how far Quaker women's activities provided a departure from traditional household norms, suggesting that a woman's call to ministry continued to be checked by her position within the household. Nevertheless, the Quaker recognition that women had a 'calling' beyond marriage and motherhood is something Larson has characterised as the 'greatest modification of the legal subordination of women to men'.[143] One of the most revolutionary features of Quaker women's position in the marital partnership was that when they felt a call to travel, their husbands were expected to support them. Even John Bowne, despite his evident reluctance, did not feel entitled to obstruct his wife's powerful call.

Much of the extant correspondence exchanged by Quaker spouses attests to the supportive and loving domestic arrangements female ministers encountered. The English Friend Isaac Hall, for instance, relayed commonplace information about the welfare of their children to his wife Alice, whilst she was travelling in Ireland:

thy Son John is grown a great lad and he is very hearty and he [goes] to the hay field and works till he Sweat he is fresh couler'd ... Sarah is hearty and fresh Couler'd and she can walk in John['s] hand unto her Grand Mothers. She has not got all her teeth yet ... My mother is very well and she helps us all she can.[144]

Although a rare example, the existence of such loving correspondence between a ministering woman and her husband, full of details about the children's progress and how they were coping during the mother's absence, suggests the implicit approval of Quaker husbands for their wives' spiritual work.

Isaac Hall's letter also hints at the important and under-acknowledged efforts of the Quaker grandmother, a type of non-itinerant female Friend who clearly had an important supportive role in the Quaker household, but

---

[142] LRSF, MS Vol 150 Luke Howard Collection, fol. 15, 'The Testimony of John Bowne Concerning His Innocent Wife and Faithful Yoke-Fellow Hannah Bowne', undated, c. 1677.

[143] Larson, *Daughters of Light*, p. 155.

[144] Isaac Hall to Alice Hall, Broughton, Cumberland, 26 July 1747, in John Hall Shield (ed.), *Genealogical Notes on the Families of Hall, Featherstone, Wigham, Ostle, Watson etc.* (Allendale, 1915), pp. 35a–37.

who rarely receives mention in the surviving sources. Since the husbands of itinerant wives were more likely to need assistance to provide for their families, it is likely that grandmothers or elder daughters were a common substitute for maternal care. This was almost undoubtedly the case when the Irish minister Elizabeth Jacob travelled to the American colonies, as revealed in a letter she sent her son Isaac dated March 1712. She reminded him not to 'disobey thy father and Grandmother and to be in anywise stuborn ... in my absence'.[145] Similarly, in October 1777, Mary Lloyd wrote a letter of thanks to her 'Honor'd Mother' Priscilla Farmer, describing how she was under 'the greatest obligation to her for the care she takes of my dear little son and Household affairs in my absence, also for her affectionate attention to my excellent Husband'.[146]

Not only did the absence of a Quaker mother prove an emotional trial for the family members they left behind, for poorer Friends it could also have a disruptive effect upon the household economy. As we shall see in Chapter 4 this was an issue exploited in the anti-Quaker press. The image of the female Quaker 'tub-preacher', for instance, depicted a laundress who had turned her washtub upside-down. This reinforced contemporary fears that such unnatural women were neglecting their families. To some extent, of course, that criticism had force. An itinerant preacher, whether female or male, was placing a burden on the rest of the household. Some correspondence hinted at the problems of a family trying to cope in the mother's absence. In 1747 Isaac Hall informed his ministering wife:

We have had about two weeks very fine we[a]ther and I have got all my hay ... and some little among the corn without hireing any but Mary Hudert two days and half. I think to get it all this week for I have got it so fare without raine. Our big [barley] and wheat will be pretty so[o]ne ripe, and I hope thou will be at home when the oats is ripe.[147]

Alice Hall clearly played a significant role in the domestic economy of the family and Isaac's remarks suggest that her presence was sorely missed.

Ruth Follows was another female minister, from a poor background, whose absence brought hardship on the family. She confessed to her husband in one letter whilst she was ministering in London in April 1760, that 'I Cannot think much of home business', admitting that 'I have never been uneasey since I Left thee about temporal affairs'.[148] She also told her

---

[145] LRSF, Portfolio MSS, vol. 41, fol. 48, Letter from Elizabeth Jacob to Isaac Jacob, Lurgan, 10 March 1712.
[146] FHL, Temp MSS 403/4/8/1/3 Arthur B. Braithwaite Family Papers, Mary Lloyd to Priscilla Farmer, Weymouth, 15 October 1777.
[147] Isaac Hall to Alice Hall, Broughton, Cumberland, 26 July 1747, in Shield (ed.), *Genealogical Notes*, pp. 36–37.
[148] LRSF, Temp MSS 127/2/5 Ruth Follows Papers, Ruth Follows to George Follows, London, 25 April 1760.

children how she and her husband, George, were partners 'at sharing last harvest', noting how they lived 'very frugally' and 'Labour Dilligently'.[149] Yet for more than forty years she repeatedly visited Meetings across the British Isles, while her supportive husband cared for their children. After her son Samuel fell into debt, Ruth reminded him that spiritual duty should be placed before outward prosperity. In one letter, she used the example of how the family depended on her labour, noting that her ministerial service 'pritty much stript [us] of many of our temporal goods'.[150] George Follows nevertheless continued to provide her with financial support and frequently made the travel arrangements at the beginning of her journeys. She also commented on the difficulties of resuming domestic life after ministerial work. In a letter to one anonymous correspondent in 1763, she described her spiritual depression following her return home, which afflicted her mind and body so much 'that I could not Do my family business'.[151] This offered a dramatic challenge to contemporary masculine ideals, for a wife would be expected to support her husband and not do anything to disrupt the economic stability of the household. Indeed, the absences of both Alice Hall and Ruth Follows seriously undermined the labour of the household and the ability of their spouses to 'make a living'. In the process, it also implicitly challenged their husbands' reputations and credit.[152]

Despite the evident disruption to the family economy, however, Quaker husbands like Isaac Hall and George Follows understood and accepted the importance of their wives' missionary work. This stands in contrast to the marital relationships of female preachers from other religious movements. For example, the Methodist preacher Sarah Ryan told how conversion had allowed her to abandon her third husband with a clear conscience.[153] Moreover, in her study of the eighteenth-century Methodist movement, Mack comments on the lack of affection between the female preachers and their husbands. Studying the extant conversion letters of the Bristol Methodist community, which were written in the 1740s, she notes that only one woman and one man described a positive relationship with a spouse.[154]

---

[149] Temp MS 127/4/14 Follows MSS, Ruth Follows to Joseph Follows, Donnington, 5 February 1775, cited in Susan E. Whyman, *The Pen and the People: English Letter Writers, 1660–1800* (Oxford, 2009), p. 145; and Temp MS 127/3/24 Follows MSS, Ruth Follows to Samuel Follows, Donnington, 19 January 1779.

[150] LRSF, Temp MS 127/3/28 Follows MSS, Ruth Follows to Samuel Follows, Donnington, 27 August 1779.

[151] LRSF, Temp MS 127/1/1/9 Follows MSS, Ruth Follows to 'Endeared Friend and Brother and Companion', Castle Donnington, 3 May c. 1763.

[152] This is something that has been recently explored in Alexandra Shepard, *Accounting for Oneself: Worth, Status, and the Social Order in Early Modern England* (Oxford, 2015), esp. pp. 232–274.

[153] Lawrence, *One Family under God*, pp. 145–150.

[154] Mack, *Heart Religion*, p. 76

It is highly probable that such encouraging letters exchanged by Quaker spouses have survived because of the positive and idealised vision of Quaker family life they evoke. However, evidence can be occasionally glimpsed of spousal conflict around the issue of the wife's public ministry. The most prominent of these scenarios tended to focus on the wives of unconverted husbands, but tension could also arise in Quaker marriages. When John Richardson arrived in Scotland and stayed with a local Friend, Peter Gardiner, he went to visit a sick woman who had experienced a calling to travel, but whose husband prevented her from going. Gardiner allegedly turned to the woman's husband and said: 'Thy wife had a concern to visit the churches in another country beyond the sea, but thou would not give her leave, so she shall be taken from Thee.' The woman died two weeks later.[155] This providential account, which was transcribed and recorded by Richardson's Monthly Meeting served as a warning for those husbands who prevented their wives from following their spiritual calling. In a famous published epistolary exchange with the German Pietist Anthony William Boehm, the minister Elizabeth Webb also drew upon providence to show the consequences of marital discord on account of spiritual service. She described how her husband prevented her from travelling to America and that she was unwilling to do so without his 'free consent'. After he refused to approve her call, she described how she was 'taken with a violent fever' and the only way she would survive was if she were carried onboard a ship bound to America, believing that 'if they would but carry me and lay me down in the ship I should be well, for the Lord was gracious to my soul'.[156]

An important comparison nonetheless exists between the position of respect and authority held by these ministering women with a Quaker spouse and those married to non-Quakers. Despite having won the grudging consent of her husband to travel to England, the Quaker minister Anne Wright was forced to carry a little notebook of advice her husband, William, had written for her 'to read and consider thrice over at least, or once every week'. In it, he reminded her of her duties and stated that once she had completed her mission she must hasten home: '[R]emember thy family, who will long to know what is become of thee; and know that thou hast some work there, which thou oughtest to look after; which all people ... know to be thy lawful work, and thy duty.'[157] William's distinction between his wife's religious and 'lawful' responsibilities suggests something of the way in

---

[155] LRSF, Box 13/4 Reynolds MSS, pp. 54–57, 'John Richardson's Account of Peter Gardiner', undated, c. 1701.

[156] Elizabeth Webb, *A Letter from Elizabeth Webb to Anthony William Boehm, with His Answer* (Philadelphia, 1781), pp. 36–37.

[157] Letter sent by William Wright to Anne Wright, Castledermot, 21 August 1670, in Leadbeater (ed.), *Biographical Notices*, pp. 63–64.

which women's spiritual callings continued to be perceived by non-Quakers. Here, Anne's relationship with the divine was viewed as something lacking natural authority.

Despite their religious differences, however, such a scenario also shows us how the domestic setting as a physical and emotive space had a formative role in shaping the relationships of itinerant women with their families. It is striking that a non-believing husband, William Wright, would consent to or at least tolerate his wife absenting herself from the family home. There is little to suggest he shared Anne's belief that her missionary calling was from God; rather, he acknowledged the strength of her conviction, and appreciated her efforts to prove herself an ideal wife in every other respect. Anne's missionary work may even have strengthened their marital bond; on her much-anticipated return she was described as 'merry and pleasant ... and very loving'.[158] That such a supportive relationship could develop between spouses of different confessions suggests the importance of women's relationships in the private space of the household. Their family life and itinerant preaching roles were interlinked and their boundaries fluid.

'GOOD EXAMPLES IN LIFE AND CONVERSATION': QUAKER MOTHERS IN ISRAEL

We have seen how itinerant women's experiences continued to be determined by their domestic identities. However, this was a reciprocal process: their positions as public prophets also had an important role in shaping the lives of their families. This is particularly pronounced after the return of the monarchy in 1660, when the movement's desire for religious toleration, combined with strict anti-Quaker legislation, focused the evangelical efforts of Friends upon the family. Mary Waite, in her 1679 *A Warning to All Friends Who Professeth the Everlasting Truth of God*, established that it was only through having an orderly household that authority would be conferred upon parents as ministers. 'If the Lord Require any Service or Testimony of any of you', she advised:

all may be cleare in your selves and justified by Gods witness, that you have stood in his Counsel and Authority in your families and been good Examples in life and conversation, by keeping your own houses in the good Order, and Ruleing their for God, then may you openly with boldness appear for the Lord.[159]

---

[158] Wright, 'A Brief and True Relation of Anne, the Wife of William Wright', p. 57.
[159] Mary Waite, *A Warning to All Friends Who Professeth the Everlasting Truth of God* (London, 1679), p. 7.

This passage underscores the oscillation between Quaker women's daily and spiritual identities, showing how their positions within and management of the household were important in conferring status upon them as ministers.

Quaker women, as Debra L. Parish has noted, were presented not simply as passive pious models but as propagators of religious advice and instruction both 'within and beyond their family spheres'.[160] This is perhaps best reflected in the figure of the 'Mother in Israel', who, according to Mack, maintained the family 'as a locus of worship, moral education, and spiritual shelter', whilst also undertaking public preaching outside of the family home.[161] The spiritual calling of the Quaker minister Joan Vokins, for example, clearly enhanced her domestic authority, as exemplified in the letters she sent to her husband and seven children during ministerial service in the American colonies. 'Remember to have an Eye over our dear Children, that they lose not the sense of Truth', she urged her husband in 1680, 'for it is my fear, now I am from them, that if thou do not supply my place in my absence, that the Spirit of this World will prevail, and hinder the Work of the Lord in their Hearts, and in thine too.'[162] Whereas a typical Puritan or Anglican marriage would emphasise that private worship was a partnership in which women were to adopt a subordinate role in determining the spiritual education of the family, Vokins's choice of phrase offers an interesting insight into the Quaker ideal of domesticity, adding weight to the idea that the promotion of domestic piety was something in which women had the primary role.

The implicit authority of Vokins's position in the religious life of her household is further demonstrated in a letter she sent the following year, reminding her husband and children to 'Forget not your Family-Meeting on First Days at Evening'.[163] Vokins worried that lack of maternal supervision might damage the spiritual welfare of her family. A significant role reversal seems to have taken place with her husband being given directions on how to deputise in her absence. Relaying expressions of love, affection, and motherly guidance enabled these women to retain maternal authority within the households from which they had withdrawn. Katharine Evans who, with her companion Sarah Cheevers, was famously held captive for more than four years by the Inquisition in Malta, offered her husband advice on

---

[160] Debra L. Parish, 'The Power of Female Pietism: Women as Spiritual Authorities and Religious Role Models in Seventeenth-Century England', *Journal of Religious History*, vol. 17, no. 1 (1992), p. 38.

[161] Mack, *Visionary Women*, p. 218.

[162] Vokins, *God's Mighty Power Magnified*, p. 52, Joan Vokins to her Husband, Richard Vokins, Rhode Island, 14 June 1680.

[163] Vokins, *God's Mighty Power Magnified*, p. 63, Joan Vokins to her Husband and Children, Nevis, 11 January 1681.

the spiritual education of their children. 'Oh my dear Husband and precious Children', she wrote, 'keep your souls unspotted of the world, and love one another with a pure heart, fervently serve one another in love ... and bear one anothers burdens for the Seeds sake.'[164]

The trials of physical separation, as Larson notes, represented not 'lack of emotional attachment but rather the denial of self', as these female ministers sacrificed their domestic duties for their wider spiritual calling.[165] This is encapsulated in the experiences of the Nottingham Friend Mabel Wigham, who set sail for Ireland in May 1777. In one letter, addressed to her nine children, Wigham expressed her deep maternal feelings and anxiety at leaving her large family behind. Her letter opened: 'It is no small concern unto me, [to know] your welfare every way, but more especially your souls Happiness.' Wigham maintained that her decision to write was motivated by 'a Duty to have a few lines in Manuscript for your consideration', whereby she hoped that 'the Reading of this [may] make some impression on your Minds, even when the calling seas may separate us'. Like Vokins, her ministerial status seems to have enhanced her authority within the marital relationship and household, for she reminded her children to be 'kind and tender over your Father in my absence'. She also described concerns that her family might be led astray without her supervision and warned of the consequences of 'forsak[ing] the Truth, and marry[ing] out of the Society', which 'wou'd be like stoning me to death'.[166] Her authority and assertive position within the household were clear. Wigham's long absence did not represent a lack of concern toward her family, but instead demonstrated that despite a higher spiritual calling, her maternal and wifely responsibilities remained an important part of her identity.

The Quaker emphasis on women's roles as religious teachers and instructors thus enabled them to occupy a position of authority within the family unavailable to their contemporaries. It has been noted that whilst some tender and religiously experienced men Friends were occasionally represented as 'nursing fathers', there was no male equivalent to the semi-official title of 'Mother in Israel'.[167] Moreover, whilst Methodists and Baptists in the eighteenth century also designated spiritually advanced women as Mothers in Israel, these were almost entirely divorced from traditional female roles.

[164] Evans and Cheevers, *This Is a Short Relation*, p. 53, Katharine Evans to her husband and children from Malta, January 1661.
[165] Larson, *Daughters of Light*, p. 168.
[166] LRSF, MS Box I3/3 Impey MSS, fol. 165, 'Mabel Wigham to Her Children (nine in number) a Few Days before She Set Out on a Religious Visit to the Meetings of Friends in the Nation of Ireland', Sunderland, 3 May 1777.
[167] Helen Plant, 'Gender and the Aristocracy of Dissent: A Comparative Study of the Beliefs, Status and Roles of Women in Quaker and Unitarian Communities, 1770–1830, with Particular Reference to Yorkshire', University of York, PhD thesis (2000), p. 70.

As Lawrence found in her study of eighteenth-century Methodism, it was celibate women who fulfilled this office.[168] These were women who devoted their lives to the Methodist cause as preachers, exhorters, and travellers. It was a lifestyle, Lawrence suggests, that 'their married sisters would have found very difficult, if not impossible'.[169] Female writers often promoted '"the single life" as a route to religious freedom' and Methodist women like Sarah Ryan and Mary Fletcher embraced 'spiritual motherhood' while avoiding its procreative counterpart.[170] The Quaker Mother in Israel, by contrast, while dedicating herself to obeying God's will, was not expected to renounce marriage or motherhood in the process.

Itinerant women's spiritual commitments had the potential to clash with their domestic duties, but many of their spiritual autobiographies sought to redirect the focus of their work onto their families and households. Though Joan Vokins spent the majority of her adult life travelling in the service of truth, she was subsequently memorialised in a domestic setting, surrounded by her husband and children. Her children's testimonial described the great care she had taken for her family and children, that 'we might be nurtur'd, and brought up in the Fear of the Lord, ... above all things in this World'.[171] Like the writings of several other female ministers, Vokins's spiritual autobiography removes the focus from her prophetic travelling work and emphasises her position as an instructor and educator of her children.[172]

The private counsel ministering women offered their children had the potential to take on far greater significance through the act of publication. Alice Curwen, for instance, justified writing and publishing her spiritual testimony by informing her readers that it was 'For the Encouragement of them that hereafter may put their Trust in the Lord'.[173] As Crawford has suggested, maternity endowed women with a powerful and distinctive voice, providing a subject on which they could publish 'without implicitly attacking conventional values'.[174] The explicit authority of female ministers like Vokins and Curwen, who addressed family discipline and childrearing practices in their writings, held particular value for second- and third-generation Quakerism. Their public status gave authority to their views on family order.

---

[168] Lawrence, *One Family under God*, pp. 151–157.
[169] Ibid., p. 151.
[170] Mack, *Heart Religion*, pp. 75–82.
[171] Vokins, *God's Mighty Power Magnified*, sig. A7r, 'Concerning Our Dear and Tender Mother, Joan Vokins'.
[172] This is something that Gill found in her study of Quaker deathbed scenes, which provided an ideal (and socially acceptable) setting for women to gain authority as religious teachers. Gill, *Women in the Seventeenth-Century Quaker Community*, pp. 147–182.
[173] Martindell et al., *A Relation of the Labour, Travail and Suffering of ... Alice Curwen*, p. 2.
[174] Patricia Crawford, 'Women's Published Writings 1600–1700', in Mary Prior (ed.), *Women in English Society 1500–1800* (London, 1991), pp. 166.

Sheila Wright has revealed that many Quaker journals, by both men and women, were consciously written to include domestic details and advice on how to deal with competing commitments to family, home, and God.[175] The leading American Friend Anthony Morris, for example, took reassurance during his travels through the colonies in 1715 because he knew that he and his wife were 'not the First that have been seperated on such ocations', and described how reading George Fox's journal had 'prov'd of some service to me'. He went on to describe the 'Abundance off [*sic*] Hardship' Fox had endured in his service to the truth, 'And how easy he seemed to part with his wife in that Service'.[176] While male Friends tended to write their journals with a general audience in mind, many female ministers consciously addressed their journals to their children. 'Having had it upon my mind for a considerable time', the Lancashire Quaker Abiah Darby began her spiritual autobiography, describing how she had felt a desire to 'leave to you my Dear Children, some Account of the gracious Dealings of the Lord towards me'.[177] The American preacher Ann More Herbert similarly explained that she had written her journal for her children, 'as a hint of gods love to me in this time of calme'.[178] By using their journals as a mechanism for instruction, these women were able to guide their children in the Quaker faith and way of life.

One surprising feature of Quaker women's ministry was that it was often passed on or down to other family members. In her study of York Monthly Meeting in the later eighteenth century, Wright notes the large numbers of active ministers whose mothers also undertook divine service. Although the movement's stress on personal revelation stood at odds with intergenerational ministry, there are instances where Quaker mothers provided 'spiritual apprenticeships' to their daughters.[179] In January 1723, Miriam Jobson acquainted Kendal Women's Meeting with her desire to visit Friends in Cumberland as her mother's companion.[180] The previous year, the Irish minister Abigail Boles was accompanied by her daughter during a visit to London. One observer described how her mother had proved a good source

[175] Wright, '"Truly Dear Hearts"', p. 100.
[176] HCQSC, MS Coll 1008 Morris-Sansom Collection, c. 1715–1925, Box 6, Anthony Morris folder, Anthony Morris to Elizabeth Morris, Chester, PA (from David Lloyd's), 13 October 1715.
[177] Abiah Darby, *Abiah Darby 1716–1793 of Coalbrookdale, Wife of Abraham Darby II*, ed. Rachel Labouchere (York, 1988), p. 1.
[178] HL, HM 66135 Ann Moore Herbert Journal (1760–1763), p. 3.
[179] Sheila Wright, 'Quakerism and Its Implications for Quaker Women: The Women Itinerant Ministers of York Meeting, 1780–1840', in W. J. Sheils and Diana Wood (eds.), *Women in the Church* (Studies in Church History, 27, Oxford, 1990), p. 408.
[180] Kendal Archive Centre (hereafter cited as KAC), WDFCF/1/46 Kendal Women's Preparative Meeting Minutes, 1719–1774, minutes for 29 January 1723.

of spiritual inspiration, so 'shee seemed agreeable to the station shee was in and behaved her selfe so discreetly that those that had any knowledge of her, had her in good esteem' and described how they had taken 'pleasure in observing her ingenuity and readiness to be serviceable to her mother'.[181]

Evidence of women passing on their spiritual gifts to their children is perhaps even more common in the eighteenth-century colonial context of Quakerism, where Quaker populations were higher and family association appeared to carry greater communal significance.[182] Of the transatlantic female ministers active between 1700 and 1775, with at least one family member involved in ministerial service, 58 per cent were raised in the colonies, 32 per cent were from England, and 11 per cent were from Ireland. Whilst biographical details of some of these colonial women are unknown, it is clear that family connections had an important role in conferring status on women as ministers. Susanna Morris, for instance, had three sisters who were approved Public Friends at Abingdon Meeting in Pennsylvania.[183] The preacher Sarah Worrell from Chester County in Pennsylvania also had four siblings who were ministers.[184] The exchange of ministerial qualities between generations of female relatives is hinted in a letter of counsel Richard Hill sent to his daughter Margaret Moore in 1721. He closed the epistle with a stress on his daughter's spiritual gifts, noting that preaching and living an exemplary pious life is a powerful tool, and 'My mother and thy Mothers Conduct in life has fixt them in my rememberance beyond words.'[185] The relationship of family and Quaker public authority, as well as the strong familial orientation of colonial Quakerism are themes explored further in Chapter 2.

The evidence presented here demonstrates that family ties and obligations continued to inform and shape the emotional, material, and spiritual lives of even the most independent of female ministers. By consistently returning the focus of their published writings and correspondence to their domestic identities, these women were able to legitimate their careers as itinerant preachers. Notwithstanding the common feminist assertion that the domestic setting was marginal in these women's writings, we can see a striking synthesis between the private space of the household and their status as public ministers, which provided a supportive accompaniment to their preaching careers. The belief that women's domestic obligations and influence in the

[181] LRSF, MS Vol 296 Watson MSS, fol. 2, Henry Gouldney to John Boles, London, 15 September 1722.
[182] I have used Larson's list of transatlantic female Quaker preachers for the sample. See Larson, *Daughters of Light*, pp. 305–319.
[183] Ibid., p. 313.
[184] Ibid., pp. 318–319.
[185] HCQSC, MS Coll 1000 Gulielma M. Howland Collection, Box 4 Hill, Richard Hill to Margaret Moore, Plantation (Madeira), 26 March 1721.

household could provide them with the status and knowledge to fulfil religious engagements was one of the most innovative aspects of second- and third-generation Quakerism. Yet this also raises the issue of whether there were any ways in which public authority could be granted to women who did not undertake itinerant service. This is the central issue in the final part of this chapter.

THE PUBLIC WORK OF THE QUAKER HOUSEWIFE

In 1911 Rufus Jones confidently declared that 'itinerant ministers were without question the makers and builders of the Society of Friends'.[186] However, this view requires serious modification when attention is directed towards those women supporting the Society (over several generations) through their roles within the household. Preserved within the volumes of Quaker sufferings and testimonies are hundreds of records attesting to the perseverance and stoicism of Quaker women in the face of hardship and persecution. Thomas Freeman has argued that the supportive role of the Marian martyrs' female relations had a decisive influence on the development of English Protestantism. Yet, he notes, the role of these 'female sustainers' remains an 'important and hitherto neglected chapter on gender and religion in English life'.[187] Existing histories of the Quaker movement also fail to give sufficient credit to those who stayed at home, sustaining the movement while ensuring the continuity of ordinary domestic life.

The posthumous testimony of Mary Taylor, published by her husband James in 1683, uncovers the striking effects of religious affiliation on family life.[188] Its main focus is the suffering Mary experienced as a dutiful wife, forced to manage her husband's affairs during his incarceration. James tells how 'she did manage the same in such care and patience until the time she was grown big with Child ... she then desired so much Liberty as to have my Company home two Weeks, and went herself to request it, which small matter she could not obtain, but was denied.' Though he was a prisoner, James judged his wife's sufferings 'far greater than mine'. For, as he recounted, 'there was never yet man, woman, nor child, could justly say, she had given them any offence ... yet must ... unreasonable men cleanse our Fields of

---

[186] Rufus Jones, *The Later Periods of Quakerism* (2 vols., London, 1921), vol. 1, p. 195.
[187] Thomas Freeman, '"The Good Ministrye of Godlye and Vertuouse Women": The Elizabethan Martyrologists and the Female Supporters of the Marian Martyrs', *Journal of British Studies*, vol. 39, no. 1 (2000), p. 9.
[188] James Taylor and Jasper Batt, *A Testimony of the Life and Death of Mary, the Daughter of Jasper Batt, and Wife of James Taylor, of Holcombe-Rogus in the County of Devon* (London, 1683), in Alice Clark, *Working Life of Women in the Seventeenth Century* (new edn, with intro. by Amy Louise Erickson, London, 1992), pp. 45–46.

Cattle, rummage our House of Goods, and make such havock as that my Dear Wife had not wherewithal to dress or set Food before me and her Children.'[189]

This poignant image of a wife unswervingly supporting her husband as a result of his religious testimony is worthy of note. Mary Taylor maintained her husband's business and financially sustained her small family during his imprisonment, in addition to travelling many miles on foot whilst heavily pregnant to petition magistrates for his release. Although not a preacher, Taylor's commitment to the movement greatly affected her daily life and outlook. Her story was recounted in 1919, along with the experiences of other 'ordinary' women, in Alice Clark's pioneering *Working Life of Women in the Seventeenth Century*.[190] While many of Clark's conclusions are disputed by modern scholars, her goal of restoring lower-status women to the historical record is still to be admired.[191] Indeed, in her examination of women's everyday lives, Clark showed how 'the exacting claims of religion' could paradoxically give women opportunities for a greater economic role within the household. She singled out the Quakers as a community that positively depicted women through their supportive domestic roles.[192] Many of the wives of persecuted husbands were forced into the position of financially and materially supporting their families and incarcerated spouses. It is striking, however, that these women, many of whom were of low social status, still remain an almost invisible element of Quaker history, and are often absent from women's history more generally.[193]

Quaker women's lives were dramatically altered by their husbands' religious beliefs. Many became indirect sufferers during 'the storms of persecution', between the passage of the Conventicle Act in 1664 and the Toleration Act in 1689, although in some places persecution persisted until the end of this period.[194] The 1691 minutes for Mountmellick Monthly Meeting

---

[189] Ibid., pp. 45–46.
[190] Clark, *Working Life*, pp. 45–46.
[191] Scholars have been particularly emphatic in countering Clark's view that the rise of capitalism eroded women's economic status and position within society. For a good summary of the critiques of Clark's work see Laura Lee Downs, *Writing Gender History* (2nd edn, London, 2010), pp. 9–17.
[192] Clark, *Working Life*, p. 44.
[193] Some exceptions to this rule are Hannah Barker and Elaine Chalus (eds.), *Gender in Eighteenth-Century England: Roles, Representations and Responsibilities* (London, 1997); Diane E. Boyd and Marta Kvande (eds.), *Everyday Revolutions: Eighteenth-Century Women Transforming Public and Private* (Newark, DE, 2008); Fletcher, *Gender, Sex, and Subordination*; Mary Beth Norton, *Separated by Their Sex: Women in Public and Private in the Colonial Atlantic World* (London, 2011); and Laurel Thatcher Ulrich, *Good Wives: Image and Reality in the Lives of Women in Northern New England, 1650–1750* (Oxford, 1983).
[194] Clark, *Working Life*, p. 44.

in Dublin provide a striking example in the testimony written by William Edmundson following the death of his wife Margaret. William recounted that Margaret 'never reflected or opposed me as touching religion, nor in my testimony against tithes and priests forced maintenance, but joyned me in all such things'. He described how Margaret had faced persecution and social ostracism as a result of his commitment to Quakerism. William recounts how she was willing to 'venture her own life' to save him from 'desperate danger'. One shocking example occurred in 1690, when 'the cruell and bloody rapperies besett our house and poured in shott on both sides in at the windows ... setting the house on fire ... and they tooke me and my two sons from her ... and left her stripped into her shift.' Edmundson recalled how, on petitioning for her family's release, the sixty-year-old Margaret was stripped 'stark naked, except shooes and she went neer two miles in the cold winter'. She was later reunited with her husband and sons, but shortly afterwards died as a result of this exposure and brutal treatment.[195] His narrative underlines women's steadfastness in their commitment to Quaker principles, and the support they provided the movement through their courage and resolution while separated from their husbands and facing harassment and violence.

The hardship experienced by Margaret Edmundson barely received attention in Joseph Besse's famous collection of Quaker sufferings. However, the forbearance of the wives of persecuted Quakers punctuated many early suffering accounts. Their trials came out of the tradition of Quaker martyrology and were presented as 'crosses' the faithful bore in Christ's name. The everyday experience of sacrifice and suffering was articulated by the Quaker leader William Penn in the second edition of *No Cross, No Crown* (1682). He drew upon 2 Timothy 3 to argue that 'bearing thy daily Cross is the only true Testimony'.[196] Quakers understood that suffering did not have to constitute physical violence or death to be worthy of the praise found in the Protestant martyrological tradition. The qualities of a faithful martyr – patient, calm, forbearing, and accepting of their fates – was presented through the physical and emotional trials of those female Friends like Mary Taylor and Margaret Edmundson who were left at home.

Suffering was an experience shared by the godly. Writing from Warwick gaol in October 1664, William Dewsbury encouraged the wives of other imprisoned Friends to endure such trials. He argued that the Lord had joined them together in marriage for a providential purpose. Parting 'with your

[195] William Edmundson, 'Margaret Edmundson (c. 1630–1691): Her Husband's Testimony', ed. Isobel Grubb, in *JFHS*, vol. 33 (1937), pp. 32–34.
[196] William Penn, *No Cross, No Crown* (2nd edn, London, 1682 printed for Mark Swaner), p. 25.

dear, tender and beloved Husbands' was one of the greatest blessings they could receive, for God had counted them 'worthy to suffer in this nature to give you such blessed Husbands, that are set as glorious Lights in the face of all People'.[197] Wives of these 'enlightened' Friends were to negate all material and emotional considerations as sacrifice to the wider spiritual calling. A striking example of this occurred in 1663 when Elizabeth Lloyd left her baby son with Friends to join her husband Charles in Welshpool gaol, where he was being held prisoner. She came 'in her fine clothes, chuseing, at that time, rather to live there with her husband in filth and inconvenience, than to dwell in her own house of Dolobran with out him'.[198] Such displays of wifely solidarity, intended as testaments for truth, were crucial to the survival of the movement.

Many male Friends depended on their wives to uphold their religious testimony whilst they were absent. Jenett Bond, for example, proudly declared to Chipping Women's Monthly Meeting, Lancashire, in 1675 that 'shee never paid Tythe nor never intends to doe, nor any thing to the Repaire of the Steeplehouse', because 'my Husband suffering for not paying Tythe, I have unity with, And never shall weaken his Testimony, but in my measure shall bee his helpe and strength in the Lord'.[199] Any woman who weakened and conformed in the face of hardship and persecution would undermine her husband's demonstration of faith, and so hinder the movement as a whole. This was encapsulated in the written advice the eighteenth-century Friend Samuel Bownas gave to male ministers in 1750. He explained that if they were facing imprisonment they should provide emotional encouragement and support to their wives, to avoid 'any *indirect* compliance with thy Adversary ... which will be a Hurt to thy Ministry, and an evil Example to thy Brethren'.[200] In 1691, William Edmundson lauded the efforts of his wife Margaret whilst he suffered. He recounted how she cheerfully bore 'all my imprissonments for truths testimony' and 'never went any indirect way to obtain my liberty, which she knew was contrary to my mind'.[201] Mary Hargreaves, by contrast, of Marsden Meeting in Lancashire described in 1684 the shame she had brought upon herself and her husband after she

---

197 William Dewsbury, *The Faithful Testimony of That Antient Servant of the Lord, and Minister of the Everlasting Gospel William Dewsbery* (London, 1689), p. 259.

198 LRSF, Temp MSS 210/1/20 Lloyd MSS, pp. 9–10, account of Charles Lloyd written by his daughter Elizabeth Pemberton, 1697.

199 Lancashire Archives (hereafter cited as LA), FRL/1/2/1/1 Lancaster Women's Quarterly MM 1675–1777, 'The Testimonies of the Women, Brought in, at a Generall Womens Meetting, at Widdow Haydockes', 23 September 1675.

200 Samuel Bownas, *A Description of the Qualifications Necessary to a Gospel Minister, Containing Advice to Ministers and Elders* (London, 1750), p. 103.

201 William Edmundson, 'Margaret Edmundson (c. 1630–1691): Her Husband's Testimony', p. 32.

allowed her non-Quaker son to pay his bail. She confessed that 'I could not truly give up my husband to go to prison from the bottom of my heart', but after admonition from her local Meeting, realised 'I hath brought my husband and my self into greater sufferings, than outward bonds in holes or dungeons'.[202]

The mutual support of Quaker spouses finds parallels in Freeman's work on the female relations of the Marian martyrs. These women, he notes, were 'sustainers' of the men in prison, providing 'physical, financial, moral, and emotional support' that enabled them to draw 'strength from each other'.[203] Similarly, many Friends would not have survived the waves of persecution without the efforts of their female relations. Some wives suffered persecution. In July 1666 Elizabeth Hughes of Montgomeryshire was imprisoned after attempting to bring her husband a clean shirt and some other provisions. Called upon to swear the Oath of Allegiance, she refused and was then imprisoned for more than a year.[204] In the same year, James Harrison asked his wife, Anne, to bring leather, patterns, and thread to Chester Castle, where he was being held a prisoner.[205] The raw materials James requested enabled him to continue his shoemaking trade, crucial for his survival, for prisoners were forced to earn money to barter for food and drink.[206] Given the conditions of Stuart prisons, the ability to work for sustenance and basic necessities was essential in preserving the life and health of persecuted Friends like Harrison.

The stigma of having a family member imprisoned or identifiable as a Quaker could seriously affect women as they went about their everyday business. Mabel Camm, for instance, who went to visit her husband John in Banbury prison in 1654, afterwards went to attend a church service in the town 'and was exceeding beaten'. As her husband described, 'she suffered for my sake', a phrase that encapsulates both the hardship endured and resilience of these little-known female Friends.[207] For many women,

---

[202] LA, FRM/1/24 Marsden Women's MM 1678–1738, paper of condemnation delivered 25 September 1684.

[203] Freeman, 'The Good Ministrye of Godlye and Vertuouse Women', p. 9.

[204] Besse, *Quaker Sufferings*, vol. 1, p. 751.

[205] 'I would have a [sole] hide and some offal leather, in the widebay you may put it, with as many [patterns] as can be spared for I have bought three pieces, for upper leathers if thou have it thou may bring me 30-or 40 shillings, ... see I would have some thread.' HSP, MS Coll 484A Pemberton Family Papers, vol. 1, p. 13b, James Harrison to Anne Harrison, Chester Castle, 21 July 1666.

[206] The Quaker Edward Coxere, for instance, described how he was forced to pursue a range of enterprises, including spinning worsted and shoemaking to barter for bread when he was imprisoned at Yarmouth in 1664. Edward Coxere, *Adventures by Sea of Edward Coxere: A Relation of the Several Adventures by Sea with the Dangers, Difficulties and Hardships I Met for Several Years*, E. H. W. Meyerstein (ed.) (Oxford, 1945), pp. 103–106.

[207] LRSF, MS Vol S 81 Caton MSS vol. 3, p. 483, John Camm to Margaret Fell, Banbury, undated, c. 1655.

simply being related to a Quaker was enough to encourage scorn. One entry in the surviving records of the Great Book of Sufferings for London and Middlesex recounts a brutal assault against Elizabeth Pocock in 1661 for being married to a Quaker. Whilst she was shopping for some meat in New Market, an angry mob ridiculed, chased, and assaulted her in what is presented as an entirely unprovoked attack. Her clothes were torn off her head and neck, she was also stabbed and left to lie in the filthy market place until a constable broke up the commotion and sent Elizabeth to gaol.[208]

The burden of Quaker men's frequent absences placed an important responsibility on the female members of the household, as they were required to labour for, as well as purchase, the provisions needed to support their families.[209] At the age of sixteen, Deborah Wynn was forced to take primary responsibility for the family business and home after her parents were imprisoned at York Castle in 1661. As their only child, 'the Management of their Trade and Business fell under her Care, and during their Imprisonment she travelled to *York*, twenty two Miles, on Foot, once in two Weeks to visit them, and to carry them what money she had got for their Support'.[210] The steadfastness of female Friends in such circumstances is a striking feature of Quaker memorials. Both John Gratton and William Edmundson remarked how their sufferings were eased by knowledge of the diligence of their wives at home. Gratton demonstrated how his imprisonment was 'made easie', for his wife Anne 'was enabled (through Mercy!) to keep Markets, and to carry on our Business for a Livelihood, she also came sometimes to see me in Prison, though it was Sixteen Miles, which was hard for her in the Winter Season'.[211] The efforts and endurance of these women were essential to the survival of Quaker households.

However, managing the family home or estate when the male householder was absent was certainly not exclusive to Quaker women. Seventeenth-century historians often remark on the independence and competence women were able to show in household management as deputies to their husbands and as widows.[212] In her study of women's agency, Rosemary O'Day has emphasised that a notion of 'active partnership' informed understandings

[208] LRSF, YM/MfS/GBS/2, Great Book of Sufferings, London and Middlesex to Yorkshire, Ireland and New England, 1650–1680, p. 15.

[209] Tim Reinke-Williams has argued that one of the main traits for which housewives were praised in early modern London was their ability to provision their households with the victuals and commodities that ensured domestic comfort. Tim Reinke-Williams, *Women, Work and Sociability in Early Modern London* (Basingstoke, 2014), p. 54.

[210] John Bell, *Piety Promoted, in a Collection of Dying Sayings of Divers of the People Called Quakers* (London, 1740), pp. 5–6, 'Deborah Wynn'.

[211] Gratton, *A Journal of the Life of That Ancient Servant of Christ*, pp. 118–119.

[212] See Mendelson and Crawford, *Women in Early Modern England*, pp. 303–313.

about marital life in early modern Britain and the colonies.[213] Moreover, Shepard's recent study of female credit in early modern England has drawn attention to the fact that men did not need to be absent from the marital home for women to have autonomy and independence over managing important financial activities.[214] Marriage, as Shepard has shown, equipped women with opportunities to undertake new economic roles and to contribute towards tasks traditionally associated with men. Wives were often given the responsibility 'for saving, increasing and accounting for goods', which, as Shepard notes, was far from 'a trivial responsibility', especially in an evolving economy increasingly dependent on credit, trust, and worth.[215]

Religious affiliation did have an important impact in determining the authority women exercised within the household. The families of Anglican and nonconformist ministers often relied upon their wives' labour within both the home and parish. Presbyterian ministers like Christopher Love, often expressed concerns about the distraction of their outward affairs to their higher spiritual calling. Love, who was executed in 1651, refused to 'entangle himself with the business of the world' and thus depended on his wife Mary to manage the business and family.[216] After the Restoration, the dissenting minister John Bunyan spent more than a decade in Bedford County Gaol, leaving his wife to care for his outward affairs, after he refused to renounce his nonconformist beliefs. As with early Friends, the hardships Bunyan's family suffered were presented as one of the trials he faced in bearing witness to the truth.[217]

However, the sheer scale of Quaker suffering and the irregularity of ministry, which could leave men absent from the family home for great lengths of time, must have pushed a large number of women into this situation. Margaret Fawcett, for instance, divulged in a testimony to Cumberland Monthly Meeting in 1680 that her husband suffered as a prisoner for nine years and it 'was only for a Hen'.[218] Similar harsh treatment over seemingly inconsequential matters is evidenced by the sheer scale of Quaker suffering in the movement's early years. Barry Reay has calculated the total number

---

[213] Rosemary O'Day, *Women's Agency in Early Modern Britain and the American Colonies: Patriarchy, Partnership and Patronage* (London, 2007), p. 189.

[214] Alexandra Shepard, 'Crediting Women in the Early Modern English Economy', *History Workshop Journal*, vol. 79, no. 1 (2015), pp. 12–14.

[215] Ibid., p. 16.

[216] Mary Love later petitioned for his release and was active in getting his condemnation overturned. Mendelson and Crawford, *Women in Early Modern England*, p. 311. See also: E. C. Vernon, 'Chrisopher Love (1618–1651)', in *Oxford Dictionary of National Biography*. Oxford: Online edn; www.oxforddnb.com/index/101017038/Christopher-Love.

[217] Alexandra Walsham, *Charitable Hatred: Tolerance and Intolerance in England, 1500–1700* (Manchester, 2006), p. 165.

[218] LRSF, MS Vol 150 Luke Howard Collection, fol. 16, 'A Coppy of the Letter to George Bowley about Margarett Fawcetts Husband's Suffering', Cumberland, 29 November 1680.

of Quaker imprisonments at 11,000 between 1660 and 1680, and other estimates put this figure much higher.[219] The incarceration of male heads of households for reasons such as refusal to pay tithes (as with Margaret Fawcett's husband) or attendance at conventicles was a great trial for many Quaker families. It could easily reduce wives and children 'to Poverty', as John Gratton feared would be the fate of his own family following a long imprisonment for refusing to pay tithes.[220]

We should not underestimate the crucial role of these non-itinerant wives in alleviating the burdens their ministering husbands faced during separation from their business associates and local affairs. The Philadelphian Quaker Ann Story appears to have had a remarkably independent role in managing her husband's business. Whilst her husband Thomas was travelling across the American colonies, she frequently sent him information about his business associates and some of the decisions she had made on his behalf, including the shipping of goods and the disbursement of money. In one letter, dated 1708, Ann wrote: 'I could acquaint thee with Severall things relating to our [own] affairs but am not willing to trouble thee with them.'[221] It was a common practice for non-Quaker wives to report to their absent husbands on what they had done in the household economy. However, as Sara Mendelson and Patricia Crawford have suggested, they were not expected to solicit advice or make too many independent decisions without the consent of their spouses.[222] Because of the length and uncertainty of spiritual service, however, many non-itinerant Quaker women were able or obliged to take on a more independent role in supporting the household economy.

These non-itinerant women also served as an important channel of communication. The surviving correspondence between ministering husbands and their wives underscores the importance of these women as stable (and reliable) points of contact with the wider Quaker community. This was powerfully encapsulated in a letter sent by William Ellis to his wife Alice in 1694, when he declared that 'truth is one, in wife and husband; and I know none fitter to do the husband's work than a wife'.[223] William frequently asked Alice to communicate messages to particular members of the Settle community in Yorkshire. In one letter of April 1698 he asked her to speak

[219] Reay, *The Quakers and the English Revolution*, p. 106. William C. Braithwaite estimates that there were 15,000 sufferers during the same period. William C. Braithwaite, *The Second Period of Quakerism* (2nd edn, rev. H. J. Cadbury, Cambridge, 1961), p. 115.

[220] Gratton, *A Journal of the Life of That Ancient Servant of Christ*, p. 40.

[221] LRSF, Temp MSS 388 Thomas Story Papers, 1702–1709, Folder 2/1 Correspondence from Ann Story to Thomas Story, Philadelphia, 22 February 1709. I am grateful to Susan Whyman for this reference.

[222] Mendelson and Crawford, *Women in Early Modern England*, pp. 309–310.

[223] William Ellis to Alice Ellis, 'Daiford, in Ireland', 26 February 1695, in James Backhouse (ed.), *The Life and Correspondence of William and Alice Ellis, of Airton* (London, 1849), p. 12.

to Elizabeth Moore 'and tell her that I am much concerned for her son John, that he may get a wife as will really love and serve Truth'.[224] Such messages show that the non-itinerant wife was far from a passive figure in the marital relationship. Alice responded to her husband's request to 'have a full account how Friends manage their affairs' by providing him with regular updates on local matters and reporting on the spiritual state of the Meetings.[225] In one letter, she informed him that 'We have had two Quarterly Meetings of Public Friends, at Settle, since thou left us, which were very precious meetings, ... I was at the Quarterly Meeting at York, and I can truly say, it was the most comfortable meeting that ever I was at there'.[226] It was crucial that these women left at home were able to communicate the minutiae of the local Quaker community to their itinerant husbands. This in turn suggests a significant and largely unacknowledged level of agency, for such women needed to know how to make effective use of social networks and sometimes also of transport arrangements to remain in contact.[227]

The efficient supervision of temporal matters was of paramount importance to ministering male Friends, who could then leave behind their worldly concerns and devote themselves to their spiritual callings. This is encapsulated in a message Anne Audland sent her husband in the 1650s. 'Take no care for us', she wrote, 'but in the worke of the Lord stand faithfull, for ... I have pure unity with [thee].'[228] These words of loving encouragement must have been significant for John Audland, who was able to leave behind his concerns for the family's welfare and devote himself entirely to the Quaker mission. Similarly, in April 1698, the Yorkshire Friend Alice Ellis communicated to her husband her concerns about a premature reunion: 'I have been a little afraid for some time, lest thou shouldest be drawn homeward over [too] soon, and thou should leave some places or Islands unvisited, which would cause uneasiness.' She went on to tell him to 'Take thy time, and perform thy service fully' and to 'Take no care for me, as for all outward things'. At the time of writing, her husband, William, was ministering in the American colonies.[229] A distinct identity evolved for those women indirectly suffering the consequences of separation on behalf of the Quaker truth. As letters between ministers and their wives show, the counsel of these

---

[224] William Ellis to Alice Ellis, Chuckatuck, VA, 19 April 1698, in ibid., p. 64.

[225] William Ellis to Alice Ellis, 'Daiford in Ireland', 26 February 1695, in ibid., p. 12.

[226] Alice Ellis to William Ellis, Airton, Yorkshire, 24 July 1698, in ibid., p. 72.

[227] How Quaker women knew how to contact their men whilst they were travelling on ships is commented on by Whyman in *The Pen and the People*, p. 60.

[228] LRSF, MS Box C4/1 Markey MSS, pp. 16–17, Anne Audland to John Audland, undated, c. 1652–1664.

[229] Alice Ellis to William Ellis, Airton, 15 April 1698, in Backhouse (ed.), *The Life and Correspondence of William and Alice Ellis*, p. 62.

non-itinerant female Friends had a decisive influence in shaping the experiences, identities, and labours of their husbands.

THE WORK OF WOMEN WITHIN THE EVOLVING QUAKER FAMILY

Whilst the context of persecution enabled female Friends to take on primary responsibility for the household, it is arguable that their domestic roles had still greater significance as the movement evolved. As already established, the mission of Quakerism as it entered its more 'quietist' and institutionalised phase from the late 1660s was redirected towards maintaining the faith within the family. Raising children who would remain faithful to Friends' beliefs and practices was essential for the survival of the Society, especially because it has been estimated that 90 per cent of Quakers were the children of Quakers by 1750. The family thus became central to 'the Quaker way of life'.[230] In 1677 the Dutch Friend Geertruyd Deriks Niesen reminded her female readers of their responsibilities as parents to raise up the next generation of ministers. She stressed that children were 'committed to us as a particular Charge and Ministry', and the mother's parental duties should therefore be considered part of her spiritual service.[231]

Quaker mothers were given a primary role in the religious socialisation of their households. In 1686, Theophila Townsend entreated women Friends to watch over their children 'and be good patterns and Holy examples to them, and use all diligence to admonish, and counsel [them]'.[232] This took on added significance in the religious climate following the 1689 Toleration Act, when Friends officially became more closely integrated into the life of wider society. Unlike many other nonconformists, who stressed a distinction between spiritual duties and more 'worldly' concerns, Friends were unequivocal in their belief that they should 'witness' the faith as part of their everyday lives. This meant that they also had to find ways to integrate their spiritual and temporal concerns. As Levy has observed, the leadership frequently expressed disquiet that Friends' active participation in local business affairs and social customs was making it hard to ensure 'the successful transference of "holy conversation" to the next generation'.[233] It was therefore doubly important for mothers to keep careful watch over their children and families to guarantee they did not lose sight of the Lord. Mabel Barker,

[230] Vann, *The Social Development of English Quakerism*, p. 167.
[231] Geertruyd Deriks Niesen, *An Epistle to Be Communicated to Friends, and to Be Read in the Fear of the Lord in Their Men and Womens Meetings* (London, 1677), p. 4.
[232] Theophila Townsend, *An Epistle of Love to Friends in the Womens Meetings in London, &c.* (1686), p. 3.
[233] Levy, *Quakers and the American Family*, p. 16.

for instance, was memorialised for 'promoting good [domestic] Order' and ensuring that 'the Church might be kept clean from the Defilements of the World', and was praised for devoting her labours to the home rather than travelling abroad on ministerial service.[234]

Such a position regarded women's labours within the household as a sacred specialised calling. Given that the home was a largely female-dominated and -managed space, the movement's focus on childrearing and discipline came to have important implications for Quaker motherhood. In emphasising a 'guarded' education for their children, Quakers identified women as the primary spiritual instructors of the household. George Fox's *A Primmer* [sic] *and Catechism for Children* advised that 'A Child left to himself bringeth his Mother to shame'.[235] His choice of expression suggests that this sort of Quaker educational material was written for the mother and that she was seen as primarily responsible for catechising and educating her children. This was reinforced by printed advice circulated by the London Yearly Meeting in 1731, which encouraged 'mothers of children … as they have frequently the best opportunities' to take particular care to instruct their children 'in the knowledge of religion and the holy scriptures'.[236] The Quaker mother's chief duty was the spiritual supervision of her children, a task facilitated by her presence within the household.

Scholarship on the post-Reformation household has stressed the ways in which Protestant teachings enhanced the position of women within the religious life of their families. It was within this space, Crawford argues, that mothers played an important role 'in socialising their children as Christians'.[237] Anglican reformers like Richard Allestree stressed the responsibility of the mother in the religious education of her family. 'All mankind is the Pupil and Disciple of Female Institution', he wrote, 'the time when the mind is most ductile, and prepar'd to receive impression, being wholly in the Care and Conduct of the Mother.'[238] However, it was only when the husband was 'absent, or negligent and careless' that she would also be expected to lead family prayers and supervise the wider religious education of the household and, even then, she was usually expected to get 'some other to performe them'.[239]

---

[234] 'A Testimony from Thirsk Monthly-Meeting in Yorkshire, Concerning Mabel Barker', in Society of Friends, *A Collection of Testimonies Concerning Several Ministers of the Gospel amongst the People Called Quakers, Deceased* (London, 1760), pp. 253–256.

[235] George Fox, *A Primmer* [sic] *and Catechism for Children: Or a Plain and Easie Way for Children to Learn to Spell and Read Perfectly in a Little Time* (London, 1670), p. 92.

[236] 'Advice to Parents and Guardians', in London Yearly Meeting, *Extracts from the Minutes and Advices of the Yearly Meeting of Friends*, p. 180.

[237] Crawford, *Women and Religion*, p. 23.

[238] Richard Allestree, *The Ladies Calling in Two Parts* (8th edn, Oxford, 1705), sig. b2r.

[239] Gouge, *Of Domesticall Duties*, p. 260.

Believing in the equality of women as teachers and instructors, Quakerism accorded its female members with a highly unusual recognised space to take a primary role in the religious instruction of their children, even when their husbands were at home. This is reflected in the circumstances in which John and Barbara Bevan of Traverigg, Glamorganshire, moved to settle in Pennsylvania. As John recounted, they emigrated after Barbara convinced him that 'it might be a good place to train up children amongst a sober people and to prevent the corruption of them here'. Whilst he was reluctant to leave his native land, he added, 'I was sensible her [Barbara's] aim was an upright one, on account of our children.'[240] Such a statement underlines the respect a pious Quaker wife could command when it came to matters relating to her children. J. William Frost cites a similar situation, when the Pennsylvania governor James Logan wanted his daughters to be educated in England, but his wife Sarah had refused.[241] Moreover, the memorial of their daughter Hannah Smith, emphasised that 'having had her self the benefit of an excellent Mothers Example, she tried to follow her [Sarah], as well in her general conduct, as a more private endearment of Family Order and Harmony'.[242] The passage underlined the centrality of the Quaker mother's role, both as a religious exemplar and through her ability to maintain a well-ordered household.

Unlike Puritan authors who emphasised the natural sinfulness of children, Quaker writers discussed their inherent perfectibility.[243] This placed the mother in an important position, with primary responsibility for maintaining a godly atmosphere within the family. The Women's Meetings we will explore in Chapter 2 offered guidance to a new generation of women, especially young mothers lacking the instruction and advice of their predecessors, and placed particular stress on the upbringing of their daughters. Lancaster Quarterly Meeting repeatedly issued advice to its female members recommending 'that all young women may be taken care of by mothers and them that have thee Rule over them that they may not go into the superfluous part ... [and] the sensable will be qualified to advise where they may see occasion'.[244] Communal mechanisms

---

[240] Quoted in Barry Levy, 'The Birth of the "Modern Family" in Early America: Quaker and Anglican Families in the Delaware Valley, Pennsylvania, 1681–1750', in Michael Zuckerman (ed.), *Friends and Neighbours: Group Life in America's First Plural Society* (Philadelphia, 1982), p. 36.

[241] J. William Frost, *The Quaker Family in Colonial America: A Portrait of the Society of Friends* (New York, 1973), p. 144.

[242] HCQSC, MS Coll 1001 Haddon-Estaugh-Hopkins Papers, 1676–1841, fol. 156, Isaac Smith folder, 'A Memorial Concerning My Beloved Wife Hannah Smith', by John Smith.

[243] See Nikki Coffey Tousley, 'Sin, Convincement, Purity, and Perfection', in Angell and Dandelion, *Oxford Handbook of Quaker Studies*, pp. 172–185.

[244] LA, FRL/1/2/1/1 Lancaster Women's Quarterly MM 1675–1777, minutes for 7 April 1721.

were in place to punish the parents of children who transgressed Quaker testimonies. In 1691, Elizabeth Dowell was condemned by the Men's Meeting in Bristol for 'entertaining and countenancing' her daughter's marriage to a non-Quaker, who the Meeting openly denounced as not being a 'friend of Truth'. Although Dowell insisted that her intentions were honest, and her daughter's suitor promised 'to follow the truth', the Bristol Friends accused Dowell of setting an 'evill Example' in encouraging young women 'to look out at and Joine with the world for [the] sake of a rich husband'.[245]

The epistles and memorials circulated between Quaker Meetings constantly asserted the importance of daily work as spiritual service. The figure of the hardworking housewife became a celebrated subject in the memorials of eighteenth-century Quaker women. The testimony written by Lurgan Monthly Meeting following the death of the Irish Quaker Mary Greer, for example, chronicled her as:

Labour[ing] much in her own Family in Gospel Love, that her Children and Servants might be preserved out of Pride and Idleness, and live in the Fear of the Lord; so that we fully believe she was faithful in discharging her Duty, according to the Gift bestowed on her.[246]

As this passage demonstrates, motherhood had been elevated to a sacred level, where Greer's spiritual calling was fulfilled by meeting the needs of her children and family, not by public ministry.

The various identities presented in these memorials fostered an important elevation of the non-itinerant female Friend. Three essential qualities were celebrated by Philadelphian Quakers in their 1765 memorial of their 'Mother in Israel' Rachel Pemberton. Firstly, her marriage to another Friend, 'who united with her in a pious concern for the prosperity and prevalence of the cause of truth'. Secondly, because of her oversight of the local Quaker community, where she 'usefully filled the station of an overseer and elder'. More importantly, she was also held in high regard for her efforts within her own family: 'being carefully concerned to rule her own family well'. This understanding of spiritual motherhood took a more prominent and public form, which is a theme to which we will return in Chapter 2. But in practical terms, Pemberton's 'rule' of her household implied her dominance over domestic life. Her memorial showed how a Quaker mother who did

[245] LRSF, MS Vol 294 Dix MSS, fol. B 17 B Men's Meeting in Bristol, 23 March 1691 and fol. G 10 B Elizabeth Dowell's paper to be read at Friends' Monthly Meetings, Bristol, 6 April 1691.

[246] 'A Testimony from the Province-Meeting at Lurgan in Ireland, Concerning Mary Greer', in Society of Friends, Collection of Testimonies, p. 169.

not undertake missionary work was expected to have primary oversight of her family's spiritual and temporal circumstances.[247]

It is possible to argue that Quakerism, in this respect, was influenced by wider cultural developments. Friends' idealisation of domestic work as a divinely appointed calling echoes the advice given by Puritan moralists, who often suggested that the duties of housewifery were as pleasing to God as preaching the gospel. William Gouge, for instance, explained that the public calling of a woman included 'a conscionable performance of household duties,' which he acknowledged 'may be accounted a publike worke'.[248] Despite such affinities, however, through the process of celebrating the domestic labours and life stories of hundreds of their female members, Quakers went considerably further. This process elevated the work of mothers whose ministerial gifts did not extend to public missionary work to an honoured position within the movement.

A similar pattern can be observed in the memorialisation of men Friends in second- and third-generation texts. Commitment to their families was often praised as an exemplary trait in their characters. Of John Fothergill it was written that he was 'a Man of Skill and Industry in managing his temporal Affairs for the Benefit of his Family, over which he had a true Paternal Care; so that it may well be said, he was a kind Husband, and tender Father'.[249] In contrast to some other nonconformist groups in the period, the family was viewed as a supportive institution for Quaker ministers, rather than distracting them from their spiritual calling. Even though they may be reluctant to draw attention to their domestic life in their spiritual writings, the hallmarks of a Quaker patriarch were his industry and strong attachment to family life. Thomas Clarkson observed that the Quaker denial of 'the pleasures of the world' had led Friends to cherish those pleasures found in domestic life:

They are long in each others society at a time, and they are more at home than almost any other people. For neither the same pleasures, nor the same occupations, separate these as others.[250]

Quaker husbands away from home often expressed in their correspondence the heavy burden their absence placed upon them. 'Parting from the[e] and our dear Children', Anthony Morris described in a letter to his wife in

---

[247] 'A Testimony from the Monthly-Meeting of Philadelphia, concerning Rachel Pemberton', in Society of Friends, *A Collection of Memorials Concerning Divers Deceased Ministers and Others of the Peopled Called Quakers* (Philadelphia, 1788), pp. 215–217.
[248] Gouge, *Of Domesticall Duties*, p. 18.
[249] 'A Testimony from Knaresborough Monthly-Meeting, Concerning John Fothergill', in Society of Friends, *Collection of Testimonies*, pp. 183–186.
[250] Clarkson, *Portraiture of Quakerism*, vol. 3, p. 258.

1715, 'was Like to Be to[o] hard for me.'[251] Likewise, Thomas Story confessed to his future wife Ann, that 'there's nothing in this life that I have ever desired more than the enjoyment of thy dear company'.[252] In emphasising the domestic as well as spiritual responsibilities of both male and female Friends, Quakerism valued those who showed deep attachment to their families and home life.

An especially strong focus on Quaker domesticity is present in the writings of eighteenth-century male Friends from Ireland. George Bewley of Cork, whose life account was first published in 1750, informed his readers of the importance of focusing their spiritual efforts on the family. 'I found it my Duty', he wrote, 'to be a good Example in the first Place to my own Family.' He stressed the necessity of 'having a watchful and tender Care over my Children and Servants' so that he could encourage and nurture their spiritual gifts, should they 'be provoked to serve the Lord in their Generation'.[253] Richard Shackleton, the Quaker schoolmaster from Ballitore, County Kildare, often stressed the importance of domestic work in his correspondence with other Friends. In 1760, he alluded to the interchangeability between 'our outward and inward habitation' in an epistle to his friend Elizabeth Pike. 'Home is the place in which we seem appointed by Providence and the center of our duties', he explained, and it is the 'place of the home', he wrote, where 'we were but favoured with divine aid ... and opening and enlarging thy understanding in the nature and path of true religion'.[254] The Quaker minister James Gough even thanked Richard Shackleton in August 1780, for encouraging him to attend to 'domestic engagements', after he felt a calling to travel overseas. Gough explained how he had followed his friend's guidance and that 'the chief view that I have before me is renewing the life and strength to my self among my Friends in visiting them, and in waiting on divine Goodness with them'.[255] Friends like Shackleton viewed nurturing and encouraging the next generation of ministers at home and within the local community as equally important to the preservation of their religious principles as missionary work.

[251] HCQSC, MS Coll 1008 Morris-Sansom Collection, c. 1715–1925, Box 6, Anthony Morris folder, Anthony Morris to Elizabeth Morris, Chester, PA (from David Lloyd's), 13 October 1715.
[252] LRSF, Temp MSS 388 Thomas Story Papers, 1702–1709, Folder 1/7 Correspondence from Thomas Story to Ann Shippen, Samuel Cheevers's at Herring Creek, 1 May 1705.
[253] George Bewley, *A Narrative of the Christian Experiences of George Bewley, Late of the City of Corke* (Dublin, 1750), pp. 32–33.
[254] UCSC, MSS 4 Ballitore Collection, Box 3/15, Richard Shackleton to Elizabeth Pike (Pim) [draft], Ballitore, 29 August 1760.
[255] HL, mssSHA Shackleton Family Correspondence, Box 4, fol. 62, James Gough to Richard Shackleton, Dublin, 17 August 1780.

The role of Quaker wives and mothers may have had particular significance in the context of early frontier life (in both Ireland and the American
colonies), when travel was difficult and much of the movement's vitality lay
in the efforts of Friends within their families. Margaret Hope Bacon, for
example, has argued that women played the primary role in the development of the Nantucket Quaker community in New England because of its
isolation and the frequent absence of husbands and fathers on whaling expe-
ditions.[256] In Pennsylvania, too, many of the early female settlers were married to Quaker merchants who spent long periods away in England, Ireland,
the West Indies, and other colonies. 'I am as a widdow before my time',
wrote the Pennsylvanian Friend Phebe Pemberton in 1695, whose husband
was often away on business. In one letter, she warned him that 'I desire thee
do not so intangle thy self for no gane, for I Had rather have thy Company
th[a]n a grate deale of outward Riches, thou art more now in bondage to
business th[a]n Ever'.[257] The experience of being alone in an unfamiliar land
added to her sense of isolation. Nevertheless, it also increased her authority
as the guardian of the family's spiritual life, as she admonished him not to
entangle himself further in the worldly concerns that were distracting him
from his religious principles. Quaker communities, as Levy notes, needed
'strong, meek, talented wives', able to guide backsliding husbands towards
the truth.[258] Such accounts underline the important position of women as
spiritual role models within the Quaker family.

Scholars have frequently emphasised the impact of the internal reform
movement on American Quakerism, which led to the disownment of
thousands of Friends in the second half of the eighteenth century.[259] The
Philadelphian Friend Ann Whitall, for example, commented in her diary
on the frustrations of being married to a man of much weaker religious
commitment. In one entry in July 1760 she confessed that one of her greatest troubles was her husband's failure to bring their children to Meetings,
noting how she went 'with a heavy heart if my children don't go to meeting
nor their father'.[260] In another entry, she described how she was 'grieved
this day because of this playing of ball and this fishing and our children

---

[256] Margaret Hope Bacon, *Mothers of Feminism: The Story of Quaker Women in America* (San
Francisco, 1986), pp. 45–46.

[257] HSP, MS Coll 484A Pemberton Family Papers, vol. 2, p. 107, Phebe Pemberton to Phineas
Pemberton, Falls, Bucks County, PA, 24 April 1695.

[258] Levy, *Quakers and the American Family*, pp. 220–221.

[259] Jack D. Marietta in his survey of the Quakers in the Delaware Valley estimated that
Pennsylvania Yearly Meeting disowned 1,426 between 1761 and 1767, equating to about
11 per cent of the estimated Quaker population of the Society in 1760. Jack D. Marietta,
The Reformation of American Quakerism, 1748–1783 (Philadelphia, 1984), p. 67.

[260] Ann Whitall, 'The Journal of Ann Whitall (1760–62)', in Hannah Whitall Smith (ed.), *John
M. Whitall: The Story of His Life* (Philadelphia, 1879), 17, diary entry for 27 July 1760.

with them'.[261] Notwithstanding her frustrations and the worldly behaviour of her husband, Whitall was clearly the custodian of the family's religious life. As a pious instructor and religious role model, she acquired an eminent position in her family and as a religious leader within the Quaker community. Such women took it upon themselves to revive the Quaker faith within their families, even as their husbands and children became ever more closely integrated with the non-Quaker world.

The language and symbolism of Quaker memorials demonstrates the extent to which the movement valued the labours of pious men and women within their homes and families. Whilst these testimonies can never accurately represent the fullness of their experiences, no comparable body of literature exists for any other group of women during this period. The women's lives followed a specific model of domesticity that was neither marginalised in Quaker history nor viewed as inferior to ministerial work. Their efforts within the home were understood as integral to the Society's development. As the autonomous guardians of the household, these spiritual housewives (and their male counterparts) shaped the public character of the movement and ensured its beliefs retained their force. Historians have often commented that the more conservative and 'quietist' phase of Quakerism in the late seventeenth and early eighteenth centuries restricted the opportunities available to women. The evidence examined, however, shows that as the movement came to rely more on transmission than conversion, Quaker women were key agents in socialising their children and instilling the Quaker faith.

The Quaker movement, as Levy has recognised, was the first to view egalitarian domestic life as a part of its religion.[262] In many ways, the Quaker family became a prism through which Quaker values were perpetuated. Whilst women's roles within the household found many parallels within wider society, especially in the Puritan tradition, Quaker culture encouraged a re-envisioning of domestic relationships in important ways. This can be seen through the emphasis Friends placed on the equality of women within the marriage partnership, whether as instructors of their children, religious teachers, or missionaries. One especially distinctive element of Friends' lives was their belief that spiritual labour authorised ministers to cede domestic responsibilities to their spouses. This meant that a recognised place was provided for women beyond their function within the family.

---

[261] Ibid., 15, diary entry for 3 May 1760.
[262] Levy, *Quakers and the American Family*, p. 182.

These women's careers clearly helped them to attain a position of authority within the marital relationship. A Quaker Mother in Israel would often take primary responsibility for the spiritual life of the household. However, unlike the women of other religious movements, a Quaker woman who dedicated herself to divine service did not have to renounce marriage or motherhood. In many dissenting communities, like the Pietists, Baptists, and Methodists, the leading female exemplars were unmarried women, committed to ascetic lifestyles, who placed spiritual service above domestic responsibility. In Quakerism, by contrast, celibacy was not a prerequisite for an active ministerial career, and familial duties were viewed as equally important to their ministerial vocations. The evidence of status accruing to ministers through their careful management of their domestic relationships underlines the interdependence of women's public and private work.

Domesticity was at the heart of the Quaker faith and, as we have seen, women were able to play multiple roles throughout their lifetimes. Even those women who did not undertake gospel service could achieve a recognised position as spiritual leaders. There were direct connections between the survival of the Quaker faith and the non-ministering female Friends whose lives were disturbed by persecution and interrupted by their husbands' religious commitments. For Quaker housewives, accepting their husbands' missionary service was an important aspect of a marital relationship in which both parties perceived domestic responsibilities as part of their joint spiritual mission. Not only did they give their husbands practical and material support, they also served as a crucial point through which their spouses could maintain contact with both the household and local community.

In a maturing Society, with a leadership placing the family at the heart of Quaker morality, women enjoyed a significant position as mothers of a future generation of believers. In the American colonies and some parts of Ireland in particular, emphasis was increasingly placed upon the correct rearing of Quaker children to ensure its survival. As motherhood became a sacred calling, some non-itinerant women were able to achieve high status within the transatlantic community. The huge number of diaries, dying words, and memorials of these women, whose lives were distinguished primarily by service to their families, attests to the determination of early Friends to memorialise exemplary wives and mothers who sustained the movement through labour within the household and not in wider public service.

The Quaker 'homemaker' as much as the traveller had a crucial role in ensuring the continuity of domestic piety and the survival of the movement. However, motherhood, was a constructed role and the duties of mothering and child care were not confined to biological mothers. The next chapter explores further the significance of the non-itinerant 'mother' within the wider Quaker community, assessing the roles available to her within the separate Women's Meetings. As we shall see, this was another aspect of female Friends' lives that was determined by their domestic identities. Their stable position within the local Quaker community and their authority as religious instructors, nurturers, and teachers within the household enabled many such 'ordinary' women to acquire a recognised public status within the 'household of faith'.

−2−

'A Government of Women': Authority and Community within the Quaker Women's Meetings

His blessed presenc[e] is with us in our Womens Meetings; and wee doe find a goeing on and prospering in that wo[r]ke which the lord hath cal[le]d many to.

LRSF, MGR 11a4 London Women's Meeting Epistles,
1671–1753, fol. 30, 30 April 1676

On 21 June 1747, a group of Irish female Friends gathered in the small Meeting House at Clonmel for the Tipperary Women's Six Weeks' Meeting. The Meeting started with the representatives of Clonmel, Cahir, Cashel, Kilcommonbeg, and Waterford giving an account of how the Society prospered in their districts.[1] The group then proceeded to their regular business. Epistles sent by their Provincial Quarterly Meeting at Cork, the Half-Year Meeting at Dublin, and the Yearly Meeting in London were read out to the women in attendance. The issue of disciplining errant members was a high priority on their agendas and those gathered considered some instructions about how to deal with members who 'run out to marry by the priests'. Business then turned to signing a certificate of removal for a young woman, Rebecca Howell, who wished to settle with her husband in London. Two women Friends had been appointed at the last Meeting to inquire into her circumstances, behaviour, and 'conversation' and had brought the certificate for the Meeting to approve and sign. The female elders also read a letter of counsel from Friends of Tortola Meeting in the British Virgin Islands. Although no comment is made by the women in their minutes, the Men's Meeting described the epistle 'from our Friends in Tortola' as containing 'good Councill and advice suitable to old and young' and hoped their members would be diligent in following their instructions.[2]

The matters put before the female Friends at Tipperary were not unusual, and their recorded minutes, like those of many across the British Isles and

---

[1] Friends of Cashell Preparative Meeting noted 'a Coolness and Indifference' in some of their female members when they attended Meetings for worship.

[2] FHLD, MMX B2 Co. Tipperary Women's MM 1735–1764; and MMX A2 Co. Tipperary Men's MM 1724–1760, minutes for 21 June 1747.

American colonies, are a repository of minutiae about the work of women in their Meetings. The aim of this chapter is to explore the nature and assess the importance of the Women's Meetings in England, Ireland, and the American colonies, challenging traditional interpretations about gender equality within second- and third-generation Quakerism. Women's Meetings were established across Britain and the American colonies from 1671, and came to dominate debates both within and outside the Society about the correct place for women within the developing sect. Although the tasks of the women of Tipperary Meeting appear rather prosaic, the formulation of a formal and collective space for women to meet together and even, at times, to advise their male brethren, made them unique within Protestantism and the subject of much debate and controversy. As I will discuss in the next section, although some nonconformist groups like the Baptists and Methodists permitted female members some role in church oversight, such as the ability to vote at church meetings, they were never granted the same level of formal institutional authority within their communities as female Friends. In 1694, the polemicist and ex-Quaker William Mather reacted with horror at the discovery of this 'Government of Women, Distinct from Men, Erected amongst some of the People call'd Quakers'. Describing them as '*Unscriptural Government*', he unscrupulously reproached the stubbornness of 'such *Women* as has a secret Command of their Husbands Purses'.[3]

Even within Quakerism, these separate spaces for women to conduct church business faced an outpouring of opposition. Central to this issue was a schism led by Quaker separatists John Wilkinson and John Story in the 1670s, who opposed the multitiered Meeting structure established by Fox and Fell, and rejected the authority of women as ministers, believing that they should be given no authority within church government outside of large cities like London and Bristol.[4] In some parts of Britain, especially in the northwest, Wilkinson-Story separatists prevented Women's Meetings being established. In 1680, the Berkshire minister Joan Vokins described ending ministerial service in New England early so that she could return home and labour for her local Women's Meeting, which 'the opposite Spirit did strongly strive' to abolish.[5] Overall, however, the schism did not hinder Quaker expansion. It nevertheless raised some fundamental ideological

---

[3] William Mather, *A Novelty: Or, a Government of Women, Distinct from Men, Erected amongst Some of the People Call'd Quakers* (London, 1694), title page.

[4] On the John Wilkinson–John Story schism and the rise of the Quaker Separatists see William C. Braithwaite, *The Second Period of Quakerism* (2nd edn, rev. H. J. Cadbury, Cambridge, 1961), pp. 290–323. On John Wilkinson, John Story, and the establishment of the Women's Meetings see also Bonnelyn Young Kunze, *Margaret Fell and the Rise of Quakerism* (London, 1994), pp. 147–158.

[5] Joan Vokins, *God's Mighty Power Magnified: As Manifested and Revealed in His Faithful Handmaid Joan Vokins* (London, 1691), p. 29.

tensions about both the future of women within the society, and how a movement driven by inner spiritual revelation could be balanced with a corporate structure. Certainly, the development of a more standardised approach to discipline and organisation, as embodied in the Meeting system, marks the 'routinization of charisma' observed by sociologists like Max Weber.[6] But its new gendered and authoritarian structures seemed to separatists like Mather, Story, and Wilkinson to be regressing into the hierarchical trappings of the religion they had rejected.

Quakers had no professionally trained full-time ministers. This meant that the responsibility for all tasks fell upon lay members. This offered potential for extensive female participation in church oversight. Whilst a few other dissenting movements permitted some women a degree of authority within church governance, Quakerism introduced a principle of gender equality into both the ministry and the conduct of church business that brought a new approach to appropriate gender roles. Despite the female elders' sometimes differing concerns, this chapter argues that the unifying experience of gathering together gave Women's Meetings across the Atlantic a shared world outlook and generated remarkably similar programmes of church oversight. They provided an important and largely overlooked alternative model of female sociability, intimately linked to the alliances that will be explored in Chapter 3 and to the domestic roles discussed in Chapter 1.

Scholars have long debated the impact of the separate Meetings on female Friends' public identities. Little is known, however, about the day-to-day activities of the Women's Meetings and their significance in the development of the Quaker faith. This chapter explores how the movement's transition from sect to denomination reshaped the roles and status of female Friends. It focuses on female elders and the tasks they undertook in the Quaker Meeting system, and provides a detailed quantitative and qualitative analysis of six Monthly Meetings spanning the British Atlantic. These comprise two Women's Monthly Meetings in northwest England – Marsden in Lancashire and Kendal in Westmorland – alongside minutes from Tipperary Six Weeks' Meeting in Ireland and three colonies in North America – Chester in Pennsylvania, Burlington in West Jersey, and Fairfax in Virginia.[7] The Meetings were selected because of the survival of a complete set of Men's and Women's Monthly Meeting minutes from the early eighteenth century through to 1750. They have also been largely neglected in the scholarship.[8]

---

[6] This is linked to Max Weber's 'sect' to 'church' thesis, as articulated in his *The Protestant Ethic and the Spirit of Capitalism* and *Economy and Society*. Max Weber, *From Max Weber: Essays in Sociology*, trans. H. H. Gerth and C. Wright Mills (London, 2013), pp. 51–55.

[7] I am grateful to Richard Allen for his suggestions concerning the Quaker Meetings in the colonies.

[8] Chester Meeting in the Delaware Valley is the only Meeting examined in this chapter that has received some acknowledgment in the scholarship, although the Women's Meetings have

This comparative approach reveals both the collective concerns and values of female Friends, and the different socio-political and demographic contexts that shaped female authority. It also uncovers another layer of the experiences of non-ministering female Friends, enabling a better understanding of their status and work within a transatlantic religious community.

'DISTINCT ... YET IN PERFECT UNITY': THE EVOLUTION OF QUAKER WOMEN'S MEETINGS

The first Women's Meeting originated in London in the early years of the Quaker movement, when Friends were still pursuing a policy of active proselytisation. The 'Box Meeting', as it came to be known (named after the 'Box' into which Friends anonymously placed their donations), became a mechanism for relieving Friends experiencing suffering and hardship. The female Quakers of London inquired into the needs of widows, orphans, and the sick and were especially concerned for those families left destitute by persecution.[9] Following the Restoration, Quaker leaders increasingly came to realise that only through better organisation and a more hierarchical structure would the movement be able to survive. It was whilst undertaking ministerial work in the American colonies in 1671 that George Fox proposed the creation of a nationwide system of separate Meetings for female Friends to sit alongside those already established for their male brethren. This development provided formal recognition of their special duties as carers, nurturers, and active overseers of their local communities. As Fox noted, women were better qualified to 'admonish and exhort, reprove and rebuke the young', and explained that 'there is many things that is proper for women to look into both in their families, and concerning of women which is not so proper for the men'.[10]

---

not been examined in depth. The surveys that have made use of Chester minutes are Barry Levy, *Quakers and the American Family: British Settlement in the Delaware Valley* (Oxford, 1988); and Jean R. Soderlund, 'Women's Authority in Pennsylvania and New Jersey Quaker Meetings, 1680–1760', *William and Mary Quarterly*, vol. 44, no. 4 (1987), pp. 722–749.

9 For more information about the first Women's Meetings and the London Women's Box Meeting see Jordan Landes, *London Quakers in the Trans-Atlantic World: The Creation of an Early Modern Community* (Houndmills, 2015), pp. 33–34; Irene L. Edwards, 'The Women Friends of London: The Two-Weeks and Box Meetings', *JFHS*, vol. 47, no. 1 (1955), pp. 3–21; and Michele Denise Ryan, '"In My Hand for Lending": Quaker Women's Meetings in London, 1659–1700', University of California, Santa Cruz, PhD thesis (2003). I am grateful to Simon Dixon for this reference.

10 George Fox, 'Friends Fellowship Must Be in the Spirit; and All Friends Must Know One Another in the Spirit and Power of God', undated, 'Book of Epistles of George Fox, 1666–1682', cited in Phyllis Mack, *Visionary Women: Ecstatic Prophecy in Seventeenth-Century England* (Berkeley, CA, 1994), p. 286.

There were many reasons behind Fox's decision to establish these segregated Meetings. One dominant strand in the scholarship argues that as the movement's leaders aimed to secure toleration, the Meeting system became a way to create the impression of a more 'respectable' movement. Kate Peters, in her analysis of Quaker printed tracts, notes that Quaker writings defending Women's Meetings and women's right to speak were attempting to 'normalise and legitimate the potentially disruptive public preaching of women in the Quaker movement'.[11] By granting men executive authority and distinguishing the work of female elders from that of their brethren, it has been suggested that the Meetings, which became characteristic of second-generation Quakerism, enabled the male leadership to limit active female participation.[12]

Yet it is no coincidence that when Fox proposed this system of female governance, women's efforts in relieving poor and suffering Friends were at their most visible, in the period of fiercest persecution. The first Meeting to be established outside of London was at Swarthmoor, the home of Fox's wife, Margaret Fell, who had been instrumental in establishing a system of relief for Quaker prisoners and families in financial distress through the Kendal Fund.[13] Fell's influence over early Quaker culture is well known and several of Fox's critics depicted him as unduly influenced by his wife.[14] Although Fell's involvement in the transatlantic Meeting system is still debated, Bonnelyn Young Kunze has argued that her role in the Quaker administrative structure was of 'equal importance' to that of her husband.[15] In establishing separate business Meetings, Fox and Fell expected Women's Meetings to collaborate with the Men's Meetings in supervising the welfare and behaviour of their female members. Crucially, they were expected to be active in their own right, departing from the exegesis that God created woman to be a helpmeet to man (Genesis 2:18, 20). They were to have their own dominion, as bodies 'distinct (as we may say in some respects,) yet in perfect unity with our brethren'.[16]

---

[11] Kate Peters, *Print Culture and the Early Quakers* (Cambridge, 2005), pp. 130–131.

[12] Mack, *Visionary Women*, pp. 283–293. See also Patricia Crawford, *Women and Religion in England, 1500–1720* (London, 1993), p. 197.

[13] For more about the Kendal Fund see Bonnelyn Young Kunze, '"Poore and in Necessity": Margaret Fell and Quaker Female Philanthropy in North-West England in the Late Seventeenth Century', *Albion*, vol. 21, no. 4 (1989), pp. 559–580.

[14] William Rogers in his tract *The Christian Quaker*, likened Margaret Fell to Eve, leading Fox into temptation and wrote "tis a Shame for a Man to become an Instrument that *Womens Meetings* should be held'. William Rogers, *The Christian-Quaker, Distinguished from the Apostate and Innovator: The First Part* (London, 1680), p. 66.

[15] Kunze, *Margaret Fell and the Rise of Quakerism*, p. 167.

[16] 'An Epistle from the Women Friends in London to the Women Friends in the Country, Also Elsewhere, about the Service of a Women's Meeting, 4 January 1674', in A. R. Barclay (ed.), *Letters, &c., of Early Friends; Illustrative of the History of the Society, from Nearly Its Origin, to about the Period of George Fox's Decease* (London, 1841), pp. 343–344.

The rise of the Quaker Meetings for discipline has met with widely vary-
ing responses from modern scholars. Historians like Christopher Hill and
William C. Braithwaite lamented the defeat of the movement's earlier radicalism.[17] In feminist and gender history too, their formalisation has been
viewed as a mechanism to suppress the actions of the first radical converts.
The segregation of men and women is often regarded as detrimental to female
advancement within the Society. Patricia Crawford declared that the rise of
'a hierarchy of male leaders', combined with the repression of the more
prophetic elements of Quaker women's ministry, made women's role in the
Society less prominent and female Friends less visible.[18] Christine Trevett,
like many historians of seventeenth-century Quaker women, lamented the
fact that the Meeting system channelled female activity into more stereotypically feminine areas.[19]

These observations echo wider trends in gender history, especially on the
impact of the Reformation on women's religious lives. In the late 1980s and
early 1990s, it was often argued that far from empowering women, cultural
changes in Reformation Europe constrained their opportunities for independent action. Reference has been made to both the closure of convents
in Protestant Europe and the enforced enclosure (*clausura*) of convents in
Catholic Europe.[20] Whilst there has been some modification to this view
in recent years, the changes brought about by the Reformation that were
traditionally regarded as limiting to women's position in early modern society persist. From this perspective, they were confined to a largely domestic
sphere controlled by men and offered only limited space for group action.
There have nevertheless been some important studies acknowledging that
women continued to exert agency within these restricted spaces through
their service to the church. Claire Walker has shown in her study of English
convent life in France and the Low Countries that the nuns were not simply
passive objects of unwelcome reform and were given plenty of opportunities
to negotiate their terms.[21] Emily Clark has also argued that many of these
religious women, including the reformer Teresa of Avila, viewed *clausura*

---

[17] Braithwaite, *The Second Period of Quakerism*, p. 324. This is discussed in Mack, *Visionary
Women*, p. 274.

[18] Crawford, *Women and Religion*, pp. 162, 193–197.

[19] Christine Trevett, *Women and Quakerism in the 17th Century* (York, 1991), p. 81.

[20] Elizabeth Rapley argued that 'reform in the Catholic church tended to be accompanied by
a hardening of its attitude toward sexuality,' which was detrimental to women. Elizabeth
Rapley, *The Dévotes: Women and Church in Seventeenth-Century France* (Montreal, 1990),
pp. 4–5. See also Lyndal Roper, *The Holy Household: Women and Morals in Reformation
Augsburg* (Oxford, 1989); and Merry Wiesner, 'Nuns, Wives, and Mothers: Women and the
Reformation in Germany', in Sherrin Marshall (ed.), *Women in Reformation and Counter-
Reformation Europe: Public and Private Worlds* (Bloomington, IN, 1989), pp. 8–28.

[21] Claire Walker, *Gender and Politics in Early Modern Europe: English Convents in France and
the Low Countries* (Basingstoke, 2003), p. 49.

as liberation from secular distractions, rather than a mechanism for patriarchal control.[22]

The denigrators of the Quaker Women's Meetings often fail to acknowledge that no comparable religious movement provided women with the opportunity for such a formal role within its organisational framework. Considerable power and authority lay with those women given committee assignments and tasked with specific acts of spiritual and moral supervision.[23] Unlike the Catholic cloister, Quakerism gave women the authority to oversee affairs beyond the walls of the Meeting House. Even those Protestant sects that allowed women to undertake some activities never went as far as to provide a formal role for them within the structure of the church. Some Baptist congregations permitted women a degree of authority in religious oversight, for example, by granting them the right to vote, and in caring for the poor and sick. However, these offices were highly circumscribed and limited to a select minority, who generally had to be sixty years of age and widowed or single. The role of deaconess, the highest position open to women in Baptist congregations, was based on 1 Timothy 5:9 and 11, where only widows could occupy the office. They were not 'under threescore years old' and were not permitted to remarry.[24] Thus, whilst Baptists offered women some authority, they continued to uphold conventional views of women and church governance; their secular roles as wives and mothers restricted their exercise of power in the movement.

Recent studies have underscored the links between female piety and church oversight. The roles available to women, however, were generally through informal, rather than official channels. Janet Moore Lindman has shown in the context of the eighteenth-century Baptist movement in Virginia and Pennsylvania that, despite the fact that women outnumbered men, they were barred from official conferences where male leaders debated issues and decided policy. Colonial Baptist church governance was an institution 'where male dominance and female subordination was the rule'.[25] A similar pattern is found in Wesleyan Methodism, where women formed 60 to 75 per cent of the movement's initial converts. When a professional clergy was created and 'the hierarchy of lay positions within the chapels became more elaborate', women were excluded from church governance. Gail Malmgreen

---

[22] Emily Clark, 'When Is a Cloister Not a Cloister? Comparing Women and Religion in the Colonies of France and Spain', in Emily Clark and Mary Laven (eds.), *Women and Religion in the Atlantic Age, 1550–1900* (Farnham, 2013), pp. 69–72.

[23] Mary Maples Dunn, 'Latest Light on Women of Light', in Elisabeth Potts Brown and Susan Mosher Stuard (eds.), *Witness for Change: Quaker Women over Three Centuries* (London, 1989), p. 82. I am grateful to Jordan Landes for this reference.

[24] Crawford, *Women and Religion*, p. 201.

[25] Janet Moore Lindman, *Bodies of Belief: Baptist Community in Early America* (Philadelphia, 2008), p. 117.

has described this transition as relegating women 'to the lowest niches' of the movement.[26] Because they could not become ministers or itinerant preachers, Methodist women were barred from the roles of 'helpers' or 'assistants', who devoted their full time and energy to the supervision of the society and the spread of the faith. Although the gender-segregated class and band meetings – a form of Methodist 'family gathering' at the lowest level of church governance – could be led by women, they were still supervised by a male community leader.[27] It was only through their role as visitors of the sick that Methodist women were allowed any authority in spiritual matters.

The transition from sect to denomination within Quakerism was thus singular in continuing to provide leadership roles for women from a range of backgrounds at all levels of the Society's hierarchy. As argued in Chapter 1, in contrast to other models of church organisation, Friends accepted that women could combine the exercise of religious and domestic responsibilities. Indeed, Quaker authors defended the Meeting system as providing an appropriate outlet for women's separate sphere of knowledge, derived from their positions within the household. William Loddington, an early supporter of separate Women's Meetings, insisted that: 'Women Friends meeting by themselves, may without the least suspition of usurping Authority over the Men, confer and reason together, how to serve Truth in their places, in such things as are most proper and suitable for them.'[28] The biblical appellation 'Mother in Israel', was often reserved for those women who attained a position of stature within their local Meetings. 'Elder women in the *Truth*', George Fox wrote in 1672, 'were not only called *Elders*, but *Mothers* ... and a *Mother in Israel*, is one that gives Suck, and Nourishes, and Feeds, and Washes and Rules, and is a Teacher in the *Church* ... an Instructer, an Exhorter'.[29]

The Mother in Israel thus denoted women who displayed a particular gift for fostering the spiritual welfare of others within their Meetings. The testimony left by Wigton Quarterly Meeting after the death of one such 'nursing *Mother in Israel*', Bridget Story, encapsulates the important role of the

---

[26] Gail Malmgreen, 'Domestic Discords: Women and the Family in East Cheshire Methodism, 1750–1830', in Jim Obelkevich, Lyndal Roper, and Raphael Samuel (eds.), *Disciplines of Faith: Studies in Religion, Politics and Patriarchy* (London, 1987), pp. 56, 67.

[27] For more about the roles available to women within the organisational structure of Wesleyan Methodism, see Paul Wesley Chilcote, *John Wesley and the Women Preachers of Early Methodism* (London, 1991), pp. 67–91; and Phyllis Mack, *Heart Religion in the British Enlightenment: Gender and Emotion in Early Methodism* (Cambridge, 2008), pp. 127–170.

[28] William Loddington, *The Good Order of Truth Justified; Wherein Our Womens Meetings and Order of Marriage (by Some Especially Opposed) Are Proved Agreeable to Scripture and Sound Reason* (London, 1685), p. 5.

[29] George Fox, *A Collection of Many Select and Christian Epistles, Letters and Testimonies* (2 vols., London, 1698), vol. 2, p. 324, Postscript of 'To All the Womens Meetings, That Are Believers in the Truth', 1672.

female elder. Story was not only 'a Pattern of Humility, Self-denial, Plainness and Circumspection, in her own Family', but also 'zealous for promoting and maintaining good Order in the Church; and in particular, concerned for the inward Growth and Preservation of the rising Generation'.[30] One of the most frequently celebrated traits of a Mother in Israel's character was diligence in attending Meetings and overseeing the spiritual growth of the younger members of her community. Deborah Wardell was memorialised in 1732 as 'an approved Mother in our spiritual Israel, for her Care, Conduct and Advice' and for being 'of good Service' in 'Meetings of Business'.[31]

Just as a household did not simply encompass the immediate family, motherhood, as Chapter 1 established, was a constructed role and the duties of mothering and child care were not confined to biological mothers.[32] It is nevertheless significant that the movement gave an accepted cultural space to those traits associated with motherhood – caring, nurturing, and teaching. Eighteenth-century Baptists and Methodists also recognised women of high spiritual stature within the community as Mothers in Israel. However, as Anna M. Lawrence has noted, they did not envision them as 'domestic figures'. They were women noted for the 'passion of their piety and the ardency of their faith', not for their ongoing roles within the household.[33]

A striking feature of the Quaker Meeting was its ability to act as a surrogate family for its members. In the early years of the movement this had resonance with those poor, orphaned, and destitute Friends, isolated from their families and suffering the effects of persecution. Even in the eighteenth century, it is clear that the Meetings provided an important space for supporting the extended Quaker family. It was expected, for example, that when a Quaker Meeting granted a certificate of travel to one of its members, they would guarantee both financial assistance towards the journey, and care for the travelling minister's family in their absence.[34] The oversight and care of Quaker children by the wider spiritual community was often extensive. Thus when Rachel and Phebe Valentine were left in Philadelphia 'almost like fatherless and motherless children', whilst their widowed father

---

[30] 'A Testimony from the Quarterly-Meeting of Wigton, Concerning Bridget Story', in Society of Friends, *A Collection of Testimonies Concerning Several Ministers of the Gospel amongst the People Called Quakers, Deceased* (London, 1760), pp. 78–79.

[31] 'Lancelot Wardell's Testimony Concerning His Dear Deceased Wife, Deborah Wardell, Who Died the 7th of the Tenth Month 1732', in Society of Friends, *Collection of Testimonies*, p. 65.

[32] Naomi Tadmor, *Family and Friends in Eighteenth-Century England: Household, Kinship, and Patronage* (Cambridge, 2001), pp. 18–43.

[33] Anna M. Lawrence, *One Family under God: Love, Belonging, and Authority in Early Transatlantic Methodism* (Philadelphia, 2011), p. 85.

[34] Margaret Hope Bacon (ed.), *Wilt Thou Go on My Errand? Journals of Three 18th Century Quaker Women Ministers* (Wallingford, PA, 1994), p. 11.

was undertaking missionary service in the British Isles, they were taken into the household of a local Quaker family.[35]

One of the most significant insights into the history of early Quakerism has therefore come from the recognition that the Quaker Women's Meetings provided an important space for the public world of the ministry and the private space of the household to converge. Barry Levy has argued that by virtue of their place within the family, eighteenth-century female Friends were already granted positions of communal authority. Indeed, according to Levy, George Fox's main reason for establishing the Meeting system was to 'ensure household discipline'.[36] Su Fang Ng has also explained how the strong familial language of fatherhood and motherhood within Quaker church culture enabled Friends to maintain hierarchy, whilst offering the potential for a more egalitarian form of community.[37] Recognising the congruity between women's public and private identities has brought a significant revision to the view that the separate Meetings suppressed women's opportunities for active participation. The home was the sphere within which women were to exercise equal ministry, and by extension, this was also the area for which they were held particularly responsible in their Meetings. After all, the first Meetings had been held within members' homes.[38] The survival of the faith, as historians have come to recognise, depended upon women's active involvement in nurturing Quaker values within their families and local Meetings. They 'combined a woman's space with a woman's sphere', by permitting a transfer of ideas from the domestic setting to the Meeting House.[39]

The work of women within their Meetings is now generally accepted as integral to the development of early Quakerism. This is particularly true of the historiography dealing with the eighteenth-century colonial context, where dramatic shifts in women's status are less evident. Rebecca Larson acknowledges that the establishment of separate Women's Meetings for business, as a counterpart to the Men's Meetings, offered an 'unprecedented inclusion of females in church government'.[40] Margaret Hope Bacon was one of the first scholars of American Quakerism to describe

[35] The two girls went to live with John Head and his wife. HL, mssRV 1–305 Robert Valentine Papers, Box 1, 1732–1783, fols. 194 and 195. Robert Valentine to 'my dear Children', London, 31 May 1782 and Settle (Yorkshire), 18 October 1782.

[36] Levy, *Quakers and the American Family*, pp. 78–79.

[37] Su Fang Ng, *Literature and the Politics of the Family in Seventeenth-Century England* (Cambridge, 2007), p. 202.

[38] The women of Chester Monthly Meeting in Pennsylvania continued to hold their Meetings in members' homes until the beginning of 1704.

[39] Dunn, 'Latest Light on Women of Light', p. 82.

[40] Larson, *Daughters of Light Quaker Women Preaching and Prophesying in the Colonies and Abroad, 1700–1775* (New York, 1999), p. 31.

the Women's Meetings for business as 'training grounds' for female leadership in the Women's Rights Movement.[41] Although Quaker women were early pioneers of the nineteenth-century campaigns for gender equality, how far the ideal of Quaker spiritual equality within their Meetings can be viewed teleologically as part of their wider political activism is debateable. It is nonetheless notable that the Meeting system equipped Quaker women with skills in record keeping, presiding at Meetings, and keeping financial accounts. Although some of these roles were part of many women's everyday lives, it is significant that these opportunities were available to female Friends within the structure of their religious community. Their exclusive female gatherings also provided a unique space in which they could act independently in their own affairs and drive forward church policy. Their ability to keep records and accounts brought them knowledge and, as Jane Whittle and Elizabeth Griffiths observe in their study of women's household account books, 'knowledge increased the ability . . . to influence decisions'.[42]

Several Quaker historians have provided helpful insights into the role of female Friends within specific Meetings.[43] But absent from these studies is any detailed investigation of the opportunities available to women to achieve status within their communities. Moreover, no study has explored the differences, or indeed, the continuities between the Women's Meetings in England and those in Ireland and the American colonies. This is a significant oversight, for much of the cohesion of the Society depended upon the successful transplantation of the Meeting structure into different social, economic, and cultural contexts. Lawrence has shown, for example, that eighteenth-century American Methodism was not simply a duplicate of the English system on American soil; rather, 'it matured within a culture of

---

[41] Margaret Hope Bacon, *Mothers of Feminism: The Story of Quaker Women in America* (San Francisco, 1986), p. 45.

[42] Jane Whittle and Elizabeth Griffiths, *Consumption and Gender in the Early Seventeenth-Century Household: The World of Alice Le Strange* (Oxford, 2012), p. 9.

[43] Soderlund explores four Women's Monthly Meetings in New Jersey and Pennsylvania: Shrewsbury, Chesterfield, Philadelphia, and Chester in 'Women's Authority', pp. 722–749; Susan Forbes has researched the Friends of New Garden Monthly Meeting in Pennsylvania in 'Quaker Tribalism', in Michael Zuckerman (ed.), *Friends and Neighbours: Group Life in America's First Plural Society* (Philadelphia, 1982), pp. 145–173; Michele Denise Ryan discusses the Quaker Women's Meetings in London in 'In My Hand for Lending'; Gareth Shaw has focused on the Meetings of seventeenth-century Ostwick, in Yorkshire in 'The Inferior Parts of the Body: The Development and Role of Women's Meetings in the Early Quaker Movement', *Quaker Studies*, vol. 9, no. 2 (2005), pp. 191–203; and Sheila Wright has researched the nineteenth-century Quaker community in York in 'Quakerism and Its Implications for Quaker Women: The Women Itinerant Ministers of York Meeting, 1780–1840', in W. J. Sheils and Diana Wood (eds.), *Women in the Church* (Studies in Church History, 27, Oxford, 1990), pp. 403–414.

exchange.'[44] It is therefore important to see if we can identify any clear pattern of divergence between the English, Irish, and colonial Quaker Meetings.

Quaker emigration certainly affected the vitality of the British Quaker Meetings, whose membership shrank dramatically over this period. It was reported, for example, that in some rural areas, the 'unsavoury precedings and runneings into Pensilvania' was 'a Cause of great weakening If not totall decayeinge of some meetings'. For these Friends, as Richard Allen argues, 'there was a general feeling that they were the "remnant" of once-vibrant Quaker communities'.[45] Moreover, the trials faced by female Friends in England and Ireland, surrounded by a resistant and, at times, hostile society must have affected their gendered roles and expectations. To appreciate how different social, cultural, economic, and demographic factors shaped the experiences of female Friends, it is necessary to undertake a more detailed comparison of individual groups in their Meetings.

THE TRANSATLANTIC QUAKER MEETING STRUCTURE

From their inception, Women's Meetings were viewed as fundamental to Quaker discipline. 'Such will be vesells fitt for the masters us[e]; to perform the servis of his hous', one epistle of 1676 declared.[46] Quaker Meetings across the British Atlantic followed the same basic pyramidal organisational structure of Preparative, Monthly, Quarterly, and Yearly Meetings. Individual local Meetings (Preparative Meetings) belonged to larger Monthly Meetings, which oversaw most of the issues relating to membership and discipline. Whilst the responsibilities of the Monthly Meetings were varied and depended on local circumstances, they generally involved issues relating to marriage, discipline, poor relief, estate management, membership requests, recording births and deaths, and providing certificates for individuals wishing to relocate. In England and the colonies, the Monthly Meetings within each county sent delegates to the regional Quarterly Meetings, to which more complicated problems were referred, especially those relating to discipline. The Quarterly Meetings also approved ministers' requests to travel abroad, sent out enquiries, and offered general guidance to Monthly Meetings about appropriate behaviour. In Ireland, delegates were sent to Province Meetings, which acted in a similar capacity to the Quarterly Meetings, but met every six weeks. Representatives were then nominated to attend the National and Half-Year Meetings in Dublin. At the top of the

---

[44] Lawrence, *One Family under God*, p. 18.

[45] Quoted in Richard C. Allen, 'Restoration Quakerism, 1660–1691', in Stephen W. Angell and Pink Dandelion (eds.), *The Oxford Handbook of Quaker Studies* (Oxford, 2013), p. 40.

[46] LRSF, MGR 1114 London Women's Meeting Epistles, 1671–1753, fol. 30, Barbados Women's Meeting to the London Women's Box Meeting, 30 April 1676.

structure was the Yearly Meeting, which met in London and the major cities of the American colonies.[47]

Across the British Atlantic, these gatherings at each level comprised separate Men's and Women's Meetings, with the roles assigned to male elders paralleled in the structure of the Women's Meetings. The officers included overseers, who in same-sex pairs supervised entire districts and cared for the Meeting's property. Overseers shared their functions with the Meeting's elders – the men and women given responsibility for the spiritual well-being of the community, through careful supervision of its members. Each Meeting also appointed a clerk and treasurer. The treasurer was responsible for the collection, care, and distribution of the Meeting's stock, whilst the clerk would record the decisions made during the Meeting, draft epistles to fellow Meetings, and prepare the business agenda. The only exception was the London Yearly Meeting, which did not officially establish a separate Meeting for its female members until 1784.[48]

'Meeting', as Thomas D. Hamm has recognised, signifies for Quakers the 'gathering of a body of believers for worship together'.[49] Each of the assemblies mentioned here would have been preceded by a mixed Meeting for worship. The male and female members would then withdraw to separate parts of the Meeting House to oversee their business. In some colonial gatherings, including the Women's Meeting at Chester, physical separation was achieved by dividing the Meeting House, using a sliding partition (see Figure 2.1). It was a symbolic statement of women's separate, but equal status within the congregation.[50] Since most business was conducted and records were kept within the Monthly Meeting, this level of church organisation forms the focus of this survey.[51] The survival of the Monthly Meeting minutes, however, has been patchy. In the American colonies, few minutes survive before 1700. Similarly, very few Irish Quaker Women's Meeting minutes exist before 1700. The records investigated here provide a far from complete picture, but they offer a valuable insight into the lives of these

---

[47] Friends residing in Pennsylvania and West Jersey alternated their Yearly Meetings at Philadelphia and Burlington, whilst Virginian Friends alternated between Levi Neck in Isle of White County and Chuckatuck in Nansemond.

[48] From 1677, a separate national Women's Meeting existed in Ireland, which met annually at the same time as the Half-Year Meeting in May. Richard L. Greaves, *God's Other Children: Protestant Nonconformists and the Emergence of Denominational Churches in Ireland, 1660–1700* (Stanford, CA, 1997), p. 293.

[49] Thomas D. Hamm, *The Quakers in America* (New York, 2003), p. 10.

[50] This is discussed by Bacon in *Mothers of Feminism*, pp. 46–47. English Friends expected their female members to retreat to a separate part of the Meeting House or a different building.

[51] Unless otherwise stated, 'Meeting' in the context of this chapter will refer to that of the Monthly Meeting for business. Greaves describes the Monthly Meetings as 'the foundation of the Friends' system of record keeping', in *God's Other Children*, p. 291.

Figure 2.1. Chester Meeting House was built in 1736 with
a moveable partition to divide the space into two. (© Haverford College
Quaker and Special Collections (Haverford, PA). Identifier HC12-15707).

ordinary women and hold the key to a more comprehensive understanding
of their place within their locales.

The English Meetings under investigation – Kendal and Marsden – were
founded during the first missionary efforts in the northwestern counties of
England from the 1650s. Kendal formed part of Westmorland Quarterly
Meeting and its first Meeting was established in 1668.[52] Marsden, a 'pocket
of Quaker enthusiasm', was formed in the same year as one of the original constituents of Lancashire Quarterly Meeting.[53] Because no membership records were kept during this period, it is almost impossible to gain
an accurate picture of the number of Friends active in these Meetings.
We might note, however, that Archdeacon Waugh was dismayed to find

---

[52] The Preparative Meetings that formed Kendal Monthly Meeting were Preston Patrick,
Grayrigg, Mislet, and Crook. For the history of Kendal Meeting and its origins see David
M. Butler, *Quaker Meeting Houses of the Lake Counties* (London, 1978), pp. 99–109.

[53] The constituent Meetings for Marsden during this period were Marsden, Trawden,
Rossendale, Oldham, and Sawley (formerly Newby). For more about Marsden Meeting see
Edwin H. Alton, 'The Story of Marsden Meeting' (LRSF typescript, 1963).

in 1747 that nearly 3 per cent of the Cumbrian population were Quakers, concentrated in about a dozen parishes.[54] Given that the Quaker community in London has been estimated at less than 1 per cent of the metropolitan population in 1720, this figure is significant.[55] There had long been a sizeable Quaker community in the northwestern counties, one that would have depended heavily on the support of fellow members in the period of persecution.

While few records survive relating to the Irish Quaker Women's Meetings during this period, Tipperary provides a detailed set of minutes of both the women's and men's activities from 1735. Tipperary, situated in southeastern Ireland, was a constituent of the Province Meeting at Munster. In contrast to the Meetings in England and the colonies, Tipperary Men's and Women's Meetings met every six weeks rather than monthly, and alternated with the Province Meetings, also held every six weeks.[56] As noted in the Introduction, the Irish Quaker community was relatively small in comparison to those in England and the American colonies.[57] Like their English counterparts, they declined in numbers between 1682 to 1750, with a considerable number emigrating to Quaker settlements in Pennsylvania and New Jersey.[58] Irish Meetings nevertheless served as important hubs for itinerant ministry. Cork Monthly Meeting recorded the names of 970 Friends who visited Ireland between 1655 and 1750.[59] Its centrality to the transatlantic mission is evident as early as 1669, when two women Friends from Virginia were said to have passed through the Meeting.[60] In 1708, the English ministers Thomas Chalkley and his companion Richard Grove stopped in Ireland on their return from Jamaica, while in 1711 the Pennsylvanian Friend Ann Chapman landed in England and later continued her mission in Ireland before returning to North America.[61]

Unlike most other colonial Monthly Meetings, Chester and Burlington, both constituents of Philadelphia Yearly Meeting, provide an unusually

---

[54] John Burgess, 'The Quakers, the Brethren and the Religious Census in Cumbria', *Transactions of the Cumberland & Westmorland Antiquarian & Archaeological Society*, 80 (1980), p. 104.

[55] Simon Dixon, 'Quaker Communities in London, 1667–c. 1714', PhD thesis, Royal Holloway, University of London (2005), p. 32.

[56] The component Meetings of Tipperary were Cahir, Clonmel, Cashel, Kilcommonbeg, and Waterford. The location of the Meetings rotated between Kilcommonbeg, Clonmel, and Waterford. Greaves, *God's Other Children*, pp. 290–291.

[57] Richard T. Vann and David Eversley, *Friends in Life and Death: The British and Irish Quakers in the Demographic Transition, 1650–1900* (Cambridge, 1992), p. 39.

[58] Albert Cook Myers, *Immigration of the Irish Quakers into Pennsylvania, 1682–1750* (Swarthmore, PA, 1902), pp. 41–42.

[59] This figure was calculated from FHLD, YM C3 Names of Friends in the Ministry in Ireland, 1655–1781. This information is detailed in Table A1.1 in Appendix 1 to this book.

[60] FHLD, YM C3 Names of Friends in the Ministry in Ireland, 1655–1781, entries for 1669.

[61] Ibid., entries for 6 May 1708 and 15 August 1711.

detailed set of minutes for the late 1690s and early 1700s. Both were thriving centres of eighteenth-century Quakerism. The first Monthly Meeting of Friends in Chester met at the house of Robert Wade on 10 January 1682, and by 1688 is estimated to have had between 538 and 561 members, making it an especially important provincial stronghold.[62] The number of Friends in Pennsylvania continued to expand throughout the late seventeenth and early eighteenth centuries. The first Meeting of Burlington Friends was established on 15 July 1678, following the 'practice in the place wee came from'.[63] The Women's Meeting was founded shortly after in 1681. By 1699 a total of 302 Quaker freeholders were listed in a survey of the inhabitants of West New Jersey.[64] Fairfax Meeting in Virginia, which also came under the jurisdiction of Philadelphia Yearly Meeting, was established in very different circumstances.[65] Founded only in 1744, it comprised a small number of Quaker families who had migrated from Pennsylvania. Disillusioned by the state of the Society there, they had travelled to this uninhabited land to perfect the religious organisation of their Society and enjoy greater authority.[66] The Fairfax Women's Meeting records begin in 1745.

OVERSEEING MARRIAGE IN THE 'TRUE CHURCH'

Women's responsibilities within their Meetings were never codified, leaving great scope for local and regional variation. Yet, this study will demonstrate that, despite some evidence of local variation and changing priorities, we find a surprisingly consistent outlook on church order and communal oversight across the English, Irish, and colonial settings. Tables 2.1 and 2.2 show the distribution of all the items of business brought before the female and male elders of Burlington, Chester, Kendal, Marsden, Fairfax, and Tipperary in their Monthly Meetings from January 1700 to December 1705, and January 1745 to December 1750.

While the data set for the 1700–1705 period is not complete in every case, the prominence of marriage issues in both sample periods is consonant

---

[62] FHL, MR-Ph 92 Chester Men's MM 1681–1721, p. 3, minutes for February 1682; and Jack D. Marietta, *The Reformation of American Quakerism, 1748–1783* (Philadelphia, 1984), p. 47.
[63] FHL, MR-Ph 60 Burlington Men's MM 1678–1737, p. 1, minute preceding business for 18 August 1678.
[64] Amelia Mott Gummere, *Friends in Burlington* (Philadelphia, 1884), p. 28.
[65] Fairfax Monthly Meeting and Fairfax Quarterly Meeting were transferred from Philadelphia to Baltimore Yearly Meeting in 1789.
[66] For more on the origins of Fairfax Meeting and the migration of Friends from Pennsylvania to Virginia see Joint Committee of Hopewell Friends, *Hopewell Friends History, 1734–1934, Frederick County: Records of Hopewell Monthly Meetings and Meetings Reporting to Hopewell* (Baltimore, MD, 1936), pp. 40–68.

Table 2.1 Items of Business in the Women's and Men's Meetings of Chester, Burlington, Marsden, and Kendal, 1700–1705

	Chester (Pennsylvania)		Burlington (West Jersey)		Marsden (Lancashire)		Kendal (Westmorland)	
	W N	M N	W N	M N	W N	M N	W N	M N
Marriage	38 (51%)	57 (38%)	46 (22%)	44 (18%)	25 (14%)	34 (11%)	56 (76%)	1 (0.3%)
Discipline	4 (5%)	24 (16%)	35 (17%)	44 (18%)	6 (3%)	25 (8%)	2 (3%)	77 (23%)
Church Oversight	16 (21%)	18 (12%)	21 (10%)	27 (11%)	31 (16%)	67 (21%)	1 (1%)	68 (20%)
Philanthropy	1 (1%)	2 (1%)	30 (14%)	4 (2%)	50 (26%)	33 (10%)	5 (7%)	3 (0.9%)
Removal and Settlement	8 (11%)	14 (9%)	14 (7%)	27 (11%)	—	5 (2%)	—	13 (4%)
Travelling Ministry	—	6 (4%)	—	5 (2%)	2 (1%)	32 (10%)	—	13 (4%)
Tithes	—	—	—	—	9 (5%)	10 (3%)	6 (8%)	25 (7%)
Accounts and Estates	8 (11%)	9 (6%)	66 (31%)	54 (23%)	8 (4%)	23 (7%)	—	31 (9%)
Advice and Queries	—	3 (2%)	—	—	58 (31%)	49 (15%)	4 (5%)	24 (7%)

(continued)

Table 2.1 (*Continued*)

	Chester (Pennsylvania)		Burlington (West Jersey)		Marsden (Lancashire)		Kendal (Westmorland)	
	W N	M N	W N	M N	W N	M N	W N	M N
Apprenticeship	–	–	–	–	–	22 (7%)	–	51 (15%)
Arbitration	–	17 (11%)	–	32 (13%)	–	7 (2%)	–	30 (9%)
Publications	–	–	–	2 (1%)	–	14 (4%)	–	–
TOTAL	75	150	212	239	189	321	74	336

Note: W = Women; M = Men; N = actual number.

See Appendix 2 for a detailed list of the activities that formed these categories.

Data extracted from the following sources: FHL, MR-Ph 98 Chester Women's MM 1695–1733; FHL, MR-Ph 92 Chester Men's MM 1681–1721; FHL, MR-Ph 63 Burlington Women's MM 1681–1747; FHL, MR-Ph 60 Burlington Men's MM 1678–1737; LA, FRM/1/24 Marsden Women's MM 1678–1738; LA, FRM/1/1 Marsden Men's MM 1678–1723; and KAC, WDFCF/1/22 Kendal Women's MM 1671–1719; KAC, WDFCF/1/13 Kendal Men's MM 1699–1723.

Table 2.2 Items of Business in the Women's and Men's Meetings of Chester, Burlington, Fairfax, Marsden, Kendal, and Tipperary, 1745–1750

	Chester (Pennsylvania)		Burlington (West Jersey)		Fairfax (Virginia)		Marsden (Lancashire)		Kendal (Westmorland)		Tipperary (Munster)	
	W N	M N	W N	M N	W N	M N	W N	M N	W N	M N	W N	M N
Marriage	62 (25%)	62 (16%)	96 (29%)	103 (22%)	46 (37%)	47 (22%)	17 (9%)	19 (6%)	56 (25%)	76 (21%)	12 (7%)	18 (4%)
Discipline	35 (14%)	116 (30%)	40 (12%)	94 (20%)	24 (20%)	72 (33%)	1 (0.5%)	5 (2%)	5 (2%)	68 (19%)	3 (2%)	89 (22%)
Church Oversight	30 (12%)	42 (11%)	27 (8%)	56 (12%)	13 (11%)	20 (9%)	27 (15%)	82 (27%)	34 (15%)	52 (15%)	8 (5%)	88 (22%)
Philanthropy	—	5 (1%)	5 (1%)	7 (1%)	—	—	58 (32%)	66 (21%)	37 (17%)	11 (3%)	31 (18%)	5 (1%)
Removal and Settlement	103 (42%)	134 (34%)	82 (24%)	107 (22%)	20 (16%)	44 (20%)	1 (0.5%)	10 (3%)	7 (3%)	43 (12%)	7 (4%)	4 (1%)
Travelling Ministry	4 (2%)	4 (1%)	1 (0.3%)	27 (6%)	—	8 (4%)	—	3 (1%)	13 (6%)	19 (5%)	1 (0.6%)	2 (0.5%)
Tithes	—	—	—	—	—	—	2 (1%)	4 (1%)	8 (4%)	—	—	—
Accounts and Estates	10 (4%)	13 (3%)	79 (24%)	32 (7%)	—	—	20 (11%)	25 (8%)	—	36 (10%)	—	83 (20%)
Advice and Queries	—	—	5 (1%)	13 (3%)	—	—	56 (31%)	57 (19%)	61 (28%)	17 (5%)	109 (64%)	90 (22%)
Apprenticeship	—	—	—	—	—	—	—	7 (2%)	—	15 (4%)	—	—

(continued)

Table 2.2 (Continued)

	Chester (Pennsylvania)		Burlington (West Jersey)		Fairfax (Virginia)		Marsden (Lancashire)		Kendal (Westmorland)		Tipperary (Munster)	
	W N	M N	W N	M N	W N	M N	W N	M N	W N	M N	W N	M N
Arbitration	–	8 (2%)	–	17 (4%)	–	4 (2%)	–	19 (6%)	–	19 (5%)	–	13 (3%)
Publications	–	2 (0.5%)	–	10 (2%)	–	–	–	10 (3%)	–	1 (0.2%)	–	3 (0.7%)
Membership	–	3 (0.8%)	–	12 (3%)	20 (16%)	21 (10%)	–	–	–	–	–	–
Sufferings	–	–	–	–	–	–	–	–	–	–	–	11 (3%)
TOTAL	244	389	335	478	123	216	182	307	221	357	171	406

Note: W = Women; M = Men; N = actual number.

See Appendix 2 for a detailed list of the activities that formed these categories.

Data extracted from the following sources: FHL, MR-Ph 98 Chester Women's MM 1733–1779; FHL, MR-Ph 103 Chester Men's MM 1745–1778; FHL, MR-Ph 63 Burlington Women's MM 1681–1747 and 1747–1799; FHL, MR-Ph 60 Burlington Men's MM 1737–1756; LA, FRM/1/25 Marsden Women's MM 1738–1760; LA, FRM/1/24 Marsden Men's MM 1746–1781; KAC, WDFCF/1/23 Kendal Women's MM 1719–1756; KAC, WDFCF/1/14 and 15 Kendal Men's MM 1727–1747 and 1747–1777; FHL, MR-B117 Fairfax Men's MM 1745–1776; FHL, MR-B119 Fairfax Women's MM 1745–1768; RSFI, MMX B2 Co. Tipperary Women's MM 1735–1764; and RSFI MMX A2 Co. Tipperary Men's MM 1724–1760.

with the expectations attached to the Women's Meetings. Unlike Anglicans and Puritans, Quakers believed that holy marriage was possible only for those willing to subordinate themselves to the will of the group, and have their characters and intentions examined by the whole community. The marriage approbation process became the primary mechanism by which the Quakers were able to sustain the faith and, as Kristianna Polder has recently argued, it proved 'to be the critical vehicle through which the Quakers held together their identity as the one and only True Church'.[67] All six of the Women's Meetings consistently involved themselves in matters relating to marriage, confirming that this was a transatlantic concern. Between 1700 and 1705, 76 and 51 per cent of Kendal and Chester women's items of business were respectively devoted to marriage. Although Table 2.2 suggests that these marriage-related tasks had declined by 1750, approving couples for marriage remained a key feature of the tasks undertaken in all six of the Monthly Meetings, especially in the American colonies.

Friends enforced a rigorous process of consent for marriage that placed female elders in an important position over both men and women.[68] Prospective partners had first to obtain permission from their parents before presenting their intentions to their local Preparative Meeting. They would then progress to the Monthly Meetings, where they would be expected to declare their intentions on two consecutive occasions. Both partners were expected to come first before the Women's Meeting, which would then grant them approval to proceed to the Men's Meeting. Each time a couple submitted a request to marry before the Women's Meeting, two female elders were appointed to investigate the 'clearness' of the woman for marriage. Clearness meant a number of different things for Friends, but in the context of marriage, it was usually in relation to whether the couple wishing to marry was free from all other engagements, whether the man and woman had the approval and consent of their parents, and whether both had sought divine guidance. In the case of a remarriage, the overseers had to ensure that neither of the parties had been widowed for less than a year and that provisions had been made for the children from previous marriages.

---

[67] Kristianna Polder, *Matrimony in the True Church: The Seventeenth-Century Quaker Marriage Approbation Discipline* (London, 2015), p. 7.

[68] The correct procedure for marriage was outlined in an epistle of the 1670s, directing all Friends to 'bring their Marriages twice to the womens meetings, and twice to the mens: the first time they are to come to the womens Meetings that the women of the meeting, do examin both the man and the woman, that they be cleare and free from all other persons, and that they have their parents, and friends and Relations, Consent; ... if any thing be found that they are not clear ... then they do not proceed, till they have given satisfaction both to the parties and friends, concerning that matter.' 'A Seventeenth-Century Quaker Women's Declaration', transcribed by Milton D. Speizman and Jane C. Kronick, *Signs: Journal of Women in Culture and Society*, vol. 1, no. 1 (1975), p. 242.

After the match had been approved, two more female elders were appointed to attend the nuptials and evening celebrations and report back on whether they had been conducted in an orderly manner. This especially centred on ensuring that the provision of food was not too covetous, to avoid associations with marriage feasts. The giving of gifts, especially of gloves, was also banned.[69] Levy has argued that Friends exhibited such rigorous control over the marriage process because of their determination to regulate the formation of new households, the primary environments in which children were raised. His findings from the Welsh Tract Meetings in the Delaware Valley support this view, with almost half of the business that came before the Meetings directly concerning marriage.[70] As Chapter 1 made clear, Quakers believed that having two parents of the same faith had a crucial role in moulding their children's character and so perpetuating the Society's values and culture.

Given that all prospective husbands and wives had to appear before the Women's Meetings before being allowed to proceed to the Men's Meetings, the process constituted an implicit challenge to patriarchy. Thus in September 1704, the Women's Meeting of Kendal delayed Jeremiah Whittnell's marriage to Margaret Harton because they judged the certificate that the young man presented was 'insufficient' to clear the truth.[71] Similarly, Chester women deferred the marriage negotiations between John Hoskins and Ruth Adkison in September 1698 because of 'some Reports concerning John'.[72] A young man (or woman) who proceeded with marriage without following the correct procedure would face charges of disorderly conduct and would be required to condemn (disavow and apologise for) their actions. The authority exhibited in this process, especially the women's ability to decide the arrangements of marriage for men, was an issue against which the dissident Wilkinson-Story Separatists reacted strongly. William Mucklow's 1673 tract, *The Spirit of the Hat*, complained that if the Women's Meeting was allowed a veto, it could deprive a man of 'a Person whom he most dearly loves'.[73] William Mather criticised the potential for disruption in such a lengthy process. He thought it 'a very hard Tryal' for men to submit to female authority in such matters, especially because unnecessary delays might drive exasperated couples to flout the

---

[69] See Greaves, *God's Other Children*, p. 322.
[70] Levy, *Quakers and the American Family*, p. 132.
[71] KAC, WDFCF/1/22 Kendal Women's MM 1671–1719, minutes for 4 August and 1 September 1704.
[72] FHL, MR-Ph 98 Chester Women's MM 1695–1733, minutes for 27 September 1698.
[73] William Mucklow, *The Spirit of the Hat, or, the Government of the Quakers among Themselves, as It Hath Been Exercised of Late Years by George Fox* (London, 1673), p. 32.

rules of the Society and go to a priest 'to rid themselves of the trouble of waiting ... any longer'.[74]

The circumstances surrounding the Quaker process of marriage discipline provided a vital space for women to act independently of their male brethren. Friends even asserted that this was a task particularly suited to women because they had greater knowledge of the circumstances in marriage and should rightly shoulder the responsibility of overseeing its orderly accomplishment. 'We are much in our families amongst our children, maids and servants', one epistle from Lancaster Women's Meeting declared, 'and may see more into their inclinations.'[75] Protestant and Catholic women often played a significant informal role in early modern marriage and courtship culture, but Quakers went much further by giving mothers and other female elders a formal role in the approbation process.[76] As I discussed in Chapter 1, it was expected that a match should be primarily driven by divine ordination. However, the consent of both parents was a compulsory feature of Quaker marriage discipline procedure, recognising the authority of the mother as well as the father over their children's futures.

Whilst marriage regulation dominated the agendas of all six of the Women's Meetings, it formed a particularly high proportion of the issues dealt with at Kendal in the period 1700–1705. Of the four Meetings from this sample period, Kendal Meeting dealt with the highest number of new marriage proposals, despite undertaking the lowest number of tasks in total. Perhaps the best explanation for this lies in the fact that up until 1704 Kendal men had little responsibility in overseeing local marriages. Women's involvement was so extensive that 98 per cent of the administration surrounding couples desiring to marry were exclusively dealt with by the Women's Meeting. By contrast, the Chester Women's Meeting, despite taking on a similar number of assignments for the same period, dealt with only 40 per cent of the total marriage arrangements within the community. This semi-independent role for the Kendal women appears more in keeping with the powers permitted

---

[74] Mather, *A Novelty: Or, a Government of Women*, pp. 11–12. The frustrations caused by such delays were encapsulated in a letter that the London Friend John Sansom sent to his recently married son, Samuel, in 1737. Here he expressed his concern that 'thou should meet with so much disapointment in passing the meetings', especially because he had thought 'the Cirtificate I had signed had been sufficient ... for I am fully satisfied in thy Choice'. HCQSC, MS Coll 1008 Morris-Sansom Collection, c. 1715–1925, Box 17, John Sansom folder, John Sansom to 'Dear Child', 16 August 1737.

[75] Highly likely to have been authored by Sarah Fell this epistle was written sometime between 1675 and 1680, transcribed by Speizman and Kronick in 'A Seventeenth-Century Quaker Women's Declaration', p. 242.

[76] Numerous examples can be found in David Cressy's chapter on 'Courtship and the Making of Marriage' in his *Birth, Marriage, and Death: Ritual, Religion, and the Life-Cycle in Tudor and Stuart England* (Oxford, 1997), pp. 233–266; and Margaret J. M. Ezell, *The Patriarch's Wife: Literary Evidence and the History of the Family* (London, 1987), pp. 24–33.

to women in the English cities, where Meetings like the independent London Box Meeting allowed women a degree of authority on certain issues without their decisions being accountable to the men. This display of female independence may also indicate the influence of Margaret Fell and her daughters in the region, for as Fell's biographer asserted, she was uncompromising in her belief that Women's Meetings should hold 'the prerogative in marriage contractual procedure'.[77]

The items of business within the Marsden Meetings during the same period, by contrast, were closer to the pattern that evolved in Ireland and the colonies. Marriage issues occupied only 14 per cent of the items of business dealt with by the Marsden Women's Meetings between 1700 and 1705. This suggests that the arrangement of marriage discipline at Kendal was a distinctly local development. This may reflect the fact that until 1704 Kendal women were limited in the range of roles they could perform because they were forced to meet and conduct business in a private building, separate from the Meeting House.[78] The small number of tasks they undertook in other aspects of church administration has therefore skewed the number of tasks relating to marriage in their favour. Whilst this division of labour may indicate that the female Friends of Kendal were not viewed as equals in their Meetings, it is significant that they were entrusted to oversee almost exclusively this particular aspect of church governance.

The pattern of marriage regulation that developed in Marsden and in the colonial Meetings suggests, however, that it was more common for the Men's and Women's Meetings to work in tandem, rather than in isolation. This is exemplified in an anonymous epistle sent to the London Women's Box Meeting, where the female correspondents declared that '[we] are workers together with them in the same faith, and only distinct as to our places, and in those particular things which most p[ro]perly appertaines unto us as women'.[79] Cooperation was particularly important when it came to the detection of specific transgressions in relation to marriage. Elizabeth Branson, for instance, brought a paper acknowledging her transgressions

---

[77] Kunze, *Margaret Fell and the Rise of Quakerism*, p. 157.

[78] As the minutes of the Men's Meetings in Kendal reveal, it was not until February 1703 that a proposal was raised for a space to be provided for the women of Kendal Monthly and Quarterly Meetings to assemble: 'Whereas it was thought necessary [that] ... a more convenient place might be provided for our women Friends of this County to keepe their Quarterly Meeting and allsoe the Womens Meet[ing] at Kendal.' The minutes for the following month declared their intention to extend the south side of the existing Meeting House and to calculate the charges incurred. However, it was not until December of that year that a general collection of £13 19s. 6d. was made to cover the costs of this undertaking. KAC, WDFCF/1/13 Kendal Men's MM 1699–1723, minutes for 5 February 1703, 5 March 1703, 26 March 1703, and 31 December 1703.

[79] LRSF, MGR 1 1a4 London Women's Meeting Epistles, 1671–1753, fol. 17, unsigned epistle to the London Women's Box Meeting, undated, c. 1671–1675.

to Burlington Women's Meeting in November 1703, to condemn her 'disorderly marriage'.[80] After inquiring into the affair, the women judged themselves 'not fully satisfied concerning it' and petitioned the Men's Meeting for advice, where it was decided that Branson should attend the following Monthly Meeting and sign a new paper of condemnation.[81] Likewise, when the overseers at Kendal 'could not give so satisfactory account' of Elizabeth Morland's clearness for marriage in 1725, occasioning 'severall questions and some uncommon discorce [sic]', it was determined that the Men's Meeting should be left to decide whether the couple should be allowed to proceed any further.[82] Whilst this reliance on the advice and counsel of the men indicates that the decisions of female elders were subject to masculine intervention, it is significant that in all instances it was the female members of the congregation who made the initial discovery of the transgression. Moreover, after the Men's Meeting had given their judgment on the matter, the Women's Meetings were entrusted to implement their advice independently.

Although clear tensions over female authority existed, this evidence reflects a collaborative relationship between male and female elders, rather than one where women were entirely subordinated to patriarchal dictates. On no occasion within these sample periods was the decision of any of these Women's Meetings in relation to marriage overturned by their respective Men's Meeting. The judgement of the female elders was respected. At Fairfax Meeting, for example, the marital proceedings of Joseph Wells and Charity Carrington were delayed by the Men's Meeting in May 1750 after the Women Friends discovered that Carrington had not acquainted her father with her intention to marry.[83] Women's involvement in the marital arrangements of their own sex even permitted them a formal place within the space of the Men's Meetings, for female overseers were expected to accompany the young women when they declared their intentions. Thus

---

[80] The denunciation of a member for misconduct was a highly charged process, not dissimilar from nonconformist models of discipline practised in England. Quaker Meetings sought to reclaim errant members and bring them to a sense of the gravity of their misconduct and followed the pattern set out in Matthew 18:15–17, moving from private admonition to presentment before witnesses and finally public condemnation. If the labours of the elders were successful, the errant member would submit a paper of acknowledgement to their Monthly Meeting for approval. If a paper was judged not to be genuine in its sincerity or satisfactory in its condemnation, then it would be returned to the individual for revision. If individuals refused to submit to the discipline of the Meeting, they were disowned. This process generated an official written condemnation.

[81] FHL, MR-Ph 63 Burlington Women's MM 1681–1747, minutes for 4 October 1703 and 4 November 1703.

[82] KAC, WDFCF/1/23 Kendal Women's MM 1719–1756, minutes for 4 June 1725.

[83] FHL, MR-B117 Fairfax Men's MM 1745–1776, p. 26 [modern pagination]; and FHL, MR-B119 Fairfax Women's MM 1745–1768, p. 19, minutes for 26 May 1750.

after Richard Holden and Ann Hellewell had been approved by Marsden Women's Meeting for marriage, two overseers were appointed to attend the wedding and to accompany the young woman to 'lay the concern before the mens Meeting'.[84] The minutes of Tortola Meeting in the Virgin Islands even suggest that the Women's Meeting had the executive decision in approving marital arrangements, as two men Friends were expected to escort a couple wishing to marry to the Women's Meeting.[85]

Colonial women demonstrated especially independent authority in supervising their female members in matters relating to marriage. When Chester Monthly Meeting heard of Jane Worrilow's so-called 'miscarridge' with Abraham Leake in February 1696, a committee of women was appointed to labour with the young woman and bring her to a sense of her 'wild doeings'. She eventually brought a paper of condemnation to the Women's Meeting, where she acknowledged that 'he did lye upon the bed Cloaths by me part of one night, I being in bed, which thing hath brought great troubell and sorrow upon me'.[86] As the circumstances surrounding this incident suggest, it was a matter the female elders took very seriously, particularly because news of the incident had spread beyond the Quaker community. The entire process from initial condemnation to the final publication of Worrilow's paper was retained within the Women's Meeting and at no point were the men Friends consulted, despite the wide publicity that the incident had gained. Similarly, when the elders at Burlington Monthly Meeting heard of Elizabeth Day's illicit marriage to 'a man that Friends did not approve of', they immediately appointed a committee to inquire into the matter and to speak with all the individuals involved. These included four female members, who were all expected to condemn their role in witnessing the marriage, as well as Day's mother, who had allegedly countenanced her daughter's behaviour. Those who refused to submit papers of condemnation were immediately suspended, among them Elizabeth Day.[87] None of the women involved in the affair was required to present her admission of guilt to the Men's Meeting, neither were the men Friends consulted in the matter. It remained entirely under the women's supervision.

---

[84] LA, FRM/1/24 Marsden Women's MM 1678–1738, minutes for 15 May 1701.

[85] One example was when Townsend Bishop and Mary Reynolds wished to declare their intentions of marriage to the Women's Meeting on 2 February 1747, the couple were accompanied by Thomas Humphries and William Gory. HCQSC, Film 128 Tortola Women's MM 1741–1762, minutes for 2 February 1747.

[86] FHL, MR-Ph 98 Chester Women's MM 1695–1733, minutes for 24 February 1696, 30 March 1696, 25 May 1696 and paper of acknowledgement issued by Jane Worrilow dated 9 May 1696.

[87] FHL, MR-Ph 63 Burlington Women's MM 1681–1747, minutes for 9 February 1703, 1 March 1704, 5 April 1704, 7 June 1703, and 6 September 1703.

ENFORCING ORDER AND DISCIPLINE

The women elders were expected to supervise their female members and ensure they complied with all aspects of church discipline. However, the contrast between the proportion of cases of delinquency dealt with by colonial women in Chester, Burlington, and Fairfax, and those by the Meetings in the British Isles, indicates a point of divergence within transatlantic Quakerism, especially in the period 1745–1750. As Table 2.2 indicates, less than 1 per cent of Marsden and only 2 per cent of Kendal and Tipperary women's energies were spent disciplining members at this time, compared to 14 per cent for Chester, 12 per cent for Burlington, and 20 per cent for Fairfax. It would appear that formal discipline was a much greater preoccupation for the women Friends of the colonies, the reasons for which I shall return to shortly.

That colonial Quaker women enjoyed greater authority than their British sisters in dealing with erring members is underlined by the fact that of the ten tasks of a disciplinary nature against female Friends that reached the agendas of Kendal Men's Meeting in the period 1745–1750, only five were ever brought to the attention of the Women's Meeting. Thus a complaint lodged in June 1747 against Sarah Sewart, who had 'committed lewdness' with John Birket, led to her suspension from the Society. This was pronounced by the Men's Meeting in September after the couple had married clandestinely – which rendered them not 'in a suitable condition at present to continue in unity'.[88] At no point during the condemnation process, however, were the women Friends involved. Instead, a short statement in the Women's Meeting book, after the incident was reported in June 1747, simply noted that 'some have born disorderly Company to thear shame and repro[a]ch'.[89] A similar scenario, with the Men's Meeting dealing exclusively with errant female members, is revealed in the Tipperary Meeting minutes. Ten cases of discipline against female members were brought before the Men's Meeting but only three reached the agendas of the Women's Meeting.

This contrast in female authority over matters of discipline should not come as a surprise when we consider the significantly different socioeconomic contexts faced by these groups of Friends. The conditions of frontier life in the American communities, much less grounded in tradition, are likely to have encouraged greater self-sufficiency, reflected in a church order permitting women more authority. The early Quakers, attempting to establish a viable supervisory and disciplinary structure, would have felt the need for everyone to play a full part. The eighteenth-century writer J. Hector

---

[88] KAC, WDFCF/1/15 Kendal Men's MM 1747–1777, pp. 1–4, minutes for 26 June 1747, 7 August 1747, and 4 September 1747.
[89] KAC, WDFCF/1/23 Kendal Women's MM 1719–1756, minutes for 26 June 1747.

de Crèvecoeur, travelling across the American frontier, viewed the Quaker women of Nantucket in New England as the rulers of their families, and commented that the frequent absence of their husbands, away at sea, had given them 'the abilities as well as a taste for that kind of superintendency, to which, . . . they seem to be, in general very equal'. This, he explained 'justly entitles them to a rank superior to that of other wives'.⁹⁰ Bacon has also noted the prominent status of Nantucket Quaker women, arguing that they were actively involved in education, poor relief, and discipline because their male counterparts were often absent for long periods on whaling expeditions.⁹¹ Local conditions thus help to explain why North American Women's Meetings were able to take on more responsibility than was perhaps originally intended.

Even in the eighteenth century, the relatively new nature of Quaker settlements, still played a role in providing colonial women with greater opportunities for involvement in disciplinary procedures. Fairfax Meeting in Virginia was founded in the 1730s by families dismayed by the declining standards of their religious Society. Their ideological focus on order and conformity to Quaker testimonies may explain why the female elders were permitted to deal independently with cases of 'disorderly walking' (as digression from Quaker doctrine became known). Between 1745 and 1750, 20 per cent of their tasks were devoted to matters of a disciplinary nature. Among the transgressors was Mary Hanby, who was disciplined by the female elders in December 1748, after reports that she had married a non-Quaker. Although she had not attended Quaker Meetings for worship for two years, two women Friends were appointed to investigate her conduct during this period of absence and decide whether to admit her or formally disown her from the Society.⁹² Other examples include Jean R. Soderlund's findings for the Monthly Meetings of Bucks County, Pennsylvania, where the women took full jurisdiction over cases of discipline without submitting disownments to the men for review.⁹³

Chapter 1 showed how an emphasis on order and stability rather than ministerial service gave colonial women greater opportunities to attain positions of authority within their local communities. English female Friends enjoyed a lesser degree of influence. This is perhaps best reflected in the issue of the Women's Yearly Meetings, where a separate Meeting for the female Friends of Pennsylvania and Burlington had been established shortly after settlement in the 1680s, whereas London women, did not get a Yearly

---

⁹⁰ J. Hector St. John de Crèvecoeur, *Letters from an American Farmer* (London, 1782), p. 197.
⁹¹ Bacon, *Mothers of Feminism*, pp. 45–46.
⁹² FHL, MR-B119 Fairfax Women's MM 1745–1768, p. 18, minutes for 30 December 1749.
⁹³ Soderlund, 'Women's Authority', p. 744.

Meeting until 1784, and only after a long and hard-fought campaign on both sides of the Atlantic. This contrast in the organisational structure of the Society has led scholars like Bacon to argue that, in the British context, women were not perceived as equals in church government.[94] In Ireland too, although women were permitted a national Half-Year Meeting, it sat less frequently than their respective Men's Meeting.[95]

From the start, Quakers in Britain had been a persecuted minority, experiencing ostracism and isolation. Facing both repression and ridicule, British Friends were more conservative in their attitudes towards women, and the establishment of the Women's Meetings marked a shift towards creating a more respectable public identity for the movement's female members. The women Friends of rural British Meetings like Marsden, Kendal, and Tipperary had fewer opportunities for independent action than their sisters in America because more executive power was held by the Men's Meeting. This is reflected in an epistle that Kendal women sent to the London Box Meeting in 1675, where they tellingly explained that their separate Meetings were 'lightly looked upon and of lit[tle] esteeme among Some who should have Strengthened us'.[96] Phyllis Mack has suggested that women in counties like Lancashire and Westmorland were particularly affected by undercurrents of opposition to them gaining positions of authority. Many of the Wilkinson-Story Separatists, who were firmly opposed to the establishment of the Women's Meetings, were from these northern regions.[97] One epistle sent in 1677 by the Quaker leader John Pennington, detailed the stance of the Kendal Men's Monthly Meeting on the issue of 'women's power to discipline'. He argued that 'the Womens Meeting cannot determine the membership of any', explaining that it would be confusing for 'offending females to be subjected to two different jurisdictions for the same offence'.[98] That cases of discipline formed a smaller proportion of the work of the Women's Meetings in England and Ireland can be explained in part by them being permitted less authority in this sphere.

---

[94] The campaign for a Yearly Meeting succeeded when a group of ten male and female representatives from the Americas, led by the Philadelphian schoolmistress Rebecca Jones, attended the 1784 London Yearly Meeting and petitioned the male elders directly to extend women's powers within the English organisational structure. Margaret Hope Bacon, 'The Establishment of London Women's Yearly Meeting: A Transatlantic Concern', *JFHS*, vol. 52, no. 2 (1995), pp. 153–154.

[95] The Men's Meeting was half-yearly until 1797. It met in May and November each year. The Women's Meeting only sat once a year at the same time as the Men's Meeting in May.

[96] LRSF, MGR 11a4 London Women's Meeting Epistles, 1671–1753, fol. 23, Kendal Women's Meeting to London Women's Meeting, 5 March 1675.

[97] Mack, *Visionary Women*, pp. 336–337.

[98] LRSF, Reynolds MSS, Box I3/4, pp. 46–47, John Pennington to John Fell, Norwich, 30 September 1677.

The colonial Friends under scrutiny here lived in a very different cultural climate, in communities formed on the basis of mutual toleration and freedom of worship. This meant they faced a different challenge: how to prevent members interacting too closely with and adopting the customs and practices of wider society. This was a source of great unease for the Meeting elders in Chester, Fairfax, and Burlington and may also explain why so many members were disciplined for transgressing from Quaker testimonies during this period. The growing non-Quaker populations in these traditional Quaker strongholds and increased opportunities for marriage to non-believers intensified the efforts of the Meeting elders to keep their members within the Quaker fold. Fairfax Men's Meeting condemned and eventually disowned Thomas Gore in 1750 after hearing reports of his 'unsavoury expressions', fighting and quarrelling. The investigation revealed that he had fallen 'into evil company' and 'did Partake ... in their Evil Practices of Dancing and Other unseemly behaviour, very Inconsistant with the Discipline of Friends'.[99] Susan Forbes has pointed to a similar concern in New Garden Monthly Meeting, in Pennsylvania, and suggests that a preoccupation with discipline was linked to rising non-Quaker populations in the region.[100]

Anxiety that Quaker order was disintegrating is also evident from the minutes of the Men's Meeting at Burlington in October 1748. When they received a report that Moses and Patience Haines had been married 'contrary to good order', two Friends were appointed to investigate. Although the source of the transgression is unclear, the signed paper of denial described the couple's 'unchasitity' before marriage, and the issue is also likely to have involved their failure to notify Friends about their intention to marry, which occurred outside the Society. To make matters worse, it became clear that Moses Haines's entire family had been negligent in attending Meetings for worship, and Friends were also appointed to speak with his father, Daniel. For the next five months Friends visited the family, and were eventually able to secure a promise that they would return to the Meeting. It was not until almost a year later, however, that they received a formal self-condemnation from Moses and Patience Haines about their transgression, followed two months later by the disownment of his brother Isaac and his wife.[101] A single transgression by a young couple had quickly triggered a thorough investigation into an entire family, resulting in public humiliation and, in some cases, excommunication.[102]

---

[99] FHL, MR-B117 Fairfax Men's MM 1745–1776, pp. 29–30 [modern pagination], minutes for 28 July 1750–24 November 1750.

[100] Forbes, 'Quaker Tribalism', pp. 167–168.

[101] The nature of their wrongdoing is not stated.

[102] FHL, MR-Ph 60 Burlington Men's MM 1737–1756, pp. 170–181, minutes from 3 October 1748–7 August 1749.

Whilst there is a strong case for believing that British Quaker women had less authority within their Meetings, we should note that English (and Irish) Women's Meetings developed different methods of ensuring conformity and dealing with errant members, without resorting to formal denunciation. These alternative procedures are very evident when we look at the number of tasks relating to 'Advice and Queries' handled by Marsden and Kendal, as well as Tipperary Women's Meetings, in the period 1745–1750, as revealed in Table 2.2. This aspect of church oversight, which usually involved reading and responding to the epistles of the Quarterly and Yearly Meetings, took up a significant proportion of the female elders' tasks (31, 28, and 64 per cent, respectively). Written Queries and Advices as a means of asserting discipline had been used by English Friends from the 1680s. The procedure involved overseers from each Meeting within the Quaker hierarchy responding to a set of about twelve questions, which were read and answered on a quarterly basis. Questions typically posed by the Women's Meetings included issues such as:

Do all who profess with us keep in plain[n]ess of Language, Apparel, Dress and Furniture?

Are the Youth among us careful, and well advised to avoid going to see any vain Shows, or even to Fairs without sufficient buesiness [*sic*]?

Are all young and unmarried Women careful that they keep no disorderly company nor in any w[ays] concern themselves upon the account of Marriage without the consent of their Parents, Guardians, or some faithful and judicious Friends of the Meeting they belong to?

Are Families visited by faithful Members for the more effectual building up of the Church?[103]

This list of queries is somewhat reminiscent of the Church of England 'Articles of Visitation' that were distributed to churchwardens before an episcopal or archdeacon's visit.[104] The Quaker stress on women keeping orderly company before marriage, for example, echoes the Anglican emphasis on the necessity of chastity before marriage.[105] The Quaker queries nevertheless had a different focus and tenor. Moreover, it is significant that, the female members of the Quaker community were actively involved in the process of obtaining these written testimonies, the answers to which would have been submitted for scrutiny to the Women's Quarterly Meeting. In the colonies,

[103] LRSF, MGR 11a4 London Women's Meeting Epistles, 1671–1753, fol. 57, Queries issued by Lancaster Women's Meeting 'To Be Observed by Women Friends in the County of Lancashire', 15 October 1748.

[104] See Kenneth Fincham (ed.), *Visitation Articles and Injunctions of the Early Stuart Church* (2 vols., Woodbridge, Church of England Record Society, 1994–1998).

[105] One of the injunctions circulated by the Prebendary John Barnston to local officials in Wiltshire in 1624 required them to ensure that no individuals residing in the parish had 'committed incontinencie before marreadge'. Ibid., vol. 2, p. xvi.

by contrast, the practice of giving written answers to specific queries was not in general usage until 1755.[106]

Through the act of regularly reading and adapting Queries and Advices, English Friends found an alternative means to encourage conformity. Occasional references in the minutes indicate the effect of this informal system of discipline. In April 1697, for instance, Marsden women asked their delegates whether all Friends were 'careful to keep their words and not run into Debt beyond what they are able to pay in one time?' The overseers of Sawley Meeting noted that Mary Tatham's thread trade had run into debt. The Meeting appointed two delegates to visit her and advise her to cease trading, to prevent getting into further debt.[107] The process of using queries as a means of admonishing members was an important instrument in ensuring conformity, without resorting to the outright condemnation prevalent in the American colonies. Many of the replies to the queries included statements such as 'the Queries was Examined and not any thing was offered by way of Complaint'.[108] David Cressy has suggested that the churchwardens' frequent employment of '*omnia bene*' (all well) should be translated to mean 'go away' or 'mind your own business', and these Quaker responses may reflect a similar wish to deal with transgressions informally.[109]

Despite differences in the handling of disciplinary matters in England, Ireland, and the colonies, it remains remarkable that female members were permitted any authority at all in the Quaker disciplinary process. As Lindman has noted, male elders administered Baptist church discipline in colonial Pennsylvania and Virginia in a spirit of rigid exclusivity. Their authority in the correction process, she argues, mirrored the traditional power of men in the family: 'to protect, reprimand, and punish dependents'.[110] Quaker women's involvement in the disciplinary process, by contrast, was deemed fundamental in providing an example to the younger generation. As the custodians of female virtue, they were expected to oversee the behaviour of their congregations, admonish them where necessary, and bring them to a sense of their errors. They aspired to be 'good Examples, to the youth

---

[106] J. William Frost, *The Quaker Family in Colonial America: A Portrait of the Society of Friends* (New York, 1973), p. 4. The English minister Samuel Fothergill reported in a letter to his wife in August 1755, that he had helped to prepare a set of Queries for Friends in Rhode Island and made arrangements for them to be sent to the Monthly and Quarterly Meetings for business, as well as to the Women's Meetings and the Meetings of Ministers and Elders in the Province. LRSF, MS Vol 329 Crossfield MS, fol. 43. Samuel Fothergill to his wife, Susanna Fothergill, Nantucket, 27 August 1755.

[107] LA, FRM/1/24 Marsden Women's MM 1678–1738, minutes for 15 April 1697.

[108] LA, FRM/1/25 Marsden Women's MM 1738–1760, minutes for 15 July 1747.

[109] David Cressy, 'Conflict, Consensus, and the Willingness to Wink: The Erosion of Community in Charles I's England', *Huntington Library Quarterly*, vol. 61, no. 2 (1998), p. 135.

[110] Lindman, *Bodies of Belief*, p. 104.

among us', and hoped that their labours would 'preserve them from the evill of those times that others runn into'.[111] Thus, although men had the final judgement in admitting or excluding members, women's involvement in the admonition and counselling of female Friends added an important dimension to the disciplinary structures. The scope they had to dictate appropriate standards is especially evident in Ireland, where all policies relating to food, apparel, and the 'ordering' of children were decided by the National Women's Meeting. The female elders' recommendations were then circulated as epistles to all local Women's (and Men's) Meetings.[112]

The surveillance of all members through a system of discipline, adjudicated by the female overseers and elders of the Meetings, became an intensive means of regulating church order. The all-female committees appointed by the Women's Meetings certainly devoted a great deal of their attention to detecting breaches of Quaker marriage discipline procedure. The surviving Meeting minutes suggest that no incident escaped the overseers' notice. Elizabeth Cadwalader was denounced by Chester Women's Meeting in 1720 for 'being over taken with strong drink and for dancing with a mans Jacket on'. She had also been seen that day 'to act unseemly with a man and in a manner most undecently and not fit to be mentioned'.[113] Similarly, in May 1715, Alice Pennell was nominated to speak to a young female member of the Meeting 'concerning the report that was made' of her 'uncivill carriage' following her marriage, 'after she went home in taking off her garters'. In September 1750, Tipperary Women's Meeting dealt with intelligence of 'disorderly behaviour' at an inn in Munster at the time of the Province Meeting by some of the female members of the Society.[114] These incidents suggest the means by which the Women's Meetings on both sides of the Atlantic gathered intelligence and reports on their members' behaviour, even in private and often intimate circumstances. They also indicate the very real public presence and communal identity of female overseers far beyond both the space of the home or Meeting House.

The fact that the Women's Meetings were granted powers of jurisdiction over their communities, and acted in tandem with their partner Men's Meetings, highlights one important way in which Friends challenged traditional gender conventions. This unusual degree of authority stood in contrast to women in Anglican and other dissenting congregations, who had limited ability to counsel their male counterparts or enforce discipline over members of their communities. Moreover, these activities were assigned and

[111] LRSF, MGR 11a4 London Women's Meeting Epistles, 1671–1753, fol. 46, Aberdeen Women's Meeting to the London Box Meeting, 21 June 1694.
[112] Greaves, *God's Other Children*, p. 318.
[113] FHL, MR-Ph 98 Chester Women's MM 1695–1733, minutes for 31 October 1720.
[114] FHLD, MMX B2 Co. Tipperary Women's MM 1735–1764, minutes for 9 September 1750.

performed within a collective female space, enabling elders to develop connections with fellow members and achieve status within their communities. The intrusive way in which the wider Quaker community monitored household order offers another example of the place of the Meetings in shaping gendered identity, as this level of oversight clearly impinged on men's abilities to govern their households independently. Thus when Fairfax Meeting in Virginia found in December 1747 that William Dodd had been encouraging a man 'not a member of our Society' to court his daughter Ann, two male Friends were appointed to visit his home and discuss the matter with him. Two months later, Dodd submitted a paper to the Meeting elders condemning his behaviour.[115]

PHILANTHROPY, MEMBERSHIP, AND SETTLEMENT

Philanthropy and the issue of settlement (granting approval for a member to move to another Meeting) were tasks that increasingly came to dominate the concerns of the Quaker Women's Meetings. In the case of Marsden and Tipperary, instances of charitable concern had even surpassed the combined totals of marriage and discipline by 1750, as demonstrated in Table 2.2. Early Quakers took a largely egalitarian view on the issue of caring for the poor, seeing property as only a temporary gift, to be shared charitably between the 'Saints in light'.[116] Early initiatives to relieve Quaker prisoners and families in financial distress underlined the Quaker sense of concern for the poorer members of their community. As previously noted, the Women's Box Meeting of London had been designed to provide financial support for the many London Friends suffering from imprisonment and poverty. This meant that from the start, the organisation and distribution of poor relief became a central concern of the Women's Meetings. George Fox argued that women should take a primary role in poor relief, because of their positions within the family and community. 'Women many times know the Condition of poor Families, and Widows, and such as are in distress, more than Men,' he wrote, 'because they are most conversant in their *Families*, and about such things.'[117] He used the biblical representation of the female elders from

---

[115] FHL, MR-B117 Fairfax Men's MM 1745–1776, p. 14 [modern pagination], minutes for 7 February 1748.

[116] 'An Epistle from the Women Friends in London to the Women Friends in the Country, Also Elsewhere, about the Service of a Women's Meeting, 4 January 1674', in Barclay, *Letters, &c., of Early Friends*, pp. 343–344.

[117] 'An Encouragement to All the Faithful Women's Meetings in the World, Who Assemble Together in the Fear of God, for the Service of Truth', 16 November 1676, in Fox, *A Collection of Many Select and Christian Epistles*, vol. 2, p. 387.

1 Timothy 5 to argue that women should be the primary carers for widows, declaring that those who do well in 'good works' were closer to God.[118]

Women's responsibilities within their Meetings were thus viewed as an extension of their private and gendered knowledge. They included visiting and relieving the sick, poor, and destitute, as well as offering care and support to widows and orphans in their Meetings. The importance of philanthropy to the female elders is evident in the fact that in all of the Meetings sampled for both periods, the philanthropic activities undertaken by the female elders consistently outstripped those of their male brethren. This form of 'practical charity' was widely viewed as an appropriate public role for pious women. Crawford argues that philanthropic acts, such as nursing the sick in hospitals, enabled abbesses and prioresses to exercise considerable independent authority within the pre-Reformation English Catholic Church.[119] Many dissenting movements also permitted women a formal place in philanthropy-based activities. The office of deaconess, which was open to women in some separatist congregations like the Baptists, involved providing relief to the sick and poor. Other groups, like the Methodists, had a designated 'sick visitor' role available to women. It was a position that Paul Wesley Chilcote suggests offered female converts 'countless opportunities for discussion of the life of faith, plain and open relations with other people'.[120]

Many researchers have suggested that this aspect of women's activities was stereotypically feminine, deemed appropriate for female members to channel their energies.[121] Malgreem, for instance, writing about eighteenth-century Methodism, noted that the rise of such 'auxiliary tasks' had the effect of driving women 'farther from the centre of affairs' within the Church.[122] However, as Michele Denise Ryan has reminded us, Quaker men could play an equally active role in poor relief as women, particularly when it came to distributing financial assistance.[123] Indeed, matters of a philanthropic nature occupied a prominent part of the business of the Men's Meetings throughout the early eighteenth century. Marsden's male overseers dealt with thirty-three cases of poor relief between 1700 and 1705, and dedicated a great deal of time to negotiating apprenticeships for young and poor members of their Society. In May 1703, for example, they read and

---

[118] Ibid., p. 389.
[119] Crawford, *Women and Religion*, p. 22.
[120] Chilcote, *John Wesley and the Women Preachers*, p. 72.
[121] Trevett described the work of the Women's Meetings in poor relief and oversight of their own sex as 'safer (and more "feminine") waters'. Christine Trevett, *Quaker Women Prophets in England and Wales 1650–1700* (Lampeter, 2000), p. 169.
[122] Malmgreen, 'Domestic Discords', p. 66.
[123] Ryan, 'In My Hand for Lending', p. 18.

approved an apprenticeship contract for a young boy, John Whittaker, in their community. They agreed to give the master £3 and Whittaker 20s., and they underwrote the agreement with a promise to cover the master's expenses should Whittaker become unable to work.[124]

Nevertheless, what made Quakerism stand out from other religious groups was the fact that the intense persecution experienced in the early years of the movement extended women's charitable roles beyond informal, moral, and spiritual support. The relief of suffering, imprisoned, orphaned, and poor members was provided through the innovation of a regular collection of a 'stock', which the Women's Meeting could dispense as necessity dictated. The accounts of the Quaker Women's Box Meeting in London testify to the concern of women Friends for suffering, including caring for members far beyond their local communities.[125] In June 1681, £7 was collected by the Box Meeting and dispatched to a 'north country friend' severely affected by his testimony against tithes. In the same meeting, they also offered money 'to a woman friend that came from Barbados' and collected an additional £5 3s. 10d. from the local Men's Meeting towards her expenses.[126] The following year, on 24 July 1682, they collected the impressive sum of £47 13s. 'for the suffering poorer friends' in Bristol and Leicestershire, and another £33 was received from the Women Friends of Ratcliff Meeting in London, which the Box Meeting sent to sufferers in Northamptonshire.[127] This rather surprising ability of women to collect, keep checks on, and distribute funds to both male and female members of their community as they saw fit was justified as necessary to perform their service. Caring for the poor was universally accepted as an appropriate responsibility for women Friends.

Economic hardship in Marsden, Kendal, and Tipperary meant that the issue of poor relief significantly affected the items of business within their Women's Meetings. As Kunze notes, 'poverty was a way of life for a considerable portion of the population' in the Lancashire and Kendal area.[128] Because many relied upon subsistence farming, the impact of localised famine, as well as financial hardship, would have severely affected many members, particularly as English and Irish Friends continued to be fined for their refusal to pay tithes and thus forfeited all claims to parish poor relief. As

[124] LA, FRM/1/1 Marsden Men's MM 1678–1723, p. 107, minutes for 20 May 1703.
[125] I have explored the activities of the Quaker Women's Box Meeting and their accounts more fully in Naomi Pullin, '"She Suffered for My Sake": Female Martyrs and Lay Activists in Transatlantic Quakerism, 1650–1710', in Catie Gill and Michele Lise Tarter (eds.), *New Critical Studies on Early Quaker Women, 1650–1800* (Oxford, 2018), chapter 6.
[126] LRSF, MGR 11a4 London Women's Meeting Account Book, 1672–1684, minutes for 13 June 1681.
[127] LRSF, MGR 11a4 London Women's Meeting Account Book, 1672–1684, minutes for 24 July 1682.
[128] Kunze, 'Poore and in Necessity', p. 564.

Table 2.2 indicates, Marsden women devoted 32 per cent of their tasks to the relief and care of poor members of their community in the period 1745–1750, equating to fifty-eight individual proceedings. Jennett Scott of Sawley, one of Marsden's constituent Preparative Meetings, received relief on an almost monthly basis. Contributions towards her care totalled the significant sum of £7 3s. 6d. between January 1745 and December 1750. Similarly, Martha Parkinson received £2 17s. 11d., some of which was paid to cover her rent, whilst other contributions were to cover the cost of the purchase of fabric to make shifts.[129] The high number of individuals in need of relief meant that a similarly high proportion of Marsden women's tasks involved raising and collecting funds to furnish the Meeting's stock. Tipperary women also allocated a significant proportion of their tasks (18 per cent) to the relief of indigent female Friends. A widow named Sarah Fennell, who had fallen on hard times, required regular financial assistance from the Meeting. Between August 1747 and the end of our sample period, the Women's Meeting made a collection at almost every Meeting for her, which funded a regular allowance of thirteen shillings every six weeks.[130] They also petitioned the Men's Meeting in March 1750 to provide an additional 6 ½d. per week towards her care.[131] The Women's Meeting showed initiative and considerable skill in raising the funds to support their female members. Their activities constituted an important and largely overlooked alternative institution for the relief of indigent members of the wider community, a theme explored in the final chapter of this book.

The wealthier colonial Meetings devoted less time to specific acts of charity, but some of their tasks involved a philanthropic element. Chester women, for instance, instructed two elders of the Meeting to visit Mary Edwards in March 1714 and 'Carry her cloath enough to make her mother two shifts'.[132] In the period 1700–1705, moreover, Burlington women exhibited great care for the needy members of their community, with 14 per cent of their tasks having a philanthropic character. These included numerous outgoings for the relief of unnamed Friends. In November 1700 £1 was donated to 'a poor widdow' and 6s. 8d. was given to 'a poor Friend'.[133] Aside from specific cases of relief, 31 per cent of Burlington women's tasks were spent dealing with what I have classified as 'Accounts and Estates' (see Appendix 2). The majority of the activities listed under this category made

---

[129] LA, FRM/1/25 Marsden Women's MM 1738–1760, see minutes between 17 January 1745 and 20 December 1750.
[130] FHLD, MMX B2 Co. Tipperary Women's MM 1735–1764, minutes for 2 August 1747, 31 October 1748, 25 September 1748, and 20 October 1748.
[131] FHLD, MMX A2 Co. Tipperary Men's MM 1724–1760, minutes for 25 March 1750.
[132] FHL, MR-Ph 98 Chester Women's MM 1695–1733, minutes for 29 March 1714.
[133] FHL, MR-Ph 63 Burlington Women's MM 1681–1747, minutes for 4 November 1700.

explicit reference to the collection of funds to go towards the Meeting stock or recorded money disbursed for cleaning the Meeting Houses at Burlington and Springfield. Whilst no indication is given about who was paid for the work, it is likely that this task provided a means of employing poorer members of the community, thus supplying them with a regular source of income. This was almost certainly also the case in Kendal, as indicated by entries in the minutes for Kendal Women's Preparative Meeting. These note, for example, that in October 1722 the Meeting appointed Ruth Knipe to clean the Meeting House in the place of Sarah Cowper. Ruth Knipe had come to the attention of Kendal women in the past and was a recipient of relief in the years running up to this appointment.[134]

The issue of relief for the poor raised the awkward problem of entitlement. Naturally, those who were declared 'out of unity' with the Meeting would forfeit any claim for support and assistance. Some Meetings, however, occasionally made an exception. When Marsden Women's Preparative Meeting was made aware of the dire need of Susan Turner, who was described as 'not being fully in society with us', it felt 'obliged to help her in her necessity' out of a sense of 'conscience'.[135] Nevertheless, under Quaker rules of settlement, members were expected to apply for a certificate of removal before joining another Meeting. This guaranteed the good character of the individual under consideration, including their clearness to marry, as well as providing reassurance on their financial affairs and creditworthiness. It also prevented charlatans from imposing on Friends' goodwill. Those who, on arrival, failed to present a certificate to their new Meeting were refused membership until they could prove they were in good standing with their former Meeting. Esther Gilbert, for instance, who desired to settle in Burlington, was advised in July 1700 by the Women's Meeting that unless she produced a certificate, 'Friends could not receive her as a member of this Meeting.'[136]

Thus while philanthropy came to dominate the activities of poorer Meetings like Marsden, it was the issue of settlement that created the most significant administrative burden for Meetings like Chester, Burlington, and Fairfax, which were generally more prosperous and did not have to contend with the continued effects of persecution. The administration surrounding members applying for and presenting certificates of removal eclipsed the

---

[134] A decision, for instance, had been made in May 1720 that her 'necessityes be enquired into' and that she be 'supplyed as its thought needfull'. On another occasion later that year, the minutes recorded how Ann Garnett was to 'give Ruth Knipe which she thinks she has occasion for, for her own use and let this Meeting know [what] she Lyes down at this time'. KAC, WDFCF/1/46 Kendal Women's Preparative Meeting 1719–1774, minutes for 4 May 1720, 1 February 1721, and 31 October 1722.

[135] LA, FRM/4/6 Marsden Women's Preparative Meeting 1698–1794, pp. 16–17, minutes for 13 February 1701.

[136] FHL, MR-Ph 63 Burlington Women's MM 1681–1747, minutes for 1 July 1700.

issue of marriage in the colonies, with settlement constituting 42 per cent of Chester, 24 per cent of Burlington, and 16 per cent of Fairfax women's duties between 1745 and 1750. These colonial Meetings had been founded by immigrant populations, and geographical mobility and resettlement may have remained commonplace. The populations in the northwestern counties of England and in Ireland were more static. Aside from a large exodus of inhabitants to the colonies in the 1680s, only a small percentage transferred beyond the bounds of their Meetings in the wake of the 1689 Toleration Act (usually for marriage). The Women's Meetings of Marsden, for instance, received and accepted only one request for removal between 1745 and 1750. This contrasts sharply with the Chester women in colonial America, who dealt with some thirty-nine separate petitions for certificates of removal and were presented with twenty-five certificates from individuals and families settling within the compass of the Meeting. Quaker women in the colonies clearly belonged to far more mobile communities.

Overseeing the resettlement of members offered great scope for female agency. It was, admittedly, subject to some limitations, for when a couple or family requested a certificate of removal, this had first to be approved by the Men's Meeting. Even so, as Betty Hagglund has argued, the ability of female Friends to confirm decisions and draft certificates resulted in an important sense of 'ownership' and 'corporate' understanding of group experience.[137] Examples can even be found of the Women's Meetings dealing independently with issues of removal, when these involved a petition from a woman desiring to remove on her own to another Meeting. Thus when the recently married Mary Delaplan requested a certificate of removal from the female elders of Burlington to settle within the compass of her husband's Meeting, a committee of women was appointed to visit her and investigate. Once satisfied, they were ordered to prepare and bring the certificate in time for the next Meeting, so that it could be signed by the women Friends present.[138] Female elders were thus able to wield considerable influence and authority over the lives of their congregation through monitoring, controlling, and authorising their removal and settlement.

Alongside managing cases of removal, the female Friends of Virginia also appear to have had significant jurisdiction in determining who could be accepted as a new member of their Meeting. In the period 1745 to 1750, Fairfax women dealt with twenty separate petitions from women wishing

---

[137] Betty Hagglund, 'Changes in Roles and Relationships: Multiauthored Epistles from the Aberdeen Quaker Women's Meeting', in Carolyn D. Williams, Angela Escott, and Louise Duckling (eds.), *Woman to Woman: Female Negotiations during the Long Eighteenth Century* (Newark, DE, 2010), pp. 140–142.

[138] FHL, MR-Ph 63 Burlington Women's Monthly MM 1681–1747, minutes for 12 August 1745 and 2 September 1745.

to join them, none of which were referred to the Men's Meeting. In July 1750 Elizabeth Everitt who had 'been under the care of friends and such of her children in their minority' for some time, asked 'for her self and them to be received as members'. Her request was approved, along with those of four other women in the same meeting.[139] In a region such as Fairfax, where there was not a long-established Quaker community, it is possible that Friends made greater efforts to convert their non-Quaker neighbours. Moreover, in consonance with the Quakers' views on marriage and charity, it is likely that the female elders were better placed than men to know about the behaviour and attitudes of their female neighbours and decide whether they should be permitted to join.

Quakerism provided a distinct and an autonomous space for its female members to involve themselves in the Society's business. As we have seen, in matters of marriage and in some cases of discipline and removal, female elders wielded considerable power over their members' lives. This leads us to ask what sort of women dominated the Monthly Meetings, and whether their status within the church hierarchy reflected the values of the wider society.

'FAVOURED WITH EXCELLENT TALENTS': THE WOMEN OF THE MONTHLY MEETINGS

Unlike many other separatist churches of the time, no official membership records were kept by Quaker Meetings before the 1830s. It is therefore almost impossible to know how many individuals were active in the Women's Meetings. This is also complicated by the fact that the elders would gather after a general public Meeting for worship. Only by creating lists of those assigned to act as overseers or members of committees can we get a sense of which women were most active. Although such data is far from comprehensive, particularly because a Friend's name would have been recorded only if he or she was assigned a particular task, it does help to create a profile of the types of women appointed to such positions.[140]

Among the most prominent female elders to emerge from this study was Grace Lloyd, wife of the Pennsylvanian politician David Lloyd, who in October 1732 was appointed to serve as clerk for Chester Women's Meeting.[141] Grace combined the traits of a well-respected elder, in good standing within the community, with the image of a capable and successful

---

[139] FHL, MR-B119 Fairfax Women's MM 1745–1768, p. 20, 28 July 1750.
[140] This approach was adopted by Soderlund in her study of eighteenth-century Pennsylvania and New Jersey Friends, enabling her to investigate the socio-economic status of the leaders within the Meetings. Soderlund, 'Women's Authority', pp. 727–728.
[141] FHL, MR-Ph 98 Chester Women's MM 1695–1733, minutes for 30 October 1732.

Quaker business woman. She was memorialised by her friend and former servant, Jane Hoskins, as one 'favoured with excellent talents', a woman of 'good understanding, sound judgment and quick apprehension', as well as possessing 'a good gift in discipline' – traits that naturally would have placed her in a good position to take on a leading administrative role.[142] As a highly literate and established member, Grace's influence over the Pennsylvanian Quaker community must have been extensive. As well as serving as clerk to Chester Women's Monthly Meeting between 1732 and 1744, she was also appointed to transcribe the proceedings of Philadelphia Women's Yearly Meetings between 1729 and 1744, and acted as an occasional scribe for Concord Women's Quarterly Meeting between 1715 and 1749.[143]

Evidence of the sway a clerk could have over the Quaker church is revealed by Grace Lloyd's private correspondence.[144] Her letters to members of the Pemberton family in Philadelphia from December 1746 reveal a dynamic woman with an appetite for both news and business ventures. A repeated theme is a desire to hear about Friends in the ministry and where they intended to travel on their missions. In one 1751 letter to Rachel Pemberton, for example, she noted that she would 'be glad to hear how our friends far[e]d at Shre[w]sbury and which way Mary Weston is gon', and in 1753, following news of Catherine Payton and Mary Peisley's ministerial travels, she declared that 'I long to hear [o]f any news of our dear Friends arrival at Carolina'.[145] Grace received regular updates from her network of female correspondents, and her letters also reveal that she was actively engaged in commercial dealings with Quaker merchants like John and James Pemberton.[146] The authority and power of her writings, even in old age, are indicative of a woman with a great understanding of the networks that bound together the social and economic lives of Friends and their communities.

[142] Jane Hoskins, *The Life and Spiritual Sufferings of That Faithful Servant of Christ Jane Hoskens* (Philadelphia, 1771), p. 30.

[143] HCQSC, B1.1 Philadelphia Women's Yearly Meeting 1692–1814, minutes for 13 November 1729 and 18 September 1744; FHL MR-Ph 136 Concord Quarterly Women's Meeting Minutes, 1695–1803, minutes for 2 May 1715, 7 November 1715, and 14 August 1749.

[144] Whether through coincidence or the time-consuming nature of the role, almost no documents relating to Grace's personal life have survived during the period she acted as clerk at Chester.

[145] HSP, MS Coll 484A Pemberton Family Papers, vol. 7, p. 142, Grace Lloyd to Rachel Pemberton, Chester, 1751; HSP, MS Coll 484A Pemberton Family Papers, vol. 9, p. 94, Grace Lloyd to Rachel Pemberton, Chester, 17 November 1754.

[146] In one letter she sent to James Pemberton in December 1753, she began by explaining that 'I have hear with sent the Remainder of the Cargoe which I cant sell to advantage … [I] shall send thee more mony as sone [*sic*] as I can gett it, have sent back 4 pieces of linen, 22 dozen Hankerchiefs, 1 ½ dozen Cotton Gloves and 3 pieces Sack Webb. I tryed 1 piece of the Yorkshire Brown, thought if it would wash and whiten I could Recomend it'. HSP, MS Coll 484A Pemberton Family Papers, vol. 9, p. 110, Grace Lloyd to James Pemberton, 19 December 1753.

Unfortunately, less information is available about the lives of the other clerks involved in Chester Meeting, or indeed, those of the other Meetings studied here. In many respects, these unusual women defy generalisation. Nonetheless, some common traits and characteristics would have been necessary to fulfil such a role. They needed to be of some stature in the Quaker community, with a high level of literacy, something that was not possible for all members. The ability to read and write was essential because they had to take rough notes of the Meeting's decisions, set the agenda, compose and sign documents, keep track of financial transactions, and copy the minutes into the official Meeting book. The clerk also needed to show leadership qualities, for she had the vital responsibility of judging the 'sense of the meeting' and representing it accordingly in the minutes. Since members were not allowed to vote on issues – instead favouring a consensus or unity to be sought through patiently waiting on the spirit – the clerk had the challenging job of discerning the 'will' of the spirit in a particular situation. A good clerk, as Hamm has explained, would have had 'the ability to find commonality among differences and to combine differing views into a solution'.[147] The role of clerk gave a female elder the potential for significant but discreet influence, and she would sometimes have to pronounce what she felt to be the will of God, even when competing arguments had been presented. Mercy Bell, the clerk of the London Women's Meeting recounted to one of her close friends the anxiety she faced in transcribing the Meeting minutes, and drafting an epistle to encourage more Friends to contribute to the Meeting's stock 'as become[s] my place as Clerk'. She was concerned that her 'plain dealing' might bring 'an army of Womens Tongues against me', but instead found that 'it has been receiv'd with approbation by those or some of those it strikes at'.[148]

Clerks were usually also well-established members of their communities who had served on committees for a number of years prior to their appointment. Grace Lloyd, for instance, had been nominated as an overseer for Chester at least eighteen years prior to being made clerk.[149] The Burlington clerk, Abigail Raper, may have been active in the Meeting for as long as forty-seven years when she stepped down from the position in 1748.[150] All of these

---

[147] Hamm, *The Quakers in America*, p. 11.
[148] LRSF, Temp MSS 403/1/2/3/22 Arthur B. Braithwaite Family Papers, Mercy Bell to Priscilla Farmer, London, undated, c. 1760.
[149] Grace Lloyd's first recorded committee assignment after settling in Chester in January 1714 was to act as a representative to the Quarterly Meeting in June 1714: FHL, MR-Ph 98 Chester Women's MM 1695–1733, minutes for 28 July 1714.
[150] Whilst it is unclear whether two individuals of the same name occupied the position of overseer, an Abigail Raper was appointed to inquire into clearness for marriage in June 1701. Another woman of the same name stepped down from the role in April 1748. FHL, MR-Ph 63 Burlington Women's MM 1681–1747 and 1747–1799, see minutes for 2 June 1701 and 2 May 1748.

women appear to have been married or widowed, although individual merit seems to have been the governing factor in judging whether a woman was suitable for the role. No evidence exists of a woman being appointed simply because her husband was clerk of the Men's Meeting, and only one instance has been identified of a husband and wife serving as clerks to their respective Meetings at the same time in this period.[151] As I shall discuss later, there are also examples of single and never-married women acting as clerks for both British and American Meetings, which indicates the emphasis Friends placed upon individual merit rather than outward circumstances.[152]

Another important and often-overlapping office was that of treasurer, who kept the accounts and retained the Meeting's stock. In some Meetings, these roles were combined. Thus when Mary Smith was appointed to act as clerk for Burlington Monthly Meeting in May 1748, the sum of £3 18s. 6d., which formed the total Meeting stock, was also placed into her hands.[153] As with the role of clerk, this was a position that required business acumen, numerical skills, and a working knowledge of basic accounting. In her thesis on the Quaker Women's Box Meeting in London, Ryan demonstrated the advanced accounting skills that the female clerks and treasurers of the Meeting displayed in their minutes. Among them was a modified style of double-entry bookkeeping, a rare skill, Ryan argues, that provides evidence of their proficiency in business.[154] This essential aspect of Quaker organisational life, which involved listing debits and credits separately, was a regular staple of Quaker Meeting minutes. Evidence even from the poorer Women's Meetings in the English countryside demonstrates regular use of calculations to confirm that the accounts were in balance.[155]

It was the overseer, however, who was at the heart of the Quaker Meeting structure. The female elders appointed to this role worked hard to maintain

---

[151] Both Abigail and Joshua Raper of Burlington Meeting appear to have been acting as clerk for the Men's and Women's Monthly Meetings at the same time. FHL, MR-Ph 63 Burlington Women's MM 1681–1747 and FHL, MR-Ph 60 Burlington Men's MM 1737–1756, p. 160, see equivalent minutes for 1 June 1747.

[152] Margaret Fell's daughter Sarah, for instance, served as clerk to Swarthmoor Meeting for a number of years before her marriage to William Meade in 1681, and the unmarried Philadelphian Friend Sarah Morris also served as clerk to Philadelphia Women's Meeting throughout the 1740s. On Sarah Fell see Kunze, *Margaret Fell and the Rise of Quakerism*, esp. pp. 91–100. On Sarah Morris see Soderlund, 'Women's Authority', p. 728; and Karin Wulf, *Not All Wives: Women of Colonial Philadelphia* (London, 2000), p. 69.

[153] FHL, MR-Ph 63 Burlington Women's Monthly MM 1747–1799, see minutes for 2 May 1748 and 6 June 1748.

[154] Ryan, 'In My Hand for Lending', pp. 137–138.

[155] The minutes of Marsden Women's Meeting for 15 May 1718, for instance, recorded that £1 5s. 8½d. had been collected from the Preparative Meetings, 5s had been disbursed to Jennet Dickinson and £1 8½d. remained in the Meeting stock. The following month, Jennet Dickinson received another payment of 5s. 4d., which left a total of 15s. 4½d. LA, FRM/1/24 Marsden Women's MM 1678–1738, see minutes for 15 May 1718 and 19 June 1718.

order and discipline. Their public accountability for the Meeting made them highly visible members of their communities. In addition to running her own household and engaging in ministerial work, the Kendal overseer Grace Chamber examined thirty-six separate couples seeking to marry, and visited numerous women to clear them for removal to other Meetings between 1705 and 1750. In this same period, she was also appointed to act as a representative for Preston Preparative Meeting and Kendal Quarterly Meeting 108 and 51 times, respectively. She visited all the Quaker households in the Preston area on a regular basis, and was occasionally nominated to support Crook and Powbank Preparative Meetings in their visitation of local families.[156] Each visitation cycle took between four and six months to complete and included family devotion, as well as opportunities to offer discreet advice to household members, both male and female.

Considerable skill in the ministry and the ability to draw upon personal experience were evidently required to fulfil the role of overseer. Grace Chamber's memorial was of a very similar tenor to Grace Lloyd's in Pennsylvania, and she was remembered as both intelligent and 'endowed with an excellent understanding'.[157] The Meeting dominated her life and outlook, reflected in the advice she sent to the travelling minister Thomas Story in 1715. Supplying him with some powder as a remedy for his coughing and shortness of breath, she added: 'A knifepoint-full (or 2) of it after a Meeting ... and at bedtime has done several good.'[158] For an elder like Grace Chamber, the place of the Meeting in her daily life was so central that she even framed her medical advice around it.

It is clear that the women occupying these roles regarded their work as a very important service for the community. A letter from James Morton in Dublin to Elizabeth and Richard Shackleton in 1781, offers a hint of the powerful role of these 'friendly visit[s]' in shaping the lives of Quaker members. Morton fondly remembered the Shackleton's great 'Care of a poore servant of the Grate master who had a Concern to visset friends meetings in the North as well as in munster but not of ability to perform it'. He described how they had 'carefully and easely' supported her spiritual calling and described their 'method of meetings' being a great help to her 'as she was not Larg in Tastamoney'.[159] These overseers had provided

---

[156] KAC, WDFCF/1/22 Kendal Women's MM 1671–1719, see, e.g., minutes from 5 September 1712 and 4 September 1713.

[157] Kendal Monthly Meeting, 'Testimony of Kendal Monthly Meeting Concerning Grace Chamber, Deceased, 1763', ed. Norman Penney, in *JFHS*, vol. 7 (1910), pp. 182–183.

[158] LSRF, MS Vol 340, The Life of Thomas Story with Original Letters, between pp. 476 and 477, Grace Chamber to Thomas Story, from Sedgwick, Cumbria, 2 June 1715.

[159] HL, mssSHA Shackleton Family Correspondence, Box 4, fol. 124, James Morton to Richard and Elizabeth Shackleton, 12 September 1781.

a young minister with the confidence and guidance to undertake ministerial service abroad and to inspire future generations. Alice Griffith, a Welsh Friend who had emigrated with her husband to Pennsylvania, was similarly remembered after her death for her services in 'Visiting friends families'. She was described as having 'Excellent talent' and a natural ability to communicate her own experience and relate divine wisdom 'to the different Circumstances of Persons and families, old or young, Rich or Poor, married or unmarried'.[160]

Overseers, as we have seen, occupied a central role in the disciplinary mechanisms of the church, with primary responsibility for investigating and reporting wrongdoing. The terms of their oversight were extensive and incorporated such matters as investigating a young couple's clearness for marriage and its orderly completion, and the visitation of members who had come to the notice of the Meeting for irregular behaviour. The position, as Levy summarises, 'required a head for genealogy, a nose for gossip and spiritually discerning eyes'.[161] The evidence suggests that family visitors were vigilant in monitoring irregular behaviour and providing accurate information about any wrongdoing. Chester Friends, for instance, were determined to secure a full account from Alice Yarnall after her child was delivered too soon after marriage. Reluctant to believe that she had come 'before her time as is supposed', a committee of women was appointed to speak to five women involved in the delivery and visitation of Yarnall after the birth and give 'the truth of what they think concerning the child'. The testimonies corroborated Yarnall's insistence that the child had been premature and the Meeting declared its satisfaction.[162] This incident reveals the extent to which the behaviour of female members was monitored outside of the Meeting House, as well as the reach of the female elders over the behaviour of their members.

Specialised forms of religious visiting, as embodied in the visiting committees, offered one of the most extensive and influential roles for the overseers of the Women's Meetings. One example of the pervasiveness of their surveillance was the issue of 'superfluity', which included both the dress of members and how they chose to furnish their houses. This was of particular concern to Irish and English Friends, who repeatedly warned members against following the 'Customes and wayes of the world'.[163] Marsden women recorded

---

160 HCQSC, MS Coll 968 Allinson Family Papers, Box 6. 'Testimony Concerning Alice Griffith' from Moses Brown to Deborah Morris, c. 1749.
161 Levy, *Quakers and the American Family*, p. 209.
162 FHL, MR-Ph 98 Chester Women's Monthly MM 1695–1733, minutes for 26 December 1715, 30 January 1716, and 27 February 1716.
163 LA, FRL/1/2/1/1 Lancaster Women's Quarterly Meeting 1675–1777, minutes for 3 July 1695.

in their minutes in 1695 an epistle from Lancaster Quarterly Meeting, which included an extensive list of fashions their female members were forbidden from buying, wearing, or selling. These included hoods with long tabs that turned back further from the cheek than from the brow; necklaces; 'figured or strip[ed] stuff'; mantuas (cloaks) lined with different coloured materials with 'small tails pinned according to the fashions of the world'; painted calico in dresses and aprons; and hatts with broad ribbons 'tyed with a bunch behind'.[164] Irish Friends even assembled groups of Quaker tradesmen to determine the official standards of 'plainness' for the community, and during family visits, overseers were expected to inspect the furnishings within Friends' homes. The tight control imposed by the Meeting over daily life is evident from the directives issued by the Half-Year Meeting in Ireland in 1671. Among their advice was guidance that pewter and brass should not be on display and that Friends should not own 'Turkey work Chaires of flousirshing Colours', large mirrors, white window curtains, polished or fine furniture of all types, and paintings, prints, and sculptures.[165]

The wealthier American Meetings, by contrast, appear to have been far less concerned with members' adherence to approved standards of plainness. As Frederick B. Tolles has noted, plainness was a relative matter for Philadelphian Friends and much depended on the wealth and circumstances of the individual.[166] I will examine this contrast more fully in the final chapter of this book, but it is worth observing here that although colonial Friends were vigilant in disciplining members for transgressions such as marrying non-believers or using law courts to sue debtors, rarely in their minutes did they seek to enforce conformity to standards of plainness and on very few occasions appointed committees to inspect Friends on this matter.

The vigorous policing of members' private lives, held up for corporate scrutiny, placed overseers in an uncomfortable position, and could create bad feeling between them and other members. In much the same way that the British Crown was forced to rely upon the voluntary authority of local magistrates and parish constables to enforce legislation in the localities, the Quaker Quarterly and Yearly Meetings left most jurisdictional authority in the hands of these unpaid male and female overseers.[167] Their intrusive activities had the potential to alienate neighbours, friends, and other family members, and raised the issue of where and to whom loyalty was primarily

---

[164] LA, FRM/1/24 Marsden Women's MM 1678–1738, minutes for 18 July 1695, copy of epistle from Lancaster Quarterly Meeting, dated 5 July 1695.
[165] Greaves, *God's Other Children*, pp. 320–321.
[166] Frederick B. Tolles, *Quakers and the Atlantic Culture* (New York, 1960), pp. 87–90.
[167] The tensions between voluntary bureaucracy and legal enforcement are explored by Alexandra Walsham in *Charitable Hatred: Tolerance and Intolerance in England, 1500–1700* (Manchester, 2006), pp. 39–105 and pp. 89–92.

owed. That individuals were sometimes reluctant to undertake disciplinary activity is suggested by evidence from the minutes, where Meetings often had difficulty finding persons willing to carry out the onerous process of conducting formal family visits. A 1704 minute from Kendal Men's Monthly Meeting, for instance, requested that volunteers come forward to undertake house-to-house visitations, noting that 'if none doe soe offer that the said Friends consider of one and return his name'.[168] Marsden Women's Preparative Meeting was forced to appoint or inquire about individuals willing to act as overseers on an almost monthly basis between 1700 and 1705, and Tipperary Six Weeks' Meeting struggled to recruit members in either the Men's Meetings or the Women's Meetings to act, even when members from other Meetings volunteered to accompany them.[169] In April 1745, for instance, a woman Friend from Limerick wrote to Tipperary Women's Meeting asking for volunteers to accompany her 'in the performance of a visit in this County to friends familys'. Enquiries were made, but the minutes of the next Meeting note that 'friends seems [sic] backward of giveing up to wholely attend said service'. The following Meeting dropped the matter altogether.[170] The nomination of individuals for committee assignments in a voluntary faith, dependent upon the spiritual consensus and unity of its members, is perhaps indicative of the elders' reluctance to undertake some of the more time-consuming aspects of this work. Ministering Friends often commented on the burdensome nature of this service. The English minister Edith Lovel, for instance, apologised to Richard Shackleton in 1781 for not writing sooner, but explained that she and her companion 'go on to visit four famlis a day' noting 'it is hard work'.[171]

Since Quaker religious culture made the need for a professionally trained clergy redundant, another important but largely overlooked moral responsibility also fell upon the members of the general congregation. Individuals who attended the Meetings but performed none of the business tasks, constituted an estimated 60 per cent of the total body that gathered on a monthly basis.[172] As much of the spiritual oversight of the congregation fell entirely and, in theory equally, upon all members, the Meeting relied heavily upon

[168] KAC, WDFCF/1/13 Kendal Men's MM 1699–1723, minutes for 4 August 1704.
[169] LA, FRM/4/6 Marsden Women's Preparative Meeting 1698–1794, pp. 10–41, minutes between 14 March 1700 and 14 February 1706.
[170] FHLD, MMX B2 Co. Tipperary Women's MM 1735–1764, minutes for 14 April 1745 and 26 May 1745.
[171] UCSC, Mss 4 Ballitore Collection, Box 3/12, Edith Lovell to Richard Shackleton, Cork, 11 December 1781.
[172] This estimate was made by Forbes in her study of New Garden Monthly Meeting in Pennsylvania, where she argues that about 60 per cent of the town Quakers attended the Meetings but performed none of the business tasks delegated by the gathering. Forbes, 'Quaker Tribalism', p. 147.

the surveillance, information, and admonition undertaken by ordinary members on an informal basis outside the Meetings House. When Anna Pole and Molly Parrock, for example, visited the household of the young Hannah Callender in January 1759, Hannah noted that 'some cautions [were] given to us Girls to take care of what Company we keept'.[173] Some women went further. 'I thought it my business', Ann Whitall wrote in her diary in 1760, 'to tell KA [Kate Andras] of Sleeping in Meetings so much as she does', leading her to question whether anything would 'rouse us up to more diligence to serve our Maker'.[174] In a culture with a strong imperative to keep members within the fold, it is likely that informal action made a significant contribution to the business of the Women's and Men's Meetings. The guidance, assistance, and knowledge of local women (and men) Friends in matters of marriage, played an important role in ensuring the spiritual vitality of their religious community.

DETERMINING COMMUNITY STATUS

As custodians of the spiritual and moral well-being of the community, the roles available for women within the Meeting system provided a range of opportunities for 'ordinary' members to act in positions of authority and leadership. For women who never experienced a spiritual calling, the Women's Meetings provided opportunities to serve in roles that rested upon their fixed residence within their locality. Considerable weight and responsibility lay on those regarded as 'elders'. The time-consuming and burdensome nature of their work, and their need to be present at almost every Monthly Meeting, underlines the important role played by non-itinerant female members in shaping the social and cultural outlook of the Society.

Yet the complex structure of the evolving Quaker movement raises the question of how status and authority were decided and conferred on the female elders who filled the roles of overseer, treasurer, and clerk. This is an aspect of the Quaker Men's and Women's Meetings rarely mentioned in the minutes and there appears to have been no formal procedure for nominating male and female elders. Thus when Chester Women's Meeting appointed a new clerk in March 1746, they simply recorded that: 'Mary Shipley desiring to be released from being clerk of this meeting: Esther Bickersdike be chosen for the service'.[175] It is likely that this

---

[173] Hannah Callender, *The Diary of Hannah Callender Sansom: Sense and Sensibility in the Age of the American Revolution*, ed. Susan E. Klepp and Karin Wulf (London, 2010), p. 86, diary entry for 13 January 1759.
[174] Ann Whitall, 'The Journal of Ann Whitall (1760–62)', in Hannah Whitall Smith (ed.), *John M. Whitall: The Story of His Life* (Philadelphia, 1879), p. 17, diary entry for 27 July 1760.
[175] FHL, MR-Ph 98 Chester Women's MM 1733–1779, minutes for 21 March 1746.

simple note obscures a far more elaborate procedure. As Quakers rejected voting, much time would have been spent carefully weighing the divine gifts, spiritual maturity, and qualifications of several potential candidates before leaving it to the will of God to determine who should fill a particular position.

The process of nominating female elders appears to have been conducted entirely within the bounds of the Women's Meeting. There is no reference in the corresponding Men's Meeting minutes of the male elders' involvement in the appointment of a new female clerk, treasurer, or overseer.[176] Even within the hierarchy of Irish Quakerism, where the Men's Meetings retained more of the executive authority than elsewhere, female elders were autonomous in determining their own constitution and leadership. This is exemplified in May 1678 when the Men's Half-Yearly Meeting approved the creation of a National Women's Meeting. Apart from prescribing what time of year it would be held, they left the provincial Women's Meetings to decide issues of governance, including the number of representatives from each province who would be required to attend.[177]

Some sociologists see the evolution of a movement from sect to denomination as acquiring those characteristics typically associated with a church, including an elite and educated leadership. Max Weber argued that the rise of institutional and organisational discipline led to the creation of an elitist movement dominated by and limited to the wealthiest and most influential members of the religious community.[178] Close analysis of the female elders who attained positions of responsibility within Quakerism, suggests that family connections, rather than social rank, were decisive in determining community status, although the two were not incompatible. Detailed family reconstitution of these Meetings is not possible because of variations in record survival and the different practices of British and colonial Friends in registering and recording births, deaths, and marriages.[179] By examining the number of Friends sharing the same surname, we can nevertheless establish a picture of how far family ties proliferated among the highest echelons of the Meetings.

[176] The only exception appears to have been the nomination of female Friends to the mixed Meetings of Ministers and Elders, which sat outside of the pyramidal Meeting structure. In April 1748, the Men's Meeting at Fairfax recorded that 'Jacob and Elizabeth Janney recommended to sit on the Quarterly Meeting of ministers and elders for testimony', but no reference to this is made in the corresponding Women's Meeting minutes for that month. MR-B117 Fairfax Men's MM 1745–1768, p. 16 [modern pagination], minutes for 30 April 1748.

[177] Greaves, *God's Other Children*, pp. 293–294.

[178] Max Weber, *The Sociology of Religion*, transl. Ephraim Fischoff (London, 1965).

[179] A good discussion of the records relating to English and Irish Quaker populations is provided in Vann and Eversley in *Friends in Life and Death*, pp. 11–31.

Table 2.3 assesses the proportion of individuals given committee assignments in the Women's Meeting with surnames corresponding to those in the Men's Meeting between 1700 and 1705 and 1745 and 1750. It shows that of the thirty-five women active in Chester Monthly Meeting between 1700 and 1705, twenty-five (71 per cent) had an identifiable spouse or probable family member sharing the same surname involved in the Men's Meeting in the same period. A similar pattern emerges in the period 1745–1750, where the number of Chester women with spouses or family members involved in the Men's Meeting constituted 67 per cent of the women actively serving in the Meeting. A total of 81 per cent of Burlington women also had a spouse or relative involved in the Men's Meetings in the period 1700–1705. Forbes observed a similar connection in her study of the Quaker community at New Garden, where those who were most active in the Monthly Meeting were easily identifiable from their family ties.[180] The emphasis on endogamous marriage and the rigour with which it was enforced, explains at least in part why such strong connections existed between the members of the separate Meetings.

This data set is likely to under-represent wider kin connections within the Meetings because of the short sample periods employed. Assessing surnames may also create false associations between members sharing the same surname but were in fact unrelated. Equally, those related but with different surnames, such as siblings, cousins, and married daughters, would also be omitted from such a survey. It also does not include non-relatives who resided in the same household (such as Quaker servants and apprentices). There is nevertheless sufficient evidence to suggest a strong positive correlation between family membership and active participation in the Meetings. Detailed searches of the Quaker birth, marriage, and death records for Burlington Meeting confirm that of the thirty-four elders active in the Women's Meeting between 1700 and 1705, twenty-seven were married to the Friend in the Men's Meeting sharing the same surname.[181] This pattern

---

[180] Forbes, 'Quaker Tribalism', p. 165.

[181] This was achieved through an assessment of the Meeting minutes, birth, marriage, removal, and death records relating to Burlington Monthly Meeting where Quaker couples were listed. For example, Rachel and William Gabitas served as overseers in the respective Men's and Women's Meetings between 1700 and 1705; and the Women's Meeting minutes record a Rachel Marshall marrying a William Gabitas in 1696. Likewise, Elizabeth Day and John Day served in Burlington Meeting, and were also listed together as the parents of Elizabeth Day, who was born in 1685. FHL, MR-Ph 54 and 55, Births and Deaths 1675–1805; MR-Ph 55 Marriage Certificates 1678–1765; and MR-Ph 54 Marriages-Approvals and Consents 1681–1856. I am grateful to Jean Soderlund for her advice about colonial Quaker family genealogy.

Table 2.3 Family Connections between Chester, Burlington, Fairfax, Marsden, Kendal, and Tipperary Men's and Women's Meetings, 1700–1705 and 1745–1750

	1700–1705				1745–1750					
	Chester	Burlington	Marsden	Kendal	Chester	Burlington	Fairfax	Marsden	Kendal	Tipperary
Individual in Men's Meeting sharing the same surname	25	42	20	22	37	43	23	29	49	9
No individual in Men's Meeting sharing the same surname	10	10	16	3	18	32	8	22	25	1
TOTAL	35	52	36	25	55	75	31	51	74	10
Total (%) of probable connection	71	81	56	88	67	57	74	57	66	90

Data extracted from the following sources: FHL, MR-Ph 98 Chester Women's MM 1733–1779, MR-Ph 92 Chester Men's MM 1721–1745 and MR-Ph 103 Chester Men's MM 1745–1778; FHL, MR-Ph 63 Burlington Women's MM 1681–1747 and MR-Ph 60 Burlington Men's MM 1678–1737; LA FRM/1/24 Marsden Women's MM 1678–1738 and FRM/1/1 Marsden Men's MM 1678–1723; KAC, WDFCF/1/22 Kendal Women's MM 1671–1719 and WDFCF/1/13 Kendal Men's MM 1699–1723 and 1747–1777; FHL, MR-B117 Fairfax Men's MM 1745–1776 and MR-B119 Fairfax Women's MM 1745–1768; and RSFI, MMX B2 Co. Tipperary Women's MM 1735–1764 and RSFI MMX A2 Co. Tipperary Men's MM 1724–1760.

is replicated across the Meeting records, suggesting that marriage in most cases linked the male and female elders together.[182]

The initial wave of conversions in the 1650s and 1660s caused many Friends to sever their familial ties. Later in the eighteenth century, when strict rules of endogamy were enforced in the face of declining numbers, Quakerism seems to have constituted a model of religious order characterised by strong family connections. This view is supported by Levy, whose assessment of Chester Friends in England led him to conclude that 'northwestern Quakers were fascinated by the potentialities of familial relations', which brought the withering of old kinship ties and the creation of 'powerful, self-contained' Quaker households.[183] The previous chapter showed how the continuing strength and coherence of the Meeting structure rested on the preservation and transmission of Quaker values, beliefs, and disciplinary structures from one generation of elders to the next. 'To understand the Meeting', writes J. William Frost, 'one needs to know the family.'[184] It became central in equipping children, apprentices, and servants with the emotional, psychological, and spiritual resources necessary to fulfil such work within their communities.

In a spiritual community that viewed itself as an extended family, the development of stable and orderly household relationships was paramount. Time and again, writers exhorted male and female elders to extend their loving and nurturing influence as heads of families over the members of their spiritual family in their separate Meetings. Catharine Whitton, for example, exhorted Friends across the Atlantic in 1681 to 'be Faithful to the Lord, and careful over his household and family'.[185] And when the elders of Kendal denounced superfluous fashions and a tendency for members to sleep in Meetings in 1713, they ordered Friends to be watchful, 'soe that we may grow up as a true family to our own comfertt and welbeing.'[186]

It was not essential, however, to have a spouse or family member in good standing in the Men's Meeting to achieve high status in the congregation. Lydia Lancaster, for instance, gained influence as both a minister and overseer

---

[182] I have been able to confirm that of the forty-nine women assigned to committee roles in Marsden Meeting between 1700 and 1705, twenty-one were married to the elder in the Men's Meeting sharing the same surname, and five of them were single at the time of appointment. These figures have been established through detailed research of the respective birth, marriage, removal,and death records relating to these Meetings, where Quaker couples are listed.

[183] Levy, *Quakers and the American Family*, pp. 50–51.

[184] Frost, *The Quaker Family in Colonial America*, p. 2.

[185] Catharine Whitton, *An Epistle to Friends Everywhere: To Be Distinctly Read in Their Meetings, When Assembled Together in the Fear of the Lord* (London, 1681), p. 6.

[186] KAC, WDFCF/1/22 Kendal Women's MM 1671–1719, minutes for 26 June 1713.

in Lancaster Monthly Meeting, despite the fact that her husband, Brian, had been disowned from the Society in 1721 for failings that included drinking in excess and running into debt.[187] Lydia, by contrast, remained a staunch supporter of her local Women's Meeting and active in its business until her death in 1761. She was memorialised as having been able to speak from experience: 'being instructed in sorrow she was favoured with a sympathizing Heart, and knew how to partake in the Affliction of others'. Perhaps even more significantly, she was revered for her ability to 'distinguish the higher obligation of spiritual unity from the ties of natural connection or general acquaintance'.[188] It is likely that Lydia Lancaster's experiences of marital hardship made her an ideal choice to advise other women in her Meetings about the dangers of entering into a rash marriage. Her story also demonstrates how any woman could excel within the organisation by virtue of her own personal qualities of leadership. Similarly, Martha Hollingsworth acted as an overseer of Fairfax Meeting in Virginia whilst Joseph Hollingsworth was being disciplined by the Men's Meeting. Between February and August 1747, Joseph was condemned for 'drinking in excess', and was formally disowned from the Society in September that year.[189] Although women's domestic experiences were never static, these examples contrast sharply with the wider societal model that measured women by their marital status and viewed them as adjuncts of their husbands.[190] Both Lydia Lancaster and Martha Hollingsworth were able to retain their status within the Women's Meetings, despite their association with disorderly family members.

In the absence of a university-trained clergy, and with a model of worship that recognised spiritual weight and inward revelation as possible for all to achieve, the Quaker Women's Meetings depended upon the participation of members from a range of backgrounds. As established in Chapter 1, despite the overtly domestic focus of the movement, its egalitarian spirit provided space for unmarried women as well as their married counterparts to attain positions of status. In her study of 'never married' women in eighteenth-century Philadelphia, Karin Wulf remarked on the compatibility between

---

[187] The disownment of Brian Lancaster is noted in the biography of Lydia Lancaster in Gil Skidmore (ed.), *Strength in Weakness: Writings of Eighteenth-Century Quaker Women* (Oxford, 2003), p. 33.
[188] LRSF, Portfolio MSS, vol. 17, fol. 65, 'A Testimony from Lancaster Monthly Meeting Concerning Lydia Lancaster'.
[189] For Martha Hollingsworth's activities see, e.g., FHL, MR-B119 Fairfax Women's MM 1745–1768, pp. 8–9, minutes for 27 June 1747 and 29 August 1747. For the condemnation of Joseph Hollingsworth see MR-B117 Fairfax Men's MM 1745–1776, pp. 9–12 [modern pagination], minutes for 28 March 1747, 30 May 1747, 30 June 1747, 29 August 1747, and 26 September 1747.
[190] Margaret J. M. Ezell, *The Patriarch's Wife: Literary Evidence and the History of the Family* (London, 1987), pp. 36–61.

singleness and positions of leadership within the Pennsylvanian Quaker community.[191] Elizabeth Norris, for instance, deliberately remained single because she felt she would be able 'to attend more closely to "truth" than could those who married'. Over twenty years she was repeatedly appointed to a range of tasks within Philadelphia Women's Monthly, Quarterly, and Yearly Meetings, including transcribing the official minute book and acting as an overseer.[192] Her contemporary Sarah Morris, also unmarried, similarly served as clerk to Philadelphia Women's Meeting in the 1740s.[193]

Perhaps the most remarkable example of a single and low-ranking woman occupying a position of influence in her Meeting is Jane Fenn, a Chester minister and servant in the household of Grace and David Lloyd. Some of the assignments she was given during this time clearly indicate that authority was not always dependent on either wealth or marital status, for she participated in Chester Monthly Meeting for at least fourteen years before her marriage to Joseph Hoskins in 1738. One of her responsibilities was reading, correcting, and transcribing the rough copies of the Monthly Meeting minutes, which she performed on a regular basis.[194] This reflects the widespread literacy accessible even to the lowliest members and suggests the influence that female ministry could have upon the organisation of the Meeting. Indeed, implicit in Jane Fenn's appointment to correct the Meeting minutes was her spiritual authority as an important minister within Chester Meeting. Arguably someone who could decipher the drawings of the spirit was seen as better placed to understand the 'sense' of the Meeting, and thus how it was reflected in the minutes.

Quakerism was clearly distinctive in advancing individuals on their own merits, rather than merely their social status or economic circumstances. Yet the evidence does also suggest a clear tendency for most leaders, in both the British and colonial Women's Meetings, to be drawn from settled and prosperous backgrounds. The importance of financial security for those women occupying the highest positions in the Meeting has been highlighted by a number of scholars. Soderlund, for example, in her survey of Pennsylvanian Meetings, noted the high number of wealthy leaders who came to dominate Quaker church governance. By the 1750s, she argues, the majority of the leaders came from households 'with above- and well-above-average wealth'.[195] Clearly, committee work and extensive family visitation were luxuries that were only available to the wealthiest members of the community.

---

[191] Wulf, *Not All Wives*, p. 68.
[192] Ibid., pp. 65–68
[193] On Sarah Morris see Soderlund, 'Women's Authority', p. 728; and Wulf, *Not All Wives*, p. 69.
[194] FHL, MR-Ph 98 Chester Women's MM 1695–1733, see, e.g., minutes for 30 March 1724.
[195] Soderlund, 'Women's Authority', p. 733.

A high level of literacy would also have been required to occupy most of the high-ranking positions within the Meeting. Whilst Quaker literacy rates were generally much higher than the eighteenth-century average, the level of education required for some of these roles would have limited the higher positions to an elite few with both the time and leisure to acquire and practise their skills.[196] Ryan, for instance, has suggested that the numerical skills and authority exhibited by the women of the London Box Meeting may have reflected their connections to the capital's wealthiest merchants.[197] Moreover, these leading figures would also have needed a significant amount of leisure time. Mercy Bell, a leading London Friend and wife of Nathaniel Bell, a schoolmaster and bookseller, often complained to her correspondents of the heavy workload associated with 'writing on the meetings account'. On one occasion, she explained that she had just completed a Letter to the Quarterly Meeting, which she had written 'three times already' and 'by order of the meeting [had] copy'd it into the Minute Book', a task she explained '[I] am quite weary of'.[198]

There were of course other reasons why women from wealthier backgrounds came to dominate the Quaker elite. In those Meetings where a considerable amount of money was distributed to the poor on a regular basis, someone with financial means would have been desirable, as they would then be able to afford to cover any deficits. Tolles demonstrated that the wealthy members of the Philadelphia Quaker community were 'disproportionately burdened' with the care of poor and sick immigrants.[199] Because charitable relief was required on an informal and ad hoc basis, female overseers were expected to dispense charitable relief to the needy under their care and then report their expenses to their Monthly Meetings, which would arrange for them to be reimbursed. Since the Meeting's ability to raise funds depended on voluntary contributions, a debt might not be paid back for several months. The female overseer would therefore need to enjoy a relative degree of financial security to take on these responsibilities. In August 1747, Sarah Rigg of Tipperary Meeting advanced 10s. 10d. to the poor widow Sarah Fennell, and £1 12s. 6d. the following month.[200] Although the female

---

[196] N. H. Keeble suggests that dissenters may have accounted for 13 to 15 per cent of the literate population despite the fact that nonconformists made up no more than 6 per cent of the total population. N. H. Keeble, *The Literary Culture of Nonconformity in Later Seventeenth-Century England* (Leicester, 1987), p. 138.

[197] Ryan, 'In My Hand for Lending', p. 21.

[198] LRSF, Temp MSS 403/1/2/3/8 Arthur B. Braithwaite Family Papers, Mercy Bell to Priscilla Farmer, London, 20 February 1757.

[199] Frederick B. Tolles, *Meeting House and Counting House: The Quaker Merchants of Colonial Philadelphia, 1682–1763* (New York, 1948), p. 66.

[200] FHLD, MMX B2 Co. Tipperary Women's MM 1735–1764, minutes for 2 August 1747 and 13 September 1747.

elders agreed to reimburse her, it was not until three months after Rigg had reported her initial concerns to the Meeting that she was fully repaid. It was almost a year later (in August 1748) before the Meeting agreed to make a regular collection to pay Sarah Fennell's 13s. allowance.[201]

Moreover, given that large donations were entrusted to the clerks and treasurers, they needed to be in a position of financial security so that the Meeting's funds were never at risk. The high personal, emotional, and financial investment that the Meetings required of their clerks and treasurers is indicated by the 1699 minutes of Barking Women's Meeting, which record with dismay that Phyllis Bush, 'who hath kept friends Booke and Stocke for some years', had stolen from the Meeting stock. Bush, having '[been] putt to some straights', made use 'of this money to her owne use; which both the Men and women Friends, doe judge to bee a wronge thing to use the poores money'.[202] A more honest replacement was immediately appointed. The incident shows how an individual's status within the community was intimately bound up with her credit and reputation. But it also indicates that wealth was not the sole determinant of leadership because a relatively poor woman Friend had been advanced to the role of treasurer.

It was generally in the more populous and wealthy Meetings of the American colonies that a more plutocratic form of government is most evident. Reconstructing the circumstances of the women involved in the English Meetings is a much harder task, owing to the disparate nature of the surviving genealogical records. Nevertheless, evidence from Marsden and Kendal Meeting minutes suggests that women from a wider range of economic backgrounds occupied positions of leadership. There are numerous instances, for example, of former overseers being forced to turn to the Meeting for relief in later life. Ellen Veepon, who had regularly served as an overseer for Marsden Monthly Meeting from 1696 and received at least eleven committee assignments between 1700 and 1705, became a regular recipient of relief from April 1730, when Friends recorded that they had disbursed '4s. to Ellen Veepon widdow'.[203] Similarly Sarah Fennell, one of the

---

[201] FHLD, MMX B2 Co. Tipperary Women's MM 1735–1764, minutes for 14 August 1748.
[202] LRSF, MGR 11b13 Ham and Waltham (Barking) Women's MM 1675–1721, minutes for 7 March 1700 and 4 April 1700.
[203] LA, FRM/1/24 Marsden Women's MM 1678–1738, minutes for 23 April 1730. Ellen Veepon was tasked with visiting every female Friend in the compass of Marsden Meeting to inspect their dresses on 21 May 1696 and was appointed to inspect Ann Hellewell for clearness to marry on 21 March 1701. The same was also the case with Susan Horrabin, who had regularly served as an elder for Marsden Preparative Meeting, but petitioned the Meeting for relief in early 1719. Her first of many payments was for 2s. 6d. in January 1719. LA, FRM/1/24 Marsden Women's MM 1678–1738, minutes for 15 January 1719. For Horrabin's committee assignments see, e.g. LA, FRM/4/6 Marsden Women's Preparative Meeting Minutes, 1698–1794, minutes for 11 April 1700.

former female elders (and a possible clerk) of Tipperary Women's Meeting, fell into poverty after her husband William died. She became the recipient of extensive relief from the Women's and Men's Meetings between 1747 and 1751.[204] It is significant that the colonial Meetings provide no comparable cases of elders becoming recipients of the relief they had once administered. The contrast further underlines the importance of local circumstances in shaping the leadership base of each Meeting.

The work of Quaker women within their Meetings made them distinctive among their sex. The nineteenth-century reformer Thomas Clarkson heralded their responsibilities as 'a new era in female history', for they had 'a public character' that 'no other body of women have'. He praised Quaker egalitarianism, explaining that in other religious congregations 'Women are still weighed in a different scale from men'.[205] Although his accolade was exaggerated, the evidence suggests that his impression of the Meetings was by no means a fantasy. The relationship that evolved between local Men's and Women's Meetings clearly affected the activities that women could legitimately undertake, but, at all levels, the space of the Meeting provided an important sphere in which women were able to develop connections with one another. It also gave them opportunities to attain positions of authority and status within their communities in new and significant ways, especially because they were able to independently manage their day-to-day activities, furnish their own Meeting stock, and oversee and manage the behaviour of the female (and male) members of their communities. Indeed, the tasks of the separate Women's Meetings in Kendal, Marsden, Tipperary, Chester, Fairfax, and Burlington reveal a dynamic and nuanced model of female oversight, reflecting the circumstances of each different group of Friends, whilst sharing a common philosophy of discipline and order.

The public religious work of Quaker women was not affected by the decline in ministerial activity that has so often led researchers to lament the opportunities available to women in the eighteenth-century movement. The surviving records make it clear that Friends had a well-structured organisation capable of exercising a great deal of authority over their members. Detailed analysis of the tasks that female Friends performed within their Meetings provides an important insight into how the concerns and priorities of the Women's Meetings evolved as they responded to different circumstances and local conditions.

---

[204] On 26 May 1745 Sarah Fennell was ordered to write to Limerick Provincial Meeting in answer to a letter they had received about conducting family visits. FHLD, MMX B2 Co. Tipperary Women's MM 1735–1764, minutes for 26 May 1745. She became the regular recipient of relief in August 1747. See minutes for 2 August 1747 onwards.

[205] Thomas Clarkson, *A Portraiture of Quakerism* (3 vols., New York, 1806), vol. 3, p. 246–249.

Whereas the Men's Meetings of England and Ireland tended to retain much of the executive power over discipline and other aspects of church administration, the conditions of the frontier environment enabled colonial women to assume a greater range of responsibilities and act more autonomously, especially when it came to disciplining errant members. Moreover, the highly mobile populations of the colonies meant that Chester, Fairfax, and Burlington Meetings tended to focus their energies on supervising the movement of members between Meetings (especially in the five years before 1750), whilst English and Irish women focused more on the relief of poorer members of their communities. Despite this geographical diversity, however, a surprisingly unified programme of order and regulation developed across the Atlantic. This can be observed not only through the activities for which women were responsible in their Meetings, but also how they worked alongside their male brethren.

The consistent model of authority that evolved on both sides of the Atlantic reveals the ongoing process of exchange and interaction dominating the experience of British and American female Friends. Moreover, it stands as testament to the durability of the Quaker Meeting system, which enabled a similar set of responsibilities and obligations to emerge within these separate male and female spaces without a bureaucratic system or hierarchy being introduced. The regulation of marriage proved to be the most prominent and consistent task for which the female elders took responsibility across our period. In many respects this should not come as a surprise, since it was a role that was particularly appropriate to women's gendered sphere of knowledge. What is striking, however, is how early Quakers established a system that enabled ordinary members to hold positions of authority within their community, by virtue of their positions within the household.

The metaphor of the family, powerful in Quaker church culture, fostered a pious community of spiritual elders, linked as much by their family connections as by their spiritual union. It also had the more practical effect of underlining the need for supportive household relationships outside of the Meeting to conduct church business efficiently and effectively. On both a material and metaphorical basis the Quaker Meeting system reflected household order, where control over the formation of new households and the need to provide exemplary guidance for Quaker children meant that regulation of marriage was to become one of the most time-consuming and important aspects of Quaker women's functions.

A strong drive to regulate the behaviour and settlement patterns of female Friends, as well as care for poor and needy members, extended women's functions from the Meeting House into the wider community. The intense and often intrusive control that female overseers exercised over the personal lives of their members demonstrated significant powers of regulation and a well-integrated presence within the wider Quaker community. In offering a separate and formal space in which to meet together and discuss church business, Quakers provided a place for women within the church hierarchy that integrated domestic responsibility with public authority. This elevation of the wife and mother was something no other dissenting or established religious movement fully realised, for it was almost always widowed or unmarried women who occupied leading positions within Baptist, Methodist, Pietist, and Catholic congregations.

The case can also be made for the meritocratic nature of the Quaker Meeting system, which elevated those members with the best spiritual and moral endowments to high-ranking roles. But we also find a strong correlation between church status and family membership. In a Society increasingly intent on regulation and discipline, it is not surprising that close kin relationships were the most significant predictor of women's involvement. On a practical level, the need for sufficient spare time and disposable income to undertake many of the tasks of the Meeting meant that positions of authority tended to be confined to the wealthiest and most literate members. Nevertheless, a strong link between active leadership and household standing was prevalent throughout the eighteenth century in the six Meetings. Whilst women did not have to be among the elite to achieve positions of authority, it was clearly important that they came from established and, in most cases, orderly Quaker households. This fits with the evidence in Chapter 1, which demonstrated a strong correlation between stable and supportive domestic environments and active ministerial service. To Friends, the family was paramount and the Quaker community was an extension of the family.

In assembling together on a weekly, monthly, quarterly, and yearly basis, these women succeeded in creating a female spiritual community – one connected to but not dependent upon their positions within households. The physical space of the Meeting House also provided an important arena for women to form connections and friendships with other members. Some of these were on a personal level, with fellow worshippers, while others were imagined or 'invisible', united only through correspondence with distant Meetings and shared religious experience. In providing an alternative form of female sociability, the Meetings gave women a sense of cohesion, friendship, and fellowship. The next chapter moves beyond the Meeting, to explore how these social connections and alliances were fashioned and experienced by women across both neighbourhood and ocean. In fulfilling their roles within Meeting, church, and family, these women participated in a shared spiritual sphere that defied class and gendered distinctions and united them across the Atlantic world of Quakerism.

−3−

'United by This Holy Cement': The Constructions, Practices, and Experiences of Female Friendship

The Sythe [*sic*] of Time, Death, parteth Friend from Friend,
But to true Friendship cannot put an end; ...
Bless'd be the Day, wherein my Love abounded,
At first to her, and Friendship firm was Founded,
In our United Hearts; my Faithful Friend!
Friendship 'twixt thee and me shall never end.

Mary Mollineux, *Fruits of Retirement*
(London, 1702), sig. B4v

In 1702 *Fruits of Retirement*, a compilation of meditations, poems, letters, and writings by the Quaker poet Mary Mollineux, was published by a group of her close friends and co-religionists. Whilst Mollineux refused to publish her writings during her lifetime, 'not seeking Praise amongst Men', her works were nevertheless designed for a public audience, 'to communicate the Exercise of peculiar Gifts amongst her near Friends and Acquaintance[s]'.[1] Manuscripts circulated by hand were her preferred form of publication. Her decision to limit the circulation of her most intimate writings only to those 'whom she knew in the Fellowship and Bond of Truth' underlines the importance of religious belief in shaping the pattern of female friendships in early Quakerism.[2] In her various poems on the subject of friendship, Mollineux emphasised the spiritual debt she owed to her friends, whose conversation had enlarged her understanding and enriched her relationship to the divine. In return, she wrote to and for her Friends – members of her religious community. This form of 'literate sociability' reflects the multifaceted experience of friendship within the early movement. Despite their rather abstract quality, one theme dominating Mollineux's verses was how the practice of friendship could be linked to a pious lifestyle. It is this complex interplay

[1] Mary Mollineux, *Fruits of Retirement: Or Miscellaneous Poems, Moral and Divine* (London, 1702), sig. A7v.
[2] Ibid.

between the language of friendship and how this translated into women's everyday experiences that will form the focus of this chapter.

Friendship and network formation within early Quakerism have received little sustained historiographical attention. In part, this is owing to the limited extent to which Quaker authors engaged with the concept of friendship, either as a philosophical idea or moral practice.[3] Indeed, the focus Mary Mollineux's compendium placed on the subject was unusual by Quaker standards.[4] The highly individualistic nature of the Quaker faith may have persuaded authors to avoid the matter altogether, as the temporal concern of maintaining relationships could be viewed as a hindrance to personal piety. Many of Mollineux's verses were composed in solitude, the 'fruits of retirement'. Yet this intense personal contemplation, as Phyllis Mack has shown, was balanced by the interactive practice of the Quaker faith.[5] Notwithstanding the inward-looking theology of Quakerism, notions of friendship and cooperation were intrinsic to the way in which Quaker communities were formed and maintained. Focusing on the various types of friendships and networks of 'Friends' that developed across the Atlantic, this chapter will show how women, through their adherence to the faith, reshaped their understandings and practices of friendship to fit their own experiences.

The multifaceted nature of Quaker friendships was facilitated through a dynamic transatlantic network of itinerant ministry, Meetings, epistolary, and commercial exchanges. We saw in the previous chapter how participation in separate Meetings offered an alternative sphere of sociability, which was dependent upon like-minded women meeting together on a weekly, monthly, quarterly, and annual basis to offer spiritual, emotional, and practical guidance to one another. This chapter will observe women's personal relationships in their broadest geographical scope. It will explore the range and meanings of friendships within the transatlantic Quaker movement, emphasising the distinctive combination of being both a personal 'friend' and a member of the religious community: a 'Friend of Truth'.

From the earliest days of the movement the word 'Friend' was in general use by Quakers to refer to those who shared the same spiritual outlook. As

---

[3] Thomas Heilke came across something similar in his study of the Swiss Anabaptists, where he noted that friendship is something not 'directly articulated' within Anabaptist writings on church community. Thomas Heilke, 'From Civic Friendship to Communities of Believers: Anabaptist Challenges to Lutheran and Calvinist Discourses', in Daniel T. Lochman, Maritere López, and Lorna Hutson (eds.), *Discourses and Representations of Friendship in Early Modern Europe, 1500–1700* (Farnham, 1988), p. 230.

[4] *Fruits of Retirement* contained ten items, both in verse and prose, with the subject of friendship in their title.

[5] Phyllis Mack, *Visionary Women: Ecstatic Prophecy in Seventeenth-Century England* (Berkeley, CA, 1994), pp. 150–151.

I acknowledged in the Introduction, a common misconception is that the term 'Society of Friends' was already in corporate use at this point in the movement's history. In fact, early Quakers preferred to describe themselves collectively as the 'Children of Light', 'Friends of Truth', or 'Friends in Truth' to distinguish one another from the rest of society.[6] Writing to her former landlady in 1752, the Quaker preacher Mary Weston explained that 'Truth makes the Friends of it, more dear to each other, th[a]n the nearest relation'.[7] In using the word 'truth' to describe their relationships, Friends were signalling their conviction that their beliefs and practices directly reflected the teachings of God. As Weston's statement suggests, Friends' spiritual compatibility and relationship to 'Truth' came before their personal connections. This tension between spiritual, temporal, and personal friendships will be explored in detail in the following discussion. Whilst adherence to Quaker testimonies in some respects restricted the types of friendship available to women, the highly mobile and literate nature of the movement also served to expand these alliances, showing how a shared religious bond could solidify friendships between women across vast distances.

The practice of friendship among early Quakers was strongly shaped by their faith. The distinctive gestures, dress, speech patterns, and cultural customs adopted by seventeenth- and eighteenth-century Friends led to an unusual code of behaviours that often stood at odds with standards of 'politeness' expected by their contemporaries. Indeed, the Quaker renunciation of polite forms of address, including the denial of 'hat honour', the abandonment of honorific titles, and their refusal to address acquaintances with greetings such as 'good morning', 'good evening', 'good day', and 'good morrow', suggested to their contemporaries that they lacked civil courtesy and sat uneasily with the manners and style of expression expected from polite discourse of the time.[8] Duty to God was always placed above custom in Quaker thought. It meant shunning the excesses and corruptions that distracted an individual believer from their higher spiritual calling. Conventional sites of sociability, such as the playhouse, theatre, coffee shop, tearoom, music hall, salon, or art exhibition, were therefore off limits for most Quaker adherents.

The task of this chapter, then, is to situate Quaker friendship within the theories and practices of friendship circulating in wider society. It seeks to

---

[6] As noted in the Introduction, the name 'Quaker', like many other derisory labels, was often used by Friends without qualification. However, it was not a term that was officially accepted by Friends, except when indicating that it was applied to them in contempt by others.

[7] HSP, MS Coll 484A Pemberton Family Papers, vol. 8, p. 56, Mary Weston to Mary Pemberton from Wapping, London, 14 September 1752.

[8] Richard Bauman, *Let Your Words Be Few: Symbolism of Speaking and Silence among Seventeenth-Century Quakers* (Cambridge, 1983), pp. 44–46.

show how Quaker friendships both conformed to and contravened non-Quaker patterns of social bonding, and will question how far there was a specifically gendered dimension to women's alliances. What made Quaker understandings of friendship distinctive, I will argue, was the distance over which women's friendships were conducted and maintained. This helped to make it possible for platonic friendships to be forged between individuals of the same sex and from a range of social backgrounds who shared nothing but a commitment to the 'truth'. Friendship, as I will discuss, encompassed a broad spectrum of relationships and had a range of meanings. To assess the ways in which Quaker friendship operated conceptually and in practice, however, this discussion will only focus upon non-kin relationships and only those formed within the movement. The connections women developed with the non-Quaker community will be interrogated in greater depth in Chapter 4.

THE QUEST FOR *AMICITIA PERFECTA*: INTERPRETING FRIENDSHIP

Friendship attracted a great deal of attention from non-Quaker writers and thinkers throughout the early modern period. It was 'perplexing', Naomi Tadmor suggests, because it entailed a range of ideas that were almost impossible 'to explain and prescribe in any consistent manner'.[9] From the days of the Ancients right up until the present age, individuals have been unable to agree on *who* should be regarded as a friend, and *what* virtues should be attached to friendship. Modern social scientists describe friendship as a voluntary relationship, often among individuals of relatively equal social status, and principally among non-kin.[10] Yet, as scholars like Barbara Caine and Tadmor have recognised, friendship had a plurality of meanings throughout the early modern period. Members of one's household, family, business associates, political affiliates, as well as personal companions, were variously described under the hypernym of 'friend'.[11] This could also refer to members of one's religious community, where connections between individuals were defined by shared religious practices.

The bonds forged within the family could also be included within this taxonomy of friendship. Kinship, as Alan Bray has stressed, turned on the same

[9] Naomi Tadmor, *Family and Friends in Eighteenth-Century England: Household, Kinship, and Patronage* (Cambridge, 2001), pp. 237–238.
[10] Jacqueline P. Wiseman, 'Friendship: Bonds and Binds in a Voluntary Relationship', *Journal of Social and Personal Relations*, vol. 3 (1986), pp. 191–211. See also Tadmor, *Family and Friends*, pp. 211–215.
[11] Barbara Caine, 'Introduction', in Barbara Caine (ed.), *Friendship: A History* (London, 2009), p. x. See also Tadmor, *Family and Friends*, esp. pp. 167–215.

axis as friendship. Like marriage, friendship created bonds between individuals, groups, and families and its effect was to 'embed the family' within 'a wider and overlapping network'.[12] The humanist scholars Desiderius Erasmus and Juan Luis Vives concluded that husbands and wives were closer than friends because they shared one body as well as one soul.[13] As explored in Chapter 1, the language of companionship helped Quaker couples to construct their understanding of marriage. Although friendship and family connections were closely linked in contemporary imagination, they were also differentiated, for the prescription of a hierarchical rather than horizontal relationship tended to define domestic experience. The indissolubility of marriage as theorised by Erasmus, for example, was based on the recognition that the authoritative husband had dominance over the weaker wife.[14] As Jeremy Taylor noted, 'this friendship and social relation is not equall, and there is too much authority on one side, and too much fear on the other to make equal friendships.'[15] Likewise, Francis Bacon noted in his essay 'Of Friendship' that unlike a father or husband, a 'true Friend' was a non-family intimate who could 'speak as the case requires' and thus offer frank and edifying counsel.[16]

As well as navigating these conflicting definitions of who should be regarded as a friend, early moderns also had to accommodate a range of attitudes and values about what constituted *amicitia perfecta*, the highest form of friendship. Leading Greek and Roman philosophers, particularly Aristotle and Cicero, continued to dominate seventeenth- and eighteenth-century theories of friendship. Prominent in their writings was the theme that the perfect unity of two individuals could only be achieved between social and intellectual equals.[17] Underlying this idealised notion of friendship was the belief that it was only available to a particular type of person – an educated elite man. Indeed, the assumption that women were naturally

---

[12] Alan Bray, *The Friend* (London, 2003), p. 214.

[13] Constance M. Furey, 'Bound by Likeness: Vives and Erasmus on Marriage and Friendship', in Lochman, López, and Hutson, *Discourses and Representations of Friendship*, p. 35.

[14] Ibid., pp. 35–36.

[15] Jeremy Taylor, *The Measures and Offices of Friendship: With Rules of Conducting It* (London, 1657), p. 68.

[16] 'A man cannot speak to his Son, but as a Father; to his Wife but as a Husband; to his Enemy, but upon terms. Whereas a *Friend* may speak as the case requires and not as it sorteth with the Person.' Francis Bacon, 'Of Friendship', *The Essays, or Councils, Civil and Moral, of Sir Francis Bacon* (London, 1696), pp. 75–76.

[17] It was Aristotle's notions of *philia* (love shared between exemplary friends) in his *Nichomachean Ethics* and Cicero's interpretation of *amicitia* (likeness in virtue) in his *Laelius de Amicitia* that early modern writers continued to utilise in their writings on friendship. Helen Berry's research into the *Athenian Mercury* found that platonic ideas of friendship were also influential during this period. Helen Berry, *Gender, Society and Print Culture in Late-Stuart England: The Cultural World of the Athenian Mercury* (Aldershot, 2003), pp. 212–234.

inferior and thus unable to become virtuous citizens continued to permeate early modern thought. Michel de Montaigne in his essay 'Of Friendship', which went through multiple editions in the seventeenth and eighteenth centuries, explained that women were incapable of perfect friendship because 'the ordinary talent of women, is not such as is sufficient to keep up that correspondence and communication, which are necessary for cultivating this sacred tye'.[18] The core values of friendship were therefore theorised within a masculine world of civic performance that was unavailable to women.[19] Jon Mee has noted that eighteenth-century women were still excluded from this world of sociability because their conversation was not deemed to meet 'the proper standards of talk underpinned by a classical education'.[20]

Nevertheless, as alternative models developed outside of this idealised, classically inspired notion of friendship, attention was increasingly focused on the possibility of friendship between women. The seventeenth-century poet, Katherine Phillips, even argued for its superiority over other types owing to the fact that, unlike marriage, it was grounded upon equality.[21] Crucially, those female writers like Phillips who defended the capacity of women for friendship appealed to traditional ideals of friendship as a meeting of equals. Using letters, diaries, and poetry to reconstruct women's affectionate bonds, scholars have successfully demonstrated the many ways in which friendship patterns enabled women from a range of social backgrounds to develop spaces in which to negotiate patriarchal constraints.[22]

This recognition of the vibrant participation of women in a culture of friendship has been supported by a scholarly interest into the emergent fields of sensibility and sociability. The appearance of new social spaces,

---

[18] Michel de Montaigne, 'Of Friendship', *The Essays of Michael Seigneur de Montaigne, Translated into English* (8th edn, 3 vols., London, 1776), vol. 1, p. 212.

[19] Laura Gowing, 'The Politics of Women's Friendship in Early Modern England', in Laura Gowing, Michael Hunter, and Miri Rubin (eds.), *Love, Friendship and Faith in Europe, 1300–1800* (Basingstoke, 2005), pp. 131–132.

[20] Jon Mee, *Conversable Worlds: Literature, Contention and Community, 1762 to 1830* (Oxford, 2011), p. 10.

[21] Penelope Anderson, '"Friendship Multiplyed": Royalist and Republican Friendship in Katherine Philips's Coterie', in Lochman, López, and Hutson, *Discourses and Representations of Friendship*, pp. 135–137.

[22] Bernard Capp's study of early modern gossips has shown us how a largely oral culture of neighbourly support and female networks could give women an active role within the early modern community. Sara Mendelson and Patricia Crawford have demonstrated how everyday interactions and life-cycle events from the birthing chamber to epistolary exchanges provided alternative spaces for women to develop relationships of intimacy outside of the family. Bernard Capp, *When Gossips Meet: Women, Family and Neighbourhood in Early Modern England* (Oxford, 2003); and Sara Mendelson and Patricia Crawford, *Women in Early Modern England, 1550–1720* (Oxford, 1998), pp. 231–251. See also Gowing, 'The Politics of Women's Friendship', pp. 131–149; and Stephanie Tarbin and Susan Broomhall (eds.), *Women, Identities and Communities in Early Modern Europe* (Aldershot, 2008).

such as the coffee house, salon, spa, and theatre, as well as new reading and writing practices, altered how women were understood as both gendered and social beings at the turn of the eighteenth century.[23] In a society where overt expressions of love, sensibility, and emotion were common in both public and private writing, the perceived emotional nature of women increasingly came to be admired. The belief that women were more emotional and thus more capable than men of sympathy and empathy corresponded with the rise of new ideas about what it meant to be a friend.[24] The emergence of prescriptive texts, such as Hannah Woolley's *Gentlewoman's Companion*, offered guidance to female readers on how to select and sustain their friendships.[25] The anonymous author of *The Ladies Dictionary*, for instance, devoted lengthy sections to the subject of friendship, arguing that 'Friendship well chosen and placed, is the greatest felicity of life'.[26] While women were excluded from the world of civic friendship, this burgeoning behavioural literature on female alliance formation indicates that they were now considered to be active participants in the culture of social exchange.

Moreover, the influence of Christian notions of friendship constituted an expansive theoretical space for close personal bonds to develop between women. Although they were viewed as inferior in terms of their mental, legal, educational, and physical capacities, in 'matters of the soul' they were often accepted as equals.[27] Amanda E. Herbert's work on women's alliance formation stresses how the idea of Christian charity (*caritas*) gave women the space to participate in a religious culture of friendship because 'followers of Christ were prompted to love one another despite their differences

---

[23] See, e.g., G. J. Barker-Benfield, *The Culture of Sensibility: Sex and Society in Eighteenth-Century Britain* (London, 1992), pp. 29–30; Susan Broomhall (ed.), *Spaces for Feeling: Emotions and Sociabilities in Britain, 1650–1850* (London, 2015); Lawrence E. Klein, 'Gender, Conversation and the Public Sphere in Early Eighteenth-Century England', in Michael Worton and Judith Still (eds.), *Textuality and Sexuality: Reading Theories and Practices* (Manchester, 1993), pp. 100–115; Sarah Knott, *Sensibility and the American Revolution* (Chapel Hill, NC, 2009); and David S. Shields, *Civil Tongues and Polite Letters in British America* (Chapel Hill, NC, 1997), pp. 11–54 and 99–140. For changing epistolary practices see James Daybell (ed.), *Early Modern Women's Letter Writing, 1450–1700* (Basingstoke, 2001); and Susan E. Whyman, *The Pen and the People: English Letter Writers 1660–1800* (Oxford, 2009), esp. pp. 112–157.

[24] Susan E. Klepp and Karin Wulf suggest that this new emphasis on sensibility gave women greater influence at social gatherings and thus in the public sphere, 'Introduction: Hannah Callender Sansom and Her World', in Susan E. Klepp and Karin Wulf (eds.), *The Diary of Hannah Callender Sansom: Sense and Sensibility in the Age of the American Revolution* (London, 2010), pp. 2–3.

[25] Hannah Woolley, *The Gentlewomans Companion: Or a Guide to the Female Sex* (London, 1673), pp. 220–230.

[26] N. H., *The Ladies Dictionary; Being a General Entertainment for the Fair-Sex* (London, 1694), p. 223.

[27] Amanda E. Herbert, *Female Alliances: Gender, Identity, and Friendship in Early Modern Britain* (London, 2014), p. 24.

and inequalities'.[28] Intimate friendships, as Sara Mendelson and Patricia Crawford have argued, could be reinforced by shared faith. They argue that religious devotion should be placed within a broader framework of 'collective feminine experience'.[29]

Recent surveys into the shared communal cultures of seventeenth- and eighteenth-century Quaker women have offered some revision in our understanding of friendship formation within Quakerism.[30] However, no study asks how the experience of friendship for Quaker women was altered by their adherence to the movement. In 1982 Nancy Tomes stated, with reference to colonial Quakerism, that 'the networks formed by women's social activities have never been given the acknowledgment they deserve'.[31] We still lack a detailed study that investigates how the terminology of friendship was used by Quaker women to add meaning to their everyday lives and relationships. This chapter seeks to rectify this historiographical omission by focusing upon how the experience of being 'Friends' shaped women's social interactions. Close examination of seemingly uncomplicated declarations of friendship, as used by early Quaker writers, reveals a multifaceted and complex picture of early modern alliance formation.

THE THEOLOGY AND LANGUAGE OF QUAKER FRIENDSHIP

The very existence of the Quaker movement was underpinned by Christian understandings of friendship: a spiritual community of believers, united by a shared religion of experience. The word 'Friend' appears repeatedly throughout Quaker writings, but its meanings vary widely. This supports Tadmor's

---

[28] Ibid., p. 26.

[29] Mendelson and Crawford, *Women in Early Modern England*, pp. 225–231.

[30] The most significant contribution has come from Herbert's recent work *Female Alliances*, which takes the special bond between travelling Quaker companions as an example of female alliance building in seventeenth-century Britain. Herbert, *Female Alliances*, pp. 142–167.

Other important contributions have come from literary studies, especially Catie Gill's assessment of Quaker women's multiple-authored texts, and from studies of later periods of Quakerism, including Sandra Stanley Holton's work on nineteenth-century Quaker women's network formations and Sheila Wright's assessment of Quaker women's friendships in the period 1750–1900. Catie Gill, *Women in the Seventeenth-Century Quaker Community: A Literary Study of Political Identities, 1650–1700* (Aldershot, 2005), pp. 184–185; Sandra Stanley Holton, 'Kinship and Friendship: Quaker Women's Networks and the Women's Movement', *Women's Historical Review*, vol. 14, nos. 3 and 4 (2005), pp. 365–384; and Sheila Wright, '"Every Good Woman Needs a Companion of Her Own Sex": Quaker Women and Spiritual Friendship, 1750–1850', in Sue Morgan (ed.), *Women, Religion and Feminism in Britain, 1750–1900* (Basingstoke, 2002), pp. 89–104.

[31] Nancy Tomes, 'The Quaker Connection: Visiting Patterns among Women in the Philadelphia Society of Friends, 1750–1800', in Michael Zuckerman (ed.), *Friends and Neighbours: Group Life in America's First Plural Society* (Philadelphia, 1982), p. 192.

claim that for early modern men and women, 'friend' was a flexible term.[32] At times, it was employed by individuals who regarded themselves as part of the Quaker community of 'Friends', and on other occasions it was reserved as a term of endearment for close personal friends, acquaintances, and, on occasion, members of the household.

Beyond its application, the lexicon of 'friendship' was also highly varied. Although 'Friend' was by far the most common and universal form of address that permeated all Quaker writings from this period, the bonds of Quaker friendship were also characterised by a multiplicity of phrases and adjectives. Quaker leaders described one another as a 'fellowship', 'family', and 'household'. In a series of letters, the early Quaker leader Richard Hubberthorne wrote to Margaret Fell, who he variously addressed as 'my dear hart', 'dear sister in the eternall power of the living god', 'dear one', and 'my dear and pretious sister'. He described their friendship as a 'fellowship which can never bee broken', a 'dear union', and 'unity' and signed his communication as 'Thy brother in the Lord'.[33]

One striking feature of early Quakerism was the diverse range of individuals addressed as 'Friends', which encompassed not only the movement's converts, but also its opponents. In a letter to William Lancaster, who had purportedly written 'a Paper of great Objection against us, the People called Quakers', George Whitehead, along with six other members of the Society, addressed him as their 'Friend'. They subscribed the letter, which was later printed in Whitehead's *An Antidote Against the Venome of the Snake in the Grass*, as 'thy Friends and Well-wishers'.[34] Jacques Derrida in his philosophical examination of friendship reminded scholars to look at friendship's binary constructions and to remember that the term implies absence and hostility, as much as its literal implications of perfection.[35] Quaker authors were notorious for their confrontational written attacks against their opponents. Yet, the decision of some Quaker authors to address their opponents as their 'Friends' implies an all-encompassing notion of friendship that could be positive and seemingly unrestricted. Alice Curwen, for example, described the mayor of Plymouth, Richard Tomes, a notorious persecutor of

---

[32] Tadmor, *Family and Friends*, p. 167.

[33] LRSF, MS Vol S 81 Caton MSS vol. 3, pp. 326–336, Copies of Richard Hubbertone letters to Margaret Fell, undated, c. 1654.

[34] Printed in George Whitehead, *An Antidote against the Venome of the Snake in the Grass* (London, 1697), pp. viii–xi, John Gratton, Samuel Watson, Thomas Lower, James Parke, John Bowater, George Whitehead, and John Vaughton to 'Friend William Lancaster', London, 3 June 1695.

[35] Jacques Derrida, *The Politics of Friendship* (London, 1997), pp. 32–33. This idea is explored in Daniel T. Lochman and Maritere López, 'Introduction: The Emergence of Discourses: Early Modern Friendship', in Lochman, López, and Hutson, *Discourses and Representations of Friendship*, p. 13.

local Quakers, as a 'Friend', requesting that he 'be not stir[r]ed up against a peaceable People that meets together singlely to worship'.[36]

In many respects, this universalised notion of friendship was an extension of the wider Christian tradition of *caritas*, which encompassed universal, brotherly, and communal love. The Bible taught individuals to 'Love your enemies' and 'do good to them that hate you' (Matthew 5:44). Theologians like Thomas Aquinas and Aelred of Rievaulx saw the 'spiritual' kinship created by baptism as a source of universal friendship, and argued that love should not be limited to a man's friends, but extended to his neighbour and fellow man.[37] This Sermon on the Mount trope continued to permeate early modern thought, as writers like Jeremy Taylor recognised the importance of Christian charity in the performance of friendship. He noted how 'there is enough in every man that is willing, to make him become our friend' and went on to explain that 'he who was to treat his enemies with forgiveness and prayers, and love and beneficence was indeed to have no enemies, and to have all friends'.[38] The religious idealisation of *caritas* viewed the love of an enemy as admirable, because it was a reflection of God's love.

However, there was a clear tension in its practical application. 'When men either are unnatural or irreligious', Taylor wrote, 'they *will not* be friends.' He also noted that strangers '*cannot be friends* actually and practically'.[39] Moreover, a preoccupation of many writings on the subject was how to discern a true friend from an enemy in disguise.[40] Henry Sacheverell's sermon on *The Perils of False Brethren*, for example, conveyed the deep-seated anxieties surrounding the deceptive influence of Satan when it came to the issues of religion and politics. Indeed, as Sacheverell explained, the Church was not only under attack from 'professed enemies', but also from those who 'pretended to defend it'.[41] The universalised notion of 'Friend' used by early Quakers, by contrast, did not need to distinguish a friend from an enemy, because all had the power to enter into divine communion. Early Quaker calls for repentance, for instance, served as affirmation of the regenerative power of the inner light, where God's grace was freely available to all and everyone was viewed as a potential friend. Grace Barwick whose 1659 printed call for repentance, *To All Present Rulers, Whether Parliament, or*

---

[36] Anne Martindell et al., *A Relation of the Labour, Travail and Suffering of that Faithful Servant of the Lord, Alice Curwen* (1680), pp. 27–28.

[37] Tadmor, *Family and Friends*, pp. 238–239; and Bray, *The Friend*, pp. 254–258.

[38] Taylor, *The Measures and Offices of Friendship*, pp. 12–13.

[39] Ibid., p. 16.

[40] Carolyn James and Bill Kent, 'Renaissance Friendships: Traditional Truths, New and Dissenting Voices', in Caine, *Friendship: A History*, p. 117.

[41] Cited in Mark Knights, *The Devil in Disguise: Deception, Delusion and Fanaticism in the Early English Enlightenment* (Oxford, 2011), p. 147.

Whomsoever of England, referred to her persecutors and unknown readers as 'Friends', whilst Esther Biddle addressed the inhabitants of London, as 'my dear beloved friends, who are friends of God' and exhorted them to 'dwell together in the life immortal'.[42] The desire to dispense with all social differences led Anne Clayton in *A Letter to the King*, to address the returning sovereign Charles II as her 'dear Friend' and 'dear Heart'.[43]

The tension inherent in this universalised notion of friendship meant that early Quakers also faced the challenge of putting it into practice. Of particular concern to early Friends, was the question of whether the highest form of friendship was available to individuals who did not share the same relationship to 'truth'. After the initial zeal of the first few decades, Friends increasingly came to view themselves as 'saints' working towards a common end. Indeed, the more 'quietist' movement of the eighteenth century has been characterised by its inward-looking focus and concomitant stress on forging alliances between believers rather than extensive missionary efforts beyond the movement. This emphasis on more selective friendship is encapsulated in an interesting exposition penned by Sophia Hume in 1750. 'The sacred and expressive name of friendship', she wrote, 'belongs only to those whose souls are united by this holy cement ... yet where this holy attraction and sacred Bond is wanting the friendship is defective, cold, incompleat and insip[i]d.'[44]

Moments of tension and conflict, at a local or national level, also severely tested the Quaker commitment to seeing enemies as potential Friends. At times, such pressures encouraged Quakers to think of persecutors as un-Christian and therefore beyond the universalism of Christian charity. Early Quakers often took glee in citing examples of providential punishment against their oppressors.[45] Elizabeth Andrews, an early Quaker preacher from Shropshire, described the 'heavy hand of God' in the circumstances surrounding the sudden death of a local persecuting priest, Tobiah Ogden. Ogden had ordered local magistrates to raid her shop and business of goods, but she noted how a few days later, Ogden was 'grievously troubled with the Stone [kidney stones] and lived not long afterwards'.[46] Although this stands

---

[42] The persecutors to whom Barwick was referring were General John Lambert 'and the rest of the Officers' and included her own husband. Grace Barwick, *To All Present Rulers, Whether Parliament, or Whomsoever of England* (London, 1659), pp. 1–2; and Esther Biddle, *A Warning from the Lord God of Life and Power, Unto Thee O City of London* (1660), p. 18.

[43] Anne Clayton, *A Letter to the King* (London, c. 1660), p. 1.

[44] HCQSC, MS Coll 1000 Gulielma M. Howland Collection, Box 6, Sophia Hume folder, Sophia Hume to unknown, undated, c. 1750.

[45] On Quakers and providential punishment see Naomi Pullin, 'Providence, Punishment and Identity Formation in the Late-Stuart Quaker Community, c. 1650–1700', *The Seventeenth Century*, vol. 31, no. 4 (2016), pp. 471–494.

[46] LRSF, Portfolio MSS, vol. 36, fol. 161, 'An Account of the Birth, and Education, with the Services and Sufferings for Truth's Sake, of That Faithful Friend Eliz[abeth] Andrews', undated, later 1690s.

at odds with universalist ideals of friendship, citing examples of providential punishment firmly placed the ability to make and break friendships in the hands of God. It was divine intervention rather than individual choice that ultimately decided whether an individual was to be a Friend or an enemy, and He would mete out justice accordingly.

The contradictions in Quaker Friendship, however, were most apparent when the movement faced its own internal crises. Among them was the schism led by George Keith in Philadelphia in the 1690s, caused by a public dispute about ministerial authority and doctrinal emphasis.[47] This split forced those who remained in the Society to question whether those 'who have given the highest Demonstrations of Their being our greatest Enemies' could be 'owned and received as Friends, as Brethren, as Preachers, as Ministers of Christ amongst us'.[48]

One of the effects of the more quietist and introspective outlook of second- and third-generation Quakerism was the still greater emphasis placed on individual piety, with members urged to refrain from all activities that distracted the mind from its focus on God. Mercy Bell, for example, warned her friend, Priscilla Farmer of the dangers of too much social interaction. 'I know its the common way to persuade People into Company', she wrote, 'indeed the company of a particular Friend may be of service, but in a general way Company is oppressive.'[49] In 1753, Richard Shackleton commented to a female acquaintance that her letter had brought him a great deal of joy. However, he also warned that 'some expressions' about the love she held for her companion, Mary Peisley, 'were more jealous than orthodox'. 'I know thou lovest Mary Peisley very well, so do I', he wrote, 'but she will love us both the better for loving her no more than we ought to do.' He advised that 'to love our dear Friends out of their places, that is; to love them to Excess and not for God's sake only' was akin to self-love.[50] Elizabeth Dennis was praised in her posthumous testimony for not being distracted from either her domestic or spiritual labours, although 'her Company was much desired by many'.[51] Similarly, the

---

[47] For more on the Keithian Schism see William C. Braithwaite, *The Second Period of Quakerism* (2nd edn, rev. H. J. Cadbury, Cambridge, 1961), pp. 482–487; and Hugh Barbour and J. William Frost, *The Quakers* (London, 1988), pp. 343–344.

[48] Thomas Ellwood, *A Reply to an Answer: Lately Published to a Book Long Since Written by W. P. Entitled, A Brief Examination and State of Liberty Spiritual*, &c. (London, 1691), pp. 11–12.

[49] LRSF, Temp MSS 403/1/2/3/4 Arthur B. Braithwaite Family Papers, Mercy Bell to Priscilla Farmer, undated, c. 1756.

[50] HL, mssSHA Shackleton Family Correspondence, Box 1, fol. 310, Richard Shackleton to Elizabeth Hutchinson, Ballitore, 23 September 1752.

[51] It was also noted how she would not leave her home, 'unless necessity, either to visit the Churches, or upon the account of her Business, called her to it'. LRSF, YM/TCDM Testimonies Concerning Ministers Deceased, vol. 1 1728–1758, pp. 285–286, 'A Testimony Concerning our Deceased Friend Elizabeth Dennis', 3 March 1749.

autobiography of the American Quaker minister Elizabeth Hudson under-scored the potential consequences of placing the needs of a friend before the needs of God:

Here I missed my way by gratifying my own will,...[and] pursued the track laid out by my companion and left that truth [which] would have opened more clear had I kept a single eye to it.

Hudson went on to warn her readers to keep 'a single eye to the Divine leader, not suffering our affections to any companion whatsoever to bias our enlightened judgements and draw us from pursuing that track truth directs us to follow'.[52] Too much focus on temporal needs and personal relation-ships would distract Friends from a greater spiritual calling.

This fitted into wider religious models that viewed all forms of temporal association as a distraction from the pursuit of godliness. Saint Teresa of Avila felt that one of her greatest faults was her attachment to her friends, until God told her, 'I will have thee converse now, not with men, but with angels.' Thereafter, her saintly lifestyle was praised because she chose to place God before all other personal relationships.[53] Moreover, the Quaker ideal also corresponded to the Calvinist model of friendship, where an indi-vidual's obedience to divine commands was placed above all other temporal connections. As a consequence, friendship was never viewed by Calvinists as anything more than a temporal pleasure or relationship of necessity. Sarah Savage, a strict Presbyterian, found that her faith prevented her from form-ing friendships with other women. Indeed, she shunned most occasions for social interaction, which she viewed as 'wasteful and decadent'. As Herbert notes, in devoting herself to an individualistic regime of personal devotion, she struggled to balance 'her duty to be friendly and loving to her female relations with the demands of her Nonconformist conscience'.[54]

As with their Predestinarian counterparts, earthly friendship for early Quakers was considered imperfect compared to their heavenly alliance. However, Quakerism was unusual in the emphasis it placed on the temporal benefits of friendship, when viewed within the context of collective salva-tion. Since Christ was present in all, friendship was with Christ, as much as with the person he inhabited. The notorious activity of quaking performed by early Friends, for example, has been characterised as a 'dissolution of

---

[52] Elizabeth Hudson, 'An Abstract of the Travels and Some Other Remarks of Eliza Hudson, from 22nd of 1st Month 1742', in Margaret Hope Bacon (ed.), *Wilt Thou Go on My Errand? Journals of Three 18th Century Quaker Women Ministers: Susanna Morris, 1682–1775; Elizabeth Hudson, 1722–1783; Ann Moore, 1710–1783* (Wallingford, PA, 1994), p. 185.

[53] Saint Teresa of Avila, *The Life of the Holy Mother Teresa of Jesus*, in *The Complete Works of St Teresa of Jesus*, ed. E. Allison Peers (3 vols., London, 1946), vol. 1, p. 155.

[54] A detailed micro-historical analysis of Sarah Savage's diaries is provided in Herbert, *Female Alliances*, pp. 168–193.

the individual personality'. It was through the 'sensation of melting', Mack argues, that a collective group identity was formed.[55] The strong, inherent preference of the early Quakers to see the possibilities of a wider, more inclusive community was reconfigured into other forms of universal association. William Penn, for instance, in his *One Project for the Good of England* (c. 1697), argued that collective interest of different religious groups could be a basis for toleration. He suggested that love of God should be the basis of a civil union between Anglicans and dissenters that would transcend self-interest and religious differences. It was not in 'the Interest of England', he wrote, 'to let a great Part of her Sober and Useful Inhabitants be destroy'd about things that concern another World'.[56] As Geoff Baldwin has argued, Penn put forward a radical view of Christian endeavour that imagined the public as a 'very close-knit community', defined by common interest rather than 'a colder, more distant, contractarian relationship'.[57] From this perspective, Quakerism opened up an important space in which it was possible to accommodate an expansive interpretation of friendship, which could create heavenly communion and recognise the spiritual benefits that close bonds between fellow believers on earth could bring to the individual.

Thus, in contrast to both the Catholic and dissenting models of friendship, Quakers managed to maintain a social cohesiveness and sense of community with other members, whilst also pursuing their own singular spiritual calling. Predestinarian doctrines emphasised the exclusivity of those able to achieve salvation and thus made it harder for those who adhered to a godly lifestyle to enter any relationship that might distract them from their higher calling. Indeed, as Thomas Heilke has found, there was 'no substantive role for friendship' in Calvin's conception of religious community.[58] The model of community proposed by Quakers, by contrast, made it entirely possible for idealised spiritual alliances between believers to coexist with more universalised notions of friendship. This was epitomised in the famous 1778 debate involving Dr Johnson and the 'ingenious Quaker lady', Mrs Knowles, who discoursed on the validity of friendship as a Christian virtue. During the discussion, which was published in James Boswell's biography of Samuel Johnson, Mrs Knowles countered Johnson's argument that all friendship involved preferring the interest of one friend over another, by explaining that God had ordered good to be done to all men, 'but especially to them who are of the household of Faith'. She then proceeded to close the debate by citing Christ's special love for John: 'our

---

[55] Mack, *Visionary Women*, p. 150.

[56] William Penn, *One Project for the Good of England* (London, c. 1679), p. 5.

[57] Geoff Baldwin, 'The 'Public' as a Rhetorical Community in Early Modern England', in Alexandra Shepard and Phil Withington (eds.), *Communities in Early Modern England: Networks, Place, Rhetoric* (Manchester, 2000), pp. 211–212.

[58] Heilke, 'From Civic Friendship to Communities of Believers', p. 227.

Saviour had twelve Apostles, yet there was *one* whom he *loved*. John was called "the disciple whom Jesus loved."'[59] Through presenting their union as something embodied in the relationship between Jesus and his disciples, Quaker theorists like Knowles reasoned that to be regarded as a true Friend an individual must share in their vision of a holy covenant or community. Nevertheless, as Knowles's argument makes clear, it was possible for special friendship to operate in conjunction with, rather than opposition to, more universalised notions of Christian charity. Everyone should be loved as friends, but intimacy was expected to be kept by a few friends who were co-religionists.

A recurring theme of Quaker women's writings was the companionship their shared religious communion brought to their relationships. Writing to Priscilla Farmer, Mercy Bell saluted her friend with the acknowledgement that 'thou art and hast of late been much the Companion of my thoughts even when [I] should sleep [I] am conversing with thee'.[60] Her conversation, as she later explained, was 'Scripture Language', which had been 'presented to my mind'.[61] The Philadelphian Friend Sarah Morris provided an important exposition of Quaker friendship in her musings on the subject. 'Where I profess Friendship, and entertain it', she wrote:

I would have it strengthen in the Root, and increase in the Genuine pleasant and beneficial fruits ... It examples, and inculcates piety; and the belief of another World ... This is Friendship imutable, a Companionship in the knowledge, love and faith of Jesus.[62]

In both cases, female Friends not only expressed the sense of companionship they experienced with their distant readers as a complementary partnership, but also as a relationship born out of a shared spiritual journey together.[63] It was powerfully expressed in a letter Sarah Taylor sent to her 'Dear Friend and Companion' Ruth Follows in 1770. Of particular importance was how she chose to sign the epistle: 'be asur'd I am in wonted near Union and affection thy real and simpathizing Friend and Sister Pilgrim'.[64]

---

[59] Mrs Knowles's famous defeat of Samuel Johnson was witnessed by James Boswell and later published in his biography of Johnson: James Boswell, *The Life of Samuel Johnson, LL.D.* (2 vols., London, 1791), vol. 2, p. 226. Boswell records the debate as occurring on 15 April 1778 during dinner at the house of John and Charles Dilly.

[60] This rather disjointed sentence has been quoted accurately from the original.

[61] LRSF, Temp MSS 403/1/2/3/4 Arthur B. Braithwaite Family Papers, Mercy Bell to Priscilla Farmer, undated, c. 1756.

[62] HSP, MS Coll 484A Pemberton Family Papers, vol. 3, p. 159, sentiments of friendship found among the papers of Sarah Morris, undated, c. 1745.

[63] Rebecca Larson has drawn attention to the importance of these bonds of friendship for Sarah Morris, who never married. In her will, she bequeathed sums to eight women ministers from different regions listed as 'esteemed friends'. Rebecca Larson, *Daughters of Light: Quaker Women Preaching and Prophesying in the Colonies and Abroad, 1700–1775* (New York, 1999), p. 131.

[64] LRSF, Temp MSS 127/1/1/13 Ruth Follows Papers, Sarah Taylor to Ruth Follows, Manchester, 28 September 1770.

The symbolic decision to describe their friendship as a 'pilgrimage' encapsulated the spiritual journey Friends believed they shared with their Quaker acquaintances. Although not physical travelling companions, it was believed that their mutual spiritual affinity would enable them to navigate the trials of their faith in this life and thus further their understanding of their lives in the next.

FRIENDSHIP AND THE 'HOUSEHOLD OF FAITH'

Tangible bonds formed between fellow members were strengthened by the allusion to a single spiritual family. A popular trope in Quaker writings across the period was the concept of Friends being united together within a 'family and Household of faith'.[65] The metaphorical 'household' implied spiritual unity and friendship, as manifested through a single body of believers. Quakers called each other 'brother', 'sister', 'father', and 'mother', and they offered one another spiritual, emotional, and economic support as imaginary family members. Crucially, this was occurring at the same time as individual members were temporarily or permanently breaking bonds with their biological families through joining the movement. New understandings of friendship were thus developed by Quakers as a means of assuaging the loss of their former personal and social alliances. Anne Audland, for instance, used deeply passionate and emotive language to describe the relationship that had evolved between herself and the Quaker leader Margaret Fell. When Anne was imprisoned at Banbury gaol in Oxfordshire in 1655, she reported her sufferings to the Quaker elder, who she variously described as 'my dear and pretious sister in whom my life is bound up', 'dear h[e]art', and 'my eternall mother'.[66] Anne's metaphorical usage of familial language and sibling bonds testifies to the ways in which rhetoric enabled women to emphasise solidarity in the face of adversity. Her choice of address to Margaret Fell as 'eternall mother' suggests the re-imagining of family, and more specifically the parent-child bond, within the writings of early Friends.

It was naturally more common for Friends to imagine themselves as part of a religious family in the earliest years of the movement, when many of their own relations were not Quakers. Nonetheless, this reconfiguration of the language of amity was still appropriated by second- and third-generation Friends. The Quaker Women's Meeting of Aberdeen, for example, addressed their 1700 epistle to the Women's Box Meeting in London to their 'Dear

---

[65] LRSF, MS Vol 335 Gibson MSS, fol. 3, Samuel Neale to Ann and Sally Kendal, Amsterdam, 10 September 1752.
[66] LRSF, MS Vol S 81 Caton MSS vol. 3, pp. 431–433, Anne Audland to Margaret Fell, Banbury Gaol, 5 February 1655.

Friends: Mothers and Sisters whome we do esteeme and Honour in the Lord and in the Everlasting Covenant of light'.[67] The image underlines the sense of familial closeness shared by Quaker Meetings, despite the distance that separated them.[68] In presenting themselves as children, they sought strength and advice as they underwent the various trials of their faith. Thus, despite the impact of changing circumstances and a sense that friendship with fellow members did not have to act as a substitute for the loss of personal relationships, Friends nevertheless continued to imagine themselves as part of a spiritualised family. A revealing letter sent from Lydia Lancaster to Samuel Fothergill in 1756, which she signed: 'thy true and faithfull friend, sister and companion in the suferings of Jesus ... acording to my measure', underscores the continued prominence of a spiritual Quaker household.[69] Moreover, after being accused of fraudulent business dealings in 1727, Israel Hale wrote a letter of thanks to his friend Sarah Lloyd. He reflected on their 'close affinity' during his incarceration, and revealingly stated that 'the Lord he Raised thee up to be as a mother to me, not only in the outward but in the thinges of God'.[70]

The metaphorical allusion to a spiritual family, however, was not exclusive to Quakerism. Baptists, Congregationalists, and many other sectarian Protestant groups referred to each other as 'Brother' and 'Sister'. The Methodists embraced very similar expressions as the Quakers, also choosing to refer to one another as 'brother', 'sister', 'father', and 'mother', which they regarded as 'the best of bonds'.[71] However, in clear contrast to the model of domestic arrangements propounded by Quakers, these Methodist spiritual families were expected to replace other temporal connections, resulting in what Anna M. Lawrence describes as a de-emphasis on the traditional family. Many women shunned their familial ties and obligations to live in same-sex communities, where friendship with other Methodist women was expected to act as a substitute for, rather than an accompaniment to, the biological family. It was important, for example, for Methodist writers

---

[67] LRSF, MGR 1104 London Women's Meeting Epistles, 1671–1753, fol. 53, epistle from Aberdeen Women's Meeting to the Women's Meeting in London, 6 April 1700.

[68] As Betty Hagglund has shown, the later-established Women's Meeting in Aberdeen initiated a correspondence with their more experienced elders in London, with a sense of being spiritually immature. Betty Hagglund, 'Changes in Roles and Relationships: Multiauthored Epistles from the Aberdeen Quaker Women's Meeting', in Carolyn D. Williams, Angela Escott, and Louise Duckling (eds.), *Woman to Woman: Female Negotiations during the Long Eighteenth Century* (Newark, DE, 2010), pp. 143–144.

[69] LRSF, MS Vol 329 Crossfield MS, fol. 59, Lydia Lancaster to Samuel Fothergill, Lancaster, 10 February 1756.

[70] LRSF, Temp MSS 210/1/165 Lloyd MSS, p. 72. Israel Hale to Sarah Lloyd, Reading, 10 December 1727.

[71] Anna M. Lawrence, *One Family under God: Love, Belonging, and Authority in Early Transatlantic Methodism* (Philadelphia, 2011), p. 72.

to see themselves as orphans separated from their natural families before they could develop relationships with their new religious family. Moreover, in contrast to early Quakers, the model of friendship idealised within Methodism continued to express these relationships in terms of traditional hierarchical bonds between family members. These terms invoked status, as fathers and mothers dominated local organisations. As a consequence, they 'replicated the titles, emotions, and supports of the nuclear family structure'.[72] The Methodist preacher Mary Bosanquet described herself as the 'daughter' of her friend Sarah Ryan, a choice of expression that enabled her to 'replace her own critical and distant natural mother with a friend whose love was both ardent and protective'.[73] Thus unlike Quakerism, the intensity of the same-sex spiritual connections that emerged in Methodist church culture meant that friendship became incompatible with the continuation of domestic relationships. Instead, Methodist women like Bosanquet and Ryan created new domestic arrangements where their enhanced opportunities for companionship led to a renunciation of traditional household order.

The notion of spiritual friendship advocated by early Friends was non-hierarchical: anyone could be a 'father' or 'mother' in the Quaker spiritual household, and they did not necessarily occupy positions of authority at the top of the movement's hierarchy. Instead of denoting status, 'father' and 'mother' were idioms commonly employed to show respect and deference to those Friends who had powerful spiritual callings. Many were elders more experienced in the faith. Thus when Quakers used the terms 'brother' and 'sister' or 'father' and 'mother', their language and actions implied the erasure of hierarchical distinctions; they acknowledged each other as 'real equals'.[74] Even where Friends like Anne Audland or the Aberdeen Women's Meeting described themselves as children, they never had to submit to the authority or rule of discipline of their spiritual parents.

One important outcome of this belief in disembodied alliances was that their spiritualised household was entirely separated from gendered distinctions, giving male and female believers extraordinary space in which to forge their friendships. The collective practice of Quaker spirituality made it possible for intimate bonds to develop between male and female believers. Lydia Lancaster, for instance, described the 'freedom to communicate to thee as a bosom friend', when recounting her spiritual experiences to Samuel Fothergill in 1756.[75] Other male writers also described sharing a

---

[72] Ibid., pp. 72–73.

[73] Phyllis Mack, *Heart Religion in the British Enlightenment: Gender and Emotion in Early Methodism* (Cambridge, 2008), p. 160.

[74] Lawrence, *One Family under God*, p. 6.

[75] LRSF, MS Vol 329 Crossfield MS, fol. 59, Lydia Lancaster to Samuel Fothergill, Lancaster, 10 February 1756.

close intimate relationship with female members of the community. In 1702, J. Alexander explained to Mary Holme, a young unmarried woman, that 'in order that we might sing prayses unto our God ... we might take hand in hand in a spiritual sense and help one [an]other on our way and so be a help and strength to each other'.[76] His revealing expressions show the powerful form in which spiritual friendships could be imagined. Indeed, the non-somatic nature of this union connecting a single man and woman was visualised through the imaginary act of taking one another by the hand and leading each other along the path to righteousness.

Read in its historical context, the idealised Quaker notion of friendship shared by men and women provided an unusual accompaniment to the wider literary and religious debate about the relationship between gender and friendship. It was a subject of continual contention within early modern society. Helen Berry's research into the world of John Dunton's *Athenian Mercury* has revealed that readers' questions throughout the 1690s were preoccupied with the issue of platonic love and whether non-sexual friendship was possible between men and women. In its reply, the periodical acknowledged that 'Platonick Love ... undoubtedly is possible', but that love and desire were usually interconnected.[77] This view of restrictive friendship between the sexes was supported by the attitudes of early modern conduct writers. Jeremy Taylor debated whether women could make such good friends as men: 'A man is the best friend in trouble ... a woman can as well increase our comforts, but cannot so well lessen our sorrows.'[78] Moreover, the author of *The Ladies Dictionary* responded to the question of whether friendship contracted by single persons could continue with 'the same Zeal and Innocence if either Marry' by noting that 'It *may*, tho Ten to One if it does; since in those Circumstances there will be great hazard that either the Innocence will spoil the Zeal, or the Zeal the Innocence.'[79] Through styling their alliances as a purely spiritual experience, outside of the body, Quakers provided an acceptable alternative space for intimate bonds to develop between men and women, without raising concerns over their moral integrity. As Sheila Wright argues, in inhabiting a shared 'spiritual sphere', Quakers established a world that was not clearly defined by 'gendered separate spheres'.[80] Thomas Lancaster, for example, argued in his testimony of the Yorkshire minister Tabitha Hornor, that an 'intimate

---

[76] LRSF, MS Vol 334 Gibson MSS, fol. 4, J. Alexander to Mary Holme Junior, Bendrigg, Kendal, 22 February 1703.

[77] Berry, *Gender, Society and Print Culture*, p. 224.

[78] Taylor, *The Measures and Offices of Friendship*, p. 103.

[79] N. H., *The Ladies Dictionary*, p. 196.

[80] Wright, '"Every Good Woman Needs a Companion of Her Own Sex"', p. 90.

acquaintance' had been made possible, because 'she was Male and Female being all one in Christ'.[81]

The ideal of Christian fellowship advocated by early Friends emphasised the indiscriminate nature of friendship shared by like-minded souls. Clearly, the changing outlook of the movement, combined with the inherent ambiguities in the practice of Christian charity, provided some tensions in how Friends performed and understood their alliances. Nevertheless, Quaker writers appear to have successfully found a theoretical balance between the pursuit of personal piety and a more universalised notion of friendship within the community of 'saints'. As Mack notes, Friends 'aimed for nothing less than the experience of a divine presence, or indwelling, in their own bodies', whilst also aspiring for 'friendship and spiritual empathy with the entire community of Quakers'.[82] This stress on the spiritualised non-physical aspects of friendship stands in opposition to Bray's observations on the ethics of friendship, which he argued centred on the symbolism surrounding the 'body' of the friend. He argued that this was the 'unifying symbol across the world', which he characterised through three familiar signs: the public embrace, the shared bed, and the common table.[83]

When examined within broader social contexts, Quakerism appears to have offered a model of friendship that was generally more spacious than those practised within other dissenting movements and wider society. The Quaker belief that enemies could be brought within their circle of amity, and thus regarded as 'Friends', is one example of this. However, it was how the relationship between men and women was expressed that constituted an important deviation from contemporary norms. Indeed, the idea that all relationships should be performed between equals, regardless of sex or race, paralleled those theories justifying women's place as spiritual authorities within the Society. The spiritualised aspect of their alliances was derived solely from God and transcended all other temporal concerns, making it easier for Quakers of the opposite sex to enter friendships with one another.

'THE SOVEREIGN BALM OF LIFE': THE PRACTICE AND MAINTENANCE OF QUAKER FRIENDSHIP

The strongest bonds of friendship were formed between those who shared the same spiritual relationship to 'truth'. However, as noted, there has been little exploration of how Quakerism altered the practice of friendship within

---

[81] LRSF, MSS Box G2/2 Hornor Family Papers, pp. 63, 65, 'Extracts from Thomas Lancaster's Testimony Concerning Tabitha Hornor', Sedbergh, Cumbria, 24 May 1747.
[82] Mack, *Visionary Women*, p. 143.
[83] Bray, *The Friend*, p. 268.

women's daily lives. Religious affiliation, as Sue Morgan has argued, offered women opportunities to develop 'sororial networks through lives bound by shared religious practices in close-knit communities'.[84] The lives of Quaker women were structured around many of the same gendered practices of sociability performed by women across early modern society, including epistolary exchange, visiting patterns, and hospitality. However, they also faced isolation and persecution for their religious beliefs, finding themselves cut off from their former acquaintances, their own families, and wider cultural customs. Joan Vokins, for instance, remarked in her life account that 'I turned my back on the World, and all the friendship and glory of it, [so] that I might obtain the favour of Jesus.'[85]

As a 'peculiar people', the customs by which Quakers differentiated their private, public, and spiritual lives from the rest of society shaped how their friendships were expressed and performed. Quaker women's adherence to a strict culture of austerity and plainness served to mark them as 'separate' from other women within their neighbourhoods and local communities. Their status as outsiders was aptly expressed by Thomas Clarkson in his appraisal of Quaker customs and habits:

It cannot be expected that persons, educated like the Quakers, should assimilate much in their manners to other people ... Excluded also from much intercourse with the world, and separated at a vast distance from it by the singularity of many of their customs, they would naturally appear to others to be close and reserved. Neither is it to be expected that those, whose spirits are never animated by music, or enlivened by the exhibitions of the theatre, or the diversions which others follow, would have other than grave countenances.

Clarkson's assessment of what he termed the Quaker 'gait' highlights the vast cultural gulf separating Friends from wider society.[86] By the eighteenth century, the leisure activities that usually afforded women opportunities to develop friendships were perceived by Friends as distractions from their higher spiritual calling. These included dancing, attending the theatre, reading romances, following the latest fashions, and socialising in places like coffee houses and salons. One 1691 epistle issued by the London Yearly Meeting warned Friends against the dangers of 'unprofitable and idle discourses' and advised members to 'watch against, and keep out, the spirit and corrupt friendship of the world'.[87] Because they were isolated from their

---

[84] Sue Morgan, 'Women, Religion and Feminism: Past, Present and Future Perspectives', in Morgan, *Women, Religion and Feminism*, pp. 10–11.

[85] Joan Vokins, *God's Mighty Power Magnified: As Manifested and Revealed in His Faithful Handmaid Joan Vokins* (London, 1691), p. 22.

[86] Thomas Clarkson, *A Portraiture of Quakerism* (3 vols., New York, 1806), vol. 1, pp. 328–329.

[87] London Yearly Meeting, *Extracts from the Minutes and Advices of the Yearly Meeting of Friends Held in London* (London, 1783), p. 25.

neighbours, Quaker women were forced to look elsewhere for sympathetic and supportive friendships: to fellow believers.

Religious worship has long been recognised for the opportunities for interaction and social solidarity it provided.[88] In the Quaker case, however, this had added significance as the Meeting House and the provision of separate Women's Meetings became important sites of female sociability. Not only did it provide a safe environment for like-minded women to physically meet, but it also offered them an opportunity to share in spiritual communion. This was revealed in an undated letter sent by Mercy Bell to Priscilla Farmer, who had been absent from their local Meeting. 'People may acceptably serve and worship the Almighty in private and its our Duty as well as in publick', she wrote, but it was essential for them to 'enjoy his presence unitedly with others of his People.'[89] The institution of separate Women's Meetings stressed the importance of female society and friendship in encouraging an emphasis on group fellowship over the individual. It was fittingly expressed by the campaigner and author Hannah More, whose poem 'Thought in a Place of Worship' encapsulated the spiritual oneness shared within a Meeting for worship:

> Most sweet it is to feel the unity
> Of such cementing love gathering in one,
> Flowing from heart to heart and like a cloud
> Of mingled incense rising to the Throne.[90]

Although More was not a Quaker, her poem was transcribed into an eighteenth-century Quaker commonplace book, suggesting that it resonated with the copyist's experiences of communal worship and the Society's values and beliefs. The prominence of the Meeting House in socialisation activities was possible because of the regular opportunities for female Friends to meet with one another; share local news; hear epistles, letters, and spiritual writings read; and collectively join in their spiritual union with God.

The significance of the Meeting as a hub of female sociability is revealed through the writings of American Quaker women. As a devout Friend, the Philadelphian diarist Hannah Callender attended Meetings for worship at least twice a week, as well as participating in the Monthly, Quarterly, and Yearly Meetings for business as an elder. Whilst silence was expected throughout the Meeting and Friends were not supposed to discuss frivolous

---

[88] Keith Thomas, *Religion and the Decline of Magic: Studies in Popular Beliefs in Sixteenth- and Seventeenth-Century England* (Harmondsworth, 1991), pp. 179–182.

[89] LRSF, Temp MS 403/1/2/3/2 Arthur B. Braithwaite Family Papers, Mercy Bell to Priscilla Farmer, London, undated, c. 1756.

[90] HCQSC, MS Coll 950 Satterthwaite Family Papers, 1696–1924, Commonplace book, 'Thought in a Place of Worship by Hannah More', undated, c. 1745–1833.

matters just before or after worship, Callender almost always used her attendance at Meetings as an opportunity to undertake social visits and often dined with visiting ministers and local acquaintances afterwards.[91] One 1758 entry in her diary encapsulated the social interaction surrounding the Meetings:

Morn: drest and gone to Eliza Barkers, found Polly Pusey there. Phebe bayly and more, after a while went to Raper's found betsey Brook there, the time passed very agreably till meetin time. went to meeting, Ann Schofeild and Sarah Marcy spoke. Polly Sandwith and I dined at John Smith's. afternoon, a women's meeting.[92]

The importance of women's social activities in maintaining group cohesion has been acknowledged as an understated aspect of Quaker history.[93] Yet, the experiences of diarists like Hannah Callender show that women played a critical role in the social interactions of their local communities. Moreover, despite its prevalence in the writings of women like Callender, the place of the Meeting in this picture has not received adequate attention. Quaker women's diaries and letters reveal a complex world of social interaction centred around their Meetings, where female Friends visited one another at home, read together, and paid close attention to one another's health, behaviour, and reputation. After a particularly intimate day with her friend Caty Howel in September 1758, Callender expressed how 'Friendship's the sovereign balm of Life'.[94]

It is important to note, however, that in contrast to the visiting customs practised in wider society, female Quakers appear to have 'observed the principle of exclusivity'.[95] The next chapter will show how this ideal was at times transgressed as a result of Quaker women's work within their communities, but they preferred not to socialise or develop close personal connections with women who did not share their faith. It was encapsulated in the testimonies and practices surrounding the circulation of Mary Mollineux's edited collection of poems, cited at the beginning of this chapter. As the testimonies in the preface of the volume made clear, intimate friendship with women outside of the Society was unimaginable for the Quaker poet. This was underlined by her reluctance to make her manuscript writings available to women outside of her close religious circle. It was also signified in her own personal connections, for it was noted how Mollineux refused to enter an intimate relationship with her childhood friend and cousin, Frances Owen, because of their 'different Principles, in matters of Religion'. As

[91] On the conduct expected of Friends before and after Meetings see J. William Frost, *The Quaker Family in Colonial America: A Portrait of the Society of Friends* (New York, 1973), p. 36.
[92] Callender, *The Diary of Hannah Callender Sansom*, p. 70, diary entry for 28 September 1758.
[93] Tomes, 'The Quaker Connection', p. 192.
[94] Callender, *The Diary of Hannah Callender Sansom*, p. 67, diary entry for 8 September 1758.
[95] Tomes, 'The Quaker Connection', p. 186.

well as being kin, the two young women shared very similar interests, personal circumstances, and an apparent compatibility in terms of their 'natural Inclinations and Tempers'. However, as Owen's testimony emphasises, Mollineux could only accept her as a 'particular Bosom Friend' after she had joined the Quaker movement.[96]

Meetings were intended to be solemn occasions, where the benefits of religious instruction were stressed over the pleasures of sociability. Friends were exhorted in 1770, for instance, to avoid all 'unprofitable association and converse', for it was believed that too 'long and frequent conversation on temporal matters' could do a great deal of damage to 'the religious mind'.[97] The practice of sociability among pious Friends like Mary Mollineux and Hannah Callender was therefore dominated by what can be termed 'godly conversation', where the main topics of discussion centred on religious discourse and issues raised in Meetings for worship. Even within these informal social spaces, Friends were exhorted to wait in silence for 'renewal of strength'.[98] Ellin Evans reminded her friend Rachel Pemberton to 'retire and spend some time in waiteing upon god' when friends were visiting, so that a 'renewing of strength ... will sit well upon thy mind when the company withdraws'.[99] Informal gatherings also afforded opportunities for solemn reflection. Frances Owen noted how she and her friend, Mary Mollineux, would often enter serious discussions whilst walking or riding together. These occasions, being 'season'd with Truth' and being 'in a Temper conversable, and concerned for the Good of others', had the effect of making their conversations 'improving and desirable'.[100] The practice of rational and edifying conversation amongst Quaker women was expected to bring believers closer to God, a matter that finds parallels in the wider dissenting tradition. Jon Mee's investigation of eighteenth-century 'conversability' shows that even in 1760, notions of conversation were still guided by ideas of an ultimate religious truth. Like female Friends, dissenting writers believed that the purpose of conversation was to seek the higher reason of Christianity, although its practice was never exclusive to their nonconformist communities.[101]

---

[96] Mary Mollineux, *Fruits of Retirement*, sig. A2r–A2v, 'A Testimony Concerning My Dear Friend and Cousin Mary Mollineux, Deceased. By Frances Owen', Reigate, Surrey, 20 May 1701.

[97] London Yearly Meeting, *Extracts from the Minutes and Advices*, p. 29.

[98] Ibid., p. 29.

[99] HSP, MS Coll 484A Pemberton Family Papers, vol. 10, p. 63, Ellin Evans to Rachel Pemberton, not dated, c. 1754.

[100] Mollineux, *Fruits of Retirement*, sig. A4v, 'A Testimony Concerning My Dear Friend and Cousin Mary Mollineux ... by Frances Owen'.

[101] The dissenter Isaac Watts, for instance, argued that the ends of reading and conversation remained 'the Conformation of our Hearts and Lives to the Duties of true Religion and Morality'. '*Free Conversation*', he argues, is designed for 'mutual Improvement in the Search of Truth.' Cited in Mee, *Conversable Worlds*, pp. 72–73.

Some disparity, however, seems to have existed between the sociability practised by American Friends and those of their British sisters. Whilst English Quaker women were involved in more functional types of social visiting, like attending births and visiting sick members of their communities, they appear not to have been so heavily invested in informal visits solely for the purpose of sociability. Ann Warder, an English-born Quaker, reflected on this in her diary, when she observed the unusual sociability of her Philadelphian co-religionists.[102] Often decrying the distraction that the time-consuming nature of social visits caused to what she deemed more important household work, she explained how 'it is a custom to visit here more than with us', remarking that 'they destroy the social freedom of it by too much dressing'. She went on to complain that 'I have now a great heap of work that decreases very slowly through gossiping about, which is unavoidable without giving my kind friends offense, for the great number before I have got once around renders it necessary to begin again'.[103] Grace Gowden, an English Friend who settled in Philadelphia, also commented on the burden of social visiting in a letter she sent to her sister in 1753 shortly after marriage. She described the whole culture as a 'ceremonious farse' and found 'the Laws of Politeness' tedious because these visits had to be reciprocated.[104] Warder and Gowden's observations underscore the significance and frequency of social calls practised by American Friends, but also hint at the irregularity of such a custom for native Englishwomen who viewed them as a distraction.

The nature of colonial life and the relative wealth of many of the Quaker inhabitants made ideal conditions for social visiting and regular interaction.[105] The frequent absence of Quaker men on business matters was regarded by the French writer Crèvecoeur as one of the principal reasons why the Quaker women of the Nantucket community engaged in social visiting. 'The absence of so many of them', he wrote, 'disposes the women to go to each other's house much oftener than when their husbands are at home;

---

[102] Ann Warder's fifteen-volume journal was written for the benefit of her sister Elizabeth, who remained in England. During their long separation, Warder described her time as a foreigner visiting America in her writings. Extracts from the diary were published by Sarah Cadbury in the *Pennsylvania Magazine of History and Biography*, vol. 17, no. 4 (1893), pp. 444–461 and concluded in vol. 18, no. 1 (1894), pp. 51–63.

[103] Ann Warder, 'Extracts from the Diary of Ann Warder (Concluded)', ed. Sarah Cadbury, *Pennsylvania Magazine of History and Biography*, vol. 18, no. 1 (1984), p. 51.

[104] HL, HM 36845–36895 Joseph Galloway Collection, fol. HM36845, Grace Gowden Galloway to Elizabeth Gowden Nickelson, Philadelphia, 6 November 1753.

[105] Although Friends were not a majority among the colonial populations, in places like Pennsylvania they remained a culturally dominant force until the end of the eighteenth century. The large number of Quaker inhabitants residing in cities like Philadelphia may have made visits of this nature more of a necessity than the more isolated Quaker communities within England.

hence the custom of incessant visiting has infected every one.' Crèvecoeur also offered an insight into the visit, describing how female Friends would always clear their own homes before setting out on 'their intended visit, which consists of a social chat, a dish of tea, and a hearty supper'. He commented on how the lack of cards, musical instruments, and songs made these Quaker friends so happy that they 'would not exchange their pleasures for those of the most brilliant assemblies of Europe'.[106]

This pattern is in quite specific contrast to the visiting customs usually observed in wider society. It is widely accepted in the scholarship on eighteenth-century sociability that it was the tea tables of Britain that set the tone for the social customs practised elsewhere in the British Atlantic. The Americas were much slower to adopt visiting rituals, which had been in place in Britain from the 1710s.[107] This disparity between 'plainness' in the English and colonial contexts is something to which I shall return in the next chapter, but as we saw in Chapter 2, colonial Meetings were reluctant to issue declarations against the clothing and goods that members were expected to buy and sell. This suggests that in contrast to their British co-religionists, in the more tolerant religious climate of the Americas, these Friends were more likely to follow the cultural practices of the society that surrounded them. In the British Isles, where Friends were always a small minority within their local communities, there may not have been the same pressure or, indeed, opportunity to undertake time-consuming social visits to local co-religionists.

It is nonetheless clear that while the evolving Society was restricting the types of activity its female members could perform within their daily lives, female Quakers on both sides of the Atlantic were finding ways to foster meaningful social interaction. The circulation of Mary Mollineux's collection of poems to a select circle of Friends reflected Quaker ideals of sociability in practice. As Tryall Ryder explained in the preface to the volume, it was during the 'Perusal of some Copies of some Verses, which she gave me,' that 'I felt such Unity of Spirit with them'.[108] The important function of this type of literate sociability in reinforcing a sense of community amongst Friends is a largely unacknowledged aspect of the movement's history. The circulation of poetry between women has been recognised as playing an important part

---

[106] J. Hector St John de Crèvecoeur, *Letters from an American Farmer* (London, 1782), pp. 198–199.

[107] The first salons based on the French model did not exist in America until the 1780s and 1790s, but had been a feature of mainstream French culture from the seventeenth century and widely adopted in Britain by the early eighteenth century. Shields, *Civil Tongues and Polite Letters*, pp. 104–126.

[108] Mollineux, *Fruits of Retirement*, sig. A7v, 'A Testimony Concerning My Dear Friend M. Mollineux by Tryall Ryder'.

in a shared culture of sociable interaction in early modern culture, bringing women together and enabling them to reflect on issues that engaged them both intellectually and emotionally.[109] Perhaps one of the reasons for the absence of this type of sociability within Quakerism was the potential threat it posed to women's spirituality. Indeed, the reading and writing of poetry was regarded by Quaker leaders as a pastime that reflected pride rather than humility and was to be avoided.[110] Unlike her contemporaries, however, whose verses reflected 'the extravagant Wits of the Age', Mollineux's poems were separated 'from the Earthly, Worthless Dross'. She was praised for making 'use of her Gift, rather to Convince and Prevail upon the Mind, to affect and raise the Soul upon Wings of Divine Contemplation'.[111]

The rise of this type of erudite friendship amongst Quaker women corresponded with the rise of other important sites of literary and intellectual interaction in early Enlightenment culture. The French salon model, which found prominence in the eighteenth-century British Atlantic, provided one such parallel. As Karin Wulf has noted, the influence of the salon was central in the practice of female sociability in the American colonies in the late eighteenth century, providing opportunities for debate, discussion, and the circulation of manuscript literature at select gatherings.[112] Elizabeth Eger's work on the bluestocking circles in eighteenth-century London has also shown how the salon came to create a sense of community for women. Their conversations were central to their sense of belonging by 'providing mutual support, identity and friendship'.[113] Like the discussions arising from the salon, Mollineux's poems served as sources of intellectual discussion for her acquaintances. Frances Owen, for instance, noted that they 'would often discourse of the present Objects [the poems], much tending to Edification'.[114]

In the Quaker context, however, the expansion of a literate culture of sociability was also facilitated by the growth of Women's Meetings. Not

---

[109] Catherine La Coureye Blecki, 'Reading Moore's Book: Manuscript vs. Print Culture, and the Development of Early American Literature', in Catherine La Coureye Blecki and Karin A. Wulf (eds.), *Milcah Martha Moore's Book: A Commonplace Book from Revolutionary America* (University Park, PA, 1997), pp. 80–81.

[110] In the 1669 edition of *No Cross, No Crown* William Penn warned Friends to avoid 'the vain Apparel and usual Recreations of the Age'. This included '*Romances, Plays, Lampoons, Poets, Montebanks, Fidlers,* and such like Buffanly conversation … which never was the Christian way of Living, but *the pastimes, of the Heathens that knew not God.*' William Penn, *No Cross, No Crown* (London, 1669), pp. 20, 23 [mispaginated as p. 17].

[111] Mollineux, *Fruits of Retirement*, sig. A6r, 'A Testimony Concerning My Dear Friend and Cousin Mary Mollineux … by Frances Owen'.

[112] Karin Wulf, 'Milcah Martha Moore's Book: Documenting Culture and Connection in the Revolutionary Era', in *Milcah Martha Moore's Book*, pp. 23–24.

[113] Elizabeth Eger, "The Noblest Commerce of Mankind': Conversation and Community in the Bluestocking Circle', in Sarah Knott and Barbara Taylor (eds.), *Women, Gender and Enlightenment* (Basingstoke, 2005), p. 292.

[114] Mollineux, *Fruits of Retirement*, sig. A4v.

only did these create a circulating library of Quaker materials, but their select gatherings were also punctuated by a constant exchange of epistles, spiritual autobiographies, and written testimonies, which were regularly discussed and reflected upon. Indeed, the intellectual benefits of the Meeting can be likened to the model of 'Amicable Society' propounded by Mary Astell, whose vision of a college of retirement was centred on her desire to create a separate intellectual space for women, who would live together in companionate scholarly friendship. Like her Quaker contemporaries, Astell emphasised the necessity of learning for the pursuit of godliness and the benefits of performing this amongst 'useful… company'.[115] The rise of a culture of literate sociability amongst Quaker women, which was supported by their Meetings, thus reflected broader social developments whilst also providing a safe public space for them to adhere to their own particularised religious beliefs.

The culture of support surrounding the births of Quaker children provides another salient example of how Quaker women could participate in a culture of sociability practised by their non-Quaker contemporaries whilst performing it within their own separate sphere. The supportive function of gossips in the early modern community has been widely documented and Quaker women also benefitted greatly from the love and comfort of those women who attended them during childbirth.[116] The extensive nature of such networks of support within English Quakerism is revealed from the Birth Notes kept by the Monthly Meetings in London from 1676, which documented the names of the women who had witnessed the births of Quaker children.[117] Daniel Wells's mother, for example, was attended by thirteen female witnesses in May 1688, whilst nine female 'gossips' were present at the birth of Maria Gandy in 1721.[118] As Ann Giardina Hess concluded from her survey of the Buckinghamshire Quaker Birth Notes, '[N]owhere was neighbourly bonding and community religious integration more evident than amongst [Quaker] women.'[119]

---

[115] Mary Astell, *A Serious Proposal to the Ladies, for the Advancement of Their True and Greatest Interest* (4th edn, 2 parts, London, 1697), vol. 1, pp. 45–48.

[116] See Capp, *When Gossips Meet*, 49–55; and David Cressy, *Birth, Marriage, and Death: Ritual, Religion, and the Life-Cycle in Tudor and Stuart England* (Oxford, 1997), pp. 84–87.

[117] The London Quaker Birth Notes, which were recorded from 1676, named the midwife who officiated at the birth, along with the witnesses who were in attendance. The National Archives (hereafter cited as NA), RG6/1626 London and Middlesex Birth Notes, 1676–1707; RG6/1627 London and Middlesex Birth Notes, 1707–1718; and RG6/1628 London and Middlesex Birth Notes, 1718–1725.

[118] NA, RG6/1626 London and Middlesex Birth Notes, 1676–1707, p. 36 and NA, RG6/1628 London and Middlesex Birth Notes, 1718–1725, p. 702.

[119] Ann Giardina Hess, 'Midwifery Practice among the Quakers in Southern Rural England in the Late Seventeenth Century', in Hilary Marland (ed.), *The Art of Midwifery: Early Modern Midwives in Europe* (London, 1993), p. 52.

Besides providing an important culture of neighbourliness this type of sociability 'typified the wider patterns of female interaction' in women's everyday lives, as Bernard Capp has noted.[120] Indeed, the role of these supportive networks within the delivery room points to an important divergence in the Quaker context, for the majority of witnesses who subscribed their names on these Birth Notes were identifiably Friends.[121] Within the rural community of Upperside in Buckinghamshire, Hess identified 160 of the 235 witnesses (68 per cent) who attended the local Quaker births as Quakers, some were Quaker maidservants from distant counties such as Yorkshire and Lancashire.[122] Such a figure is surprising because Quaker families were much more widely dispersed than they were in London. Thus, despite the fact that it would have been difficult to gather a group of Quaker women to attend a delivery at short notice, at least two-thirds of witnesses were from the mother's religious community. This contrasts with the gossip networks studied by Capp, where female support during childbirth was determined mainly by physical proximity and a 'culture of good neighbourliness', rather than religious affiliation.[123]

The intimacy and exclusivity of these events for Quaker women is evident in the London Birth Notes, where the conditions were favourable for gathering a select group of women at short notice. Margaret Cross was attended by six gossips at the birth of her daughter Margaret in March 1720 and, in the fifteen years that followed, the same group of gossips were listed as present at numerous Quaker births. A more detailed account of these networks is provided in Appendix 3. On all occasions where Margaret Cross attended a Quaker birth, they were exclusive to those gossips who had witnessed her own lying-in.[124] This was also a mobile network, demonstrated by the fact that Margaret Cross and her husband, Josiah, moved to three different parishes during this period – from St Saviour's to St Olave's, and from there to St Martin Orgar's – but continued to be supported by the same group of gossips. This suggests that religious ties rather than neighbourly support were significant in forming these alliances. Gossiping, as Capp argues, 'was about bonding and belonging'.[125] Indeed, if we follow his suggestion of everyday supportive networks being manifested in the delivery room, we can see how Quaker women stood outside or on the margins of this culture of

---

[120] Capp, *When Gossips Meet*, p. 51.
[121] The presence of non-Quaker women at Quaker births will be discussed in more detail in Chapter 4. It is worth noting, however, that where a non-Quaker woman was in attendance at a Quaker birth, it was usually the skilled midwife and her assistant.
[122] Hess, 'Midwifery Practice among the Quakers', p. 53.
[123] Capp, *When Gossips Meet*, pp. 50–57.
[124] NA, RG6/1628 London and Middlesex Birth Notes, 1718–1725, p. 622; and RG6/1629 London and Middlesex Birth Notes, 1725–1769.
[125] Capp, *When Gossips Meet*, p. 57.

neighbourly support. The choice of godparents or 'gossips', for example, was used to strengthen friendship and reinforce kinship and patronage, but was a custom that Quakers regarded as superfluous and not in keeping with their testimonies.[126] This reinforced the bonds between believers whilst also distancing them from the networks of family and patronage that ensured the survival of individual families.

It is highly probable that many of the women present at Quaker births were forced to travel longer distances than their non-Quaker neighbours to help their co-religionists. This is something that Hess found for Buckinghamshire Quaker midwives, whose preference for delivering Quaker mothers meant that they were much more mobile than other midwives.[127] When the New York Friend Mary Bowne believed herself 'to be quickened', she expressed her desire to see her distant friend, Phebe Pemberton, during this difficult time, explaining that 'I greatly want thy Company and assistance ... I see my Los[s] more ... and more and thy motherly advise would be a great Comfort to mee here'.[128] The supportive relationship expressed in this exchange had added significance, for Mary Bowne had recently relocated from Bucks County, Pennsylvania, where the Pembertons resided, to New York.[129] After the birth of her third child two years later, Bowne expressed similar hopes of seeing her distant friend when she faced problems with breastfeeding, believing that both Phebe and her husband would be a great comfort to her in her time of need.[130] The shared experiences of settlement and religious affiliation were crucial in this context, for Bowne chose to turn to her distant co-religionists for emotional support and advice at this difficult time. This underlines not only the difficulties associated with settlement, but also the strength of communal bonds shared by female Friends during important life-cycle events.

In their everyday lives, Quaker women shared many of the same kinds of cultural exchange as their non-Quaker contemporaries, whether through worship, gossiping, or literary discussion. Nevertheless, within these alliance-building practices, we can also see how religious belief altered how they were expressed and experienced. What made Quaker women's friendships unusual was the exclusivity of their social interactions, as well as the austere

---

[126] Ralph A. Houlbrooke, *The English Family 1450–1700* (London, 1984), p. 131.

[127] Hess, 'Midwifery Practice among the Quakers', p. 69.

[128] HSP, MS Coll 484A Pemberton Family Papers, vol. 2, p. 98b, Mary Bowne to Phebe Pemberton, August 1693.

[129] Bowne was writing from Flushing in New York and Pemberton was living in Bucks County in Pennsylvania.

[130] 'I am so bad a [nurse] that I thinck the child does not get [one fourth] part of its mentenance from the brest and what it gets is with much dife[c]ulty and hard ship.' HSP, MS Coll 484A Pemberton Family Papers, vol. 2, p. 113, Mary Bowne to Phineas and Phebe Pemberton, Flushing, New York, 9 August 1695.

nature of their exchanges. Despite some geographical variation, these occasions of informal interaction became spaces in which female Friends monitored one another's behaviour, indicating the degree to which the ideal of an internally open and visible community life transcended concepts of public and private space. Above all, however, faith permeated Quaker women's social worlds at every level, physically separating them from the wider 'world', whilst cementing the bonds between spiritual equals. Local ties had far less significance than religious affiliation.

'THIS ACT OF PURE FRIENDSHIP': FEMALE COMPANIONSHIP IN QUAKER MISSIONS

Looking beyond Quaker women's life-cycle events and everyday exchanges, one of the most powerful examples of how Quaker doctrines encouraged an alternative model of friendship was the intimate bonds shared by women during their itinerant travels. The presence of supportive companions during missionary service is a prominent feature of itinerant women's writings. Because Quakers modelled their journeys on the labours of the early Apostles, these same-sex partnerships encapsulate how spiritual friendship could be incorporated into women's alliances. A number of themes emerge from the study of Quaker companionships, including the concept of a union of spirits, the biblical friendship of Jonathan and David, and the influence of providence. Quaker friendships incorporated some traditional elements, as theorised and practised in wider society. The unparalleled circumstances in which these women found themselves, however, created a distinctively nuanced experience of friendship.

The word 'companion' appears repeatedly throughout female ministers' spiritual autobiographies, showing that their same-sex partnerships were a formative influence in the construction of their writings. The English minister Catherine Payton, for instance, used the word 'companion' 107 times in her 300-page memoir.[131] The same term, by contrast, was only used 81 times by the English minister Thomas Story in his 750-page life account.[132] Both were English Public Friends who undertook missionary work to the

---

[131] This figure has been calculated from a keyword search of the word 'companion' in her spiritual autobiography. Only discrete uses of the word in reference to her same-sex partners have been recorded. Payton only ever referred to her travelling partners as 'my dear friend' or 'my companion', so this keyword search is not excluding a broader lexicon of meanings associated with their friendship. Catherine Phillips, *Memoirs of the Life of Catherine Phillips* (London, 1797).

[132] This figure has also been calculated from discrete uses of the word 'companion' in Thomas Story's life account: Thomas Story, *A Journal of the Life of Thomas Story: Containing an Account of His Remarkable Convincement of, and Embracing the Principles of Truth* (Newcastle, 1747).

American colonies in the eighteenth century.[133] Whilst this does not mean that the experience of companionship was any less important or meaningful for male Friends, it does indicate how the physical and emotional burdens of travel could shape women's writings. As we observed in Chapter 1, Quaker men like Story appear to have been much less inclined to make reference to their domestic relationships in their life accounts, preferring to emphasise their own spiritual progress and journeys. The unconventional nature of Quaker women's work made it harder for them to relinquish personal ties. This may account for the important role of their 'spiritual yokemates' in their writings, for they became substitutes for their absent families at a time when they were expected to eschew all connections to complete the Lord's work.[134]

Ostensibly, there were a multiplicity of other adjectives Quaker writers might use to describe their relationship with their companions. Katharine Evans, who was held in captivity in Malta with her companion Sarah Cheevers between 1558 and 1662, had a whole range of expressions for referring to her 'dear Friend', including 'fellow and labourer in the Work of God', 'dear Sister in Christ Jesus', 'dearly beloved Yoke-mate', 'dear heart', and 'right dear, precious and Heavenly one'. However, this broad lexicon was the exception rather than the norm in most Quaker writings published after 1670. Catherine Payton, for instance, only ever described her companion Mary Peisley, with whom she travelled across the American colonies for three years, as 'my dear friend' or 'my companion'. This is because spiritual accounts by Quaker ministers tended to be formulaic in their construction, conveying the details of their journeys in a plain and direct manner.

Moreover, a close study of how these friendships were expressed in Quaker women's autobiographies reveals the gendered nature of their relationships. Of particular prominence was the idea that the messages articulated by a companion reflected the writer's spiritual calling. Catherine Payton described the spiritual unity she attained with her American companion, Sarah Barney, as 'that sincere love to Truth which dwelt in her, [and] united her to my spirit'.[135] In articulating messages that complemented the words spoken by their companions, ministers could be reassured about the divine origin of their own message. The American minister Jane Hoskins explained that 'where companions in this solemn service are firmly united in

---

[133] Catherine Payton was an active Quaker minister from 1748 up until her death in 1794 and visited America with the Irish Minister Mary Peisley from 1753 to 1756. Story travelled and lived in the American colonies for fifteen years and was an active Public Friend between 1696 and 1742.

[134] The idea of Quaker yoke-mates is discussed in detail in Herbert, *Female Alliances*, pp. 163–166.

[135] Phillips, *Memoirs of the Life of Catherine Phillips*, p. 127.

the true bond of christian fellowship, it must tend to confirm that authority of their message, testifying their joint consent to the doctrine they teach'.[136] In contrast, very few references are made by male Friends to the idea of spiritual service being shared by companions. Like many other male Friends, not one mention is made in Thomas Story's life account of the messages he shared with his travelling companions. Instead, the emphasis was on the message *he* preached and how it was received. Quaker women, however, reserved the highest praise for their companions when they vocalised one another's most intimate thoughts. A common trope in Katharine Evans and Sarah Cheevers's 1661 account of captivity in Malta, for example, was how they 'were guided by one Spirit'. When their captors tried to turn them against one another, it was noted that both friends spoke 'one and the same thing in effect, so that they had not a jot nor tittle against us'.[137] In preaching the same message, the spiritual foundation of their friendship was at its strongest. At a time when independent female travel was treated with suspicion, the spiritual unity emphasised by itinerant women reinforced the divine inspiration of their mission since their message carried more weight when it was expressed as a shared spiritual instinct that could only have come from God.

One of the dominant themes of Quaker women's writings was how the intense spiritual connections formed by female companions supported them through extraordinary trials and life-threatening situations. Evans and Cheevers's fragmentary account of their four-year imprisonment in Malta provides a striking example of how their love and care for one another offered a positive accompaniment to their narrative of suffering. Their travails included separation from their natural families and native land, as well as confinement in a tiny airless cell without access to light, water, or regular supplies of food. 'Their mutuality', as their biographers have written, 'confirmed and generated the emotional and spiritual strength which, along with their belief, allowed them to endure physical suffering and spiritual attack.'[138] One telling instance occurred after their captors first attempted to separate them. In an act of defiance, Evans took Cheevers by the arm and declared that: 'The Lord hath joined us together, and wo be to them that should part us ... I rather chuse to dye there with my friend, than to part from her.'[139] This was reminiscent of the words spoken at the Church

---

[136] Jane Hoskins, *The Life and Spiritual Sufferings of That Faithful Servant of Christ Jane Hoskens* (Philadelphia, 1771), p. 30.

[137] Katharine Evans and Sarah Cheevers, *This Is a Short Relation of Some of the Cruel Sufferings (for the Truths Sake) of Katharine Evans and Sarah Chevers in the Inquisition in the Isle of Malta* (London, 1662), p. 17.

[138] E. Graham, H. Hinds, E. Hobby, and H. Wilcox (eds.), *Her Own Life: Autobiographical Writings by 17th Century Englishwomen* (London, 1989), p. 117.

[139] Evans and Cheevers, *A Short Relation ... of Katharine Evans and Sarah Chevers*, pp. 13–14.

of England marriage service, when the minister pronounced that 'those whom God hath joined together, let no man put asunder'.[140] Such, a choice of expression, has been argued by Herbert to have figured them as 'devoted, long-term companions who shared an identity of religious purpose'.[141] Like the marriage service, it also had a sense of finality: they could only be parted in death. The account was a product of collaborative endeavour, and the voices of the two women are often hard to discern because of the continual veering between 'I' and 'we', a linguistic trope that Catie Gill argues merged their voices and indicates their unity of purpose in the face of the inquisitorial efforts to silence them.[142] Their captors were unable to break the immutable spiritual bond shared by these two women, and they were eventually released in 1662.

Outside the context of persecution, the profound spiritual connections between women who had joined together 'in gospel labour' was a central feature of their writings. This shared special bond was powerfully expressed by the American minister Susanna Morris who, with her companion Sarah Lay, travelled to the British Isles in 1745 and suffered a dangerous crossing and shipwreck. '[W]e were so in fellowship one with another', Morris recorded in her journal, 'that she [Sarah] held fast hold on me and said if she then must die she would go off with me.' Lay's physical presence and attentiveness to the needs of her companion testify to the extraordinary singularity of their bond. Their union was heightened by their anticipation of heavenly communion. As Morris explained, '[T]he living Lord was a comforter to me and my dear companion' who 'wrought wonders for my deliverance.'[143] Similarly, Joan Vokins, who suffered from poor health for most of her ministerial career, described her companions as 'Heavenly Relations'. Like Sarah Lay's pledge of devotion to her companion, this choice of expression emphasised the transcendence of their alliance. They knew that even if she departed this life, they would be reunited in the next.[144]

The experience of companionship served to create powerful and enduring alliances that lasted far beyond the duration of the mission. 'My heart seemed rent within me on parting with thee', wrote Mary Weston to her former companion and Philadelphian landlady Mary Pemberton in 1752.[145]

---

[140] Cressy, *Birth, Marriage, and Death*, p. 289.

[141] Herbert, *Female Alliances*, p. 143.

[142] Catie Gill, '"Bad Catholics": Anti-Popery in *This Is a Short Relation* (Katherine Evans and Sarah Cheevers, 1662)', in Paul Salzman (ed.), *Expanding the Canon of Early Modern Women's Writing* (Cambridge, 2010), p. 236.

[143] Susanna Morris, 'An Account of Part of the Travels of Susanna Morris', in Bacon, *Wilt Thou Go on My Errand?*, p. 72.

[144] Vokins, *God's Mighty Power Magnified*, p. 50.

[145] HSP, MS Coll 484A Pemberton Family Papers, vol. 8, p. 56, Mary Weston to Mary Pemberton, Wapping, London, 14 September 1752.

Her choice of expression indicated the lasting character of their friendship despite the temporary nature of their ministerial work together.[146] As Herbert has noted, seventeenth- and eighteenth-century Quaker companions addressed one another with expressions that emphasised the 'common spirituality' as well as the 'lifelong bond' they shared.[147] The long-term nature of companionate friendship was effectively conveyed in a letter sent by the Pennsylvanian Friend, Grace Lloyd, to her former companion, Abigail Boles, shortly after recovering from a life-threatening illness. In her letter, Lloyd noted how Boles was 'daily in My Mind', and declared that she would rather pass what time she had left with her former companion than with friends or family: 'Noe friend. Nor Relation in the world I Should [be] So glad to see. Espesaly in my Sickness I wo[u]ld have given abboundance to have one hours time with thee.'[148]

Parting from a companion, after the impulse to preach was satisfied, often proved a great source of anguish for itinerant ministers. Mary Weston explained when she joined in ministerial service with Mary Peisley in 1749, that 'the longer I was with her the harder it was to part'; and when Mary Peisley parted temporarily from Catherine Payton during their service in the American colonies, she underwent a great spiritual crisis. In one particularly evocative letter she wrote: '[W]hat now adds to my trial is that I have got no second self to whome I might disclose my Joys [and] my griefs.'[149] Peisley's expression 'second self' recalls the long-established ideals of friendship between men, where the virtuous friend was idealised as 'another himself'.[150] The second self, as Keith Thomas explains, became a 'mirror', by which an individual could better understand himself through contemplating his friend.[151] In contrast to the traditional formulation of the second self, however, the view of companionship propounded by ministers like Mary

[146] The two women only travelled together for a few weeks for the small section of Mary Weston's voyage between Philadelphia and New York.

[147] Amanda E. Herbert, 'Companions in Preaching and Suffering: Itinerant Female Quakers in the Seventeenth- and Eighteenth-Century British Atlantic World', *Early American Studies: An Interdisciplinary Journal*, vol. 9, no. 1 (2011), pp. 109–110.

[148] LRSF, MS Vol 296 Watson MSS, fol. 3, Grace Lloyd to Abigail Boles (later Watson), Chester, PA, 26 September 1727.

[149] LRSF, Portfolio MSS, vol. 4, fol. 49, Mary Weston to Peter Peisley, Wapping, London, 10 November 1749; and HCQSC, MS Coll 859 Shackleton Family Papers, 1707–1785, Mary Peisley folder, Mary Peisley to Elizabeth Shackleton, Christiana, PA, 16 November 1754.

[150] Aristotle viewed *amicitia perfecta* as an intimate and affective relationship, where the virtuous friend became 'another himself'. See Dirk Baltzly and Nick Eliopoulos, 'The Classical Ideals of Friendship', in Caine, *Friendship: A History*, p. 23. This idea continued to permeate early modern notions of friendship. Francis Bacon remarked in his essay on friendship '*That a Friend is another himself; for that a Friend is far more than himself.*' Francis Bacon, 'Of Friendship', p. 75.

[151] Keith Thomas, *The Ends of Life: Roads to Fulfilment in Early Modern England* (Oxford, 2009), p. 194.

Peisley was entirely spiritual and served to enhance the minister's knowledge of the divine, rather than personal self-knowledge. Indeed, Peisley's anxiety about being separated from her 'second self' stemmed from her own uncertainty as to whether the calling she had experienced was genuine. In one letter, her sense of crisis and loss was exemplified through her presentation of herself as 'a poor backslideing child … who donte see her self in the light thou do[es]'.[152]

The language used by these women is reminiscent of what Constance M. Furey has termed 'more abstract notions of perfect friendship', conveyed through the classical description of friends as 'one soul in two bodies'.[153] The most powerful example of the intimate and personal love shared by Christian friends was the story of David and Jonathan, whose souls, according to the first book of Samuel, were 'knit together'.[154] Many Quaker ministers compared their relationships with their companions to that of David and Jonathan. The American minister Elizabeth Hudson, for example, stated that her friend Elizabeth Norris had been made 'an useful instrument in the hand of the Lord … for our hearts became truly united to each other [and] I believe not inferior to that degree of friendship which subsisted betwixt Jonathan and David'.[155] In one letter, Mary Weston also noted the 'cementing vertue' of friendship, 'which as David saith passeth the Love, that I need not name'.[156] The story of Jonathan and David provided a powerful model for women to illustrate their close personal and emotional alliances, for it was friendship at its most perfect: based on a foundation of unshakeable commitment to each other and to their shared religious ideals. However, it was a surprising allusion given their gender, leading us to question why they preferred to model their relationship on two men, rather than find an appropriate scriptural example of a close bond between two women.[157] It is best explained by Mack, who suggests that in their roles as prophets, Quaker women transcended their gendered identities and felt free to assume the personalities of men.[158]

---

[152] HCQSC, MS Coll 859 Shackleton Family Papers, 1707–1785, Mary Peisley folder, Mary Peisley to Elizabeth Shackleton, Christiana, PA, 16 November 1754.
[153] Furey, 'Bound by Likeness', p. 31.
[154] '[T]he soul of Jonathan was knit with the soul of David, and Jonathan loved him as his own soul', 1 Samuel 18:1 (King James version).
[155] Hudson, 'An Abstract of the Travels and Some Other Remarks of Eliza Hudson', pp. 131–132.
[156] HSP, MS Coll 484A Pemberton Family Papers, vol. 8, p. 56, Mary Weston to Mary Pemberton, Wapping, London, 14 September 1752.
[157] The story of Ruth and Naomi, for example, provided another important example of friends being united through their love of God, despite their differences in language, age, culture, and understanding.
[158] Mack, *Visionary Women*, p. 10.

The Quaker transformation of sociability through close spiritual alliance also had important implications for Quaker masculinity. Like many ministers, John Audland and John Camm were described as being 'firmly knit together, as David and Jonathan, by the bond of unspeakable love'. They declared that their shared emotional relationship was so strong and their 'hearts being perfectly united and knit together, in that love that's everlasting' that it surpassed 'the love of women'.[159] Bray argues that the rhetoric of male friendship 'occupied an impossible space' because of its implied sexual connotations and violation of hierarchies and honour codes.[160] Thus the ability of Quaker men to forge such powerful bonds with members of the same sex through their shared spiritual alliance is striking, especially given that Audland and Camm were married men. As Alexandra Shepard has argued in her seminal study on early modern manhood and masculinity, 'close contact between men, in the form of either friendship or homosexual intimacy' often became blurred in the early modern mind, becoming dangerous to the social and gender order.[161] Thus when Friends like Samuel Bownas addressed their companions as 'My Dearly Beloved', they were delicately balanced between spiritual respectability and temporal opprobrium.[162]

Quaker women's emphasis on friendship as a meeting of the 'souls' was part of a long-standing tradition dating back to Aristotle. It was an integral concept in influential early modern treatises on friendship, such as Anglican cleric Jeremy Taylor's *The Measures and Offices of Friendship* (1657). Friendship, for him too, was to be celebrated as a 'union of souls'.[163] The biblical story of Jonathan and David also continued to permeate such religious ideals of friendship. The eighteenth-century Methodist movement, for instance, also appropriated this alliance to express the emotional bonds shared by believers. However, as Lawrence has shown, for the Methodists this story took on greater emotional significance because it provided an example of how religious bonds between godly people could overthrow natural family bonds.[164] Specific examples of the friendship formed by Methodist women show how their newfound spiritual alliances could be used as a justification for severing familial relationships. Sarah Ryan, for instance, confessed in her autobiography that her desire to pursue a celibate

---

[159] Thomas Camm and Charles Marshall (eds.), *The Memory of the Righteous Revived: Being a Brief Collection of the Books and Written Epistles of John Camm and John Audland* (London, 1689), sig. C3r.

[160] Bray, *The Friend*, p. 199.

[161] Alexandra Shepard, *Meanings of Manhood in Early Modern England* (Oxford, 2003), pp. 115–116.

[162] LRSF, MS Vol 334 Gibson MSS, fol. 55, Samuel Bownas to James Wilson, Bridport, Dorset, 3 October 1751.

[163] Taylor, *The Measures and Offices of Friendship*, pp. 82–83.

[164] Lawrence, *One Family under God*, pp. 123–124.

lifestyle with her female co-religionists allowed her to abandon her husband.[165] Quaker women (and men), as I have already noted, never used their spiritual alliances as a justification for relinquishing other personal relationships. Their lives and domestic arrangements were traditional, and their companionate alliances proved a supportive accompaniment to a godly lifestyle during their temporary removal from the family home.

The distinctive aspects of itinerant Quaker women's self-fashioning of their friendships can thus be attributed to the providential element of their undertakings: it was their relationship to 'Truth', rather than to each other, that served to unify their message. As Sarah Crabtree has noted, Public Friends did not come from a particular socio-economic class, but were a 'diverse group of people unified by a religious calling'.[166] For itinerant Quakers, the purest form of spiritual friendship could be achieved by women of very different social backgrounds. Mary Peisley, the daughter of an Irish farmer, joined with Mary Weston, the wife of a wealthy London merchant, in ministerial service across England in 1749. Weston described her time with her Irish companion as 'this act of pure friendship'. In a letter to Peisley's father she wrote that 'I know none to equal her of the rising generation' and later went on to declare that 'I own I love her beyond expression, and would do any thing in my power to serve her by night or day, should think it a blessing to have her continually with me'.[167] Not only was Peisley of a lower social rank than Weston, but she was also seven years her junior and unmarried. Weston's willingness to place herself in service to a lower-status woman underscores the authority conferred on Friends who displayed a particularly powerful spiritual gift.

In some ways, this accords with an ambiguity in Aristotelian ideals of friendship, where equality of virtue and talent could be placed above hierarchical bonds. However, as Aristotle goes on to stress, friendship of opposites (for example, between rich and poor, ignorant and learned, old and young) tended to be friendships of utility or convenience.[168] It was generally accepted in seventeenth- and eighteenth-century ideals of sociability that friendship was only possible for individuals who were of similar social standing.[169] Thomas explains that one of the necessary conditions for perfect friendship in early modern thought was equal social status, so

---

[165] Ibid., pp. 145–146.

[166] Sarah Crabtree, '"A Beautiful and Practical Lesson of Jurisprudence": The Transatlantic Quaker Ministry in an Age of Revolution', *Radical History Review*, vol. 99 (2007), p. 54.

[167] LRSF, Portfolio MSS, vol. 4, fol. 49, Mary Weston to Peter Peisley, Wapping, London, 10 November 1749.

[168] Lorraine Smith Pangle, *Aristotle and the Philosophy of Friendship* (Cambridge, 2003), pp. 62–64.

[169] See Berry, *Gender, Society and Print Culture*, pp. 212–234; and Baltzly and Eliopoulos, 'The Classical Ideals of Friendship', pp. 17–19.

that the bonds defining the relationship were horizontal and not vertical.[170] The primacy that Quaker ministers gave to the religious rather than practical dimensions of their union therefore stood in contrast to wider social expectations.

The uncontrollable power of providence was seen as the overriding force in determining companionate friendship. Mary Weston, for example, explained in a letter to her cousin, Abigail Watson, in 1749 that after having no view of a companion for her proposed ministerial work to the American colonies, she was resolved to submit to the will of God in the hope that 'my good master will provide me one when the time comes'.[171] The lack of individual choice in selecting a suitable companion stood in contrast to eighteenth-century conduct literature, which advised female readers to move cautiously and choose their friends carefully. Indeed, literate women, as Herbert notes, were expected to ponder carefully in private the individual merits of potential female companions before they trusted them with friendship.[172] *The Ladies Dictionary* advised its readers to enter into their friendships with 'the greatest Wariness imaginable, since you are to be responsible to the World for the Miscarriages of those in some measure that you contract an Intimacy with'.[173] Quaker women, too, were expected to enter into their alliances with caution. However, their motivations for doing so were very different from the advice their non-Quaker contemporaries were given. In 1752, the young Catherine Payton noted her reservations about forming a relationship too hastily with the Lancashire minister Rachel Wilson, whom she accompanied to London. She remarked that this rather sudden union 'brought a great exercise upon my mind' because she knew her relations 'were desirous that I might steadily move in the counsel of God; and perhaps might fear my running too fast, which I also dreaded'.[174] Whereas her contemporaries emphasised the potential damage that could be done to a woman's reputation should she enter a friendship too hastily, Payton's concerns stemmed from a fear of offending God by not patiently waiting for his guidance.

Similarly, the lack of reciprocity and material support in Quaker women's friendship formation stood in contrast to contemporary norms, for a companion's compatibility was judged entirely by divine guidance. In 1681 Joan Vokins travelled to the colonies without a companion, '[Y]et the Lord so ordered it, that I had still some honest Woman, or Maiden Friend, both by

[170] Thomas, *The Ends of Life*, p. 196.
[171] LRSF, MS Vol 296 Watson MSS, fol. 13, Mary Weston to Abigail Watson (Boles) from Wapping, London, 25 November 1749.
[172] Herbert, *Female Alliances*, p. 46.
[173] N. H., *The Ladies Dictionary*, p. 224.
[174] Phillips, *Memoirs of the Life of Catherine Phillips*, p. 27.

Sea and Land.'[175] The spiritual underpinning of her ministry was evidenced through God's provision of suitable female companions throughout her journey. Divinely inspired friendship is further evidenced by the circumstances that brought Catherine Payton together with her companion, Mary Peisley, in the early 1750s. As Payton explained in her spiritual autobiography, her calling to travel to America manifested itself with an 'apprehension that I must go with my dear friend Mary Peisley'. It was to her great surprise that she shortly after received a letter from Peisley, enquiring whether she knew of a female Friend with an inclination to travel to the American colonies. 'I am almost at a loss', wrote Payton in her reply, 'to find terms to express the laborious thought which has possessed my soul; for it seems to me, that providence designs I should accompany thee.'[176] The singular impulse these women experienced to travel to a distant part of the world stood as powerful testament to the providential nature of their friendship. It functioned as a reminder of the divinely inspired nature of their service, which transcended all other considerations.

This trust in providence was all pervasive and affected how companionship was formed between male Friends. Thomas Story, for instance, devoted an entire section in his journal to detailing how he joined with his companion, Roger Gill. 'I found my Mind very free towards him', he stated, 'and discovered something of my Concern to him for *America* ... and asked him if he knew of any ministering Friend concerned for those Parts, for I wanted a Companion: To which ... he replied "It is now long since I was first concerned that way."'[177] Companionate friendship nevertheless had specific value for itinerant Quaker women. Travel to unknown and distant lands during this period was dangerous for a multitude of reasons, and women who travelled without an official companion were more vulnerable, especially as their unusually public roles opened them up to physical and verbal attack. Herbert cites the example of the young Quaker woman Elizabeth Ashbridge, who in 1732 became trapped into indentured servitude when attempting to secure a crossing from Ireland to the American colonies.[178] A more colourful example of the dangers inherent in travel without an official companion appears in the spiritual autobiography of the American minister Elizabeth Hudson, who had travelled to the British Isles on religious service. In 1749, shortly after separating from her companion, she lost her way in Edinburgh, entered a local house, and asked for the master to send word to a local Quaker of her arrival, not knowing where she was 'or in

[175] Vokins, *God's Mighty Power Magnified*, p. 46.
[176] Phillips, *Memoirs of the Life of Catherine Phillips*, pp. 47–51.
[177] Story, *The Life of Thomas Story*, pp. 149–150.
[178] Herbert, *Female Alliances*, pp. 159–160.

what sort of hands'. Her concerns were fully justified for, as she described later in a carefully worded account, the door swung open to reveal 'divers others of these little rooms with men and women in them in such positions as to give me an insight into what sort of house we were in, and also of the necessity of our departure'.[179]

Seventeenth- and eighteenth-century Quakers believed that their companions were critical to their ministry and spiritual growth. The close bonds they formed provided a powerful model of female sociability that reconfigured traditional notions of friendship by providing a degree of respectability to women's itinerant service at a time when the radical act of leaving the family home continued to be viewed by society with suspicion. Unlike other types of religious female friendship, the Quaker model was particularly flexible in enabling women to pursue these intense spiritual alliances in conjunction with their traditional domestic relationships. It provided a positive accompaniment to a female minister's own personal and emotional trials, particularly when it could be understood as a providentially ordained union. As Deborah Bell characterised her journey to Scotland with her unnamed female companion: '[W]e having travelled together this long journey in much love and true unity, always being willing, according to the strength given, to help to bear one another's burdens.'[180]

IMAGINARY FRIENDS: QUAKER WOMEN'S OVER-OCEAN ALLIANCES

Keith Thomas has argued that friendship was 'largely determined by proximity'.[181] However, we have seen how shared religious observation between fellow Quakers had the potential to alter the geographical and physical scope of their alliances. Adherence to the movement enabled female Friends to move beyond worldly concerns and fixed spatial boundaries, a fact that is powerfully demonstrated through the long-distance networks of support that evolved within the early movement. The itinerant nature of early Quakerism, combined with strong epistolary and mercantile networks, gave women Friends outside of the context of public ministry frequent opportunities to enter alliances with other members of their Society.

The distance that often separated Quaker women opened an important space for them to develop close alliances with little physical contact. This was particularly evident in the epistles exchanged by the Women's Meetings

---

[179] Hudson, 'An Abstract of the Travels and Some Other Remarks of Eliza Hudson', p. 182.
[180] Deborah Bell, *A Short Journal of the Labours and Travels in the Work and Ministry, of That Faithful Servant of Christ, Deborah Bell* (London, 1776), p. 31.
[181] Thomas, *The Ends of Life*, p. 211.

across the Atlantic, which illuminate a remarkable network of support, despite the fact that the majority of these letter writers had never met.[182] The Women's Meeting in Maryland in 1678 described the 'Spirituall Comfort, and great Satisfaction in the truth' that they received after their sisters in London started a correspondence with them and sent them some books. 'Wee are but weake, and few in nomber', they wrote, 'and oure outward beinges far distant one from another.' But they declared their 'true love and heavenly fellowship' and begged their distant friends to pray for their continued spiritual growth.[183] Mendelson and Crawford have stressed how the power of female piety and prayer should be viewed within a broader cultural framework of collective female endeavour.[184] Indeed, in their mutual quest for salvation, the simple act of assisting one another with spiritual advice, admonition, and prayer gave female Friends the opportunity to enter into supportive relationships with one another.

With the same spiritual outlook and theological presuppositions, a degree of intimacy could be immediately assumed between unknown and distant members of the community. Mary Pemberton, writing from Philadelphia in 1754, explained to the Yorkshire Friend Susanna Fothergill, whom she had never met, that she felt 'a degree of that Love that makes the Friends of truth near to each other in a spiritual Relation tho Personally unacquainted'. At the time of Mary's writing, Susanna's husband, Samuel, was undertaking ministerial service in the American colonies. 'Though tis a Considerable tryal to be deprived of the [company] of an agreeable Companion and Indulgent Husband', Mary wrote, 'tis a Circumstance which has heretofore frequently fallen to my Lot In which at times I have happily experienced the exercise of Patience and Resignation.'[185] The shared experience of writer and recipient served as a foundation on which women's friendships could develop. 'The Continuance of such a valuable Friendship', as Mary Pemberton explained in a later letter to Susanna, certainly helped to lessen the burden both women were experiencing as a result of their husbands' absences.[186] Inhabiting a shared culture of religious belief, these women were able to

---

[182] The transatlantic nature of their alliances is particularly effectively demonstrated in a little-known extant collection of epistles sent to the Quaker Women's Box Meeting in London between 1675 and 1753, comprising about sixty-four letters from Meetings across the British Isles, the American Colonies, and the West Indies. LRSF, MGR 1 1a4 London Women's Meeting Epistles, 1671–1753.

[183] LRSF, MGR 1 1a4 London Women's Meeting Epistles, 1671–1753, fol. 37, epistle from the Women's Meeting in Maryland to the Women's Meeting in London, 22 September 1678.

[184] Mendelson and Crawford, *Women in Early Modern England*, pp. 225–231.

[185] LRSF, MS Vol 329 Crossfield MS, fol. 34, Mary Pemberton to Susanna Fothergill, Philadelphia, 16 October 1754.

[186] Ibid., fol. 63, Mary Pemberton to Susanna Fothergill, Philadelphia, 18 October 1757.

imagine an intimate alliance without physical contact. This represented a radical departure from contemporary norms, for, as we have seen, the highest form of friendship was thought possible only between intimates who occupied a similar, political, cultural, and social world. The bodily symbolism of friendship, through sharing common gestures and physical space, was stressed by Bray as its most important and enduring characteristic.[187]

The extensive body of transatlantic ministers presented perhaps the most important opportunity for intimate connections between distant individuals. The act of hosting travelling ministers was also performed in the name of 'Friendship' and provided further opportunities for long-distance female alliances to develop, despite the often-fleeting nature of their initial encounters. Mary Weston, for example, was not acquainted with any Friends in America before her arrival in Philadelphia, but was hosted by co-religionists across the colonies throughout her two-year journey. The letters of thanks sent by Weston's husband, Daniel, during her stay in America, speak of the 'repeated acts of the greatest Friendship to her, which has made her passage in that Land much Easier th[a]n it would otherwise have been'.[188] In 1738, the Yorkshire Friend Tabitha Hornor wrote a letter to the minister Abigail Watson, in the hope that she would be 'Ingaged in mind to pay us another visitt here'. Noting how 'that near fellowship and simpathy between us cannot admit decay', she described how her thoughts for this ministering Friend were 'often revived upon my mind with that brightness which is the soul ravishing'.[189]

Hospitality, or 'guest-friendship', had long been regarded as an important act of cultural significance in early modern England.[190] The Christian notion of universal benevolence, from which Quakers drew much of their rhetoric, was central to the construction of a culture of support and mutual assistance. Indeed, it was the table, as Bray aptly comments that 'perhaps most of all transformed the stranger into the friend'.[191] However, as Felicity Heal found in her seminal work on hospitality, the notions of Christian charity underpinning early modern ideals of conviviality came to be replaced by a more discriminatory system where family, kin, and neighbours were placed at the forefront of charitable concern, and friends and strangers, as well as

---

[187] Bray, *The Friend*, pp. 140–176.

[188] HSP, MS Coll 484A Pemberton Family Papers, vol. 7, p. 25, Daniel Weston to Israel Pemberton, London, 30 March 1751.

[189] British Library, Add MS 71116 Jacob Family: Correspondence of the Irish Quaker Family of Jacob; 1701–1802, fol. 11, Tabitha Hornor to Abigail Watson (Boles), Leeds, 7 August 1738.

[190] See in particular, Felicity Heal, *Hospitality in Early Modern England* (Oxford, 1990), esp. pp. 192–222; and Baltzly and Eliopoulos, 'The Classical Ideals of Friendship', pp. 1–64.

[191] Bray, *The Friend*, p. 150.

enemies, were placed on the outer circles of this amicability.[192] The networks of hospitality that evolved within early Quakerism, by contrast, were almost always constructed between complete strangers. Indeed, a greater degree of support and intimacy appears to have been offered to a Quaker woman's co-religionists (even if they were strangers) than to their non-Quaker neighbours or kin.

Whilst male Friends also opened their homes to travelling ministers, and many hosts were married couples, the greatest burden arguably fell upon women Friends.[193] Their household labours meant that they were ideally placed to provide a supportive environment for visiting ministers, whether in supplying food or accommodation, or making arrangements during their stay. On hearing of the arrival of the English ministers Catherine Payton and Mary Peisley in South Carolina, Rachel Pemberton ordered that their chests, bedding, and possessions be conveyed from London and Charlestown to her home in Philadelphia. 'An appology for sending them under my care is altogether needless', she explained in one letter dated 9 January 1754, 'being glad of the Opportunity of doing this or any other service in my power for you.' She also expressed her hopes that when the two women arrived in Philadelphia, they would choose to stay at her home, where 'you may be assured of an hearty wellcome'.[194] The fact that Rachel initiates this generous act of hospitality with two complete strangers shows the central role that women played in this culture of support. Rachel's husband, Israel, was an important member of the Philadelphian merchant community, with access to the necessary contacts to make such arrangements possible. However, it was the woman of the household who had heard of the two ministers' travels, initiated contact with them, and arranged for the conveyance of their luggage across the Atlantic.

The centrality of women within networks of hospitality has often been recognised as an important part of early modern religious culture. In a context of persecution, the private space of the household was important because it was the only place where religious dissent could be safely

---

[192] This process was encapsulated in the growing seventeenth-century tendency to give money to the needier members of communities, rather than provide more intimate forms of assistance, like food, drink, and lodging. Heal, *Hospitality in Early Modern England*, pp. 16–19.

[193] The role of men in Quaker hospitality networks is revealed in a letter of recommendation sent from Catherine Payton to Ruth Follows, which advised the minister about travel in Ireland. In this letter of recommendation, Catherine directed Ruth to lodge with an 'antient' Friend in Dublin, adding that if 'thou should have an account of his being Dead, go to William Tayler who lives with him, and by his will is appointed to succeed him in the service of entertaining ministering Friends and to live in the same House he does'. LRSF, Temp MSS 127/1/1/3 Ruth Follows Papers, Catherine Payton to Ruth Follows, Dudley, 29 July 1761.

[194] HSP, MS Coll 484A Pemberton Family Papers, vol. 9, p. 129, Rachel Pemberton to Mary Peisley and Catherine Payton, Philadelphia, 9 January 1754.

practised. Households harbouring Catholic priests during the late sixteenth and seventeenth centuries, for instance, were dependent upon wives of recusant Catholics receiving priests into their homes. The 'abnormally large part' played by wives and widows was stressed by John Bossy in his study of the Catholic community before 1620. This went beyond mere domestic tasks, and was both active and proselytising in its character.[195] Paralleling the models of hospitality provided by female Friends, these women, usually made the arrangements for a priest's arrival and his secret stay.[196] Methodist women also came to play a prominent role within household dissent because unpaid ministers were continually forced to rely upon the charity of the female members of their circuits for food, lodging, and supplies as they travelled from place to place. Mary Bosanquet Fletcher's home in Madeley was renowned for hosting a constant stream of Methodists. She compared her home in Yorkshire to 'a pilgrims inn'.[197] Whilst Quaker women's hospitality was not unfamiliar in the context of religious dissent, it was unusual for women to participate in both the role of visiting minister and host. Both Catholicism and Methodism subscribed to a model of religious orthodoxy that promoted a celibate class of single men in ministerial roles, to the exclusion of women. Even the relatively liberal ethos of the Wesleyan Methodists did not extend as far as granting women the authority to undertake transatlantic service. This meant that their friends and social acquaintances were usually situated within their own localities.

Clearly, there was also a localised supportive element to Quaker women's connections, which involved an exchange of goods, care, emotional support, and natural affection. Yet Quakerism provided unparalleled opportunities for women Friends from across the Atlantic to meet through the act of hospitality and initiate enduring friendships. Mary Weston, for instance, an English minister who had travelled to the American colonies in 1750 without a female companion, forged a lifelong relationship with her Philadelphian landlady, Mary Pemberton. A letter in 1752, sent shortly after her return home, revealed her longing to be reunited with her 'sympathising Friend'. 'I have just immagin'd my self personally present with thee', Weston wrote, 'as often am in spirit, tho perhaps may never behold the faces one of another more.'[198] Friendship in this respect was a powerful

---

[195] John Bossy, *The English Catholic Community 1570–1850* (London, 1975), pp. 152–160. See also Marie B. Rowlands, 'Recusant Women 1560–1640' in Mary Prior (ed.), *Women in English Society, 1500–1800* (London, 1991), pp. 112–135.

[196] Diane Willen, 'Women and Religion in Early Modern England', in Sherrin Marshall (ed.), *Women in Reformation and Counter-Reformation Europe: Public and Private Worlds* (Bloomington, IN, 1989), p. 156.

[197] Lawrence, *One Family under God*, p. 80.

[198] HSP, MS Coll 484A Pemberton Family Papers, vol. 8, p. 56, Mary Weston to Mary Pemberton, Wapping, London, 14 September 1752.

accompaniment to ministerial work because it enabled women Friends to continue to offer spiritual support and counsel to one another long after the initial period of service was over. Like Mary Pemberton, the Irish Friend Elizabeth Shackleton took great pleasure in the company of 'Religious friends' who visited her home in Ballitore. In her memoirs, she commented that 'divers have written me encouraging letters' after leaving her home, implying the long-term nature of the relationship despite the transience of their first encounter.[199]

The sense of spiritual equality shared by Quaker believers also meant that the host could be placed in a position of authority within the relationship, despite her non-itinerant status. As Weston communicated to her, 'Dear Landlady', Pemberton's 'Judgments in spiritual things [I] prefer to most' and begged for 'the help of thy spirit, in Joynt travel for Enlargement of heart'.[200] John Griffith explained in his testimony of Susanna Morris, how he had 'once made my Home at her House induced thereto by an expectation of receiving Help by her good Company, and Example in my religious Progress in which I was not disappointed'.[201] It is interesting that hosts like Mary Pemberton and Susanna Morris could achieve a position of spiritual authority, despite a status theoretically inferior to that of their ministering visitors. It certainly stood in contrast to the guest-host relationships that emerged within the context of Catholicism or Methodism, where an itinerant, educated, paid minister was immediately placed in a dominant position within the relationship. Indeed, if we take the contemporary view that intimate friendship was only available to equals, it would never have been possible for a close relationship to develop between a laywoman and a Catholic or Methodist minister because of the inequality of their relationship. The provision of hospitality thus provides an important insight into how ideas of friendship among early Quakers became inseparable from their ideas of community: these networks were dominated both by women performing their benevolent duties as Friends, and by women sharing intimacies as friends.

The powerful transatlantic networks of support that emerged within early Quakerism offer conclusive proof of the importance of female sociability within a religious culture that denigrated many of the traditional customs

[199] Mary Leadbeater (ed.), *Memoirs and Letters of Richard and Elizabeth Shackleton, Late of Ballitore, Ireland* (London, 1849), p. 16.

[200] HSP, MS Coll 484A Pemberton Family Papers, vol. 8, p. 56, Mary Weston to Mary Pemberton, Wapping, London, 14 September 1752.

[201] HCQSC, MS Coll 968 Allinson Family Papers, 1710–1939, Box 6, 'A Brief Account of Part of Susanna Morris's Second Journey through Sundry Parts of Great Britain to Which is Prefixed a Few Remarks Concerning Her, by John Griffith', undated, c. 1775.

of friendship. As Sandra Stanley Holton argues, in guarding one another against the dangers of the material world, Quaker women were forced to focus upon the 'shared pursuit' of spirituality within their daily lives.[202] This served to influence not only how friendships were maintained by Quaker 'friends', but also the distance over which the most intimate of alliances could operate.

To hostile observers, Quaker doctrines appeared to be shunning the conventions of politeness and sociability, and belonging to the movement enabled many isolated, persecuted, and suffering Friends to form new and meaningful relationships with other members of their religious community. In the first few decades of the movement, this played an important role in compensating for the loss of their former personal connections following conversion. As the movement developed, however, its social cohesiveness came to rest on the complex web of friendship and kinship networks, which enabled Friends to imagine themselves as part of a unified spiritual family. As I discussed in the Introduction to this book, the term 'Society of Friends' didn't emerge until at least 1793, but it nevertheless captures the spirit of the early movement, for membership immediately gave Friends access to a network of obligation and reciprocity that, like ties of blood, was characterised by an unconditional love for their co-religionists.

While always honouring social obligations to their spiritual kin, however, Friends generally secluded themselves from wider practices of sociability. The 'quietism' that has come to characterise many depictions of the second- and third-generation movement also reflects the Quakers' determination to distinguish themselves from those outside their circle. Yet, rather than subordinating the ideal of friendship altogether, as their Calvinist contemporaries did, early Quakers recognised its value for their union with God in the life to come. The simple acts of offering one another spiritual advice, admonition, prayer, and written encouragement gave Quaker women the opportunity to form powerful sororal networks of support in their mutual quest for salvation.

Traditional practices of sociability were reconfigured into an alternative framework of 'polite Quakerliness', which balanced social interaction with co-religionists with the expanding social and cultural opportunities increasingly available to their contemporaries. However, even the most informal social gatherings, whether in the tearoom or the birthing chamber, became exclusive sites of religious devotion, where women could meet solemnly together to give praise to God. The spiritual dimension of all their relationships, sometimes transnational in scope, enabled Quaker women to imagine as much as experience their friendships. One of the most distinctive elements

---

[202] Holton, 'Kinship and Friendship', pp. 367–368.

of Quaker women's social alliances is the distances over which many were conducted.

Whilst historians have demonstrated how friendship connections were usually reinforced through ties to kin and neighbours, the Quaker case shows how believers could gain immediate access to a transatlantic network of Friends with whom they often formed strong and enduring bonds. It was this 'imaginary' aspect of Quaker women's alliance formation that constituted the most significant deviation from contemporary understandings of friendship. Rather than physical proximity, careful consideration, mutual benefit, or social equality, it was the emphasis they placed on divine providence and the shared pursuit of spirituality that guided Quaker women in initiating close and enduring friendships. This is particularly apparent in the experience of travelling ministry, where the compatibility between having a singular spiritual calling and a sympathetic partner with whom to share the physical, emotional, and spiritual burdens of itinerant ministry was a compelling feature of their alliances. Female public ministry was still widely viewed with suspicion, so it is unsurprising that itinerant women appear to have placed greater value than male itinerants on their travelling companions. Women travelling together gave one another an invaluable sense of solidarity and support when they were undergoing great hardships and sufferings for their faith.

The important role of female alliances in reinforcing a sense of community amongst Friends has been largely unacknowledged in the movement's history. As this chapter has shown, religious belief played a significant part in shaping the social bonds that developed between these women, and were as much a part of their everyday experiences as their domestic arrangements. The networks forged by Quaker women illustrate the intermediacy of their religious community in the structuring of everyday encounters and personal relationships. Nevertheless, Quaker women did not live in a social vacuum. Their lives were defined by the world beyond their religious communities as well as through their friendships with their co-religionists. How these attitudes towards friendship affected Quaker women's interactions with the non-Quaker world is therefore the focus of the final chapter of this book.

−4−

'In the World, but Not of It': Quaker Women's Interactions with the Non-Quaker World

Hail happy virgin of celestial race,
Adorn'd with wisdom, and replete with grace ...
Too long indeed our sex has been deny'd.
And ridicul'd by men's malignant pride; ...
Redeem the coming age, and set us free
From that false brand of Incapacity.

A Young Lady, 'On the Noted and Celebrated
Quaker Mrs Drummond',
Gentleman's Magazine: Or, Monthly Intelligencer,
vol. 5 (September 1735), p. 555

The emergence of the Quakers shattered the early modern consensus on the role of ordinary men and women in church hierarchies. Over the seventeenth and eighteenth centuries, Quakerism functioned as both a negative 'other' for mainstream religious groups and as a subject of interest and intellectual curiosity. In July 1735, the *General Evening Post* reported that a Scottish Quaker preacher, May Drummond, had lately had the 'Honour to preach' before Queen Caroline. Renowned for her oratory, the 'celebrated Mrs Drummond['s]' audience with the Queen only added to her reputation, as the English press detailed her progress around the nation.[1] The Bristol excise official John Cannon noted in his diary the popular appeal of her Meetings, describing how huge crowds had come 'far and near for novelty's sake to hear her'.[2] Cannon's observations were supported by another report from October 1735, which described the throngs of people that gathered to hear her preach at the Friars Meeting, near Broadmead in Bristol. It was so well attended with

---

[1] *General Evening Post* (London), 3 July 1735, p. 3; *London Daily Post and General Advertiser* (London), 22 April 1736, p. 1. Drummond's tours across England were reported in the *General Evening Post*; *London Daily Post and General Advertiser*; *Daily Journal*; and *London Evening Post*.

[2] John Cannon, *The Chronicles of John Cannon Excise Officer and Writing Master, 1734–1743*, ed. John Money (2 vols., Oxford, 2010), vol. 2, p. 313, original fol. 320 entry for 18 October 1737.

'great Numbers of different Perswasions' that reinforcements allegedly had to be added to the gallery 'to prevent any Accident by its falling'.[3]

May Drummond's popular appeal is far removed from the scorn and intolerance experienced by the first female Quakers in Bristol. In 1681, four women were abused at the hands of local magistrates and crowds for attending the same Friars Meeting. An account of their sufferings described how an 'ancient Woman', Susanna York, was badly injured after being thrown down, and how Mary Page, who was heavily pregnant, suffered 'great danger to her Life' after being violently pulled from the Meeting House. To add to their humiliation, local boys were incited to throw dirt and heckle them, calling them '*ugly Whores, Bitches, Jades*, and the like'.[4] Just more than fifty years later, May Drummond encountered a dramatically different reception at the same Meeting. Her 'celebrated' status implied a high public standing, whilst her ability to attract mixed audiences indicates curiosity and tolerance at the popular level.

It is, however, notable that at the very moment when May Drummond was enjoying mass public attention, the wider Quaker movement was debating how far it should be integrating with the non-Quaker world. We saw in the previous chapter how dissociation from the wider world altered how Quaker women's alliances were formed. Yet Quaker theology also offered an all-encompassing notion of friendship, for the ubiquitous nature of the inner light meant that spiritual friendship was attainable to all. The decades following the introduction of formal toleration in 1689 brought about an identity crisis for the transatlantic movement. Mid-eighteenth-century Quaker leaders, argues James Emmett Ryan, were undergoing a 'crisis in their membership that exposed fault lines in the Society'.[5] As discussed in Chapter 2, the Quaker Meetings expected members to carefully balance their testimonies of simplicity and plainness with commercial, charitable, political, and social activities within their mixed communities. But this led to the question of how to be 'in the world, but not of it'.[6]

This book has thus far emphasised the relationships female Friends developed with other members of their religious community. In this chapter, I will move beyond confessional boundaries to trace Quaker women's bonds with the non-Quaker world, both as preachers and members of local

---

[3] 'Country-News. Bristol, October 4', *General Evening Post* (London), 4 October 1735–7 October 1735, p. 1.

[4] Besse, *Quaker Sufferings*, vol. 1, p. 57. This incident is also reported in LRSF, YM/MfS/GBS/3/1 Great Book of Sufferings, Berkshire to Lincolnshire, 1650–1686, Bristol 1681, p. 32.

[5] James Emmett Ryan, *Imaginary Friends: Representing Quakers in American Culture, 1650–1950* (London, 2009), p. 90.

[6] Emma J. Lapansky, 'Plainness and Simplicity', in Stephen W. Angell and Pink Dandelion (eds.), *The Oxford Handbook of Quaker Studies* (Oxford, 2013), p. 336.

communities. Eighteenth-century Quakerism has often been defined by its 'quietist' and introspective nature; as Friends sought to withdraw from the world rather than compromise their religious identity and beliefs.[7] Yet, as the example of May Drummond shows, being an outsider did not preclude acceptance from wider society. Historians examining the 'sociology of deviance' have captured this complex phenomenon. Alexandra Walsham, for instance, has warned historians about the dangers of viewing tolerance and intolerance as simple binaries.[8] Moreover, in his reflections on 'Insiders and Outsiders' in modern European, German, and Jewish history, Steven Aschheim has observed that the balance between 'full integration' and the 'maintenance of a distinctive, separate identity' for marginal groups is both fluid and exceedingly fragile. Exclusion is often dependent upon having a connection to the normative 'inside'.[9] It is therefore necessary to embrace the complex and often contradictory facets of Quaker women's lives, shaped both by their confessional affiliation and their interactions with wider society. I will present a multiplicity of images that could be attached to Quaker women in different social contexts across the British Atlantic and suggest how they changed over the movement's first century.

The issue of women's assimilation into seventeenth- and eighteenth-century society is an important but overlooked aspect of Quaker history. Rebecca Larson has argued persuasively that by the closing decades of the eighteenth century, non-Quaker reactions to female preachers were overwhelmingly positive. The favourable reception of ministers such as May Drummond proved that attitudes towards public female preachers had softened. Larson attributes this changing reception, in both England and New England, to the Toleration Act of 1689, which reshaped the image of Friends in society, politics, and business affairs.[10] The assimilation of the movement into wider society and its newfound 'respectability', she argues, resulted in 'a new visibility of their spiritually "gifted" females'.[11]

However, focusing only on female preachers overlooks the significant relationships of Quaker women with non-Quakers in different social and

---

[7] On Quaker 'quietism' see Robynne Rogers Healey, 'Quietist Quakerism, 1692–c. 1805', in Angell and Dandelion, *The Oxford Handbook of Quaker Studies*, pp. 47–62.

[8] Alexandra Walsham, *Charitable Hatred: Tolerance and Intolerance in England, 1500–1700* (Manchester, 2006), pp. 1–5. Walsham explores the relationship between tolerance and intolerance in chapter 6, showing how the separate dichotomies of 'sect' and 'denomination'; and 'assimilation' and 'separation' are part of a continuous spectrum and not mutually exclusive of one another.

[9] Steven Aschheim, *At the Edges of Liberalism: Junctions of European, German and Jewish History* (Basingstoke, 2012), pp. 145–155.

[10] Rebecca Larson, *Daughters of Light: Quaker Women Preaching and Prophesying in the Colonies and Abroad, 1700–1775* (New York, 1999), pp. 247–258.

[11] Ibid., p. 290.

economic contexts. The majority of women attracted to Quakerism did not undertake ministerial travel or radically alter their domestic, social, or economic responsibilities. Little is known about these women at the very 'grass-roots' of the Society. Patricia Crawford has suggested that 'the loss of neighbourliness was a handicap' for nonconformist women, who experienced 'social ostracism' following the withdrawal of female support in their daily household tasks.[12] This raises the question of how women were able to survive and function in their communities after they converted to Quakerism. Questions also arise about the evolving movement and how far strict isolation characterised Quaker women's position with those outside their religious Society.

The picture is further complicated when we turn our attention across the Atlantic, particularly to the setting of eighteenth-century Pennsylvania. Remarkable religious diversity had characterised the colony from its earliest years. Yet distinct Quaker practices, such as their peace testimony and desire to develop peaceable relations with the indigenous population, antagonised their non-Quaker neighbours. Quaker refusal to bear arms, for instance, led to their forced withdrawal from colonial government in the mid-eighteenth century and, during the Revolutionary Wars, resulted in frequent accusations of illicit pacts with the British.[13] The experience of being a female Friend within Penn's 'Holy Experiment' was therefore markedly different for colonial Quaker women. Though they were usually tolerated by wider society, the stance the movement took in particular social and political circumstances clearly bought to light the fragile boundaries between religious pluralism and full assimilation.

To draw a clear distinction between 'tolerance' and 'intolerance' is therefore, to quote Walsham, 'both intractably difficult and a matter of perspective'.[14] This chapter will assess the character of popular intolerance alongside the co-existence experienced by seventeenth- and eighteenth-century female Friends. It will begin by assessing negative representations of female Quakers, especially in printed and visual sources. Next, it will discuss evidence of British and American Quaker women's assimilation at a local level, offering many examples of mutual and supportive relationships that female Friends maintained with individuals outside their religious community: as neighbours, in their professional roles, through philanthropic work, and as preachers. The chapter will close by assessing the ways in which

---

[12] Patricia Crawford, *Women and Religion in England, 1500–1720* (London, 1993), p. 191.
[13] The various crises that affected colonial Quakerism are explored in Hugh Barbour and J. William Frost, *The Quakers* (London, 1988), pp. 119–151. See also Sarah Crabtree, *Holy Nation: The Transatlantic Quaker Ministry in an Age of Revolution* (Chicago, 2015), esp. pp. 31–60.
[14] Walsham, *Charitable Hatred*, p. 264.

Quaker women came to be the subjects of admiration in wider society following intellectual developments that regarded both female Friends and religious women more widely as 'respectable' citizens. This thematic organisation is deliberately flexible to avoid a teleological narrative describing a simple transition from persecution to toleration with 1689 as the defining moment in this relationship. Indeed, as Simon Dixon noted in his study of the Quaker communities of London, Quaker strategies of separation and integration do not reflect more general patterns of sectarian development.[15]

Naturally, any study dealing with a broad range of women's representations and experiences across a large geographical space brings with it methodological challenges. It is always much easier to identify instances of conflict, division, and public scandal in the archives than to find evidence of communal harmony. Difficulties also arise from any survey utilising printed and visual sources to understand attitudes towards a movement or idea. In particular, they raise questions about the reception of such opinions and whether they were representative of broader social values. Moreover, given low levels of female literacy at this time, polemical accounts had a strong gender bias, as they were largely written by men for a male audience. Nevertheless, written and visual sources, as Adam Fox has argued, formed part of a 'dynamic continuum' with local ideas, customs, beliefs, and intellectual trends.[16] Many of the authors discussed prided themselves on the veracity of their reports and the trustworthiness of their sources. As I will show, despite their evident partiality and exaggeration, these printed materials are useful for understanding changing popular and intellectual ideas about Quaker women.

Non-Quaker writings can also provide a strong indication of changing attitudes and understandings of female Friends on an international scale. However, because very few publications hostile to Quakerism originated in Ireland and the American colonies, it is important to note some geographical imbalance in relation to where they were printed and circulated. This can partly be linked to the slower development of regional printing even in the more established cities of Dublin, Boston, and Philadelphia.[17] It is also plausible that the liberal principles of colonies like Pennsylvania, where religious plurality was part of the everyday life of the colony, discouraged Quaker opponents from engaging in printed debate. Nevertheless, the colonies were never entirely cut off from the cultural practices of Britain, and many of the publications sold by booksellers and merchants in London

---

[15] Simon Dixon, 'Quaker Communities in London, 1667–c. 1714', Royal Holloway, University of London, PhD thesis (2005), pp. 104–108.

[16] Adam Fox, *Oral and Literate Culture in England, 1500–1700* (Oxford, 2000), p. 50.

[17] Michael Warner, *The Letters of the Republic: Publication and the Public Sphere in Eighteenth-Century America* (London, 1990), p. 31.

found their way to Ireland, Scotland, and the colonies. Thus, despite the limited development of a domestic book trade, around 120,000 books and pamphlets were shipped annually from English ports to the North American colonies by the 1770s.[18]

The variety of printed and manuscript sources that form the focus of this chapter show us how the transformation, or reformulation of female Friends by wider society, was part of a dynamic process of exchange deeply affected by developments in both Britain and the colonies. The task of this chapter, then, is to chart the impact of confessional difference within a range of social and economic contexts. It will show how understandings of women's place within religious dissent were being transformed across Atlantic culture.

'DELUSIONS OF THE DEVIL': WOMEN IN EARLY ANTI-QUAKER POLEMIC

When Quakerism first emerged in Britain, it provoked a large backlash in print, with a dual purpose of discouraging others from joining the sect and casting Quaker adherents as outsiders. Popular understandings of Quakerism as particularly attractive to women meant that female Friends were often the targets of satire and were used to represent excess and the menace that the movement posed to established conventions. According to the Cambridge Platonist Henry Hallywell, '[M]any heretics have diffused and spread their desperate Errors by insinuating them first into women.' And this, as he went on to explain, 'has been a very great help in the Propagation of Quakery, by making the Woman first in the Transgression, who by her continual Solicitation and Importunity ... wins the good man to betray himself into the hands of these uncircumcised Philistines'.[19] Underlying Hallywell's statement is a genuine alarm about the role of women in the propagation and spread of the Quaker faith.

Printed tracts published by the Quakers have played a vital role in shaping our understanding of women in the early movement. Kate Peters's *Print Culture and the Early Quakers* provides a particularly important contribution to this debate. Peters demonstrates a crucial link between Quaker published tracts and the movement's successful missionary campaign.[20]

---

[18] James Raven, 'The Importation of Books in the Eighteenth Century', in Hugh Amory and David D. Hall, *The Colonial Book in the Atlantic World* (Chapel Hill, NC, 2007), p. 184.

[19] Henry Hallywell, *An Account of Familism as It Is Revived and Propagated by the Quakers* (London, 1673), pp. 122–123.

[20] Kate Peters, *Print Culture and the Early Quakers* (Cambridge 2005), pp. 252–253. See also Catie Gill, *Women in the Seventeenth-Century Quaker Community: A Literary Study of Political Identities, 1650–1700* (Aldershot, 2005); and Hagglund, 'Quakers and Print Culture', in Angell and Dandelion, *Oxford Handbook of Quaker Studies*, pp. 477–491.

The question of how attitudes towards Quaker women manifested in seventeenth- and eighteenth-century print culture has received surprisingly little attention in the history of the movement.[21] Anti-Quaker literature had a sustained presence throughout this period, demonstrated by the large number of anti-Quaker prints that appeared shortly after the movement's establishment. More than 500 pamphlets and books were published against Friends between 1650 and 1750, and Joseph Smith's famous nineteenth-century compilation, *Bibliotheca Anti-Quakeriana*, contains the names of more than 150 different authors who published texts 'adverse to the Society of Friends'.[22] These texts helped to shape the image of Quakerism presented to the non-Quaker public. A number of themes run throughout the anti-Quaker material relevant to women, including their negative impact on family relationships; ignorance and credulity; scolding and sexual licentiousness; and witchcraft and madness. We should note, however, that many of these slurs were not exclusively applied to Friends and formed part of a long tradition of antagonism towards religious deviance.

One of the most common tropes in early anti-Quaker polemic was the argument that adherence to the faith was undermining the unity of the family. Chapter 1 made reference to the destructive (and violent) consequences of divided households, affected by the conversion of one spouse, or a child, to Quakerism. But it was the potential repercussions of female-initiated conversion that early critics seemed to fear most. Anna M. Lawrence argues, with reference to anti-Methodist polemic, that this stemmed from a belief that women were leading their families into 'new, delusional religious and moral spheres'.[23] Likewise, evidence from anti-Quaker literature suggests that writers were keen to defend traditional domestic values, which the disruptive excesses of Quakerism seemed to be disturbing. This was evidenced in 1725 when William Walker's wife converted to Quakerism against his wishes. In his published account, Walker explained that this had created 'a

---

[21] One exception is Mark Knights, *The Devil in Disguise: Deception, Delusion, and Fanaticism in the Early English Enlightenment* (Oxford, 2011), esp. pp. 77–94. See also Ryan, *Imaginary Friends*.

[22] Knights, *The Devil in Disguise*, p. 77; Charles L. Cherry, 'Enthusiasm and Madness: Anti-Quakerism in the Seventeenth Century', *Quaker History*, vol. 73, no. 2 (1984), pp. 10–11.

For the purposes of this discussion I have searched for references to women in the hostile anti-Quaker texts published between 1650 and 1750. These have been identified through a number of catalogues, including a search of 'Quaker women' in the English Short Title Catalogue and a subject search of 'Antiquakeriana' on Tripod catalogue, which combines the archival material held at Haverford College, Bryn Mawr College, and Swarthmore College libraries. This search has led to the identification of more than 700 texts (including editions) relating to anti-Quaker polemic published in England and the colonies between 1650 and 1750.

[23] Anna M. Lawrence, *One Family under God: Love, Belonging, and Authority in Early Transatlantic Methodism* (Philadelphia, 2011), p. 98.

House of Confusion'. He warned that by being accountable to another man, his wife was no longer willing to submit to his authority, leading to a situation of 'Divide and Rule'.[24]

An anonymous pamphlet published in 1700 detailed a series of errors linked to the 'Quaker-Craft', accusing Quaker preachers of seducing 'silly Women', who would then initiate the conversion of their families.[25] It was 'not only an easie, but a very important Conquest', the author warned, 'for the *Quakers* having made sure of the Wife, they seldom miss of the Husband, who can never be at quiet till he hath Complied with her by renouncing of his Faith.'[26] The biblical trope of 'silly women' was a slur linked to more general notions of the female constitution, since they were more prone to the deception of heretics. Women's perceived emotional nature and inability to discern truth from error required their subjection in marriage and matters of religion. Anti-Catholic literature from earlier in the century had made reference to 'Romanists who creep into great houses to lead captive "simple women laden with sinnes"', a rhetoric that Arthur F. Marotti suggests was enhanced by the harbour and hospitality that English recusant women provided for Jesuit priests.[27] The intensity with which the family became the focus of anti-Quaker writings, however, suggests a strong underlying recognition of the Quaker mother's position within family piety. Writing in 1653, Francis Higginson remarked on the deception of 'silly women' in their homes as one of the chief reasons for the proliferation of the sect in northern England, noting their success 'in subverting whole houses, and overthrowing the faith of so many'.[28] The sheer number of women associated with Quakerism, combined with the fact that they could adopt public and itinerant roles independent of patriarchal authority, must have made the disruptive effects of conversion on household order seem all the more menacing.[29]

---

[24] William Walker, *A True Copy of Some Original Letters, Which Pass'd between John Hall of Monk-Hesleden in the County of Durham, an Eminent Quaker Teacher, and William Walker* (Newcastle, 1725), p. 51.

[25] The term 'Silly Women' had biblical origins. 2 Timothy 3:6 on evil in the last days described how traitors 'of this sort are they which creep into houses, and lead captive silly women laden with sins, led away with divers lusts' (King James version).

[26] Anon., *Remarks upon the Quakers: Wherein the Plain-Dealers Are Plainly Dealt With* (London, 1700), p. 3.

[27] Arthur F. Marotti, *Religious Ideology and Cultural Fantasy: Catholic and Anti-Catholic Discourses in Early Modern England* (Notre Dame, IN, 2005), pp. 53–56.

[28] Francis Higginson, *A Brief Relation of the Irreligion of the Northern Quakers* (London, 1653), sig. A5v–A6r.

[29] As in many congregational churches, women often outnumbered men in Quaker congregations. Keith Thomas remarked that rumours had even spread in the years before 1660 that the Quaker sect was confined to women alone. Keith V. Thomas, 'Women and the Civil War Sects', *Past and Present*, vol. 13 (1958), p. 47.

As a 'little commonwealth', divisions within the home could only be a sure sign of the conflict within society that was to come, rending the bonds of obedience that held both family and state together.[30] It was the potential repercussions of female-initiated conversions on household order that early critics of the sect seemed to fear most. The French mystic Antoinette Bourignon described the revelations experienced by one Quaker woman, who had prophesied that her husband would die and that she would marry a young man nearly half her age, as 'Delusions of the Devil'.[31] She also recounted one scenario of a man who had been abused by his wife and her friends. The couple separated when the wife refused to turn away her Quaker servant. It was even revealed that the woman had 'loved her Servant more than her Husband ... and was ready, upon Occasion, to beat her Husband rather than her Servant'.[32] The scandalous implication of such a story was that in a divided household female servants might be elevated to positions above their male masters. It underlined the ill-effects of a woman favouring her co-religionists over her family. In violating the marital bond and splitting households, Quaker beliefs were condemned as both disruptive and corrosive to traditional social relationships.

Approbation of public female preaching, which went against Pauline precepts of women remaining silent in church, was a radical component of Quaker theology and, predictably, became a target of much anti-Quaker polemic. Phyllis Mack has suggested that negative reactions to female prophets stemmed from a popular fear of disorder.[33] One 1655 publication by Donald Lupton underscored the divisive nature of public female speech. 'They like not Saint *Pauls* advise', the author wrote, but 'presume so far, even to *Railing* and *Scolding* ... women are called houswives [*sic*], they should in modesty keep at home'.[34] Such concerns for domestic order are symbolised through hostile propaganda that discredited female prophets as 'tub-preachers', such as the one presented in Figure 4.1. This image was linked to laundresses who, according to Mack, had turned their washtubs upside down as makeshift pulpits to preach disorder and disobedience.[35] The tub had symbolic resonance, for in adopting such a public role, critics could argue that women were literally upturning their domestic responsibilities. It also resonated with the image of a 'world turned upside down',

---

[30] William Gouge, *Of Domesticall Duties* (London, 1622), p. 18.

[31] Antoinette Bourignon, *A Warning Against the Quakers: Wherein the Errors of That Sect Are Plainly Detected* (London, 1708), p. 16.

[32] Ibid., pp. 126–129.

[33] Phyllis Mack, *Visionary Women: Ecstatic Prophecy in Seventeenth-Century England* (Berkeley, CA, 1994), p. 249.

[34] Donald Lupton, *The Quacking Mountebanck or the Jesuite Turn'd Quaker* (London, 1655), p. 19.

[35] Mack, *Visionary Women*, p. 56.

Figure 4.1. *The Quakers Meeting*, engraved by Marcel Lauron
after Egbert van Heemskerck I, c. 1640–1680. (© Religious
Society of Friends (Quakers) in Britain. LRSF 88_AXL70).

suggesting an inversion of traditional social, hierarchical, and gender roles.
The original design for this image, attributed to the Dutch artist Egbert
van Heemskerck, was copied at least thirty-three times, appearing as oil
paintings, drawings, etchings, and high-quality mezzotints, suggesting broad
appeal to a middling and wealthy urban market.[36]

It was not only the potential for wifely insubordination after conversion to Quakerism that shocked authors and printers, but the economic
disruption caused to the family unit by such behaviour. If we are to take
Mack's suggestion that 'tub-preachers' represented humble washerwomen,
then these women embodied the tension between the private realm of the

[36] This figure was calculated through examination into the surviving 'Quakers Meeting' prints
in the British Museum Collection and the holdings at the Library of the Religious Society
of Friends, London. See also Harry Mount "Egbert van Heemskerck's Quaker Meetings
Revisited", *Journal of the Warburg and Courtauld Institutes*, vol. 56 (1993), p. 212; and
Robert Raines, "Notes on Egbert van Heemskerck and the English Taste for Genre",
Walpole Society, vol. 53 (1987), pp. 136–141.

household and women's public work. Their inversion of the tub confirmed that in neglecting their employment, they were also disrupting the household economy. The example discussed in Chapter 1 of Alice Hall's husband anticipating her return from preaching in Ireland in time for harvesting the oats, illustrates the damaging effect that female itinerancy could have on the economic life of the household.[37] Another example of female ministers' inverted priorities was offered by a correspondent in the *Spectator*, who explained that he was 'one of those unhappy Men that are plagued with a Gospel-Gossip ... Lectures in the Morning, Church-Meetings at Noon, and Preparation-Sermons at Night, take up so much of her Time, 'tis very rare she knows what we have for Dinner'.[38]

Others criticised the control that Quaker wives had over their husbands' resources. One text ironically claiming to be an almanac for a Quaker audience, outlined a brief chronology of 'very memorable Things' relating to the year 1677. It noted that the wife of one man had 'invited the Brotherhood and Sisterhood to a Collation', who proceeded to eat all his hard-earned roast meat.[39] Another anonymous author warned in 1700 that once the Quakers 'have got the heart of the Wife, they'll never want the Husbands Purse. For 'tis a certain Rule amongst the *Quakers*', he wrote, 'to support themselves by means of the Women, who think it no Sin to rob their Husbands, to pay the Speaker'.[40] This image was doubly satirical as it presented Quaker preachers who renounced paid ministry as hypocrites who took advantage of the more vulnerable members of their congregations. The 1679 *Yea and Nay Almanack*, authored by William Winstanley, satirised Quaker plainness testimonies by suggesting that rather than dressing in finery, female Friends' inward pride led them to steal money from their 'Husbands pockets' and give it to their unpaid preachers.[41] This was paralleled in criticisms of women in anti-Methodist literature. The scandalous actions of the cobbler's wife in *The Mock Preacher* (1739), for instance, are emphasised by her appropriation of the family finances to support a George Whitefield-like figure whilst her family starved.[42] Such slurs showed how

---

[37] Isaac Hall to Alice Hall, Broughton, Cumberland, 26 July 1747, in John Hall Shield (ed.), *Genealogical Notes on the Families of Hall, Featherstone, Wigham, Ostle, Watson etc.* (Allendale, 1915), pp. 35a–37.

[38] *The Spectator*, no. 46, 23 April 1711, in Donald F. Bond (ed.), *The Spectator* (5 vols., Oxford, 1987), vol. 1, pp. 198–199.

[39] Anon., *Poor Robin 1677: Or A Yea-and-Nay-Almanack for the People Called by Men of the World Quakers* (London, 1677), sig. A2r.

[40] Anon., *Remarks upon the Quakers*, p. 7.

[41] William Winstanley, *Yea and Nay Almanack, for the People Call'd by the Men of the World Quakers* (3 vols., London, 1678–1680), vol. 1 (1679), sig. A5r.

[42] Anon., *The Mock-Preacher: A Satyrico-Comical-Allegorical Farce* (London, 1739), pp. 15–17.

the social and economic stability of the household could be undermined by female sectarianism.

Women in anti-Quaker polemic were viewed as a dangerous threat to the established gender hierarchy. Public female speech, as David Underdown has recognised, was explicitly associated with women who defied the authority of their husbands.[43] This was linked to an age-old fear that women whose tongues were loose in public were also likely to have loose morals in private. The readiness of contemporary literature to equate sectarianism with sexual licentiousness is demonstrated forcefully in the figure of Martha Simmonds, who gained notoriety for her role in the scandalous James Nayler affair in 1656. She was labelled by polemicists as the movement's 'chief *Virago*' and more suited to a 'Cucking-stool than a speaking place'.[44] The suffering of Margaret Newby and Elizabeth Courten at the hands of Evesham magistrates also encapsulated this association between public speech and sexual immorality. According to one account, the two women were set with their legs rather than their arms in the stocks 'near a yard one from another', and when they requested a block to sit on, the mayor thrust it between their legs.[45] Catie Gill has suggested that this humiliating act was used for symbolic effect, supposedly acting as 'a substitute' for the sexual gratification that the women sought from their public speech.[46]

The unorthodox public nature of the female preacher negated traditional feminine roles and helps to explain the popular hostility women experienced in the early years of Quakerism. Their polluting behaviour made them 'agents of contamination'.[47] This is supported by a strong body of anti-Quaker polemic linking Quaker membership with sexual deviance. The 1679 *Yea and Nay Almanack* satirically warned of the rampant lechery of Quaker women in the spring months. The story of one Friend who had caught 'the Pox' from 'an unclean Sister' was expected to act as a warning to other Quakers to keep their wives under control.[48] Another hostile

---

[43] David Underdown, 'The Taming of the Scold: The Enforcement of Patriarchal Authority in Early Modern England', in Anthony Fletcher and John Stevenson (eds.), *Order and Disorder in Early Modern England* (Cambridge, 1985), p. 127.

[44] Lupton, *The Quacking Mountebanck*, p. 19; and John Deacon, *An Exact History of the Life of James Naylor* (London, 1657), p. 25. For more on James Nayler see the Introduction to this book. For a detailed account of Martha Simmonds see Crawford, *Women and Religion in England*, pp. 166–180.

[45] Humphrey Smith, *Something Further Laid Open of the Cruel Persecution of the People Called Quakers by the Magistrates and People of Evesham* (1656), p. 6.

[46] Gill, *Women in the Seventeenth-Century Quaker Community*, pp. 59–60.

[47] Michele Lise Tarter, 'Quaking in the Light: The Politics of Quaker Women's Corporeal Prophecy in the Seventeenth-Century Transatlantic World' in Janet Moore Lindman and Michele Lise Tarter (eds.), *A Centre of Wonders: The Body in Early America* (New York, 2001), pp. 151–152.

[48] Winstanley, *Yea and Nay Almanack*, vol. 1 (1679), A7r.

account described how a Yorkshire woman 'came naked from her own Bed to another womans husband'. On arriving, she 'bid him, *Open his Bed to her, for the Father had sent her to him*'. To add to the scandal, moreover, it was alleged that 'The man had at that time another man lying in Bed with him, who rose to give place to this woman.' In linking Quakers to aberrant sexual proclivities, polemicists sought to limit their influence upon the rest of society. The author insisted that 'no rational person' would conclude that Quakers were anything other than 'deluded people, taking their own Dreams and Melancholick Fancies for Divine Inspirations'.[49]

The scandal associated with female Quaker prophets served as proof for hostile observers that Quakerism was dangerous to the moral and social order. They were portrayed dually as seductresses and propagators of false opinions, who 'emitted unclean excretions in body and tongue'.[50] Writers like Thomas Danson catalogued numerous incidents of women subverting female modesty. In 1659, for instance, Danson reported that Mary Todd of Southwark had 'pull'd up all her cloaths above her middle, exposing her nakednesse to the view of all that were in the Room, and walked so up and down a while, using several expressions about her practise'.[51] Thomas Underhill described in 1660 the actions of one Quaker maid-servant who came into her master's parlour 'stark naked' when he was dining with friends.[52] The act of 'going naked for a sign' in imitation of the prophet Isaiah was one of the least understood aspects of Quaker testimony and seemed to confirm the validity of charges of delusion. This was reinforced by one broadside image widely circulated in the seventeenth century, which depicted a Quaker woman seeking guidance from her inner light with a lustful horned devil standing behind her (see Figure 4.2). The text surrounding the image reprimands the female preacher for giving into the temptations of the devil and for her failure to 'mind hir housewifery'. It was an image that 'crystallised contemporary anxieties', to quote Walsham.[53] Not only did it delegitimise the divine authority of the Quaker inner light, but also it preyed upon more general fears about the public authority of women who would have less time to devote to their housekeeping.

[49] Hallywell, *An Account of Familism*, pp. 110–111. The account was also published in Higginson's *A Brief Relation of the Irreligion of the Northern Quakers*, p. 30; and in Deacon's *An Exact History of the Life of James Naylor*, p. 42 [mispaginated].

[50] Tarter, 'Quaking in the Light', p. 151.

[51] Thomas Danson, *The Quakers Wisdom Descendeth Not from Above: Or a Brief Vindication of a Small Tract Intituled, the Quakers Folly Made Manifest to All Men* (London, 1659), Appendices, p. 4, 'A Narrative'.

[52] Thomas Underhill, *Hell Broke Loose: Or an History of the Quakers Both Old and New* (London, 1660), pp. 32–33.

[53] Walsham, *Charitable Hatred*, p. 124.

Figure 4.2. A Quaker woman is seduced to preach by the devil.
A Quaker attributed to Richard Gaywood, c. 1665–1675.
(© Religious Society of Friends (Quakers) in Britain. LRSF Q1).

The Quakers' contempt for authority, their marginalisation of the scriptures, and their rejection of the established Church were axiomatic, in that all were rooted in their adherence to the 'light within'. That the divine impulses of female preachers like the woman depicted in Figure 4.2 could be construed by opponents as demonic has frequently been noted by scholars. The idea of the witch as a female challenger of religious order only added to this image. Peter Elmer has noted the 'inordinate frequency' with which accusations of diabolical witchcraft were levelled against Quakers.[54] Rather than Quakers being divinely inspired, Ralph Farmer observed in 1658 that 'the souls of *beasts* had transmigrated, and shifted themselves into the bodies of *women and* maidens', who would then lift 'up their voices in the very

---

[54] Peter Elmer, '"Saints or Sorcerers": Quakerism, Demonology, and the Decline of Witchcraft in Seventeenth-Century England', in Brian P. Levack (ed.), *Demonology, Religion, and Witchcraft: New Perspectives on Witchcraft, Magic and Demonology* (6 vols., London, 2001), vol. 1, p. 437.

streets and *publike* Congregations'.[55] The association of the female preacher with beastly imagery accentuated the unnaturalness of her public activities. In employing bestiality to represent female converts, authors sought to dehumanise their subjects, underlining the gulf between women's natural behaviour as quiet, civil, and meek citizens and the loud, scolding, and raving preachers. The 1655 sensationalist account, *Quakers Are Inchanters and Dangerous Seducers*, described the bewitching of Mary White after attending Meetings and reading Quaker texts. Witnesses described how 'something within her body did run up and down, and in her Fits sometime[s] she roared like a Bull, sometime[s] barked like a Dog, and sometime[s] blared like a Calf'.[56] Such shocking images served to make the external threat of Quakerism appear even more menacing.

Evidently, the boundaries between religious nonconformity and other types of aberrant behaviour were easily blurred. However, the association of religious deviance with sexual amorality, and charges of heresy and witchcraft were nothing new to early modern audiences. Numerous studies have drawn attention to slurs of a very similar tenor against other 'outsider' groups, like Catholics, Baptists, Huguenot refugees, and Methodists.[57] The first Friends were often alleged to be Catholics in disguise, and anti-Quaker polemic deliberately blurred the movement with other separatist groups. Figure 4.3, for example, used a portrait of the Fifth Monarchist plotter Thomas Venner to blacken Quakers and Anabaptists. At the top of his halberd is a tablet entitled 'A strange gathering of Anabaptists and Quakers', depicting a naked woman standing before a pulpit. The association between religious radicalism and female-initiated excess is at its most powerful despite the different affiliations of the participants. One image adapted from the depiction of the Quaker prophet in Figure 4.2, branded the Fifth Monarchist prophet Hannah Trapnel as 'a Quaker, and

---

[55] Ralph Farmer, *The Imposter Dethron'd, or, the Quakers Throne of Truth Detected* (1658), p. 17.

[56] Anon., *Quakers Are Inchanters and Dangerous Seducers: Appearing in Their Inchantment of One Mary White at Wickham-Skyeth in Suffolk, 1655* (London, 1655), p. 7.

[57] For Catholics see Colin Haydon, *Anti-Catholicism in Eighteenth-Century England, c. 1714–80: A Political and Social Study* (Manchester, 1993); Peter Lake, 'Anti-Popery: The Structure of a Prejudice', in Richard Cust and Ann Hughes (eds.), *Conflict in Early Stuart England: Studies in Religion and Politics, 1603–1642* (London, 1989), pp. 72–106; and Marotti, *Religious Ideology and Cultural Fantasy*, pp. 55–65.

For the Huguenots see Penny Roberts, 'Peace, Ritual and Sexual Violence during the Religious Wars', in G. Murdock, P. Roberts, and A. Spicer (eds.), *Ritual and Violence: Natalie Zemon Davis and Early Modern France* (Oxford, 2012), pp. 75–99.

For the Methodists see A. M. Lyles, *Methodism Mocked: The Satiric Reaction to Methodism in the 18th Century* (London, 1960); Emma Major, *Madam Britannia: Women, Church, and Nation 1712–1812* (Oxford, 2011), esp. pp. 130–152; and John Walsh, 'Methodism and the Mob in the Eighteenth Century', in G. J. Cuming and Derek Baker (eds.), *Popular Belief and Practice* (Studies in Church History, 8, Cambridge, 1972), pp. 213–227.

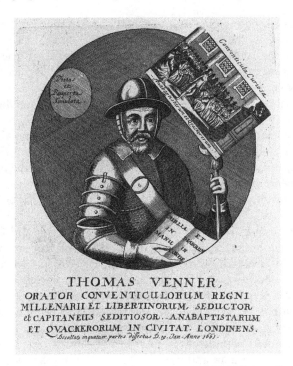

Figure 4.3. *Thomas Venner*, Anon., c. 1662. (© Religious Society
of Friends (Quakers) in Britain. LRSF 80_N128).

pretended Prophetess'. Trapnel's plain Quaker attire, combined with a devil
supposedly inspiring her preaching, shows how the public behaviour of
female prophets could spark concerns over the preservation of the moral
and religious order.⁵⁸ Such damning tropes suggest the combined power of
religious sectarianism and public female speech in generating fear and para-
noia across seventeenth-century society, to the point where distinct sectarian
identities often became blurred.

'KEEPING HER LIGHT WITHIN': CHANGING
UNDERSTANDINGS OF WOMEN IN ANTI-QUAKER SATIRE

The images used to discredit female adherents of Quakerism were not uniform across the period. Indeed, the associations of Quakerism with going

---

⁵⁸ *Hannah Trapnel, a Quaker, and Pretended Prophetess*, attributed to Richard Gaywood,
reprint c. 1823. ICV No 7499. Held in the Wellcome Library Collection, London.

naked for a sign, performing miracles, and accusations of witchcraft were mainly confined to the movement's first decade. The shift can largely be attributed to the outward presentation of Quakerism in the years following the Restoration. The movement's leadership increasingly sought to limit dramatic styles of proselytisation, requiring members to engage with non-Quaker audiences in less publicly offensive and combative ways. Second-generation leaders like William Penn and Robert Barclay rejected flamboyant activities such as performing miracles, running through the streets naked, and disrupting church ceremonies, dismissing them as the actions of eccentrics operating outside of 'respectable' Quaker behaviour.[59] As a consequence, there was a significant decline in the number of accounts published in Britain after the late 1660s that alluded to Quaker witchcraft, sorcery, or nudity.

In accounts coming from the American colonies, however, anti-Quaker satire linking religious enthusiasm to diabolic possession continued to appear much later. For example, the New England clergyman Increase Mather described in 1684 how Mary Ross was seduced by the devil to join the 'Singing' Quakers in Plymouth, New England. It was reported that she had 'made her self naked, burning all her Clothes; and with infinite Blasphemy said that she was Christ, and gave names to her Apostles ... declaring that she would be dead for three dayes, and then rise again'. She later allegedly danced naked with a man and woman during a ritual sacrifice of a dog.[60] As late as the 1690s, reports of Quaker women being possessed by devils and worshipping Satan were in circulation in New England, suggesting that sensationalist Quaker-witch accounts continued to find an audience. This was at the very time when historians have argued learned demonology was in decline in England, and matches a broader pattern in the scholarship on witchcraft that sees accusations and persecutions persisting much later in North America than England.

The association of the Quakers with other 'outsider' groups in the American colonies endured throughout our period. As Michele Lise Tarter has argued, by the end of the seventeenth century, Quaker women stood as the wayward 'other' to whom the ideal of the Godly Puritan wife was compared. She explains how New England commentators came to link Quaker worship to other 'outsiders' and evil influences, especially the paganism of the Native Americans.[61] The clergyman John Norton, for example,

---

[59] For a detailed discussion of the later movement's refutation of the more 'eccentric' elements of Quaker worship and testimony see Rosemary Moore, *The Light in Their Consciences: Early Quakers in Britain, 1646–1666* (University Park, PA, 2000), pp. 214–228.

[60] Increase Mather, *An Essay for the Recording of Illustrious Providences Wherein an Account Is Given of Many Remarkable and Very Memorable Events Which Have Hapned [sic] This Last Age, Especially in New-England* (Boston, 1684), pp. 346–347.

[61] Tarter, 'Quaking in the Light', pp. 155–156.

evocatively described Quaker testimonies as 'the pernicious waters of old heresyes, till then out of mind for many hundred yeares'.[62] Whilst the relationship of Quakers with wider society was overwhelmingly peaceful in comparison to the suffering experienced by their counterparts in Britain, the mid-eighteenth century did bring about a renewed print crusade against prominent Pennsylvanian Quakers. This was because they refused to bear arms or defend the colony against attacks by Native Americans. One satirical print by Henry Dawkins entitled *An Indian Squaw King Wampum Spies* (1764) encapsulated the rage of the Pennsylvanian inhabitants by depicting Israel Pemberton as the lustful 'King Wampum', seducing a Native American woman. Pemberton was a leading Quaker Philadelphian merchant and politician, who had founded the Friendly Association with the Indians in 1755. The print preyed upon fears that Friends were an outsider group with too much influence over colonial government, posing a threat to the inhabitants' safety because they were more willing to side with enemies than their own people.[63] These tensions would eventually lead to the forced withdrawal of Friends from Pennsylvanian political life.

Such derogatory slurs, as I have already established, were not used exclusively against the Quakers, but the large number of anti-Quaker prints on this theme suggests a very wide public fascination with the group. However, some noticeable changes in anti-Quaker rhetoric occurred in the closing decades of the seventeenth century, especially in Britain. The rise of rationalism and a greater impetus towards empirical observation diminished fears of witchcraft and diabolism. Influenced by new scientific understandings, a shift also began to occur in what authors believed were the causes of such eccentric behaviour. The highly derogatory tract *The Quakers Art of Courtship*, first published in 1689, could offer only one explanation why some 'She-Friends' had decided to go to Rome in 1667 to deliver their address to the Pope, where they had allegedly saluted him as the '*Man of Sin, Whore of Babylon, The Scarlet Whore* sitting on the Beast with Seven Heads, with many other Apocalyptick Greetings'. It was not a demonic inspiration that caused them to greet the Pope in such a brazen manner, but 'some sort of Hypocondriack Distemper'. The two women were allegedly treated by physicians before they returned home, 'having left much of their Disease behind them'.[64]

In a period when piety could easily be confused with delusion, we see a transition in how the female body was understood. Increasingly, women's

---

[62] John Norton, *The Heart of N-England Rent at the Blasphemies of the Present Generation* (Cambridge, MA, 1659), p. 2.

[63] Crabtree, *Holy Nation*, p. 40.

[64] Anon., *The Quakers Art of Courtship, or the Yea-and-Nay Academy of Complements* (London, 1689), pp. 16–18.

association with the excesses of radical religion moved away from demonic explanations to an inversion of the reasoned mind, leading to madness. In part, this alteration can be observed through the emergence of groups like the Methodists in the eighteenth century, whose stress on intense emotional experience became associated with the traits of madness, such as melancholy, hysteria, and distraction.[65] John Langhorne's widely published *Letters on Religious Retirement* (1762), related the cautionary tale of one young woman called Eleanora, who fell 'prey to the monster *Superstition*'. She was persuaded by a maiden aunt to attend Methodist meetings and fell into a 'stupefying melancholy', which 'affected her constitution; and she languished away in the bloom of life, a Sacrifice to Fanaticism'.[66] Mental instability was replacing demonic pacts as the major explanation for religious deviance in anti-sectarian propaganda. One broadside entitled *Harlequin Methodist* offered a satire of the preacher George Whitefield, depicting him as a Harlequin in a play. The crowd surrounding him is dominated by women, and the set in the background offers a view of the lunatic asylum of Bedlam.

Despite Quakerism's changing public image, English anti-Quaker polemic continued to criticise women for their disruption of the family order. But the tone of these attacks gradually shifted from fear to ridicule and contempt, much of it with a misogynist flavour. One recurring theme was the highly sexualised nature of Quaker men and the friction between them and their absurdly righteous wives. *The Secret Sinners*, for instance, depicted in dialogue form how a frustrated husband could justify committing adultery with his maidservant because his wife spent so much time in religious meetings. Indeed, his ministerial wife was completely off-limits for 'she hath kept all her Light within, and held none forth till now of late, it has dried her up ... she is stricken in years and regardeth not the Flesh'.[67] This type of dialogue between a Quaker and his maid was published in multiple forms throughout the period, all claiming that over-zealous female elders had driven their lustful husbands to commit adultery.[68] The depiction of women as fanatical

---

[65] See, e.g., Phyllis Mack, *Heart Religion in the British Enlightenment: Gender and Emotion in Early Methodism* (Cambridge, 2008), pp. 14–28.

[66] John Langhorne, *Letters on Religious Retirement, Melancholy, and Enthusiasm* (London, 1762), pp. 54–58. This text is also discussed in Major, *Madam Britannia*, p. 143.

[67] Anon., *The Secret Sinners: Or, a Most Pleasant Dialogue between a Quaker and His Maid, and His Wife Sarah* (c. 1675), in Roger Thompson (ed.), *Samuel Pepys' Penny Merriments* (London, 1976), p. 151.

[68] Similar accounts were also published in Anon., *Moll and Her Master: Or, a Dialogue between a Quaker and His Maid* (London, 1675); Anon., *The Unconstant Quaker: Or, Sweet Susan His Servant, Unworthily Left in the Lurch, After He Had Tickl'd Her Fancy* (c. 1664–1703); Anon., *A Yea and Nay Mouse-Trap: Or, the Quaker in Darkness, Being a True, But Comical Account of an Eminent Quaker in Southwark* (London, 1701); and Anon., *A Merry Conversation That Lately Pass'd between a Very Noted Quaker of This City and His Maid, upon a Very Merry Occasion* (London, c. 1739).

zealots was especially hostile, often focusing on their preposterous appearance and outward demeanour. Thomas Brown's 1688 dialogue surrounding *The Reasons of Mr Bays Changing His Religion* offered one of the most savage criticisms of women attending Quaker Meetings, explaining that 'it is as impossible for a Woman to be a *Quaker* any time and handsome'. The author described how one Quaker woman's zeal 'had certainly discoloured and sowr'd her countenance, and made her look like the rest of her Sex in those *Pagan* Assemblies'.[69]

Such rigid conformity to the movement's testimonies increasingly became the focus of anti-Quaker satire against women. One such theme was the scolding wife who bullied her husband into submission. Drawing upon the Quaker rejection of superfluity and luxurious apparel, the London journal *True and Domestick Intelligence* published in 1680 the comical story of an adulterous Quaker whose pious wife prevented him leaving the house in a velvet coat on Christmas day, hiding the coat from him. The story ends with her discovery of his mistress and her decision to go to the local justice for a warrant, resulting in his imprisonment and eventual conveyance to a lunatic asylum.[70] Two similar instances are reported in the chronology of 'very memorable Things' to have happened in the year 1677 in the satirical *Yea-and-Nay-Almanack*. One Quaker wife was condemned for burning her husband's box of lace, worth £10 'to the destruction of pride'. Another was criticised for stripping her husband 'of his Superfluous Garments'.[71] The husband became a similar figure of scorn in Antoinette Bourignon's *Warning Against the Quakers*, first translated into English in 1708. One 'bigotted' Quaker woman, for example, was criticised for reproaching her husband after he began to doff his hat to his friends and to 'say *Goodmorrow* to his Neighbours'.[72] The comedic undertones of such accounts served to make the male Quaker a subject of ridicule and mockery *because* of the overpowering fanaticism of his too-pious wife, who placed zealotry before her family loyalties.

The outward apparel of Quakers was one of the ways in which female members identified themselves as spiritually pure. I will return later to the tension inherent in the evolving movement about how to avoid succumbing to the pleasures and riches of the societies of which they were a part. These were matters the movement's elders frequently discussed in their Meeting epistles. However, the visible frivolity of members was also becoming a topic of biting satire from the movement's critics, who revelled in

---

[69] Thomas Brown, *The Reasons of Mr Bays Changing His Religion* (London, 1688), p. 29.
[70] *True Domestick Intelligence or News Both from City and Country* (London), 9 January 1680, p. 2.
[71] Anon., *Poor Robin 1677*, sig. A2r.
[72] Bourignon, *Warning against the Quakers*, pp. 102–104.

drawing attention to Quaker dishonesty. In December 1709, an anonymous author of the *Female Tatler* – writing under the pen name Arabella – used a public tea room as the setting for observations about 'two sanctified sisters', who were compared to vain and pompous aristocratic ladies in their dress, deportment, and lustful behaviour. They 'enquir'd for *Fine Tea-Tables*, *Gilded Cabinets* ... and all the richest Things, more proper to adorn the *Palace* of *a Prince*', but were also barely identifiable from the other aristocratic ladies: '[T]heir Cloaths were *Costly* without making any *Show*, and tho' they abominate Profane *Pinners* and *Topknots*, yet by the Disposition of their *Locks* and *artful Crimping* of their *Hoods* upon *Wyres*, they show'd themselves equally Vain.' The hypocrisy of the sanctimonious female protagonists was presented as the main rationale for the issue's publication. After observing their behaviour, the authors concluded that 'Quakers are the most designing, deceitful sect of creatures in the world, who assume more pride and exact more homage from their seeming sanctity, than the truly pious.'[73]

The association of Quaker women with dominant and sanctimonious behaviour was noticeably transformed in anti-Quaker accounts from the 1670s, after the formal establishment of the Quaker Meeting system. The rise of separate Women's Meetings for business, as explored in Chapter 2, provided women with unparalleled liberties in the organisational life of the Society. Indeed, they were a feature of Quaker church culture deeply contested and feared by commentators both within and without the movement. As we saw, the rise of this 'government of women' was feared because of the authority that this system gave female elders over the private affairs of men.[74] This was encapsulated in one hostile account published in 1715 by Henry Pickworth, an ex-Quaker, who faced condemnation after he tried to attend his wife during childbirth, but was refused by a leading member of the Women's Meeting, Frances Ostill. He described her as 'a starch'd *Quaker Pharisee*, who ... took upon her to rebuke me for my said kindness to my Wife'. Ostill had allegedly associated Pickworth's presence in the birthing chamber with his wife having been twelve hours longer 'in her Labour than otherwise she would have been'. Members of the Men's Meeting had advised lenience, but Pickworth noted that when the matter came before the Women's Meeting 'the *Pharisaical* Zealots amongst them,

---

[73] *The Female Tatler by a Society of Ladies*, issue no. 67 (London), 9 December 1709, pp. 197–198.

[74] These accounts against the Women's Meetings, often written by former members, included William Mather, *A Novelty: Or, a Government of Women, Distinct from Men, Erected amongst Some of the People Call'd Quakers* (London, 1694); William Mucklow, *The Spirit of the Hat, or, the Government of the Quakers among Themselves as It Hath Been Exercised of Late Years by George Fox* (London, 1673); Henry Pickworth, *A Charge of Error, Heresy, Incharity, Falshood* (London, 1715); and William Rogers, *The Christian-Quaker* (London, 1680), esp. part 1.

being the Majority, ... would by no means be prevailed on to cease their Prosecution, till they had drawn up their Paper of my Condemnation'.[75] The rise of the Meeting system, which served to centralise and consolidate Quaker testimonies, seemed to hostile critics to be placing women in unnatural positions of authority.

Whilst sexual slurs were often used against female Friends, in contrast to other anti-sectarian propaganda, little reference is made in anti-Quaker polemic to the activities or behaviour of women in their separate Meetings. Anti-Catholic and anti-Methodist writings, for example, depicted cloisters and 'love feasts' as sites of debauchery and railed at unchaste disorderly women. Authors denouncing the Quakers, in comparison, rarely speculated about the behaviour of female Friends when they met together in their segregated gatherings.[76] Quaker Meetings were often open and public, whereas the more private Catholic convents of Europe and Methodist 'love feasts' created the conditions for greater speculation in the British press. 'The connection of the private with the sexual and secret', argues Emma Major in relation to anti-Methodist satire, 'gave carnal resonances to Methodists' "private revelation"', and was linked to anti-Catholic satires viewing confession 'as an intimate and erotic exchange'.[77] Instead, what occupied a central place in anti-Quaker accounts was how women's authority in church governance affected other aspects of their relationships with men.

The female elders of the Meetings were frequently presented as over-zealous shrews, wielding an unhealthy amount of authority over their male brethren. These sometimes bawdy satires played on popular fears of gender subversion and the effect female ascendancy in matters of religion might have upon the patriarchal order. The tragic story of the *Quaker Turn'd Jew* (1675), for instance, detailed how a Quaker preacher had seduced a godly female Friend, but felt so guilty afterwards that he circumcised himself. His act of contrition, which involved presenting his 'unruly member' to the Men's and Women's Meetings, was rejected by the so-called 'She Friends', who opposed his readmission. The author recounts how these women had claimed 'no person unfit for the Work of Generation, ought to be admitted to their Communion'.[78] This rejection served to deepen the man's status as

---

[75] Pickworth, *A Charge of Error, Heresy, Incharity, Falshood*, pp. 246–248. Almost all contemporaries, of course, would have been shocked by the idea of a husband being present at his wife's labour.

[76] The negative depictions of convent life are explored by Claire Walker in *Gender and Politics in Early Modern Europe: English Convents in France and the Low Countries* (Basingstoke, 2003), pp. 53–54. See also Haydon, *Anti-Catholicism*, pp. 254–255; and Marotti, *Religious Ideology and Cultural Fantasy*, pp. 1–34.

[77] Major, *Madam Britannia*, p. 137.

[78] Anon., *The Quaker Turn'd Jew: Being a True Relation, How an Eminent Quaker in the Isle of Ely, on Monday 18 April 1675 Circumcised Himself* (London, 1675), esp. p. 7.

an outcast. The control of the Women's Meeting over the disciplinary process and readmission of transgressors underscored suppressed fears about female authority within church governance.

The command female Friends held over their husbands and other male members of the Society was a theme that pervaded the *Yea and Nay Almanack*, published annually by William Winstanley between 1677 and 1680. Whilst retaining many of the tropes about Quaker women found in earlier anti-Quaker satire, the author acknowledged their unusual power by juxtaposing a chronology and calendar with sardonic comments about the movement. One section, which satirised Quaker testimonies in the form of a catechism, questioned whether there were any occasions when Quakers might pull off their hats. The answer: 'Yea, yea, we pull them off when we go to Bed with our Yoke-fellows, because we Honour the Woman as the weaker Vessel, nay we Honour them so much as we often times [go] down on our knees to them.'[79] The rise of gender-segregated Meetings altered the way in which Quaker women were understood and presented in satirical literature. No longer were they vulnerable women apt to confuse sexual urges with religious enthusiasm. Instead, they were assertive viragos predisposed to subverting their place within both the household and the church by ruling over men.

NEGOTIATING THE NON-QUAKER WORLD: FEMALE FRIENDS AND THEIR NEIGHBOURS

The damning image of female Friends in print was only enhanced by the suffering they experienced at the hands of brutal mobs and local officials. This is an aspect of their experiences hinted at in Chapter 1, when we saw the ways in which women often suffered indirectly from their male relatives' religious testimonies. Historians have also pointed to the all-encompassing hostility Quaker women experienced, cutting horizontally across political, social, and religious divides, which has dominated our understanding of their relationships with wider society.[80] The Quaker preacher Barbara Blaugdone, for instance, recorded how a butcher 'swore he would cleave my Head in twain', when she preached at a marketplace in Cork.[81] Mack, in her assessment of the early Quaker women prophets, has drawn attention to the theatrical nature of women's sufferings, which carried with them different social and sexual connotations from the sufferings experienced by men. One

---

[79] Winstanley, *Yea and Nay Almanack*, vol. 3 (1680), sig. C6v.
[80] Barry Reay, *The Quakers and the English Revolution* (London, 1985), pp. 62–78.
[81] Barbara Blaugdone, *An Account of the Travels, Sufferings and Persecutions of Barbara Blaugdone* (1691), p. 27.

example is the New England Friend Hored Gardner, who was whipped in 1658 whilst holding an infant to her naked chest.[82]

But the focus on dramatic or sensationalist suffering accounts, often coloured by 'martyrological hyperbole and distortion', has come at the expense of other aspects of Quaker women's experiences.[83] After all, even the most radical of Quaker prophets were exhorted to lead ordinary lives as part of their service to God. As early as 1658, the Quaker leader George Fox believed that members must thrive within, rather than isolate themselves from, their local communities. He stated that spiritual or 'particular growth' could only occur by leading godly lives and making use of opportunities to convert neighbours, for 'Truth hath an honour in the hearts of people that are not Friends'.[84]

This doctrinal tension has led to much debate about how far Friends were assimilated into wider society in this period. The highly cohesive nature of the 'quietist' eighteenth-century movement and the desire of Friends to mark themselves as separate from the rest of the world, both in terms of who they socialised with and how they behaved, was traditionally characterised as a deliberate policy of isolationism. Second- and third-generation Friends preferred to live within the bounds of their own closed community, rather than corrupt their spiritual purity with the customs of 'the world'.[85] Revisionist interpretations, however, have effectively challenged this view, showing that Quakers were not hermetically isolated after the 1689 Toleration Act and were far more integrated into their local communities than previously believed.[86] Whilst these studies have faced some criticism for underplaying continued prejudices, a range of evidence has been presented of charity, harmony, and peaceful co-existence between Friends and their non-Quaker neighbours throughout this period.[87] Evidence has also been uncovered of

---

[82] Mack, *Visionary Women*, p. 132. The story of Hored Gardner's persecution was included in James Bowden's *The History of the Society of Friends in America* (2 vols., London, 1850–1854), vol. 1, pp. 141–142.

[83] Walsham, *Charitable Hatred*, p. 84.

[84] George Fox, *The Journal of George Fox*, ed. John L. Nickalls (Cambridge, 1952), pp. 340–341, George Fox's Address to Friends in the Ministry, given at John Crook's house, 31 May 1658.

[85] This is explored by Bill Stevenson in 'The Social Integration of Post-Restoration Dissenters, 1660–1725', in Margaret Spufford (ed.), *The World of Rural Dissenters, 1520–1725* (Cambridge, 1995), pp. 360–361; and Michael Mullett, 'From Sect to Denomination? Social Developments in Eighteenth-Century English Quakerism', *Journal of Religious History*, vol. 13, no. 2 (1984), pp. 168–191.

[86] On Quaker integration see Adrian Davies, *The Quakers in English Society, 1655–1725* (Oxford, 2000); Simon Dixon, 'Quaker Communities in London'; David Scott, *Quakerism in York, 1650–1720* (York, 1991); Bill Stevenson, 'The Social Integration of Post-Restoration Dissenters', pp. 360–387; and Walsham, *Charitable Hatred*, esp. chapters 5 and 6.

[87] Evidence of the continuation of local hostilities can be found in Knights, *The Devil in Disguise*, esp. chapter 4; and John Miller, '"A Suffering People": English Quakers and Their Neighbours c. 1650–c. 1700', *Past and Present*, 188 (2005), pp. 71–103.

moderation on the part of English law enforcement officials in enacting statutes against Friends.[88] This changing perspective has been influenced by studies foregrounding the ways in which other religious minorities successfully integrated into their local communities.[89]

That members of the public could be sympathetic to Quaker women's maltreatment is a persistent but often unremarked presence in the suffering literature. Numerous accounts of suffering recorded the actions of neighbours who came to the aid of Friends during times of hardship, an aspect of late-Stuart law enforcement that Craig Horle characterises as 'pivotal' in determining the treatment of Quakers.[90] Anne Upcott was cruelly treated by her family for working on the Sabbath, and her brother, the local constable, instigated her arrest and set her in the stocks. However, the sympathy of local neighbours was aroused when her father and other brothers came to jeer and mock her whilst she sat stocked in the marketplace. Such callous behaviour, it was reported, made 'some of the neighbors weepe to see there unnaturalnesse'. One stranger proclaimed 'hee was ashamed to see such a thinge donne by her father and brothers haveinge never knowne the like before'.[91] The episode is telling of the divisive potential within families following conversion to Quakerism. It also suggests some public sympathy towards female sufferers, and a sense that family (and perhaps communal) ties should override or at least soften religious differences.

In some instances, the persecution experienced by Quaker women was enough to prompt intervention by members of the public. When Elizabeth Braithwaite, aged only seventeen, was sent to prison in May 1684, it was reported how 'severall of her Neighbours ... were sorely grieved that she should go to Prison, blaming the Officers for Presenting her, telling them, it was a shame for them, she being ... an innocent Maid, and had done no evil nor harm to any'.[92] Female neighbours, moreover, intervened when local justices raided the house of John and Deborah Wynn in the 1670s. Having already distrained almost all their goods, the persecutors had attempted to take the bed from under Deborah as she lay in childbirth, 'but the neighbouring Women abhorring the Inhumanity of such an Attempt interrupted

[88] Craig W. Horle, *Quakers and the English Legal System, 1660–1688* (Philadelphia, 1988), pp. 255–274.
[89] Walsham, *Charitable Hatred*, esp. chapters 5 and 6. Evidence of religious dissidents living peaceably within their communities was at the centre of Spufford (ed.), *The World of Rural Dissenters*.
[90] Horle, *Quakers and the English Legal System*, p. 265.
[91] Norman Penney (ed.), *Record of the Sufferings of Quakers in Cornwall 1655–1686* (London, 1928), pp. 17–19.
[92] Anon., *A Brief Relation of the Life and Death of Elizabeth Braytwhaite, a Maid of the Age of about Seventeen Years* (London, 1684), p. 2.

their Design, and would not suffer it'.[93] The birthing room is regarded as an important space in which early modern women could exercise communal support and care for one another.[94] The intervention of Wynn's female neighbours demonstrated that such intimacy did not wholly dissipate despite the different religious beliefs of the participants. This supports Barry Reay's suggestion that it was Quaker outsiders rather than close neighbours who suffered the brunt of persecution. 'It was the idea of the Quaker', he notes, rather than the individual 'that was hated and feared'.[95]

Even persecutors showed occasional sympathy towards their Quaker neighbours, as Elizabeth Stirredge noted in her autobiography. She explains how local officers had come to the family shop to demand money for her violation of the Conventicle Act. However, seeing her and her family at their 'lawful Calling', the constable 'leaning his head down upon his Hand' had said: 'It is against my Conscience to take their Goods from them.'[96] As we have seen, these responses were occurring at the same time that women were being vilified in the anti-Quaker press as disrupters of parish life. But this shows that families were sometimes able to maintain amicable neighbourly relations that protected them during periods of persecution, showing that some degree of local toleration existed before the introduction of the 1689 Act. This confirms Horle's findings that legal officials, law enforcement officers, and churchmen often acted with moderation towards Quakers.[97] Moreover, as the case of Stirredge suggests, a desire for communal harmony may have acted as a disincentive for local officials to take action against their Quaker neighbours.

Although not adhering to the same principles, non-Quakers could be sympathetic to some Quaker testimonies. The movement's refusal to pay tithes was one policy that appeared to gain widespread interdenominational admiration from its earliest years, especially because it was an issue that other groups like the Levellers, Fifth Monarchists, and Diggers had foregrounded in their campaigns for greater social equality during the Civil Wars. The female Friends who composed the petition *These Several Papers*, signed by more than 7,000 women and presented to Parliament in 1659, claimed its

---

[93] John Bell, *Piety Promoted, in a Collection of Dying Sayings of Divers of the People Called Quakers* (London, 1740), pp. 6–7, 'Deborah Wynn'.

[94] See Chapter 3 of this book. See also Bernard Capp, *When Gossips Meet: Women, Family and Neighbourhood in Early Modern England* (Oxford, 2003); and David Cressy, *Birth, Marriage, and Death: Ritual, Religion, and the Life-Cycle in Tudor and Stuart England* (Oxford, 1997), pp. 84–87.

[95] Reay, *The Quakers and the English Revolution*, p. 66.

[96] Elizabeth Stirredge, *Strength in Weakness Manifest: In the Life, Various Trials, and Christian Testimony of that Faithful Servant and Handmaid of the Lord, Elizabeth Stirredge* (London, 1711), pp. 43–44.

[97] Horle, *The Quakers and the English Legal System*, pp. 255–265.

circulation was driven by widespread anti-tithe feeling.[98] The document, which was divided into twenty-nine sites of regional protest across the country, is testament to an extraordinary feat of organisation. The petition was also signed by women who were not affiliated to the movement, but shared the Quakers' hostility to the tithe system and resented the financial burdens associated with it. A sense of the scale of this interdenominationalism is provided by Stephen Kent, who suggests that only about 50 per cent of the signatories for Lincolnshire appear in Quaker records. More remarkably, only 35 per cent of the women who signed the Chester petition can be identified as Quakers.[99] The large number of non-Quaker signatories testifies to a high level of social interaction between female parishioners of different denominations. It also supports research into the female petitioners of the Civil War period, who were motivated by both secular and religious concerns.[100] *These Several Papers* is a powerful example of how household issues could draw women into the political process, and on a large scale. It also supports Ann Marie McEntee's suggestion that such petitions are evidence of the increasing political sophistication of ordinary women during this period.[101]

Quaker opposition to tithes is one striking example of how the movement's testimonies could cross denominational boundaries. Another, is the integrity and trustworthiness contemporaries came to associate with Quakers' 'plain dealing', often viewed as an explanation of their success in business.[102] This made both female and male members stand out from their contemporaries as scrupulously honest people. One case recorded in the Old Bailey hints at the value placed on a Quaker woman's word as early as 1677. The woman in question was a servant who had purportedly stolen

[98] Mary Forster et al., *These Several Papers Was Sent to the Parliament the Twentieth Day of the Fifth Moneth [sic], 1659: Being above Seven Thousand of the Names of the Hand-Maids and Daughters of the Lord* (London, 1659).

[99] Stephen A. Kent, 'Seven Thousand "Hand-Maids and Daughters of the Lord": Lincolnshire and Cheshire Quaker Women's Anti-Tithe Protests in Late Interregnum and Restoration England', in Sylvia Brown (ed.), *Women, Gender, and Radical Religion in Early Modern Europe* (Leiden, The Netherlands: 2007), pp. 87–88.

[100] See especially, Patricia Higgins, 'The Reactions of Women, with Special Reference to Women Petitioners', in Brian Manning (ed.), *Politics, Religion and the English Civil War* (London, 1973), pp. 179–224; Ann Marie McEntee, '"The [un] Civill-Sisterhood of Oranges and Lemons": Female Petitioners and Demonstrators, 1642–53', *Prose Studies: History, Theory, Criticism*, vol. 14, no. 3 (1991), pp. 92–111; and Amanda Jane Whiting, *Women and Petitioning in the Seventeenth-Century English Revolution: Deference, Difference, and Dissent* (Turnhout, Belgium, 2015). This form of collective action also links back to a much longer tradition of women's involvement in food and enclosure riots and crowd activities. See E. P. Thompson, 'The Moral Economy of the English Crowd in the Eighteenth Century', *Past and Present*, vol. 50, no. 1 (1971), pp. 115–120.

[101] McEntee, '"The [un] Civill-Sisterhood of Oranges and Lemons"', pp. 92–93.

[102] Frederick B. Tolles, *Quakers and the Atlantic Culture* (New York, 1960), pp. 55–64.

goods valued at £50 from her master and mistress. As the testimony reveals, she had been accepted into the household because she had pretended to be a Quaker. 'On which account', the prosecution noted, 'her Master and Mistriss the more freely trusted her'.[103] This is indicative of the respectability and integrity non-Quakers associated with Friends from an early stage. It also suggests that non-Quakers might be happy to employ Quaker servants in their households, even when the movement was legally outlawed. The growing moral reputation of Quakerism shaped the representation of its female members in a variety of contexts. The sympathetic response of neighbours and members of the public to Quaker women's suffering and their testimonies exemplifies the existence of amicable social relations during the movement's fraught beginnings.

'USEFUL AND LOYAL MEMBERS OF SOCIETY': QUAKER WOMEN'S PROFESSIONAL RELATIONSHIPS

Religious isolationism could not always be put before the practicalities of daily life. The rising economic profile of Quakers was one of the most important underlying reasons for their acceptance in society. Numerous examples attest to women's continued involvement in the economic life of their communities, despite their religious affiliation. Daniel Fleming, a High Tory Anglican from Westmorland, noted his wife's willingness to buy goods from local Quakers, recording in his account book that she had paid 'Jane (a Quaker)' 3s. for six pairs of stockings in October 1667.[104] Elizabeth Andrews detailed in her spiritual autobiography how she had opened a shop in 1672 with her brother in Broseley, Shropshire, where 'no Friends had lived before we came'. The town was an important trading centre and Andrews frequently discoursed with her customers on matters of religion. In one passage, she notes 'many were Convinced of the Truth, and some stand faithful to this day'.[105] A similar scenario is observable in the journal of the Lancaster Quaker businessman William Stout, who was at the centre of economic life in the northwestern counties of England. His sister, Elin, was responsible for much of the day-to-day management of the retail business, as well as attending market days and fairs, all of which provided her with

---

[103] Old Bailey Sessions Papers (Online), 12 December 1677, trial for theft: grand larceny (t16771212-9); www.oldbaileyonline.org/.

[104] 'Extracts from Daniel Fleming's Great Book of Accounts' in *The Flemings in Oxford, Being Documents Selected from the Rydal Papers in Illustration of the Lives and Ways of Oxford Men, 1650–1700*, ed. John Richard Magrath (3 vols., Oxford, 1904), vol. 1, p. 434.

[105] LRSF, Portfolio MSS, vol. 36, fol. 161, 'An Account of the Birth, and Education, with the Services and Sufferings for Truth's Sake, of That Faithful Friend Eliz[abeth] Andrews', undated, later 1690s.

opportunities to interact with individuals outside of the Society.[106] In fact, the commercial interactions of these women serve as evidence of integration at its most effective. Through their everyday work, they were able to present their religious testimonies and peculiar ways of life to a broad cross-section of society.

Quaker women could not easily withdraw from their economic obligations. Instead, they needed to be flexible to thrive within their communities. Jane Metford's public identity as a Quaker schoolmistress working in Somerset in the 1730s serves as a particularly useful example of such pragmatism. The diarist John Cannon described how Metford taught elementary reading at a Church of England charity school, which served as a preparatory school or 'nursery'. The 'best readers' were then selected and transferred to Cannon's school.[107] This shows how female Friends actively furthered their involvement with the world, rather than isolating themselves from it. Indeed, Metford liaised with the local churchwardens, supervising the school's arrangements. She also taught her pupils a curriculum that complemented their progression to Cannon's Anglican school. The school run by Richard Shackleton and his wife, Elizabeth, in Ballitore in County Kildare, continually attracted families beyond the Quaker community. In May 1772, Elizabeth Shackleton reported that she had returned from a journey to find 'two quite strangers not of our society who had brought a son to school'.[108] The school at Ballitore gained an international reputation for its quality, and many American Quakers sent their children to be educated there. Its success, however, owed much to the fact that people from different denominational backgrounds were willing to place their children under the Shackleton's care.[109] Their daughter recounted one scenario where a young boy from considerable fortune had been brought to the school by his mother, but neither parent had 'seen one of the people called Quakers'. When Elizabeth Shackleton queried why she had 'brought her son among a people who were such strangers to her', the woman answered 'that she had heard a good character of them, although they differed from the Church of England concerning baptism and the supper'.[110] Since many opportunities to participate in civic life were closed to Quakers because of their refusal to swear oaths, it is interesting to see women's involvement in their local communities in this

[106] William Stout, *The Autobiography of William Stout of Lancaster, 1665–1752*, ed. J. D. Marshall (Manchester, 1967), see, e.g., entries for 1688: pp. 90–91, 96, and 1691–1692: pp. 102 and 105.

[107] Cannon, *The Chronicles of John Cannon*, vol. 2, p. 202, original fol. 199, entry for 1733.

[108] HL, mssSHA Shackleton Family Correspondence, Box 3, 1772–1775, fol. 201, Elizabeth Shackleton to Elizabeth Pike (Pim), Ballitore, 17 May 1772.

[109] One of the more famous of the Shackleton's pupils was Edmund Burke.

[110] Mary Leadbeater (ed.), *Memoirs and Letters of Richard and Elizabeth Shackleton Late of Ballitore, Ireland* (London, 1849), p. 25.

professional capacity.[111] It shows that when it came to economic matters, the reality could never match the Quaker isolationist ideal or government restrictions. Women like Jane Metford and Elizabeth Shackleton clearly had a vital role in working with children and families beyond their religious community.

Midwifery was another important role that enabled a Quaker woman to integrate into her community. Its practice was a source of much anxiety for the Quaker leadership. It was feared that women who attended non-Quaker births would be exposed to and corrupted by profane customs, such as participating in the 'gossips feast', the 'sprinkling of children' (baptism), or receiving offerings or gifts.[112] Quaker midwives were also legally prohibited from mixing with non-Quakers because they would not swear the oath of office and refused to baptise a child if its life seemed at risk. They were therefore prevented from obtaining an ecclesiastical licence to practise their profession.[113]

However, Quaker affiliation did not have a wholly negative effect on their livelihoods. Edmund Verney, for example, repeatedly employed the skilful Quaker midwife Frances Kent to attend to his sickly wife during childbirth. She was paid fees of £5, £10, and £20, but, as he notes, she refused traditional gifts from the godparents.[114] The Bristol excise officer John Cannon also employed a Quaker midwife and her assistant to deliver his wife Susannah in 1717 and 1719.[115] This suggests a degree of compromise on the part of both midwife and parents, who were able to set aside religious differences within the walls of the birthing chamber. Although succumbing to persecution, one 'ancient widow' named Hewlings from Cirencester was described in Joseph Besse's compendium of Quaker suffering as a 'useful Woman in the Neighbourhood, a skilful Midwife, and ready to do Good to all'.[116] The inhumanity of her suffering was enhanced by the service she

---

[111] Richard T. Vann argues that the Quakers' testimony against oaths 'cost more Friends their lives than any other'. Richard T. Vann, *The Social Development of English Quakerism 1655–1755* (Cambridge, MA, 1969), pp. 189–190.

[112] Anon., 'At a Meeting of the Midwives in Barbadoes, 11.xii.1677', *JFHS*, vol. 37 (1940), p. 22.

[113] The training and licencing of midwives in the American colonies is less-widely documented, but those who practised without a licence would also have been subject to fines or excommunication. However, owing to the dispersed nature of colonial settlements and the practical barriers resulting from this distance, the licencing system would have been weaker. Jane B. Donegan, *Women and Men Midwives: Medicine, Morality and Misogyny in Early America* (London, 1978), p. 12.

[114] Cited in Ann Giardina Hess, 'Midwifery Practice among the Quakers in Southern Rural England in the Late Seventeenth Century', in Hilary Marland (ed.), *The Art of Midwifery: Early Modern Midwives in Europe* (London, 1993), pp. 64–66.

[115] Cannon, *The Chronicles of John Cannon*, vol. 1, pp. 146 and 156, original fols. 140, 146, entries for 1717 and 1719.

[116] Besse, *Quaker Sufferings*, vol. 1, p. 216.

offered to the general community and not just other Friends. This reaffirms Doreen Evenden's conclusion that 'the universal and elemental drama' shared by women during childbirth could temporarily create stronger ties than those imposed by religion.[117]

Dixon's research into Friends and the London livery companies of the late seventeenth century also supports this evidence. He concludes that London Quakers were establishing themselves as 'useful and loyal members of society' and becoming more integrated into the mainstream of everyday life.[118] The livery companies were willing to admit Quakers, despite their refusal to swear oaths.[119] Whilst Quaker midwives were not granted ecclesiastical licences, a good reputation could outweigh such handicaps. Moreover, evidence from the Quaker London Birth Notes between 1676 and 1750 even indicates that a high proportion of Quaker births were attended by women granted an ecclesiastical licence. The Anglican midwife Elizabeth Clarke, for instance, attended almost 12 per cent of the births recorded between 1680 and 1690 (see Table A4.1 in Appendix 4). This suggests that non-Quaker midwives were often deliberately chosen by parents for the task, and not simply employed in an emergency situation when a Quaker midwife was unavailable.

The value of a skilful non-Quaker midwife willing to attend Quaker births could be placed by female Friends above religious affiliation. A 1750 letter of introduction, written by Sophia Hume on behalf of Mary Sincrey, who was both a 'stranger' to the writer and 'not a Friend', reveals that Quaker women might be willing to promote the services of non-Quaker midwives. Hume was an active minister in the transatlantic Quaker community, a native of South Carolina who had settled in London. In the letter, Hume explained that Sincrey 'professes midwifery' and was planning to emigrate to Philadelphia, having heard of a shortage of 'skilful practical midwi[ves]' in the city. Hume was willing to endorse a non-Quaker's profession despite the detrimental impact it might have on the livelihoods of other members of her Society. She confessed to her recipient that the recommendation could 'Disadvantage ... our Friends Professing that Business' and asked not to be mentioned in relation to the matter.[120] Underpinning Hume's recommendation is a clear sense that that the position of the midwife in seventeenth- and eighteenth-century society had the potential to transcend religious affiliations.

---

[117] Doreen Evenden, *The Midwives of Seventeenth-Century London* (Cambridge, 2000), p. 97.
[118] Dixon, 'Quaker Communities in London', p. 224.
[119] Ibid., pp. 212–220.
[120] HSP, MS Coll 484A Pemberton Family Papers, vol. 6, p. 19, Sophia Hume to Mary Pemberton, London, 26 April 1750.

QUAKER PHILANTHROPY AND THE BRISTOL WORKHOUSE

As with their involvement in childbirth, Quaker women's work was under-pinned by a strong sense of charity and good neighbourliness. Second- and third-generation 'quietist' Quakerism was strongly focused on providing members with economic and spiritual support, but female Friends were also actively involved in causes that reached beyond their own community. Jacalynn Stuckey Welling has suggested that the experience of suffering and persecution had the counter-effect of sensitising Friends to the 'plight of the disenfranchised'.[121] Much of this effort was channelled into poor relief and later prison reform – matters that many of the early sufferers had experi-enced first-hand.

Within England, Quaker women undertook a range of philanthropic ventures to assist the poorer members of their communities. The extant records of the Quaker workhouse in Bristol provide a fascinating example of the extensive nature of female-led philanthropy and Quaker integra-tion in practice. The independent Quaker workhouse was modelled on the utopian vision of the London cloth merchant John Bellers, who wanted a subscription-funded 'Colledge of Industry' to provide the poor with use-ful employment.[122] Bellers, like many Friends, viewed wealth as a moral rather than material issue and pressed for direct involvement by encourag-ing the poor to join these institutions voluntarily and gain the education necessary for self-improvement.[123] What made the Bristol workhouse differ from contemporary institutions was its emphasis on self-help, rather than compulsory labour. It was to act as a supplementary voluntary exercise to facilitate the education of poor children, so that they could acquire the skills and resources necessary to become useful and successful citizens.[124] Production and sale of goods were negotiated through the workhouse man-ager Sarah Chubb, who took over its administration from her husband George in 1704.[125]

---

[121] Jacalynn Stuckey Welling, 'Mission', in Angell and Dandelion, *Oxford Handbook of Quaker Studies*, p. 309.
[122] See Mark Freeman, 'Quakers, Business, and Philanthropy', in Angell and Dandelion, *Oxford Handbook of Quaker Studies*, p. 423. See also Bristol Yearly Meeting, *Minute Book of the Men's Meeting of the Society of Friends in Bristol, 1686–1704*, ed. Russell Mortimer (Bristol, 1977), pp. xxviii–xxx.
[123] Deborah Valenze, *The Social Life of Money in the English Past* (Cambridge, 2006), pp. 119–144.
[124] The Corporation of Bristol was a similar contemporary scheme implemented by John Cary, which included the founding of two new workhouses from 1698. *An Account of the Proceedings of the Corporation of Bristol* (London, 1700), pp. 11, 17; and E. E. Butcher, *Bristol Corporation of the Poor, 1696–1898* (Bristol, 1972), esp. pp. 10–11 and 15.
[125] The extant accounts and correspondence of the Bristol Workhouse were consulted in the following repositories: LRSF, MS Vol 294 Dix MSS, fols. B 1 B–B 33 B; Bristol Record Office, SF/A/9/1 Records of the Workhouse and New Street Mission, 1697–1809.

Whilst the workhouse aimed to offer education, paid employment, and comfortable accommodation for poor Friends, many of the merchants and traders who corresponded with Sarah Chubb were outside the Society. Moreover, the type of fabrics they ordered suggests that the Quaker-produced goods were not manufactured merely for Quaker customers. In a letter sent from Cornwall in 1710, Alice Beeling Jr ordered eighty yards of stole fabric. Like many of Sarah Chubb's customers, she enclosed a sample with specific instructions about its appearance, explaining that 'in ste[a]d of strip[e]s of black it must be a dee[p]e Red'.[126] It is unlikely that such bright or patterned fabric would be primarily targeted at Quaker consumers because Quaker Meetings continually warned Friends against wearing 'Gaudy Colour[s]'. An epistle from Lincolnshire Women's Meeting in 1721 recommended that 'green' was 'very decent and becoming us as a people'.[127] Likewise, Friends were continually warned against the buying and selling of any 'striped or flowered stuffs'.[128] When the merchant Benjamin Bond attached a piece of striped red fabric to an order in 1714, requesting 'the Best Canteloones to this Pattern', it is unlikely that such a product was intended for Friends.[129] Naturally, frequent references to 'modist coloures' suggest that some buyers had Quaker customers in mind when they made their requests, but it is clear that the outputs of the workhouse extended beyond the direct local community of Friends.[130] Sarah Chubb collaborated with non-Quaker merchants, and oversaw the manufacture of goods intended for wider society.

In channelling their wealth into philanthropic endeavours, commentators have suggested that Quakers were conforming to a 'Protestant ethic' that combined Christian motivations with economic and social advancement.[131] This morality was evident in other nonconformist groups, whose simplicity in personal life often became associated with an attachment to 'industry and frugality'.[132] But such activities demonstrate how Friends' concerns for

---

[126] LRSF, MS Vol 294 Dix MSS, fol. B 10 B, Alice Beeling Junior to Sarah Chubb, Penryn, Cornwall, 14 January 1710.

[127] LRSF, Temp MSS 747 Cash Papers, fol. 17 'Extracts from the Minutes of Lincolnshire Quarterly Meeting', 22 June 1721.

[128] KAC, WDFCF/1/13 Kendal Men's Monthly Meeting Minutes, 1699–1723, minutes for 4 February 1704.

[129] Cantaloons were a type of lightweight worsted fabric manufactured at the Bristol workhouse. LRSF, MS Vol 294 Dix MSS, fol. B 31 B, Benjamin Bond to the Bristol Workhouse, 26 April 1714.

[130] When Francis Place requested 'a peece of the best Cantaloon' from the workhouse in 1715 for his mother, he specified that this should be of 'modist coulers'. LRSF, MS Vol 294 Dix MSS, fol. B 33 B, Francis Place to Sarah Chubb, Minehead, Somerset, 11 December 1715.

[131] See Matthew Niblett, 'The Death of Puritanism? Protestant Dissent and the Problem of Luxury in Eighteenth-Century England', *Studies on Voltaire and the Eighteenth Century*, vol. 6 (2008), pp. 251–259.

[132] Freeman, 'Quakers, Business, and Philanthropy', p. 422.

their own kind could be channelled into other philanthropic activities. It also underscores the unusually active place of Quaker women in administering public charity. In many respects, it was an extension of their roles in their separate Meetings for business, discussed in Chapter 2, where relief of poorer members of the community was a dominant concern for the elders of the English Meetings. One example was evidenced in 1679, when John Bellers purchased and provided the London Women's Meeting with cloth and flax so that they could fashion them into clothing for the poor.[133] Not only were they able to lessen the burden of poor relief on local rate payers through caring for their own religious community, they were also finding innovative solutions to the problem of poverty within wider society. The similarities between the Quaker workhouse in Bristol and those workhouses set up by the Bristol Corporation of the Poor, testify to the influence of Friends in shaping local poor relief initiatives. An unnamed Quaker woman from Edinburgh, for instance, was commended in the national press in 1725 for her proposal to establish a woollen manufactory in the city. This 'Act of great Charity' found strong support in the *Weekly Journal*, for the woman intended to 'employ all the Beggars in Work, and to give them Food and Rayment [*sic*]', which would be of 'great Service to the City'.[134] Such undertakings epitomise the acceptance that Quakers had attained within British society by the early eighteenth century.

In Pennsylvania, where cooperation and tolerance were enshrined in the colonial charter, Friends were encouraged to live in harmony with other settlers, as well as with the indigenous population. In cities like Philadelphia, where the general wealth of Friends meant that there was less direct need for Quaker poor relief, women appear to have taken an active interest in the plight of poorer members of the wider community. They joined with others to oversee the establishment of institutions like the Philadelphia Almshouse in 1713, for the employment and relief of the able-bodied poor, and the Pennsylvania Hospital in 1751, for the aid of the sick poor and insane.[135] The Philadelphian Quaker diarist Hannah Callender frequently visited the Pennsylvania Hospital, where she provided material and financial relief to the sick inmates.[136] Ann Warder also incorporated visits to the hospital and workhouse into her social itinerary when visiting the city. In May 1786, she

---

[133] Valenze, *The Social Life of Money*, p. 122.
[134] *Weekly Journal or British Gazetteer* (London), 27 February 1725, issue no. 9, p. 5.
[135] Barbour and Frost, *The Quakers*, pp. 127–128 and 164–167.
[136] Hannah Callender, *The Diary of Hannah Callender Sansom: Sense and Sensibility in the Age of the American Revolution*, ed. Susan E. Klepp and Karin Wulf (London, 2010), pp. 68, 98–99, 132, 247: diary entries for 19 and 20 September 1758, 10–12 April 1759, 13 November 1759, 27 and 29 March 1770.

visited both institutions after a day trip to the Philadelphia Public Library.[137] Their activities show that there was an underlying recognition that poor non-Quaker citizens needed support and assistance.

Concern for 'outsider' communities is also evidenced in Friends' later activities against slavery and the establishment of their Friendly Association for Regaining and Preserving Peace with the Indians, founded in 1755. Its creation formalised the concerns of the Pennsylvanian Quaker community for the welfare of Native American populations. But its establishment has been viewed as marking a change in Quaker attitudes towards reform, as members proved that they were willing to use external and voluntary institutions to contribute to the societies in which they lived.[138] Thus by the mid-eighteenth century, Quakers in both Britain and the Americas were actively involved in the world around them, taking up positions of responsibility within their communities.

FEMALE PREACHERS AND QUAKER 'PLAINNESS' TESTIMONIES

The preacher or 'Public Friend' provides a compelling example of women's liminality between the private world of the Quaker Meeting and the wider non-Quaker world. In fact, the denotation of 'Public Friend' shows how Quakers understood the work of ministers to mean interaction with those who were not of their Society. Whilst the highly unorthodox behaviour of female preachers often met with criticism and scorn, their labours could also encourage conversion. The anonymous author of *Remarks Upon the Quakers* criticised the movement as late as 1700 for using female preachers as a means of attracting large audiences. 'The Meeting not thronged so much as it used to be, what a subtle Art the *Quakers* have to regain the Company, and fill the House afresh', for 'a Woman is to Speak the next time, which sets the People a madding and makes them all for coming again'.[139] Whilst the cynicism of this author is clear, it is significant that non-Quaker writers attributed the success of the movement to the novelty of female preachers. This is supported by anecdotal evidence from Quaker women's spiritual autobiographies. For example, shortly before her conversion to Quakerism in 1680, Alice Hayes attended a Meeting because she had 'heard a Report about the Neighbourhood of a *Woman-Preacher*, that was esteemed of

---

[137] Ann Warder, 'Extracts from the Diary of Mrs. Ann Warder (concluded)', ed. Sarah Cadbury, *Pennsylvania Magazine of History and Biography*, vol. 18, no. 1 (1894), pp. 53–54.

[138] Barbour and Frost, *The Quakers*, pp. 126–128.

[139] Anon., *Remarks upon the Quakers*, p. 13.

greatly among the *Quakers*' and had gone with some neighbours to see her 'in Curiosity'.[140]

Encounters of this sort appear to have occurred on an even greater scale in the American colonies. The status of female Friends as itinerant preachers, travelling from place to place, naturally aroused much suspicion. Mary Weston, for instance, described in her journal concerns about visiting Connecticut because the people 'were very much Strangers to Friends and their principles, and indeed some few years ago were bitter Enemies Against them'. She noted the aversion of the inhabitants to women's preaching, which she admitted 'brought my Mind very low'.[141] Circumstantial evidence nevertheless suggests that her presence was often welcomed as a novelty. During a visit to Newport, Rhode Island, in 1750, Weston reported that between '4 and 5 thousand people' had attended a Meeting where she preached.[142] Because the population of Newport at this time could not have much exceeded this figure, Weston's estimate is almost certainly exaggerated.[143] Nevertheless, the writings of other women who undertook missionary work in the Puritan colonies suggest that they had enjoyed a similarly generous reception. For example, Mary Peisley noted on her journey to New England that the people had 'thronged' to the Meetings in 'unbounded curiosity' to hear her speak, despite the hot weather. She remarked that 'it was exceeding hard to fit them, and much more trying to speak in them'.[144] Quaker women ministers might not only achieve eminence within their own religious society but also attain status in the non-Quaker community, as objects of interest and wonder.

The acceptance and hospitality offered to female preachers during their itinerant work was frequently acknowledged by women in their spiritual autobiographies. The scarcity of Friends in some regions, combined with long distances between Quaker Meetings, often meant that preachers had to rely on the kindness of non-Quaker strangers. Recalling such conditions during missionary service to the colonies in 1753, Catherine Payton noted that after travelling through 'a wilderness country for several days', she came upon a 'lodging at some planters; who, though not of our Society, readily gave us admittance into their houses, and freely entertained us according to their manner of living'.[145] Mary Peisley even claimed that her missionary

[140] Alice Hayes, *A Legacy, or Widow's Mite; Left by Alice Hayes, to Her Children and Others: With an Account of Some of Her Dying Sayings* (London, 1723), p. 18.

[141] LRSF, MS Vol 312 Journal of Mary Weston, p. 116.

[142] Ibid., between pp. 70 and 71, Mary Weston to Daniel Weston, New York, 9 December 1750.

[143] See Lynne Withey, *Urban Growth in Colonial Rhode Island: Newport and Providence in the Eighteenth Century* (New York, 1984), p. 115.

[144] Mary Peisley, *Some Account of the Life and Religious Exercises of Mary Neale, Formerly Mary Peisley* (Philadelphia, 1796), p. 104.

[145] Catherine Phillips, *Memoirs of the Life of Catherine Phillips* (London, 1797), p. 73.

work in Ireland had been more effective amongst non-Quakers than those of her own Society. When she visited the town of Sligo in Connaught in July 1751, for example, she commented that 'there seemed much more openness to declare the truth amongst those of other societies, than amongst them that go under our name'.[146] In such instances, necessity, combined with a desire to preach to an audience beyond co-religionists, overcame denominational restrictions.

As Public Friends, ministers were placed in a precarious position: at whom and for what purpose should their message be directed? Female ministers often commented upon the difficulty of addressing the spiritual state of large mixed crowds in their journals. Deborah Bell, for instance, observed that her popularity in Lancashire 'added much to the weight of my present exercise'.[147] Undoubtedly, the tenor of their religious exhortation might be different when addressing a largely non-Quaker audience. However, concerns about the popularity of particular preachers could also prove a source of conflict within the introverted eighteenth-century movement. Female preachers who felt called to exhort non-Quaker audiences could face condemnation from their own Society. May Drummond, for instance, was forbidden from preaching in her native Meeting in Edinburgh after Friends judged that her public speech was not spiritually edifying. The criticisms she faced were remarkably hostile, with one Friend declaring that 'we have farr better meetings in thy absence than when thou art present'.[148]

The 'burden' Friends reportedly experienced with Drummond's preaching was explained as the reason for her forced removal from this office. However, it is almost certain that her popularity with non-Quaker audiences also contributed to this stigmatisation. This tension was encapsulated in an anonymous publication from 1750, called *A Scheme for a General Comprehension of All Parties in Religion*, which satirised Drummond as the only woman presiding over a mock committee wishing to alter the Anglican liturgy. The text portrayed her as having departed from Quaker culture because she was willing to compromise and negotiate with 'the several principal sects and Parties of Christians, or reputed Christians'.[149] Similar criticisms were levelled at the Staffordshire preacher Frances Henshaw, who became a recognised minister in 1737, but faced criticism for the 'popularity

[146] Peisley, *Some Account of the Life and Religious Exercises*, pp. 61–62.
[147] Deborah Bell, *A Short Journal of the Labours and Travels in the Work in the Ministry, of That Faithful Servant of Christ, Deborah Bell* (London, 1776), p. 13.
[148] William Miller to May Drummond, Abbay, 3 April 1765, in William F. Miller, 'Episodes in the Life of May Drummond', *JFHS*, vol. 4 (1907), p. 107.
[149] Anon., *A Scheme for a General Comprehension of All Parties in Religion* (London, 1750), pp. 7–13.

and applause' that her ministering efforts enjoyed, leading some Friends to accuse her of spiritual vanity.[150]

The evangelical and almost messianic quality of Quaker exhortation had disappeared from the English movement by the mid-eighteenth century. Moreover, the reaction of leading Friends against Drummond's and Henshaw's public preaching reflects a more general anxiety that members were becoming too integrated into the world. Such concerns are revealed in a 1744 letter sent by William Cookworthy, where he reported upon Drummond's preaching. Commenting on the 'learned' style of her ministry, he observed that 'some of her epithets rather swell too much' and were 'a little theatrical'. He went on to explain that 'She has a perfect acquaintance with the world'.[151] One critic of Frances Henshaw accused her of following the example of 'M. Drummond', noting that 'it is the Peculiarity, indeed of the Quakers to distinguish themselves more by attending the Private Mammon, than the Public Divertions or Fashions of their neighbours'.[152] Underlining these observations are veiled warnings that eighteenth-century ministers were becoming too integrated into non-Quaker culture and thus polluting themselves with 'worldly' behaviour. Interestingly, no comparable example exists of colonial Friends criticising a female minister for the popularity of her preaching. This suggests that those female preachers who attained too much acclaim among non-Quaker audiences were censured primarily within the British context. One possible explanation for this disparity is that the colonial Quaker community was more tolerant of religious diversity and difference because they had not continued to experience the effects of suffering and persecution.

The fluidity with which testimonies were adapted and understood by different groups of Quakers is evidence of the tension between the movement's public presentation and its efforts to encourage members to lead pure lives. However, it was not just the itinerant preachers who were transgressing these boundaries. One of the most visible examples of the growing 'worldliness' within the Quaker rank and file was through their outward dress and deportment. Noting increasing disparities between Quaker prosperity and precepts of plain living, Voltaire perceived the movement's decline in England, describing how 'the children, whom the industry of their parents has enrich'd are desirous of enjoying honours, of wearing buttons and ruffles; and [are] quite asham'd of being call'd Quakers'.[153] The French writer

---

[150] Frances Dodshon (née Henshaw), *Some Account of the Convincement and Religious Experience, of Frances Dodshon* (London, 1804), p. 36.

[151] William Cookworthy to Richard Hingston, Plymouth, 1 August 1744, in Miller, 'Episodes in the Life of May Drummond', pp. 60–61.

[152] LRSF, MSS Vol 332 Toft MSS, fol. 15, letter on behalf of Frances Henshaw for Joshua Toft, undated, c. 1736.

[153] François-Marie Arouet Voltaire, *Letters Concerning the English Nation* (London, 1733), p. 29.

Brissot also lamented the extravagance of a younger generation of female Pennsylvanian Friends, who fussed over curling their hair and expensive fabrics. 'These observations gave me pain', he wrote, for 'these young Quakeresses, whom nature has so well endowed ... are remarkable for their choice of the finest linens, muslins, and silks'.[154] A fondness for luxury and ostentatious living was a recurring concern for the developing movement, showing how wealthy Friends struggled to balance the material status associated with their position in society with a plain and circumspect lifestyle.

We saw in Chapter 2 how standards of 'plainness' varied greatly over time and in different places. It was a matter relative to wealth and, as I observed, many of the affluent colonial Meetings were more tolerant of members transgressing plainness testimonies. This tension was highlighted in the reflections of Ann Warder, an English-born Quaker, who observed the unusual sociability and fashionable dress of her Philadelphian co-religionists in a journal she kept for her sister. She frequently commented on the un-Quakerly fashions of the female Friends of the city, criticising her visitors for failing to distinguish themselves from wider society, and for wearing outfits 'elegant enough for any bride'. During one hot summer, she had endeavoured to make 'no alteration in my dress on account of the weather' since godly 'resolution would not let me wear short gowns, which are common here'.[155] English and Irish Friends appear considerably more vigilant than their colonial sisters in discouraging members and preachers from emulating the fashions and pleasures of the rest of the 'world'. Irish Quakers were especially uncompromising in their standards of plainness, devoting more time to discussing 'appropriate standards of dress' in their national and provincial Meetings than any other social issue, aside from marriage. Regular committees of merchants, clothiers, and tailors were gathered together at the National Meeting in Dublin to specify standards for Quaker clothing.[156]

The gap between theory and practice, that is what was expected of members and how they behaved, was a cause of continual concern for the Society. An increasing acceptance of the movement by the rest of society led, in the eyes of its leadership, to potential for greater transgressions. Above all, it serves to remind us that a rigorous code of ethics was difficult to enforce within a movement whose membership base spanned such a broad social and geographical cross-section of the Atlantic world. Interaction with their non-Quaker neighbours was a very real and unavoidable element of Quaker

[154] J. P. Brissot de Warville, *New Travels in the United States of America Performed in 1788* (Dublin, 1792), pp. 380–381.

[155] Ann Warder, 'Extracts from the Diary of Mrs. Ann Warder', ed. Sarah Cadbury, *Pennsylvania Magazine of History and Biography*, vol. 17, no. 4 (1893), pp. 447 and 453.

[156] Richard L. Greaves, *God's Other Children: Protestant Nonconformists and the Emergence of Denominational Churches in Ireland, 1660–1700* (Stanford, CA, 1997), pp. 318–319.

women's lives. Having explored some facets of the assimilation of female Friends at a local level, I will now turn to consider the admiration that some female Friends were able to attain on a wider scale: in non-Quaker writings and political discussions.

'SWEETNESS... IN YOUR SOCIETY': QUAKER WOMEN AND EARLY ENLIGHTENMENT THOUGHT

The public roles given to female Friends naturally continued to fuel the debate about the relationship between gender and authority in the national Church, as women continued to occupy a public and visible place within the Quaker movement. Yet the representation of female Friends in many non-Quaker writings from the eighteenth century was very different in character to those anti-Quaker discussions I explored earlier. Indeed, one of the most striking features of eighteenth-century anti-Quaker polemic is how infrequently the movement's female members are discussed at any great length. At least 227 tracts hostile to Quakerism were published between 1700 and 1750.[157] However, only a handful explicitly targeted Quaker women.[158] This discrepancy is surprising, especially because there is evidence of women becoming more visible in Quaker culture and taking on leading organisational roles during this period.[159] The absence of women from printed debates suggests that the public response to female Friends was changing. Indeed, the opening example of May Drummond's status as a 'celebrated' preacher reminds us that eighteenth-century Quaker women were acquiring eminence not only within their own religious society but also as public figures beyond the Quaker community.

It is difficult to identify precise reasons why the behaviour of Quaker women attracted less attention in the non-Quaker press, though it is

---

[157] This figure has been calculated by doing a subject search of 'Antiquakeriana' on the Haverford, Bryn Mawr, and Swarthmore combined 'Tripod' catalogue. This figure is not comprehensive and may also include some texts that were sympathetic to Quakerism, but were responding to a specific anti-Quaker text. It nevertheless gives an indication of the scale of continued anti-Quaker feeling during this period.

[158] These were Anon., *A Comical New Dialogue between Mr. G-F A Pious Dissenting Parson, and a Female-Quaker (a Goldsmith's Wife) Near Cheapside* (London, 1706); Walker, *A True Copy of Some Original Letters, which Pass'd between John Hall of Monk-Hesleden ... and William Walker*; and Anon., *A Dissertation upon the Liberty of Preaching Granted to Women by the People Call'd Quakers* (Dublin, 1738). Other tracts published during this period did include references to the movement's female members, but very few engaged in sustained debate about their roles within the movement. This included the highly derogatory anonymous tract *The Quakers Art of Courtship*, which contained extensive negative portrayals of female Friends and went through multiple editions during this period.

[159] A detailed discussion of this is provided in the Introduction. See also Larson, *Daughters of Light*, p. 63; and Sarah Apetrei, *Women, Feminism and Religion in Early Enlightenment England* (Cambridge, 2010), p. 14.

important to observe that concerns about the preservation of the Protestant faith were renewed with fierce intensity during the eighteenth century. It was not Quakerism that was the source of concern for mainstream commentators, however, but the challenge posed by female religiosity closer to home, namely through the rise of Methodism, a radical reformist group based within the national Church.[160] The Methodist appeal to private feeling was attractive to women from a range of social backgrounds, and attacks on female members became a pronounced feature of the polemical literature from the mid-eighteenth century. Major has persuasively argued that Methodist women became integral to debates about the membership and definition of the national Church, as writers searched for 'a female figurehead that would distinguish the Church of England and its women from Methodism and its female followers'.[161] This shift from an external to an internal religious challenge may explain why Quaker women were eclipsed by their Methodist counterparts in the public world of polemic.

New political ideas and discussions were also influencing a new generation of non-Quaker writers who perceived the movement and female piety in far more positive ways. In this context, female participation in religious life took on particular social and political significance. The idealisation of female Friends was pronounced in the remarks of French philosophes and travellers, who had immersed themselves in colonial Quaker customs and culture. This was especially true of Pennsylvania, where William Penn's 'Holy Experiment' became a model that many thinkers observed and admired. As Barry Levy argues, such a reception was part of a broader French admiration for new forms of egalitarian domestic life.[162] It was also motivated by a desire to observe the effects of religious toleration on social relations and to consider new social, religious, and political approaches to governance and worship. In his *New Travels in the United States*, Brissot brought the nuances of American Quaker life to European society in 1788.[163] He commented in detail on the lifestyle of American Friends during his stay on a Quaker farm in Pennsylvania, where he attended Meetings and funerals and interviewed a number of Quakers. Like many of his contemporaries, he believed that Quaker women occupied a separate sphere of moral and social life, as paragons of femininity and virtue. They were 'faithful to their husbands, tender to their children, vigilant and economical in their household, and simple in their ornaments'. Moreover, their sober dress and outward

---

[160] Methodism did not secede from the Church of England until 1795.
[161] Major, *Madam Britannia*, p. 125.
[162] Barry Levy, *Quakers and the American Family: British Settlement in the Delaware Valley* (Oxford, 1988), pp. 7–9.
[163] Brissot, *New Travels in the United States*, pp. 375–420.

appearance meant that they were able to 'reserve all their accomplishments for the mind'.[164] Underlying such a declaration was a strong sense that Quaker principles and the behaviour of female Friends were compatible with Enlightenment values, as both emblems of affective female religion and with the rational virtues of citizenship.[165]

Ryan has described the French philosophes' admiration for Penn's 'Holy Experiment' as a 'lengthy infatuation'.[166] Here, Quaker women were particularly visible in public life because Friends formed the third-largest religious group and dominated Pennsylvanian government.[167] A letter of 1723 to 'the venerable Doctor Janus' by an anonymous 'Traveller', remarked on the general happiness of the Quaker communities he had encountered during his travels in the colonies. The letter, published in the *New England Courant*, praised Friends for their speech, honesty, integrity, and simplicity. The commentator reserved his warmest praise for the modesty of the women; 'the neatness and decency of their *Apparel*', he notes, 'is very delightful to the Eye'. 'Who ever saw a *Quaker-Slut?*', he asks, 'Tis a Contradiction in Terms'.[168] Even in London, Quakers were attracting positive attention from 'enlightened' commentators. In his *Letters Concerning the English Nation* (1733), for example, Voltaire devoted more attention to the Quakers than any other religious movement. He brought the London Quakers to the attention of the world, as an 'extraordinary people' respected for their honesty, virtue, moderation, peaceable nature, and rational approach to religion.[169] This picture stands in sharp contrast to the sexual slurs and other criticisms about Quaker customs used by earlier writers to discredit female preachers. Moreover, it underlines how the Quaker utopian vision carried great weight for those enlightened travellers seeking alternative models on which to base their own social programmes.

Praise for the Quakers during the eighteenth century, however, was not limited to a narrow circle of French thinkers commenting on Quaker domesticity. A large number of intellectuals were also giving a surprising amount of positive attention to public female preachers. This is powerfully demonstrated in a letter John Locke sent to two Quaker women, Rebecca Collier and Rachel Buckon, after attending a Quaker Meeting in London where they had both preached. The letter, dated November 1696 and accompanied by a packet of sweetmeats, showed great admiration for Quaker

---

[164] Ibid., pp. 376–377.
[165] Crawford, *Women and Religion*, pp. 204–208.
[166] Ryan, *Imaginary Friends*, p. 90.
[167] Larson, *Daughters of Light*, p. 303.
[168] *New England Courant* (Boston) 6 May–13 May 1723, p. 1.
[169] Voltaire, *Letters Concerning the English Nation*, pp. 1–29.

female preaching. Commenting on 'the sweetness I found in your society', Locke wrote:

Outward hearing may misguide us, but internal knowledge cannot err. We have something here, of what we shall have hereafter, to know as we are known; and thus we, with our other Friends, were even at first view mutual partakers . . . Women, indeed, had the honour first to publish the resurrection of the spirit of love, and let all the disciples of our Lord rejoice therein, as doth your partner. John Locke.[170]

The original version of the letter no longer survives, and its authenticity can be questioned.[171] However, Locke's sympathetic attitude towards Quakers like Benjamin Furly and William Penn is well documented.[172] Much can be inferred from the remarkable language employed in the letter. Of particular note is the apparent shift in how intellectuals like Locke viewed the Quakers' inner light. Instead of associating the movings of Quaker preachers like Rebecca Collier as 'delusions of the Devil', these internal promptings became characteristic of the reasoned mind. Under both the formulation of the 'light within' and 'reason', the 'light' functioned as a primary source of truth and authority, which could be accessed by the individual in an unmediated way.[173] Locke's words thus reflect a new approach to religion, no longer viewing unorthodox individual conscience as inherently heretical. It is interesting that he chose the personal pronoun 'we' to refer to the collective experience he felt with his two female readers, as if he too had been touched by what he felt during their Meeting for worship. This was heightened by his choice of salutation 'partner' to close the letter.

Like his attitudes towards women more generally, Locke's position on women's public speech was never consistent and often fell short of modern feminist ideals.[174] His endorsement of female preaching at this Meeting is nonetheless significant, as he linked the Gospel story of the women spreading news of Christ's resurrection to the proselytising activities of women in Quaker Meetings for worship. Moreover, the manuscript account in which the letter was transcribed claimed that after hearing Rebecca Collier preach,

[170] LRSF, Temp MS 745 Robson Papers, Vol. 37, Box 1, p. 92, 'A Letter from John Locke to Rebecca Collier and Rachel Buckon' (copy), Gray's Inn, London, 21 November 1696.

[171] In his edited collection of Locke's correspondence, E. S. De Beer questioned the authenticity of the letter because it is sometimes dated as 1699 and no other record of Rebecca Collier (or Collins) and Rebecca Brecon (or Buckon) exists. E. S. De Beer, *The Correspondence of John Locke in Eight Volumes* (vol. 5, Oxford, 1979), p. 718.

[172] For more on Locke's relationship with other leading Friends, see Jeffrey Dudiak and Laura Rediehs, 'Quakers, Philosophy and Truth', in Angell and Dandelion, *Oxford Handbook of Quaker Studies*, pp. 510–511; and W. Hull, *Benjamin Furly and Quakerism in Rotterdam* (Swarthmore, PA, 1941).

[173] Dudiak and Rediehs, 'Quakers, Philosophy, and Truth', p. 513.

[174] The Bristol Quaker Benjamin Coole engaged in a public printed debate in 1717 about the presentation of female preaching in his *Paraphrase and Notes*. Benjamin Coole, *Some Brief Observations on the Judicious John Lock's Paraphrase and Notes on the Texts* (London, 1715).

Locke was inspired to alter a passage in his *Paraphrase and Notes*.[175] In the final version, published posthumously, he modified St Paul's view that women should keep silent in church, explaining that where a woman was directly inspired by God, she might speak and prophesy.[176] We can never be certain that Locke made a conscious decision to adapt his interpretation of St Paul based on this encounter. But it underlines how leading intellectuals could admire the public presence of women within Quaker Meetings. At least three eighteenth-century copies of the letter have found their way into the collections held at the Library of the Religious Society of Friends in London.[177] This suggests that even if the letter wasn't genuine, this scenario of a great political thinker responding positively to these female preachers had become part of collective Quaker memory. It also attests to the importance of individual women like Rebecca Collier in transforming ideas and knowledge.

The new intellectual climate could sometimes be accommodating and open-minded towards the idea of the female preacher, and there were now many religious options available in the eighteenth-century Atlantic. The 'religious marketplace', as Carla Gardina Pestana suggests, led religion to become a commodity that was 'sold and consumed'.[178] In the expanding British Atlantic world, women with prophetic gifts did not just act as 'representivites of specific religious communities', but were also 'participants in religious networks that crossed sectarian lines'.[179] Widespread religious experimentalism is underlined from reports following the conversion of May Drummond in 1731, which allude to the broad public acceptance she received whilst preaching in London. She was described as popular 'amongst those of other societies, who were much drawn to the Meetings she attended'.[180] In 1753, a Quaker commentator noted how 'the kind Treatment, and good Reception, she had with the *Queen*' had 'spread so in City and Country, that many Thousands flocked to hear her, and more of

---

[175] LRSF, Temp MS 745 Robson Papers, Vol. 37, Box 1, p. 92, 'A Letter from John Locke to Rebecca Collier and Rachel Buckon' (copy), Gray's Inn, London, 21 November 1696.

[176] '[T]hat the spirit of God and the Gift of Prophesie should be poured out upon Women as well as Men, in the time of the Gospel is plain.' John Locke, *A Paraphrase and Notes on the Epistles of St Paul to the Galatians, I and II Corinthians, Romans, and Ephesians* (London, 1707), I Corinthians Section VII, p. 65.

[177] I have located copies of this letter in the following collections: LRSF, Temp MS 745 Robson Papers, Vol. 37, Box 1, p. 92; LRSF, MS Vol S 487 Eighteenth Century Commonplace Book, p. 23; and TEMP MSS 57/15 Notebooks and Papers.

[178] Carla Gardina Pestana, 'Between Religious Marketplace and Spiritual Wasteland: Religion in the British Atlantic World', *History Compass*, vol. 2 (2004), p. 1.

[179] Elizabeth Bouldin, *Women Prophets and Radical Protestantism in the British Atlantic World, 1640–1730* (Cambridge, 2015), p. 154.

[180] William F. Miller, 'Episodes in the Life of May Drummond', *JFHS*, vol. 4 (1907), pp. 55–56.

the Gentry and Nobility than ever was known before to our Meetings'.[181] This suggests an increasing desire on the part of educated and elite men and women to participate in different forms of religious worship.

The competition between different religious ideas was particularly prevalent in the American colonies, where the diversity of religious life and absence of a national church encouraged individuals to seek new spiritual experiences. Female Friends were also willing to consider other worship practises and religious cultures, a fact often recorded by colonial women in their writings. The Quaker diarist Elizabeth Drinker attended a Methodist meeting during an evening walk, remarking that the audience 'appear'd quiet and attentive'.[182] Her contemporary Hannah Callender documented a journey with relatives and other Philadelphian Friends to stay at the Moravian settlement at Bethlehem, Pennsylvania, in August 1761. Although she disagreed with their values, Callender was sympathetic to the settlement, commenting on the way of life and order of the inmates, as well as the decor and interior furnishings. 'The great order, decency, decorum and conveniency is hardly to be expressed', she wrote, and explained that 'we left this pleasant place with due thanks to the minister'.[183] The fluidity of religious identity and ability of individuals to 'alter their beliefs and dabble in other faiths' is an often-unacknowledged feature of eighteenth-century religious culture.[184]

This climate of religious exchange may also be linked to a much broader change underway in eighteenth-century society that saw women dominating aspects of religious life. The Protestant churches, as I noted in the Introduction, were becoming feminine institutions, at least in numerical terms. Work by historians of American religion has estimated that between the late seventeenth and mid-nineteenth centuries 60 to 75 per cent of the church members and of those 'responding to revivalist "awakenings" were women'.[185] Movements like the Methodists, Moravians, Philadelphians, French Prophets, German Pietists, Behmenists, and Baptists advocated some form of official role for women in the public life of their churches. Major notes that an average of 57.8 per cent of English Methodist members

[181] Thomas Chalkley, *A Journal or Historical Account of the Life, Travels, and Christian Experiences of … Thomas Chalkley* (3rd edn, London, 1751), pp. 279–280.

[182] Elizabeth Drinker, *The Diary of Elizabeth Drinker: The Life Cycle of an Eighteenth-Century Woman*, ed. Elaine Forman Crane (Boston, 1994), p. 228: diary entry for 2 September 1800.

[183] Callender, *The Diary of Hannah Callender*, pp. 152–156: diary entries for 27–31 August 1761.

[184] Annette Laing, 'Crossing Denominational Boundaries: Two Early American Women and Religion in the Atlantic World', in Emily Clark and Mary Laven (eds.), *Women and Religion in the Atlantic Age, 1550–1900* (Farnham, 2013), p. 121.

[185] Gail Malmgreen, 'Domestic Discords: Women and the Family in East Cheshire Methodism, 1750–1830,' in Jim Obelkevich, Lyndal Roper, and Raphael Samuel (eds.), *Disciplines of Faith: Studies in Religion, Politics and Patriarchy* (London, 1987), p. 56.

between 1759 and 1770 were female, and that in some regions the number of single women attending Methodist meetings was considerable.[186] Liberal writers even came to praise and admire the authority that Quakers permitted their female members. Thomas Clarkson, for instance, defended Quaker women in his *Portraiture of Quakerism* as more spiritual than the men and acknowledged that they have 'that which no other body of women have, a public character'.[187]

This 'feminisation' of religion was also influenced by the domestic sphere: the space in which much of the day-to-day aspects of religious life were performed. The place of the family in advancing religious teachings has been viewed as a positive effect of the Protestant Reformation, which gave women frequent opportunities to exercise domestic religious power.[188] The influence of women in the spiritual education of their families was central to eighteenth-century devotional life. Susanna Wesley, for example, shaped the spiritual upbringing of her sons Charles and John Wesley, who went on to found Methodism.[189] The strong domestic focus of colonial Quakerism may have transformed the image non-Quakers held about female Friends. No longer were they characterised as dangerous deviants with the power to lead their families into new delusional spheres, but instead were praised by writers for their devotion and attentiveness to their families' spiritual welfare. 'In consequence of denying themselves the pleasures of the world', wrote Clarkson, Friends 'have been obliged to cherish those which are found in domestic life.'[190] The high regard travellers held for colonial Friends, Levy argues, was linked to the belief that Quaker political and economic success was due to their formation of 'special families' that created and perpetuated 'sacred lives'.[191]

An evident change had clearly taken place in how eighteenth-century audiences understood the place of the female preacher. The epigraph to this chapter cites part of a poem 'On the noted and celebrated Quaker Mrs Drummond', written by a young woman, and published in September 1735 in *The Gentleman's Magazine*. The poem, which compared Drummond to the mystic Saint Teresa of Avila, was originally intended to celebrate Mary

---

[186] Unmarried women swelled the ranks of some London congregations by almost two thirds. Major, *Madam Britannia*, p. 143.

[187] Thomas Clarkson, *A Portraiture of Quakerism* (3 vols., New York, 1806), vol. 3, p. 288–289.

[188] See, e.g., Natalie Zemon Davis, *Women on the Margins: Three Seventeenth-Century Lives* (London, 1995); and Steven E. Ozment, *When Fathers Ruled: Family Life in Reformation Europe* (London, 1983).

[189] As Lawrence notes, she was the evangelical head of her family and instituted weekly meetings with her children to examine them on their spiritual well-being. Lawrence, *One Family under God*, p. 28.

[190] Clarkson, *Portraiture of Quakerism*, vol. 3, p. 257.

[191] Levy, *Quakers and the American Family*, p. 17.

Astell.[192] It is curious that this text was applicable to both women, who came from such different social, religious, and political backgrounds. Astell was among the first to equate 'women's spiritual capacities with their intellectual potential'.[193] Nevertheless, it was Drummond, the missionary from Scotland, who was hailed in the twenty-four lines of couplets as a 'generous heroine' brought to reform the nation's corrupt morals and values. She was praised for her 'pious maxims' and 'wisdom', and for showing 'your sex's aptitude and worth', freeing women from 'that false brand of Incapacity'.[194]

The recognisably public position of the female preacher was increasingly viewed as compatible with the advancement of proto-feminist causes. Cartesian philosophy, after all, had come to discern the reasoned mind as 'naturally equal' in all human beings. The concept of rational thought gave female advocates like Astell the confidence to believe that women should share the same access to learning and religious instruction as men. This led to her proposal for an all-female college for 'Religious Retirement', a kind of 'secular convent' where women could lead an independent intellectual life devoted to study, contemplation, and religious devotion.[195] Her ideas had some affinity with Quaker theology, which viewed the female mind as equally receptive of divine guidance. Moreover, as Mark Knights observes, it was an issue taken up by many Quaker authors, who believed in 'the importance of education or learning as a means carving out a legitimate role for women'.[196] The structure of Quaker worship and discipline, with its gender-segregated Meetings for business, had parallels to the communities of women envisioned by writers like Astell.

This new form of 'polite Quakerliness' demonstrates the changing ways in which Friends engaged with the non-Quaker public about their beliefs.[197] The rise of both spoken and printed discussion found a celebrated example in the figure of the Quaker Mary Knowles, who became famed for debating with Dr Johnson.[198] One such occasion occurred in April 1778, when Knowles disputed with Johnson over the right of women to independently join religious movements. The dialogue, recorded by James Boswell in his

---

[192] Larson, *Daughters of Light*, p. 288.
[193] Apetrei, *Women, Feminism and Religion*, p. 7.
[194] A Young Lady, 'On the Noted and Celebrated Quaker Mrs Drummond', *Gentleman's Magazine: Or, Monthly Intelligencer*, January 1731–December 1735, September 1735, p. 555.
[195] Ruth Perry, 'Mary Astell and Enlightenment' in Sarah Knott and Barbara Taylor (eds.), *Women, Gender and Enlightenment* (Basingstoke, 2005), p. 360.
[196] Knights, *The Devil in Disguise*, p. 123.
[197] Judith Jennings, *Gender, Religion, and Radicalism in the Long Eighteenth Century: The 'Ingenious Quaker' and Her Connections* (Aldershot, 2006), p. 16.
[198] For more on Knowles and Johnson see Jennings, *Gender, Religion, and Radicalism*, pp. 49–72.

Life of Johnson and published by Knowles in *The Gentleman's Magazine* in 1791, allegedly began after Johnson criticised a young woman, Jane Harry, for renouncing the Church of England and joining the Quakers.[199] Clearly old stereotypes about Quaker ensnarement of naive individuals had not gone away, for Johnson began by declaring aggressively: 'I hate the odious wench for her apostasy: and it is you, Madam, who have seduced her from the Christian Religion.' Knowles, however, begging leave 'to be heard in my own defence', countered with a justification of Quakerism, which she insisted was not a departure from Christianity. 'As an accountable creature', she argued, Harry had every right to 'examine and to change her educational tenets whenever she supposed she had found them erroneous'.[200] By assuming what Amanda Vickery has described as 'the mantle of politeness', Knowles was able not only to defend her religious beliefs within a largely male setting, but also to present Quaker doctrines clearly and coherently for both her listener and readers.[201] This new form of proselytisation, no longer depended upon an uncompromising and confrontational approach to Quaker opponents in public places.

Polite public and epistolary conversations were viewed as potential arenas for converting others and relaying Quaker opinions to a wider audience. This is evidenced in letters exchanged between the Irish Quaker Elizabeth Shackleton and the Scottish philosopher David Hume.[202] Shackleton initiated a point-by-point defence of the Quaker movement in a letter addressed to 'Friend Hume', dated May 1770. She commented on his failure to represent Quakers 'in a true light' in his *History of England* (1754–1761) and his 'Essay on Superstition and Enthusiasm', published in *Essays Moral, Political and Literary* (1742–1754). She was affronted by his failure to properly identify Quaker doctrine, especially in relation to the question of whether Quakers could be considered Deists. Friends' practices, she argued, were both 'agreeable to Scripture, and no way prejudicial to civil society' and explained that 'perhaps thou hast taken thy account of them from the writings of some of their adversaries'. Shackleton stressed that Hume's conclusions should have

---

[199] The account Boswell published of the debate between Knowles and Johnson is radically different from Knowles's version of the events. Indeed, according to Knowles, it was Boswell's failure to accurately represent the conversation that forced her to publish the 'Truth' in the *Gentleman's Magazine*: James Boswell, *The Life of Samuel Johnson, LL.D.* (2 vols., London, 1791), vol. 2, pp. 231–232; and Mary Knowles, 'An Interesting Dialogue between the Late Dr. Samuel Johnson and Mrs. Knowles', *Gentleman's Magazine and Historical Chronicle, January 1736–December 1833*, June 1791, pp. 500–502.

[200] Knowles, 'An Interesting Dialogue between the Late Dr. Samuel Johnson and Mrs. Knowles', pp. 500–501.

[201] Amanda Vickery, *The Gentleman's Daughter: Women's Lives in Georgian England* (London, 1998), p. 9.

[202] This was published by Shackleton's daughter in Leadbeater (ed.), *Memoirs and Letters of Richard and Elizabeth Shackleton*, pp. 52–54.

been drawn from evidence, personal experience, and rational observation, telling him that an author who did not ascertain information based on 'his own experience, or by right information' would damage his reputation and brand his work 'with the imputation of being written by a partial or prejudiced person'.[203] Hume graciously responded two months later, defending his description of the Quaker movement, and claiming that he had the intention of doing the movement 'the greatest honour, by putting them on the same footing with Socrates, Plato, Cicero, Seneca, and the wisest men in all ages'. He saw the Quaker rejection of priests and stress on morality as positive aspects of their theology, and explained that he had 'a great regard for that body of men, especially for the present members', seeing them as 'peaceable, charitable and exemplary'.[204] Through the skilful employment of the conventions of female politeness and 'rational conversation', Shackleton was effectively able to use her correspondence to enter into dialogue with non-Quaker intellectuals. Moreover, like many other female authors from this era, she showed her skill in taking a religious subject and extending it into a philosophical debate about religious truth.[205]

The religious and intellectual content of many Quaker women's published writings and letters, enabled them to achieve status as 'enlightened' thinkers. Sophia Hume, for instance, in her publication addressed to the inhabitants of South Carolina, justified its mass circulation because she had 'the Testimony' of a good conscience. She also claimed to have come to a 'rational conclusion'.[206] Such statements indicate the way early Enlightenment ideas about rationality and reason could be appropriated for women's radical proselytising. The Quaker preacher Elizabeth Webb entered an epistolary debate with the German Pietist Anthony William Boehm, published in 1781. Despite Webb's Quaker identity, Boehm remarked that it was refreshing to meet 'a fellow pilgrim' in Philadelphia and expressed his desire to continue corresponding with her, adding that 'I shall always be ready to answer your kindness'.[207] The term 'fellow pilgrim' to refer to individuals of different religious persuasions fits into a tradition that Pink Dandelion suggests marks

---

[203] Leadbeater, *Memoirs and Letter of Richard and Elizabeth Shackleton*, p. 52, Elizabeth Shackleton to 'Friend Hume', Ballitore, May 1770.
[204] Ibid., pp. 53–54, David Hume to Elizabeth Shackleton, Edinburgh, 5 July 1770.
[205] Such writers included Mary Astell, Aphra Behn, Susanna Cenlivre, Damaris Masham, Catherine McCauley, and Catherine Talbot. They are discussed in Apetrei, *Women, Feminism and Religion*; Sarah Apetrei and Hannah Smith (eds.), *Religion and Women in Britain, c. 1660–1760* (Farnham, 2015); Sarah Knott and Barbara Taylor (eds.), *Women, Gender and Enlightenment* (Basingstoke, 2005); Major, *Madam Britannia*; and Karen O'Brien, *Women and Enlightenment in Eighteenth-Century Britain* (Cambridge, 2009).
[206] Sophia Hume, *An Exhortation to the Inhabitants of the Province of South Carolina, to Bring Their Deeds to the Light of Christ* (London, 1752), p. 13.
[207] Elizabeth Webb, *A Letter from Elizabeth Webb to Anthony William Boehm, with His Answer* (Philadelphia, 1781), p. 44.

a distinction between guarded Quakerism and worldly piety.[208] Indeed, as Tessa Whitehouse's research into the eighteenth-century dissenters has shown, authors like Boehm were influenced by a new model of religious expression that sought to move beyond 'institutional walls'. In engaging in literary debates, women like Elizabeth Webb had become part of this wider culture of religious exchange, guided by the ideas they held in common with others about 'useful godly service'.[209] In other words, Quakerism, like other religious movements, was forced to negotiate and adapt the public presentation of its beliefs to the non-Quaker world, in the hope that some might be instructed and perhaps even 'enlightened' by the debates that ensued.

Viewing both the individual and collective experiences of female Friends in relation to the societies in which they lived, brings to light the fluidity and continual reconfiguration of the borders between 'belonging and non-belonging' so often observed by sociologists, anthropologists, and cultural historians. In embracing a Quaker lifestyle, female Friends could never live an exalted spiritual life in isolation from the rest of society. As Elizabeth Webb explained in her letter to Boehm: '[W]e are grown to be a mixed multitude, much like the children of Israel when they were in the wilderness.'[210] The Christian foundation of the Society, combined with a need to survive within rather than apart from the world, left great scope for connections and bonds to be forged with individuals beyond the immediate community of believers. This meant that women's relationships and interactions with the non-Quaker world were dynamic, complex, and at times contradictory. It is the very flexibility of the relationships that Quaker women could develop with their non-Quaker contemporaries that this chapter has explored. At times, their place within society depended upon their resilience to withstand attacks and aggressive responses from members of the public. At others, both non-Quaker reactions to female Friends and their own attitudes towards the rest of the 'world' appear surprisingly flexible as they negotiated life as members of communities while still adhering to the movement's testimonies.

Clearly aspects of Quaker behaviour antagonised and distanced them from the rest of society. We have seen a variety of images and stereotypes that gained currency throughout the seventeenth and eighteenth centuries, helping to shape both popular and intellectual attitudes. Critics of Quakerism

---

[208] Pink Dandelion, 'Guarded Domesticity and Engagement with "the World": The Separate Spheres of Quaker Quietism', *Common Knowledge*, vol. 16, no. 1 (2010), pp. 104–105.

[209] Tessa Whitehouse, 'Godly Dispositions and Textual Conditions: The Literary Sociology of International Religious Exchanges, c. 1722–1740', *History of European Ideas*, vol. 39, no. 3 (2013), p. 401.

[210] Webb, *A Letter from Elizabeth Webb to Anthony William Boehm*, p. 24.

understood and utilised a variety of images, ideas, and representations to discredit Quaker women in print. Their campaign was shaped both by the movement's behaviour and their own assumptions. Very few of these stereotypes were unique to Quakerism, having resonance and connections to a range of other religious nonconformists. However, the large number of anti-Quaker prints suggests a wide public fascination with the movement's female adherents. Moreover, as the movement and its testimonies became more widely understood, there was a repositioning of Quaker women in the popular press. This is particularly true of accounts discussing the rise of the separate Women's Meetings, which had an important place in shaping the printed representation of female Friends.

Evidence nevertheless exists of a strong supportive context in which women were able to maintain amicable relationships with their neighbours in spite of their religious affiliation. This was true of the emotional and material support provided to some families during the height of persecution, as well as the inter-denominational appeal that certain Quaker testimonies received, such as the issue of tithes and, later, female preaching. This meant that they were frequently forced to interact with individuals outside of the Society. Women's involvement in business and philanthropic activities provides perhaps the strongest examples of their participation in the economic structures of their communities – providing goods and services, as well as charitable relief to non-Quaker neighbours. In fact, it was the increasing wealth of the urban Friends that seems to have provided the most pronounced opportunities for women to both participate in and embrace broader societal trends. Such extensive assimilation into everyday life, however, was a matter of great concern to the Quaker leadership. At the very time the world was coming to accept Quaker virtues, fewer Friends were living up to the rigorous standards expected by the movement's leadership.

We have observed, too, how social and intellectual changes also altered how Quaker women were understood and represented. These were primarily influenced by new political theories and discourses, which Larson has suggested served to transform 'the "heretics" of the seventeenth century into exemplars of the Age of Reason'.[211] The Quaker movement certainly saw women in much more prominent roles than any other religious group during this period. It is not surprising that eighteenth-century thinkers increasingly held up the Quaker model as a means of questioning and debating the place of women within religious culture more generally. Whilst admiration for Quaker life did not necessarily equate to imitation or conversion, patterns of Quaker worship evidently altered attitudes towards female Friends. In the early years, their actions were often regarded as immoral and depraved;

---

[211] Larson, *Daughters of Light*, pp. 249–250.

later, the pious 'otherness' of Quaker women came to be viewed as something that could be emulated and admired.

Associated increasingly with virtue and moderation, second- and third-generation female Friends were understood and presented to the non-Quaker world in a completely different way. These trends ran parallel to Quaker understandings of the reasoned mind, as well as the place of educated women as preachers, teachers, and equals in the church. The increasing acceptance of Quaker women preachers within elite and educated circles revealed how they had successfully adapted their proselytising activities outside their own religious community by assimilating new forms of polite sociability and positioning themselves within established socio-cultural frameworks. Women, however, were not passive recipients of these changing cultural shifts, and one theme that has run throughout this discussion is the agency of individual female Friends in shaping ideas and knowledge about female piety and religious doctrine.

Reactions to Quakerism were the product of female Friends' social and cultural assimilation throughout the period and thus emblematic of their participation in, rather than separation from, wider society. It is clear that female Friends in Britain and the Americas were never as geographically or economically isolated from the rest of society as traditional histories of Quakerism would lead us to believe. This meant that despite their best efforts, polemicists and persecutors were never able to destroy the movement. Equally, Friends were never able to live the fully segregated lives to which the Quaker leadership aspired. Rather than being isolated or shunned by the world, Quakers underwent a complex process of assimilation, continually forced to renegotiate and balance their lives both with one another and with the wider world.

Conclusion:
Quakerism Reconsidered

The central argument of this book has been that to understand the experiences of women within seventeenth- and eighteenth-century Quakerism, we have to look beyond their roles as radical preachers. Narratives that seek to chart how the Quaker transition from 'sect' to 'denomination' limited women's involvement within the Society do not merely run the risk of eclipsing the broad range of activities women undertook outside of their missionary service; they also undervalue the important work that Quaker women undertook within their separate Meetings. If the period after 1670 was poised to focus its efforts on preserving the distinct identity of its members, it was also marked by many powerful restatements about the importance of the home, family, and Meeting in defending the Quakers' unusual theology and 'peculiar' way of life. And by focusing on women's identities, as preachers, wives, mothers, companions, friends, hosts, overseers, clerks, philanthropists, and neighbours, we have discovered the range of ways in which even the most 'ordinary' women could be vital actors in making and sustaining transatlantic Quakerism.

In their Meeting epistles, female Friends often described how their roles within the religious community continued to grow. Their success was proclaimed by the Women's Meeting in London, when they addressed their sisters in Pennsylvania in July 1747. Noting their spiritual oneness, they saluted their distant readers by describing the 'Union of Spirit, that ... abounds in our hearts', spreading 'over sea and land', and making 'as one family the whole household of faith'.[1] Almost a century after the movement's creation, these female authors continued to invoke the power of spiritual fellowship. But it was not as prophets that they envisaged their unity over this vast distance, but through their positions within the Quaker family and their own roles within the household.

---

[1] LRSF, MGR 11a4 London Women's Meeting Epistles 1671–1753, fol. 55, epistle from the Women's Meeting in London to Pennsylvania Women's Meeting, 27 July 1747.

This book has explored how Quaker women adapted and brought meaning to their relationships within and without the transatlantic world of Quakerism. The lives and experiences of women in England, Ireland, and the American colonies were deeply affected by joining the movement and adhering to its peculiar injunctions. From evidence in their writings – in correspondence, spiritual autobiographies, memorials, epistles, Meeting minutes, and life accounts – we have seen how these women successfully fashioned their identities on the very margins of society. As the epistle of the London Women's Meeting suggests, they were able to bring meaning to traditional domestic concerns whilst simultaneously participating in a radical culture of sectarian dissent that brought them into remarkably public roles as leaders and spiritual elders within the Society. I have attempted to uncover the lived experience of Quakerism for seventeenth- and eighteenth-century women. By using relationships as a category of analysis, each chapter has aimed to reinscribe meaning into the lives of 'ordinary' Quaker women (and men), who were generally not from elite backgrounds, did not undertake ministerial service, and were not necessarily in a position to document their experiences in a spiritual autobiography. My intention has been to show how these non-elite early modern men and women were active in shaping their identities and how they became important historical actors in their own rights.

At its centre, this book has argued that female visibility and the evolution of the Quakers into a settled denomination were not in competition with one another, but mutually reinforcing. Quakerism offered a unique model of gender relations that saw married and unmarried women from a range of social backgrounds leading household worship, undertaking itinerant missionary service, and occupying positions of leadership within the local, national, and international Meeting hierarchy. This degree of equality was present from the movement's radical beginnings and evolved into something that was both positive and empowering for its female members. The task of this conclusion is to focus on a final claim: that when viewed from the perspective of female relationships, the classic chronological, geographical, confessional, and even social boundaries of Quaker history need to be reconsidered.

This study began by examining the impact of the movement's transition from 'sect' to 'church' on women. It explored the complexity of Quaker theology within an Atlantic context and the ambiguity with which the separate Women's Meetings were interpreted by historians who had admired the energetic and fierce outpourings of the first female prophets. The rationalisation of the Quaker community into these gender-segregated spaces has often been viewed by scholars as limiting to female freedom. The question arises, then, about what changed for preaching and non-preaching women as the movement made its transition from its first to second generations. The answer is that the introduction of separate Men's and Women's Meetings marked the culmination of three decades of spiritual equality. Male leaders recognised that women had a distinct contribution to make to the religious Society and should be responsible for the spiritual education and instruction of the female members of their communities. They did not have to be itinerant preachers to lead these Meetings, they simply had to be active within their districts and willing to oversee the conduct, domestic affairs, and charitable relief of Quaker families. So, in many respects, the changing nature of early Quakerism did not mean a decline in women's status, but instead confirmed and perhaps even enhanced the role of 'ordinary', non-itinerant female Friends as protectors of the spiritual life of the community.

In this sense, it was the mother as religious teacher and instructor who became an increasingly more prominent part of the movement's central ideology. In the earliest years of the movement, it was accepted that family ties would need to be broken to spread the faith abroad. The biological family was reconfigured into the spiritual family. As Quakerism entered its second and third generations, however, it was the family that was to become the main site of spiritual activity. Parents were the guardians of Quaker orthodoxy and the home was the site of Quaker spiritualisation efforts. Mothers were expected to bring their children up in the faith and were disciplined when transgressions in domestic life came to the attention of their local Women's Meetings. Women's efforts within the household were thus seen as central to sustaining the wider household of faith. The Quaker family and household became the 'twin bulwarks in the struggle to maintain the membership and spiritual vitality of the movement'.[2]

This has been a book about the permeability of the home, Meeting, and wider Quaker movement, all of which can be said to have broken down the separate spheres of life for early female Friends. The key difference for Quaker women was not between the private life of the household and the public realm of politics, but between the Quaker way of life and the society that surrounded it. The differing extent to which Quakers interacted with those outside their religious community provides another noticeable change in Quaker relationships over this period. If formal toleration had removed the impetus for persecution, the ever-closer cooperation of Friends with their non-Quaker neighbours had the paradoxical effect of accentuating Quaker difference. Those who adhered to Quakerism needed to distinguish themselves clearly from the world that surrounded them. What members wore, how they spoke to those outside the movement, how they conducted

---

[2] Helen Plant, 'Gender and the Aristocracy of Dissent: A Comparative Study of the Beliefs, Status and Roles of Women in Quaker and Unitarian Communities, 1770–1830, with Particular Reference to Yorkshire', University of York, PhD thesis (2000), p. 61.

their business relationships, and who they married were the many aspects of daily life that increasingly came to be monitored by Monthly and Quarterly Meetings. We have seen that in England and Ireland, where Friends had experienced prolonged and unusually high levels of persecution, the desire to attain this separate identity was more strictly enforced by local Meetings than those in the Americas. However, even in the colonial context, Friends still encountered problems with the authorities, for example by refusing to muster for militia drills and for refusing to swear oaths. The Quaker desire to protect household purity, moreover, resulted in the excommunication of a large number of members and their families in the latter part of the eighteenth century.[3]

Thus whilst we see these changes in domestic life and wider society taking place over our period, they appear to be more refinements of first-generation Quaker practice and belief rather than dramatic breaks with the movement's more enthusiastic and less regulated early decades. Repeatedly, we have been able to trace the highly respected status of non-missionary eighteenth-century Quaker women back to the 1650s and 1660s. Indeed, without the movement's earliest stress on the spiritual equality of men and women within their families, the elevated role of the Quaker housewife after the 1670s would not have been attainable. Moreover, even if some Friends were coming to be admired by their contemporaries, they were never a fully 'tolerated' community. This came to have symbolic significance during the American War of Independence, where the fissures created by this conflict proved that Quakers continued to be regarded as a dangerous movement posing a direct threat to political stability. A number of Friends who were unwilling to offer financial or military support to the war effort, once again found themselves under public scrutiny and the subjects of harassment, persecution, and widespread opposition.[4]

Much can also be said of the geographical uniformity of transatlantic Quakerism. There have been a great many invaluable studies of local Quaker communities, which have foregrounded the uneasy tension between coexistence and full integration for seventeenth- and eighteenth-century Friends. Likewise, one of my objectives when approaching this study was to document and observe the peculiar geographical disparities between English, Irish, and colonial Quaker communities. I wanted to question whether being a second- or third-generation Friend living in the Americas was fundamentally different from being a Friend in Britain. Certainly, the communities

---

[3] Between 1750 and 1790, almost 50 per cent of young members of Philadelphia Monthly Meeting were disowned. Barry Levy, *Quakers and the American Family: British Settlement in the Delaware Valley* (Oxford, 1988), p. 16.

[4] See Sarah Crabtree, *Holy Nation: The Transatlantic Quaker Ministry in an Age of Revolution* (Chicago, 2015).

that surrounded each group of Friends were diverse and, as we have seen, Quaker inhabitants were forced to adapt their customs and ways of life to survive within these environments. In Chapter 2, for instance, we saw that colonial female elders appear to have had a greater degree of authority over their families and local affairs than British Friends, whilst imposing fewer restrictions on the behaviour of their female members. Irish women Friends, by contrast, had less authority to discipline transgressors, but like their brethren, were much more rigorous in their enforcement of standards of 'plainness' and overseeing the behaviour of their members.

Certainly, the remarkably different environments that Friends living in England, Ireland, and the Americas encountered over this long period should not be understated. Yet, I want to suggest that it is not the variant forms of church organisation that developed within Quaker communities that fundamentally marks the experiences of female Friends, but the remarkable consistency in the models of order and regulation that developed across the Atlantic. Despite the fact that the movement, which was divinely inspired and intensely personal, was unable to provide an overarching bureaucratic authority, a coherent order and way of life developed in both Britain and the Americas over an extended period. Overwhelmingly, Quakers took on the common trappings of a religious denomination, where members identified themselves by separation from what surrounded them, which meant that they were forced to seek alternative forms of communal expression. This often meant looking to their distant co-religionists for guidance and support.

One feature of Quakerism explored throughout this book is that there is a case for seeing the Meeting system not as a uniform organisational structure, but as part of a series of extended overlapping networks. The mass emigration of Friends to the colonies from the 1680s forged a powerful network of families and friends whose correspondence and connections helped them 'maintain a sense of shared family membership and common national identity'.[5] Sandra Stanley Holton has suggested that the sense of belonging to a 'peculiar people' encouraged Quaker women of the late eighteenth and early nineteenth centuries to develop what she terms 'a cosmopolitanism that encouraged transnational as well as national networks'.[6] Such connections were reinforced by several factors, which encouraged the growth of intimate relationships and networks of support across the Atlantic, among them the frequent exchange of Quaker ministers and their spiritual writings; the trade

[5] David Cressy, *Coming Over: Migration and Communication between England and New England in the Seventeenth Century* (Cambridge, 1987), p. 213.
[6] Sandra Stanley Holton, *Quaker Women: Personal Life, Memory and Radicalism in the Lives of Women Friends, 1780–1930* (London, 2007), p. 228.

routes and migration networks that grew up between British and American Friends; and complex patterns of intermarriage among Quaker families. Much also depended upon the sociability of the male and female members who attended their local Meetings. In the context of the more mobile communities of the American colonies, new members brought knowledge and experience to the different places in which they settled.

These long-distance exchanges, moreover, were facilitated by powerful webs of correspondence and epistles. As a non-hierarchical movement dispersed across the Atlantic, physical ties between members were often weak. Through letters and epistles, however, close bonds of community were woven between Meetings, individuals, and local Quaker populations. The exchange of correspondence between Meetings meant that English and American Friends were repeatedly forced to compare their experiences and adjust their practices and behaviour accordingly. This helps to explain why Quaker women's everyday customs and practices were so uniform without order being imposed from any central organisational structure. When the Women's Meeting of London composed an epistle in 1749 reporting on the spread of 'truth' within the English Meetings, they did so to emphasise the value and emotional power they placed on their transatlantic spiritual alliance. 'It is not possible', they wrote, 'to be unmindful of each other: the ground, and cement of [our] Fellowship, being that divine Charity.'[7] The intimate relationships they shared within the 'household of Faith', despite never having met, created a sense of common identity that transcended national borders and united a dispersed and socially diverse community of women across the Atlantic world.

We can see how an experience of theological convergence shaped the lives of eighteenth-century colonial Friends with the events of the 1775 Revolution. Being part of a transatlantic religious community impinged directly on how they positioned themselves in relation to the emerging American nation for, more than any other colonists, they were so closely connected with their co-religionists in the British Isles that the idea of independence was almost unthinkable. Following 1775, as Sarah Crabtree has persuasively argued, Quaker leaders reinvigorated their shared spiritual bonds and detached themselves from the events taking place around them. This posed a significant challenge to American state-building efforts because it enabled American Friends to justify non-intervention in the war effort and thus to challenge the united American 'citizenry' that was being constructed.[8] Thus at the very moment when we would expect transatlantic

---

[7] LRSF, MGR 11a4 London Women's Meeting Epistles, 1671–1753, fol. 58, Women's Yearly Meeting in Philadelphia to Women's Yearly Meeting in London, 20 September 1749.
[8] Crabtree, *Holy Nation*, pp. 1–8.

Quakerism to be drifting further apart, it was the shared imagined community that reinvigorated the connection between these distant groups of believers. Their adoption of the ancient Jewish concept of 'Holy nationhood', argues Crabtree, did not merely provide consolation to a divided community, but 'was a forceful articulation of political resistance' in direct response to a strengthening state.[9] It proves that even more than a century after the first Friends settled in the colonies, they continued to have more in common with distant groups of believers than with their close neighbours.

In many ways, the early Quakers also shared much with other dissenting Protestant movements, and we find that the experiences of being a woman within early Quakerism overlapped with many other religious groups that recognised the spiritual authority of their female members, such as the Baptists, Methodists, and Pietists. But Quakerism was peculiar for several reasons. First, and most important, was the balance that members managed to achieve between their spiritual and everyday lives. As Phyllis Mack has argued, Quaker theology was based upon the assumption that every aspect of daily life, whether in the household or Meeting House, was spiritualised. Once 'in the light', she argues, the individual's outward behaviour would automatically answer to divine standards.[10] In fact, one of the most unusual elements of early Quakerism was not so much the radical roles it gave to its women as public preachers, but its recognition that such work should be combined with the traditional elements of everyday life within the household and the family. Unlike other religious denominations like the Methodists, Baptists, Pietists, and Catholics, the demands of daily life became a key theme in the construction of Quaker narratives of obedience to God. It was mothers, rather than celibate unmarried women, who came to perpetuate Quaker values and ensure group cohesion.

A second aspect of Quakerism that was highly unusual was the remarkable organisational ability of Friends through their multi-tiered Meeting system. This played a considerable part in holding a disparate movement together and ensuring the movement's continued expansion after its evangelical phase had come to an end.[11] Quaker women's power within their Meetings was never uniform. Local circumstances as well as changing relationships with their male brethren affected the types of tasks that women oversaw in their Monthly Meetings. But more significant is that the rise of gendered spaces in Quaker church order offers an important example

---

[9] Ibid., p. 3.

[10] Phyllis Mack, *Visionary Women: Ecstatic Prophecy in Seventeenth-Century England* (Berkeley, CA, 1994), p. 260.

[11] Craig W. Horle, *Quakers and the English Legal System, 1660–1688* (Philadelphia, 1988), p. 15.

of an alternative form of female sociability operating in practice. Quaker devotion was intensely personal, linked to solitary prayer and private contemplation, but as I have established its practice was highly collaborative. Although worldly pleasures were regarded as a distraction, as they were within Methodist, Puritan, and Pietist congregations, individual Quaker believers were never expected to isolate themselves from their religious or local communities.

The networks of the separate Women's Meetings demonstrate the importance of female society and friendship in encouraging the individual to adhere to the collective corporate outlook. The language of friendship, where all members addressed one another as 'Friends', was replete with the lexicon of spiritual equality, encompassing anyone willing to embrace the 'truth'. The powerful spiritual bond forged between believers therefore encouraged the formation of close transatlantic ties, unparalleled in any other religious movement of the time. Many friendships were formed between individuals who had no formal acquaintance and whose only essential commonality was their desire for salvation. Like the previously quoted communication sent by the Women's Meeting in London to Pennsylvania, female Friends viewed themselves as being united in the spirit, despite being absent in body and were thus able to develop relationships of mutual love and support without physical contact. The networks of hospitality that developed across the Atlantic, which were dominated by female Friends renowned for their generosity to strangers, enabled non-itinerant women to have a central place in the developing community. The intense spiritual sociability that characterised such relationships provides conclusive proof of alternative forms of female friendship operating in practice. Their shared spiritual alliance reinforced their sense of religious community, overcoming the great distances that separated them.

Whilst the movement retained a reputation for eccentric, unrestrained, and uncivilised behaviour, a final way in which Quakerism can be distinguished from other nonconformist movements of this period is through the relationships they developed with the world that surrounded them. All Quakers were expected to continue to serve God through the ordinary interactions of daily life, making complete isolation from wider society almost impossible. At times, female Friends were despised for their unusual principles and peculiar ways of life, gaining notoriety for their idiosyncratic customs in dress, language, lack of social etiquette, and public preaching. On other occasions, they came to be admired by some of the greatest thinkers of the age for their educational attainments, sobriety, and family centeredness. As we saw in Chapter 4, many female Friends remained bound to their Anglican and dissenting neighbours by ties of love, friendship, family, and neighbourhood that 'blurred the confessional divisions that theoretically divided them'.[12] It therefore seems possible to conclude that despite its increasingly introspective nature, Quakerism was successful in balancing an exclusive spiritual piety with significant participation in community life. As Mack observes, Quaker theology allowed men and women to live '"in the body" without regarding the bodily aspect of their existence as necessarily polluting'.[13] Eager to act as moral examples to individuals outside of their religious community, Quakers were able to find a balance between their private faith and the need to reach out to non-believers. This meant that both ordinary members and preachers could often attain a surprising level of harmony with women of other religious denominations.

This all points to a much deeper conclusion: that the transition from radical sect to settled church did not diminish the position of women within early Quakerism. For them, the spheres of religion and everyday life were co-extensive, and Quaker ideals within the household and the structure of the movement were mutually reinforcing. The Quakers' domestic lives were harmonised with their spiritual authority, whilst affiliation with the Society reinforced and could expand their network of personal relationships. Quaker women's domestic identities should thus be celebrated as the pivotal force of their experiences as religious dissenters. Their roles as wives, mothers, 'sustainers', elders, Meeting overseers, philanthropists, Friends, hosts, and preachers enabled them to transform their experiences within the household into public action. At the same time, a constant exchange of ideas and practices influenced the way Quakerism found expression on both sides of the Atlantic.

When viewed through the lens of women's relationships and by drawing attention to 'ordinary' members of specific religious communities, we may be able to infer similar conclusions for other religious denominations across time and beyond the context of the British Atlantic. Certainly, the ideal of gender relations advocated by Quakerism was never divorced from its theological origins and was never cited by later feminist authors as an acceptable basis for sexual equality.[14] Nevertheless, the praise that mainstream authors reserved for Quaker women's behaviour and conduct shows how their daily lives both shaped and were shaped by their relationship to the wider world. The establishment of the Women's Meetings, for example, created a form of institutionalised sectarian authority that thinkers like Mary Astell were arguing should be available to women more generally. The radical lifestyle

---

[12] Alexandra Walsham, *Charitable Hatred: Tolerance and Intolerance in England, 1500–1700* (Manchester, 2006), p. 309.

[13] Mack, *Visionary Women*, p. 246.

[14] This is discussed by Patricia Howell Michaelson in 'Religious Bases of Eighteenth-Century Feminism: Mary Wollstonecraft and the Quakers', *Women's Studies*, vol. 22, no. 3 (1993), pp. 281–295.

that Quakers promoted for their female members arguably provided an important complement to, or strand within, broader debates on the place of women in public life.

It therefore seems fitting to conclude that the lives of Quaker women, both as preachers and homemakers, reveal how religious radicalism could challenge the institutions and values articulated at the heart of early modern society. Whether undertaking ministerial work or remaining at home, Quaker women helped to strengthen their family relationships and the social networks that operated in early Quakerism. They communicated a set of values, ideas, and beliefs that distance could not impede, and which ultimately helped to usher in a new era in which women and the household were placed close to the very centre of religious and public life.

Appendix 1
Male and Female Friends Ministering in Ireland

Table A1.1 Proportion of Male and Female Ministers Who Visited Ireland between 1655 and 1750

	Male	Female	Total	(%) Female
1655–1660	14	5	19	26
1661–1670	24	5	29	17
1671–1680	42	5	47	11
1681–1690	35	3	38	8
1691–1700	157	30	187	16
1701–1710	119	20	139	14
1711–1720	107	54	161	34
1721–1730	94	44	138	32
1731–1740	68	55	123	45
1741–1750	38	51	89	57
TOTAL	**698**	**272**	**970**	

Note: Figures calculated from FHLD, YM C3 Names of Friends in the Ministry in Ireland 1655–1781.

Appendix 2
Tasks Undertaken by the Women's and Men's Monthly Meetings

Tables 2.1 and 2.2 provide a numerical breakdown of each of the tasks listed under each grouping for the two sample periods. Because of large variations in the number of tasks performed by each Meeting, the types of activities were grouped under the headings of Marriage; Discipline; Church Oversight; Philanthropy; Removal and Settlement; Travelling Ministry; Tithes; Accounts and Estates; Advice and Queries; Arbitration; Apprenticeship; Publication; Membership and Sufferings.

BREAKDOWN OF TASKS UNDER EACH ACTIVITY

Marriage: Intentions for marriage presented for the first or second time; reports from overseers after the marriage has taken place; certificate requested to marry a Friend of another Meeting; certificate for marriage produced by Friend of another Meeting; papers requested after courtship has ended (after broken marriage intentions).

Discipline: Friend to be disciplined or admonished for courting or marrying a non-Quaker; for clandestine marriage, i.e. marriage by priest or magistrate; for fornication before marriage; for attending a 'disorderly marriage' (i.e., acting as a witness); for general misconduct; petition of repentance by Friend wishing to be reunited to the Meeting; paper of denial produced against a member and to be made public.

Church Oversight: Appointments to attend the Quarterly Meeting; new clerk, treasurer or overseer(s) appointed for a particular Meeting/locality; arrangements to be made for purchase of Meeting books; Friend(s) appointed to sit in the Meeting for Ministers and Elders; arrangements made for transfer of Minute and Account Books between elders; Friend(s) appointed to view, correct, and transcribe the clerk's rough minutes into fair copy; Friend(s) appointed to attend regional Yearly Meeting; formation of new/change to existing structure of Preparative Meetings; Friends to inspect attendance at Meetings (especially weekday Meetings).

Philanthropy: Money or practical assistance given to relieve a poor or sick Friend; necessity of poor inquired into by Meeting; overseers appointed to visit family and see if they stand in need of relief; money loaned for relief of Friends during hardship.

Removal and Settlement: Certificate of removal (outgoing) requested by Friend and produced and signed by overseers; warning issued to Friend(s) who joined with Meeting without certificate; certificate of removal (incoming) presented to Meeting; certificate requested for travel relating to trading ventures.

Travelling Ministry: Friend(s) acquaints Meeting with drawings to visit another Meeting and requests certificate; Friend(s) return from visit, return the certificates attesting to behaviour, and make a report to the Meeting about how they found things; certificate requested for Friend to act as companion to a minister from another Meeting.

Tithes (English Meetings only): Account given by overseers of a Friend's clearness in relation to tithes; report given to Meeting of Friends suffering on account of tithes; separate Meeting to be appointed to inquire into clearness of Friends from paying tithes and church rates.

Accounts and Estates: Collections ordered to be made to cover the cost of relief/administration; recording of legacies; accounts inspected and balanced; money collected and sent to the Quarterly or Yearly Meeting; money paid out of Meeting stock; new trustee appointed to hold bonds of Meeting; Province fee discussed in Meeting and money raised by Friends to cover costs (Irish Meetings only).

Advice and Queries: Advices of the Quarterly or Yearly Meeting to be read and implemented; queries read and reports given, over issues such as: neglect in attending Meeting on weekdays and at hour appointed; drowsiness and sleeping in Meetings; moderation at births, marriages, and burials; against superfluity and needless fashions; and against keeping company with those of other societies.

Apprenticeship: Enquiry made by master to Meeting about apprentice; child offered as an apprentice to master; child in need of master; Meeting enquires into care of child as an apprentice; Meeting to cover expenses of poor apprentice; Meeting negotiates terms of apprenticeship on behalf of child; no master found for apprentice, matter referred to Quarterly Meeting.

Arbitration: Complaint made that money is owed from a legacy; Meeting has intervened in dispute between two or more persons to avoid law suit in courts; Friends appointed to investigate claims made in dispute and determine next steps; dispute not resolved because parties refused to accept terms of agreement.

Publications: Meeting received publications from Provincial or Yearly Meetings; Meeting makes decision about quantity of books to purchase from Provincial or Yearly Meeting.

Membership: Individual residing in locality petitions Meeting to join with them and become a member of the Society; Quaker who has been disowned or declared 'out of unity' with the Meeting offers contrition for behaviour and requests to return to the Society.

Sufferings: Meeting orders for accounts of suffering to be collected and sent to the Quarterly/Province Meetings; Meeting receives and reads accounts of suffering; member of Meeting nominated to copy accounts of suffering for Quarterly/Province Meeting.

Appendix 3
A Recurring Network of Gossips

The original copies of Friends Birth Notes for London and Middlesex are unique in the details they provide of the witnesses attendant at the birth of Quaker children. From the original documents a database was created, entering the names of those witnesses whose names could be identified from the signatures entered on the births notes between the years of 1720 and 1735.

The act of witnessing births was clearly reciprocated by women like Margaret Cross, who attended only the deliveries of her fellow gossips. The enduring friendship networks surrounding the births of Margaret Cross's children can be seen in the following text. They indicate that close networks of support operated between Quaker women at this most intimate and local level. For clarity, recurring names of the female gossips have been highlighted in **bold**.

Margaret Cross was attended by the following women at the birth of her daughter Margaret in March 1720 at St Saviour's parish: Elizabeth **Earle** (midwife), Elizabeth Hawkes, **Elizabeth Willet, Mary Knight, Sarah Mason**, Elizabeth [], and **Mary Bockett**.

The following witnesses attended the birth of Margaret Cross's daughter Sarah on 5 October 1723 at St Olave's parish: **Elizabeth Stapleton** (midwife); **Elizabeth Willett**, and **Mary Knight**.

The following witnesses attended the birth of Margaret Cross's son Joseph on 26 October 1724 at St Olave's parish: **Elizabeth Stapleton** (midwife), Elizabeth Curtis, and **Elizabeth Willett**.

The following witnesses attended the birth of Margaret Cross's daughter Mary on 26 September 1725 at St Olave's parish: **Elizabeth Stapleton** (midwife), **Elizabeth Willett**, Ann Hill, and **Mary Knight**.

The following witnesses attended the birth of Margaret Cross's son Peter on 8 January 1727 at St Olave's parish: **Elizabeth Stapleton** (midwife), **Elizabeth Willett**, and Elizabeth Drinkwater.

The following witnesses attended the birth of Margaret Cross's daughter Margaret on 15 June 1728 at St Olave's parish: **Elizabeth Stapleton** (midwife), **Mary Bockett,** and Abigail Fennley.

The following witnesses attended the birth of Margaret Cross's daughter Margaret on 8 September 1730 at St Martin Orgar's parish: **Elizabeth Stapleton** (midwife).

The following witnesses attended the birth of Margaret Cross's son Joseph on 17 September 1732 at St Martin Orgar's parish: **Elizabeth Stapleton** (midwife), **Mary Knight, Barbara Willett,** and **Elizabeth Willett.**

The following witnesses attended the birth of Margaret Cross's son John, on 18 November 1733 at St Martin Orgar's parish: **Elizabeth Stapleton** (midwife), **Elizabeth Willett, Mary Knight, Barbara Willet,** and Hannah [].

The following witnesses attended the birth of Margaret Cross's son John, on 4 November 1734 at St Martin Orgar's: **Elizabeth Stapleton, Elizabeth Willett, Mary Knight, Barbara Willet,** Hannah Willet, and Frances Rudd.

Of the births that Margaret Cross is listed as having attended between 1720 and 1730 she appears on the following records:

4 June 1720 at the birth of Elizabeth Knight, daughter of **Mary Knight,** at St Butolph's parish, with the following witnesses: **Elizabeth Earle** (midwife), **Elizabeth Willet,** and Ann King.

26 December 1720 at the birth of Margaret Mason, daughter of **Sarah Mason,** at St Saviour's parish, with the following witnesses: Mary Draper (midwife), Hannah [Routh], Rachel Bowman, and Elizabeth Fawcett.

11 October 1721 at the birth of John Knight, son of **Mary Knight,** at St Butolph's parish, with the following witnesses: **Elizabeth Willett** and **Elizabeth Knight.**

2 May 1723 at the birth of Mary Knight, daughter of **Mary Knight,** at St Butolph's parish, with the following witnesses: **Elizabeth Earle** (midwife), **Elizabeth Willett,** and **Elizabeth Knight.**

24 October 1724 at the birth of Priscilla Knight, daughter of **Mary Knight,** at St Butolph's parish, with the following witnesses: **Elizabeth Stapleton** (midwife) and **Elizabeth Willett.**

25 November 1725 at the birth of Samuel Knight, son of **Mary Knight,** at St Butolph's parish, with the following witnesses: **Elizabeth Stapleton** (midwife) and **Elizabeth Willett.**

13 September 1734 at the birth of Wilmer Willett, son of **Barbara Willett,** at St Lawrence Jewry's parish, with the following witnesses: Margaret Sparrow (midwife), **Mary Knight,** Margaret Lucan, and Elizabeth [].

Appendix 4
Ecclesiastical Licensed Midwives at Quaker Births, 1680–1690

Table A4.1 Midwives Attendant at Quaker Women's Births between 1680 and 1690, as Recorded in the London and Middlesex Birth Notes

Name of Midwife	Known Ecclesiastical Licence?*	Number of Births Attended, 1680–1690	Years
Albrighton, Anna		7	1683–1689
Basket, Ann		1	1687
Benett, Mary	Yes	1	1689
Berrisford, Barbara		1	1690
Boulton, Alice		1	1689
Bridges, Margaret		1	1686
Clarke, Elizabeth	Yes	5	1682–1689
Douglas, Rebekah		1	1689
Gibson, Elizabeth		1	1688
Grand, Annbell		1	1682
Harrison, Margaret		12	1682–1689
Hoard, Dorothy		1	1682
Howell, Mary		2	1689–1690
Kendal, Martha		1	1688/9
Lovell, Elizabeth		1	1687/8
Spencer, Elizabeth		1	1688
Whyte, Elizabeth	Yes	2	1683–1689
Unknown**		3	
TOTAL			
18	3	43	

Note: Data extracted from RG6/1626 London and Middlesex Birth Notes, 1676–1707.
 * Information about ecclesiastical licences extrapolated from Table 3.3. Licensed Midwives Who Delivered Quaker Mothers in Doreen Evenden, *The Midwives of Seventeenth-Century London* (Cambridge, 2000), p. 96.
 ** Includes those records where folios are either damaged or the name of the midwife is illegible.

BIBLIOGRAPHY

MANUSCRIPT SOURCES

Bristol Record Office

SF/A/9/1 Records of the workhouse and New Street Mission: Papers Illustrating the Management of the Workhouse, 1697–1809

British Library

Add MS 71116 Jacob Family: Correspondence of the Irish Quaker Family of Jacob, 1701–1802

Friends Historical Library Dublin

YM C3 Names of Friends in the Ministry in Ireland, 1655–1781
MMX A2 County Tipperary Men's Monthly Meeting Minutes, 1724–1760
MMX B2 County Tipperary Women's Monthly Meeting Minutes, 1735–1764

Friends Historical Library, Swarthmore College,
Swarthmore, Pennsylvania

MR-Ph 60 Burlington Men's Monthly Meeting Minutes, 1678–1737
MR-Ph 60 Burlington Men's Monthly Meeting Minutes, 1737–1756
MR-Ph 63 Burlington Women's Monthly Meeting Minutes, 1681–1747
MR-Ph 63 Burlington Women's Monthly Meeting Minutes, 1747–1799
MR-Ph 92 Chester Men's Monthly Meeting Minutes, 1681–1721
MR-Ph 98 Chester Women's Monthly Meeting Minutes, 1695–1733, with Papers of Condemnation
MR-Ph 98 Chester Women's Monthly Meeting Minutes, 1733–1779
MR-Ph 136 Concord Quarterly Women's Meeting Minutes, 1695–1803
MR-B117 Fairfax Men's Monthly Meeting Minutes, 1745–1776
MR-B119 Fairfax Women's Monthly Meeting Minutes, 1745–1768

Haverford College Quaker and Special Collection, Haverford, Pennsylvania

MS Coll 968 Allinson Family Papers, Box 6
MS Coll 955 Edward Wanton Smith Papers, 1681–1971, Box 5
MS Coll 1000 Gulielma M. Howland Collection, Boxes 4 and 6
MS Coll 1001 Haddon-Estaugh-Hopkins Papers, 1676–1841
MS Coll 1008 Morris-Sansom Collection, c. 1715–1925, Boxes 6, 17, and 18
B1.1 Philadelphia Women's Yearly Meeting Minutes, 1692–1814
MS Coll 950 Satterthwaite Family Papers, 1696–1924
MS Coll 1100 Scattergood Family Papers, 1681–1903
MS Coll 859 Shackleton Family Papers, 1707–1785
Film 128 Tortola Women's Monthly Meeting Minutes, 1741–1762
MS Coll 971 Yearly Meeting Epistles and Extracts, 1698–1842, London Yearly Meeting to Friends at Their Quarterly and Monthly Meetings in Great Britain, Ireland &c

Historical Society of Pennsylvania

MS Coll 484A Pemberton Family Papers, Volumes 1–10

Huntington Library, San Marino, California

HM 66135 Ann Moore Herbert Journal (1760–1763)
HM 36845 Joseph Galloway Collection
mssRV 1–305 Robert Valentine Papers, Box 1 1732–1783
mssSHA Shackleton Family Correspondence, Boxes 1–4

Kendal Archive Centre

WDFCF/1/13 Kendal Men's Monthly Meeting Minutes, 1699–1723
WDFCF/1/15 Kendal Men's Monthly Meeting Minutes, 1747–1777
WDFCF/1/22 Kendal Women's Monthly Meeting Minutes, 1671–1719
WDFCF/1/23 Kendal Women's Monthly Meeting Minutes, 1719–1756
WDFCF/1/46 Kendal Women's Preparative Meeting Minutes, 1719–1774

Lancashire Archives

FRL/1/2/1/1 Lancaster Women's Quarterly Meeting Minutes, 1675–1777
FRM/1/1 Marsden Men's Monthly Meeting Minutes, 678–1723
FRM/1/24 Marsden Women's Monthly Meeting Minutes, 1678–1738
FRM/1/25 Marsden Women's Monthly Meeting Minutes, 1738–1760
FRM/4/6 Marsden Women's Preparative Meeting Minutes, 1698–1794

Library of the Religious Society of Friends, London

MS Vol 364 Abraham ManMSS

Temp MSS 403/1/2/3/1–39 and Temp MSS 403/4/8/1 Arthur B. Braithwaite Family Papers
Temp MSS 747 Cash Papers
MS Vol S 81 Caton MSS, Volume 3
MS Vol 329 Crossfield MS
MS Vol 294 Dix MSS
MS Vol 334–335 Gibson MSS Volumes 1 and 2
YM/MfS/GBS/3/1 Great Book of Sufferings, Berkshire to Lincolnshire, 1650–1686
YM/Mfs/GBS/2/5 Great Book of Sufferings, London and Middlesex to Yorkshire, Ireland and New England, 1650–1680
MGR 11b13 Ham and Waltham (Barking) Women's Monthly Meeting Minutes, 1675–1721
MSS Box G2/2 Hornor Family Papers
MS Box I3/3 Impey MSS
MS Vol 312 Journal of Mary Weston
MS Vol 340 The Life of Thomas Story with Original Letters
MGR 11a4 London Women's Meeting Account Book, 1672–1684, Volume 1
MGR 11a4 London Women's Meeting Epistles, 1671–1753
MS Vol 150 Luke Howard Collection
Temp MSS 210/1 Lloyd MSS
MS Box C4/1 Markey MSS
MS Box 6.18 Pocket Almanac for 1751 carried by Mary Weston on her travels to the Americas
Portfolio MSS, Volumes 4, 17, 36, and 41
Box I3/4 Reynolds MSS
Temp MS 745 Robson Papers (Joshua Wheeler), Volume 37, Box 1, Notebooks of Thomas Robson
Temp MSS 127 Ruth Follows Papers, Box 1/1–2
YM/TCDM Testimonies Concerning Ministers Deceased, Volume 1, 1728–1758
MSS Vol 332 Toft MSS
Temp MSS 388 Thomas Story Papers, 1702–1709
MS Vol 296 Watson MSS

The National Archives

RG6/1626 London and Middlesex Birth Notes, 1676–1707
RG6/1627 London and Middlesex Birth Notes, 1707–1718
RG6/1628 London and Middlesex Birth Notes, 1718–1725
RG6/1629 London and Middlesex Birth Notes, 1725–1769

University of California Santa Barbara Special Collections

Mss4 Ballitore Collection, Boxes 1, 3, and 4

ONLINE PRIMARY SOURCE COLLECTIONS

The Proceedings of the Old Bailey, 1674–1913 (www.oldbaileyonline.org/)

PRINTED PRIMARY SOURCES

Periodicals

The Female Tatler by a Society of Ladies
General Evening Post (London)
Gentleman's Magazine: Or, Monthly Intelligencer
Gentleman's Magazine and Historical Chronicle
London Daily Post and General Advertiser (London)
New England Courant (Boston)
The Spectator, in Donald F. Bond (ed.), The Spectator (5 vols., Oxford, 1987)
True Domestick Intelligence or News Both from City and Country (London)
Weekly Journal or British Gazetteer (London)

Books and Pamphlets

*All titles were published in London unless otherwise stated.
Allestree, Richard, *The Ladies Calling in Two Parts* (8th edn, Oxford, 1705).
Anon., *A Brief Relation of the Life and Death of Elizabeth Braytwhaite, a Maid of the Age of about Seventeen Years, Who Died in Prison for the Testimony of a Good Conscience, in the Town of Kendal in Westmorland, the 26th of the 7th Month 1684* (1684).
Anon., *Certain Quæries and Anti-Quæries, Concerning the Quakers, (So Called) in and about Yorkshire* (1653).
Anon., *A Comical New Dialogue between Mr. G-F A Pious Dissenting Parson, and a Female-Quaker (a Goldsmith's Wife) Near Cheapside* (1706).
Anon., *A Dissertation upon the Liberty of Preaching Granted to Women by the People Call'd Quakers* (Dublin, 1738).
Anon. [N. H.], *The Ladies Dictionary; Being a General Entertainment for the Fair-Sex* (1694).
Anon., 'At a Meeting of the Midwives in Barbadoes 11.xii.1677', *Journal of the Friends' Historical Society*, vol. 37 (1940), pp. 22–24.
Anon., *The Mock-Preacher: A Satyrico-Comical-Allegorical Farce* (1739).
Anon., *Moll and Her Master: Or, a Dialogue between a Quaker and His Maid* (1675).
Anon., *Poor Robin 1677: Or a Yea-and-Nay-Almanack for the People Called by Men of the World Quakers* (1677).
Anon., *Quakers Are Inchanters and Dangerous Seducers: Appearing in Their Inchantment of One Mary White at Wickham-Skyeth in Suffolk, 1655* (1655).
Anon., *The Quakers Art of Courtship, or the Yea-and-Nay Academy of Complements Calculated for the Meridian of the Bull-and-Mouth* (1689).
Anon., *The Quaker Turn'd Jew: Being a True Relation, How an Eminent Quaker in the Isle of Ely, on Monday 18 April 1675 Circumcised Himself, Out of Zeal for a Certain Case of Conscience, Renounced His Religion, and Became a Prosolited [sic] Jew* (1675).
Anon., *Remarks upon the Quakers: Wherein the Plain-Dealers Are Plainly Dealt With* (1700).
Anon., *A Sad Caveat to All Quakers: Not to Boast Any More That They Have God Almighty by the Hand, When They Have the Devil by the Toe* (1657).

Anon., *A Scheme for a General Comprehension of All Parties in Religion: And Proposals for a Committee to Meet on That Occasion* (1750).

Anon., *The Secret Sinners: Or, A Most Pleasant Dialogue between a Quaker and His Maid, and His Wife Sarah* (c. 1675), in Roger Thompson (ed.), *Samuel Pepys' Penny Merriments* (1976), pp. 147–152.

Anon., 'A Seventeenth-Century Quaker Women's Declaration', trans. by Milton D. Speizman and Jane C. Kronick, *Signs: Journal of Women in Culture and Society*, vol. 1, no. 1 (1975), pp. 231–245.

Ashbridge, Elizabeth, *Some Account of the Early Part of the Life of Elizabeth Ashbridge* (Philadelphia, 1807).

Astell, Mary, *A Serious Proposal to the Ladies, for the Advancement of Their True and Greatest Interest* (4th edn, 2 parts, 1697).

Avila, St Theresa, 'The Life of the Holy Mother Teresa of Jesus', in E. Allison Peers (ed.) *The Complete Works of St Teresa of Jesus* (vol. 1, 1946), pp. 1–300.

Bacon, Francis, 'Of Friendship', in Francis Bacon (ed.), *The Essays, or Councils, Civil and Moral, of Sir Francis Bacon* (1696), pp. 69–76.

Bacon, Margaret Hope (ed.), *Wilt Thou Go on My Errand? Journals of Three 18th Century Quaker Women Ministers: Susanna Morris, 1682–1775; Elizabeth Hudson, 1722–1783; Ann Moore, 1710–1783* (Wallingford, PA, 1994).

Banks, John, *A Journal of the Labours, Travels, and Sufferings of That Faithful Minister of Jesus Christ, John Banks* (2nd edn, 1798).

Barclay, A. R. (ed.), *Letters, &c., of Early Friends; Illustrative of the History of the Society, from Nearly Its Origin, to about the Period of George Fox's Decease* (1841).

Barclay, Robert, *An Apology for the True Christian Divinity* (1678).

Barwick, Grace, *To All Present Rulers, Whether Parliament, or Whomsoever of England* (1659).

Bell, Deborah, *A Short Journal of the Labours and Travels in the Work in the Ministry, of That Faithful Servant of Christ, Deborah Bell* (1776).

Bell, John, *Piety Promoted, in a Collection of Dying Sayings of Divers of the People Called Quakers* (1740).

Besse, Joseph, *A Collection of the Sufferings of the People Called Quakers* (2 vols., 1753).

Bewley, George, *A Narrative of the Christian Experiences of George Bewley, Late of the City of Corke* (Dublin, 1750).

Biddle, Esther, *A Warning from the Lord God of Life and Power, Unto Thee O City of London* (1660).

Blaugdone, Barbara, *An Account of the Travels, Sufferings and Persecutions of Barbara Blaugdone* (1691).

Boswell, James, *The Life of Samuel Johnson, LL.D. Comprehending an Account of His Studies, and Numerous Works, in Chronological Order* (2 vols., 1791).

Bourignon, Antoinette, *A Warning against the Quakers: Wherein the Errors of That Sect Are Plainly Detected* (1708).

Bowden, James, *The History of the Society of Friends in America* (2 vols., 1850–1854).

Bownas, Samuel, *An Account of the Life, Travels, and Christian Experiences in the Work of the Ministry of Samuel Bownas* (1756).

——*A Description of the Qualifications Necessary to a Gospel Minister, Containing Advice to Ministers and Elders* (1750).

Brissot de Warville, J. P., *New Travels in the United States of America Performed in 1788: Translated from the French* (Dublin, 1792).

Bristol Yearly Meeting, *Minute Book of the Men's Meeting of the Society of Friends in Bristol, 1686–1704*, ed. Russell Mortimer (Bristol, 1977).

Brooksop, Joan, *An Invitation of Love unto the Seed of God, throughout the World, with a Word to the Wise in Heart, and a Lamentation for New England* (1662).

Brown, Thomas, *The Reasons of Mr Bays Changing His Religion Considered in a Dialogue between Crites, Eugenius, and Mr Bays* (1688).

Bunyan, John, *The Pilgrim's Progress: From This World to That Which Is to Come Delivered under the Similitude of a Dream* (1678).

Callender, Hannah, *The Diary of Hannah Callender Sansom: Sense and Sensibility in the Age of the American Revolution*, ed. Susan E. Klepp and Karin Wulf (2010).

Camm, Thomas and Charles Marshall (eds.), *The Memory of the Righteous Revived: Being a Brief Collection of the Books and Written Epistles of John Camm and John Audland* (1689).

Cannon, John, *The Chronicles of John Cannon Excise Officer and Writing Master, 1734–1743*, ed. John Money (2 vols., Oxford, 2010).

Cary, John, *An Account of the Proceedings of the Corporation of Bristol, in Execution of the Act of Parliament for the Better Employing and Maintaining the Poor of That City* (1700).

Chalkley, Thomas, *A Journal or Historical Account of the Life, Travels, and Christian Experiences of ... Thomas Chalkley* (3rd edn, 1751).

Clarkson, Thomas, *A Portraiture of Quakerism, Taken from a View of the Education and Discipline, Social Manners, Civil and Political Economy, Religious Principles and Character of the Society of Friends* (3 vols., New York, 1806).

Clayton, Anne, *A Letter to the King* (c. 1660).

Coole, Benjamin, *Some Brief Observations on the Judicious John Lock's Paraphrase and Notes on the Texts, Relating to Women's Praying and Prophesying* (1715).

Coxere, Edward, *Adventures by Sea of Edward Coxere: A Relation of the Several Adventures by Sea with the Dangers, Difficulties and Hardships I Met for Several Years*, ed. E. H. W. Meyerstein (Oxford, 1945).

Danson, Thomas, *The Quakers Wisdom Descendeth Not from Above: Or a Brief Vindication of a Small Tract Intituled, the Quakers Folly Made Manifest to All Men* (1659).

Darby, Abiah, *Abiah Darby 1716–1793 of Coalbrookdale, Wife of Abraham Darby II*, ed. Rachel Labouchere (York, 1988).

Deacon, John, *An Exact History of the Life of James Naylor* (1657).

De Crèvecoeur, J. Hector St. John, *Letters from an American Farmer* (1782).

De Montaigne, Michel, 'Of Friendship', in *The Essays of Michael Seigneur de Montaigne, Translated into English* (8th edn, 3 vols., 1776).

Dewsbury, William, *The Faithful Testimony of That Antient Servant of the Lord, and Minister of the Everlasting Gospel William Dewsbery* (1689).

Dodshon, Frances, *Some Account of the Convincement and Religious Experience, of Frances Dodshon* (1804).

Drinker, Elizabeth, *The Diary of Elizabeth Drinker: The Life Cycle of an Eighteenth-Century Woman*, ed. Elaine Forman Crane (Boston, 1994).

Edmundson, William, 'Margaret Edmundson (c. 1630–1691): Her Husband's Testimony', ed. Isobel Grubb, *Journal of the Friends' Historical Society*, vol. 33 (1937), pp. 32–34.

Ellis, William and Alice Ellis, *The Life and Correspondence of William and Alice Ellis, of Airton*, ed. James Backhouse (1849).

Ellwood, Thomas, *A Reply to an Answer: Lately Published to a Book Long Since Written by W. P. Entitled, A Brief Examination and State of Liberty Spiritual, &c.* (1691).

Evans, Katharine and Sarah Cheevers, *This Is a Short Relation of Some of the Cruel Sufferings (for the Truths Sake) of Katharine Evans and Sarah Chevers in the Inquisition in the Isle of Malta* (1662).

Farmer, Ralph, *The Imposter Dethron'd, or, the Quakers Throne of Truth Detected* (1658).

Fleming, Daniel, *The Flemings in Oxford, Being Documents Selected from the Rydal Papers in Illustration of the Lives and Ways of Oxford Men, 1650–1700*, ed. John Richard Magrath (3 vols., Oxford, 1904).

Fletcher, Mary, *Jesus, Altogether Lovely: Or a Letter to Some of the Single Women in the Methodist Society* (1766).

Follows, Ruth, *Memoirs of Ruth Follows, Late of Castle Donnington, Leicestershire; For Sixty Years a Minister in the Society of Friends with Extracts from Her Letters*, ed. Samuel Stansfield (1829).

Forster, Mary, et al., *These Several Papers Was Sent to the Parliament the Twentieth Day of the Fifth Moneth [sic], 1659: Being above Seven Thousand of the Names of the Hand-Maids and Daughters of the Lord* (1659).

Fox, George, *A Collection of Many Select and Christian Epistles, Letters and Testimonies* (2 vols., 1698).

——— *The Journal of George Fox*, ed. John L. Nickalls (Cambridge, 1952).

——— *A Primmer [sic] and Catechism for Children: Or a Plain and Easie Way for Children to Learn to Spell and Read Perfectly in a Little Time* (1670).

——— *Saul's Errand to Damascus with His Packet of Letters from the High-Priests, against the Disciples of the Lord* (London, 1653).

Gouge, William, *Of Domesticall Duties* (1622).

Gratton, John, *A Journal of the Life of That Ancient Servant of Christ, John Gratton: Giving an Account of His Exercises When Young, and How He Came to the Knowledge of the Truth* (1720).

Hallywell, Henry, *An Account of Familism as It Is Revived and Propagated by the Quakers Shewing the Dangerousness of Their Tenets, and Their Inconsistency with the Principles of Common Reason* (1673).

Haydock, Roger, et al., *A Collection of the Christian Writings, Labours, Travels and Sufferings of That Faithful and Approved Minister of Jesus Christ, Roger Haydock* (1700).

Hayes, Alice, *A Legacy, or Widow's Mite; Left by Alice Hayes, to Her Children and Others: With an Account of Some of Her Dying Sayings* (1723).

Higginson, Francis, *A Brief Relation of the Irreligion of the Northern Quakers* (1653).

Hoskins, Jane, *The Life and Spiritual Sufferings of That Faithful Servant of Christ Jane Hoskens* (Philadelphia, 1771).

Hume, Sophia, *An Exhortation to the Inhabitants of the Province of South Carolina, to Bring Their Deeds to the Light of Christ, in Their Own Consciences* (1752).

Jacombe, Thomas, *Hooinh Egzainiomnh, or, a Treatise of Holy Dedication Both Personal and Domestick the Latter of Which is (in Special) Recommended to the Citizens of London* (1668), part 2.

Kendal Monthly Meeting, 'Testimony of Kendal Monthly Meeting Concerning Grace Chamber, Deceased, 1763', ed. Norman Penney, in *Journal of the Friends' Historical Society*, vol. 7 (1910), pp. 182–183.

Langhorne, John, *Letters on Religious Retirement, Melancholy, and Enthusiasm* (1762).

Leadbeater, Mary (ed.), *Biographical Notices of Members of the Society of Friends Who Were Resident in Ireland* (1823).

———*Memoirs and Letters of Richard and Elizabeth Shackleton, Late of Ballitore, Ireland* (1849).

Locke, John, *A Paraphrase and Notes on the Epistles of St Paul to the Galatians, I and II Corinthians, Romans, and Ephesians* (1707).

Loddington, William, *The Good Order of Truth Justified; Wherein Our Womens Meetings and Order of Marriage (by Some Especially Opposed) Are Proved Agreeable to Scripture and Sound Reason* (1685).

London Yearly Meeting, *Epistles from the Yearly Meeting of Friends, Held in London to the Quarterly and Monthly Meetings in Great Britain, Ireland, and Elsewhere, from 1681 to 1817* (1818).

———*Extracts from the Minutes and Advices of the Yearly Meeting of Friends Held in London, From Its First Institution* (1783).

Lucas, Margaret, *An Account of the Convincement and Call to the Ministry of Margaret Lucas, Late of Leek, in Staffordshire* (1797).

Lupton, Donald, *The Quacking Mountebanck or the Jesuite Turn'd Quaker: In a Witty and Full Discovery of Their Product and Rise* (1655).

Martindell, Anne, et al., *A Relation of the Labour, Travail and Suffering of That Faithful Servant of the Lord, Alice Curwen* (1680).

Mather, Cotton, *Ornaments for the Daughters of Zion, on the Character and Happiness of a Woman* (1694).

Mather, Increase, *An Essay for the Recording of Illustrious Providences Wherein an Account Is Given of Many Remarkable and Very Memorable Events Which Have Hapned [sic] This Last Age, Especially in New-England* (Boston, 1684).

Mather, William, *A Novelty: Or, a Government of Women, Distinct from Men, Erected amongst Some of the People Call'd Quakers* (1694).

Miller, William F., 'Episodes in the Life of May Drummond', *Journal of the Friends' Historical Society*, vol. 4 (1907), pp. 55–61, cont. 103–111.

Mittelberger, Gottlieb, *Gottlieb Mittelberger's Journey to Pennsylvania in the Year 1750 and Return to Germany in the Year 1754*, trans. Carl Theo. Eben (Philadelphia, 1898).

Mollineux, Mary, *Fruits of Retirement: Or Miscellaneous Poems, Moral and Divine. Being Some Contemplations, Letters &c. Written on a Variety of Subjects and Occasions* (1702).

Moore, Milcah Martha, *Milcah Martha Moore's Book: A Commonplace Book from Revolutionary America*, ed. Catherine La Courreye Blecki and Karin A. Wulf (University Park, PA, 1997).

Mucklow, William, *The Spirit of the Hat, or, the Government of the Quakers among Themselves, as It Hath Been Exercised of Late Years by George Fox* (1673).

Niesen, Geertruyd Deriks, *An Epistle to Be Communicated to Friends, and to Be Read in the Fear of the Lord in Their Men and Womens Meetings* (1677).

Norton, John, *The Heart of N-England Rent at the Blasphemies of the Present Generation: Or a Brief Tractate Concerning the Doctrine of the Quakers* (Cambridge, MA, 1659).

Parnell, James, *The Lambs Defence Against Lyes* (1656).

Pearson, Jane, *Sketches of Piety: In the Life and Religious Experiences of Jane Pearson* (York, 1817).

Peisley, Mary, *Some Account of the Life and Religious Exercises of Mary Neale, Formerly Mary Peisley: Principally Compiled from Her Own Writings* (Philadelphia, 1796).

Penn, William, *No Cross, No Crown, or Several Sober Reasons against Hat-Honour, Titular-Respects, You to a Single Person, with the Apparel and Recreations of the Times* (1669)

——*No Cross, No Crown, or Several Sober Reasons against Hat-Honour, Titular-Respects, You to a Single Person, with the Apparel and Recreations of the Times* (2nd edn, 1682, printed for Mark Swaner).

——*One Project for the Good of England: That Is, Our Civil Union Is Our Civil Safety, Humbly Dedicated to the Great Council, the Parliament of England* (c. 1679).

——*The Select Works of William Penn* (3rd edn, 5 vols., London, 1782).

——*Some Fruits of Solitude: In Reflections and Maxims Relating to the Conduct of Human Life* (1693).

Penney, Norman (ed.) *Record of the Sufferings of Quakers in Cornwall 1655–1686* (1928).

Pepys, Samuel, *The Shorter Pepys*, ed. Robert Latham (Harmondsworth, 1987).

Phillips, Catherine, *Memoirs of the Life of Catherine Phillips: To Which Are Added Some of Her Epistles* (1797).

Pickworth, Henry, *A Charge of Error, Heresy, Incharity, Falshood, … Mostly Exhibited, and Offered to Be Proved against the Most Noted Leaders &c. of the People Called Quakers* (1715).

Pike, Joseph, *Some Account of the Life of Joseph Pike, of Cork, in Ireland, Who Died in the Year 1729*, ed. John Barclay (1837).

Rogers, William, *The Christian-Quaker, Distinguished from the Apostate and Innovator: The First Part* (1680).

Shield, John Hall (ed.), *Genealogical Notes on the Families of Hall, Featherstone, Wigham, Ostle, Watson etc.* (Allendale, 1915).

Smith, Humphrey, *Something Further Laid Open of the Cruel Persecution of the People Called Quakers by the Magistrates and People of Evesham* (1656).

Smith, John Jay (ed.), *Letters of Doctor Richard Hill and His Children: Or, the History of a Family, as Told by Themselves* (Philadelphia, 1854).

Society of Friends, *A Collection of Memorials Concerning Divers Deceased Ministers and Others of the Peopled Called Quakers* (Philadelphia, 1788).

——*A Collection of Testimonies Concerning Several Ministers of the Gospel amongst the People Called Quakers, Deceased* (1760).

Stirredge, Elizabeth, *Strength in Weakness Manifest: In the Life, Various Trials, and Christian Testimony of That Faithful Servant and Handmaid of the Lord, Elizabeth Stirredge* (1711).

Story, Thomas, *A Journal of the Life of Thomas Story: Containing an Account of His Remarkable Convincement of, and Embracing the Principles of Truth, as Held by the People Called Quakers* (Newcastle, 1747).

Stout, William, *The Autobiography of William Stout of Lancaster, 1665–1752*, ed. J. D. Marshall (Manchester, 1967).

Taylor, James and Jasper Batt, *A Testimony of the Life and Death of Mary, the Daughter of Jasper Batt, and Wife of James Taylor, of Holcombe-Rogus in the County of Devon* (1683), in Alice Clark, *Working Life of Women in the Seventeenth Century* (new edn, with intro. by Amy Louise Erickson, 1992), pp. 45–46.

Taylor, Jeremy, *The Measures and Offices of Friendship: With Rules of Conducting It* (1657).

Townsend, Theophila, *An Epistle of Love to Friends in the Womens Meetings in London, &c.* (1686).

Travers, Rebecca, et al., *The Work of God in a Dying Maid Being a Short Account of the Dealings of the Lord with One Susannah Whitrow* (1677).

Underhill, Thomas, *Hell Broke Loose: Or an History of the Quakers Both Old and New* (1660).

Vokins, Joan, *God's Mighty Power Magnified: As Manifested and Revealed in His Faithful Handmaid Joan Vokins* (1691).

Voltaire, François-Marie Arouet, *Letters Concerning the English Nation* (1733).

Waite, Mary, *A Warning to All Friends Who Professeth the Everlasting Truth of God* (1679).

Walker, William, *A True Copy of Some Original Letters, Which Pass'd between John Hall of Monk-Hesleden in the County of Durham, an Eminent Quaker Teacher, and William Walker of East-Thickley in the Same County, Farmer, Whose Wife Had the Misfortune to Be Seduc'd to Quakerism* (Newcastle, 1725).

Warder, Ann, 'Extracts from the Diary of Mrs. Ann Warder', ed. Sarah Cadbury, *Pennsylvania Magazine of History and Biography*, vol. 17, no. 4 (1983), pp. 444–461.

——'Extracts from the Diary of Mrs. Ann Warder (Concluded)', ed. Sarah Cadbury, *Pennsylvania Magazine of History and Biography*, vol. 18, no. 1 (1984), pp. 51–63.

Webb, Elizabeth, *A Letter from Elizabeth Webb to Anthony William Boehm, with His Answer* (Philadelphia, 1781)

Whitall, Ann, 'The Journal of Ann Whitall (1760–62)', in Hannah Whitall Smith (ed.), *John M. Whitall: The Story of His Life* (Philadelphia, 1879), pp. 13–22.

Whitehead, George, *An Antidote against the Venome of the Snake in the Grass* (1697).

Whiting, John, *Early Piety Exemplified, in the Life and Death of Mary Whiting: A Faithful Handmaid of the Lord* (1681).

Whitton, Catherine, *An Epistle to Friends Everywhere: To Be Distinctly Read in Their Meetings, When Assembled Together in the Fear of the Lord* (1681).

Wilson, Thomas, *A Brief Journal of the Life, Travels and Labours of Love, in the Work of the Ministry of That Eminent and Faithful Servant of Jesus Christ, Thomas Wilson* (Dublin, 1728).

Winstanley, William, *A Yea and Nay Almanack, For the People Call'd by the Men of the World Quakers* (3 vols., 1678–1680).

Woolley, Hannah, *The Gentlewomans Companion: Or a Guide to the Female Sex* (1673).

SECONDARY SOURCES

Adcock, Rachel, *Baptist Women's Writings in Revolutionary Culture, 1640–1680* (London, 2015).

Anderson, Penelope, '"Friendship Multiplyed": Royalist and Republican Friendship in Katherine Philips's Coterie', in Daniel T. Lochman, Maritere López, and Lorna Hutson (eds.), *Discourses and Representations of Friendship in Early Modern Europe, 1500–1700* (Farnham, 1988), pp. 132–146.

Angell, Stephen W. and Pink Dandelion (eds.), *The Oxford Handbook of Quaker Studies* (Oxford, 2013).

Apetrei, Sarah, 'Masculine Virgins: Celibacy and Gender in Later Stuart London', in Sarah Apetrei and Hannah Smith (eds.), *Religion and Women in Britain, c. 1660–1760* (Farnham, 2015), pp. 41–59.

Women, Feminism and Religion in Early Enlightenment England (Cambridge, 2010).

Apetrei, Sarah and Hannah Smith (eds.), *Religion and Women in Britain, c. 1660–1760* (Farnham, 2015).

Armitage, David and Michael J. Braddick (eds.), *The British Atlantic World, 1500–1800* (Basingstoke, 2002).

Aschheim, Steven, *At the Edges of Liberalism: Junctions of European, German and Jewish History* (Basingstoke, 2012).

Bacon, Margaret Hope, 'The Establishment of London Women's Yearly Meeting: A Transatlantic Concern', *Journal of the Friends' Historical Society*, vol. 57, no. 2 (1995), pp. 151–165.

——*Mothers of Feminism: The Story of Quaker Women in America* (San Francisco, 1986).

Baldwin, Geoff, 'The "Public" as a Rhetorical Community in Early Modern England', in Alexandra Shepard and Phil Withington (eds.), *Communities in Early Modern England: Networks, Place, Rhetoric* (Manchester, 2000), pp. 199–215.

Baltzly, Dirk and Nick Eliopoulos, 'The Classical Ideals of Friendship', in Barbara Caine (ed.), *Friendship: A History* (London, 2009), pp. 1–64.

Barbour, Hugh, 'Quaker Prophetesses and Mothers in Israel', in J. William Frost and John M. Moore, *Seeking the Light: Essays in Quaker History in Honor of Edwin B. Bronner* (Wallingford, PA, 1986), pp. 41–60.

Barbour, Hugh and J. William Frost, *The Quakers* (London, 1988).

Barker, Hannah and Elaine Chalus (eds.), *Gender in Eighteenth-Century England: Roles, Representations and Responsibilities* (London, 1997).

Barker-Benfield, G. J., *The Culture of Sensibility: Sex and Society in Eighteenth-Century Britain* (London, 1992).

Bauman, Richard, *Let Your Words Be Few: Symbolism of Speaking and Silence among Seventeenth-Century Quakers* (Cambridge, 1983).

Berry, Helen, *Gender, Society and Print Culture in Late-Stuart England: The Cultural World of the Athenian Mercury* (Aldershot, 2003).

Bossy, John, *The English Catholic Community 1570–1850* (London, 1975).

Bouldin, Elizabeth, *Women Prophets and Radical Protestantism in the British Atlantic World, 1640–1730* (Cambridge, 2015).

Boyd, Diane E. and Marta Kvande (eds.), *Everyday Revolutions: Eighteenth-Century Women Transforming Public and Private* (Newark, DE, 2008).

Brailsford, Mabel Richmond, *Quaker Women, 1650–1690* (London, 1915).

Braithwaite, William C., *The Beginnings of Quakerism* (2nd edn, rev. H. J. Cadbury, Cambridge, 1961).

——*The Second Period of Quakerism* (2nd edn, rev. H. J. Cadbury, Cambridge, 1961).

Brant, Clare, *Eighteenth-Century Letters and British Culture* (Basingstoke, 2006).

Bray, Alan, *The Friend* (London, 2003).

Broomhall, Susan (ed.), *Spaces for Feeling: Emotions and Sociabilities in Britain, 1650–1850* (London, 2015).

Burgess, John, 'The Quakers, the Brethren and the Religious Census in Cumbria', *Transactions of the Cumberland & Westmorland Antiquarian & Archaeological Society*, 80 (1980), pp. 103–111.

Butcher, E. E., *Bristol Corporation of the Poor, 1696–1898* (Bristol, 1972).

Butler, David M., *Quaker Meeting Houses of the Lake Counties* (London, 1978).

Caine, Barbara (ed.), *Friendship: A History* (London, 2009).

Capp, Bernard, 'Gender, Conscience and Casuistry: Women and Conflicting Obligations in Early Modern England', in Harald E. Braun and Edward Vallance (eds.), *Contexts of Conscience in Early Modern Europe, 1500–1700* (Basingstoke, 2004), pp. 116–131.

———*When Gossips Meet: Women, Family and Neighbourhood in Early Modern England* (Oxford, 2003).

Chedgzoy, Kate, *Women's Writing in the British Atlantic World: Memory, Place and History, 1550–1700* (Cambridge, 2007).

Cherry, Charles L., 'Enthusiasm and Madness: Anti-Quakerism in the Seventeenth Century', *Quaker History*, vol. 73, no. 2 (1984), pp. 1–24.

Chilcote, Paul Wesley, *John Wesley and the Women Preachers of Early Methodism* (London, 1991).

Clark, Alice, *Working Life of Women in the Seventeenth Century* (new edn, with intro. by Amy Louise Erickson, London, 1992).

Clark, Emily, 'When Is a Cloister Not a Cloister? Comparing Women and Religion in the Colonies of France and Spain', in Emily Clark and Mary Laven (eds.), *Women and Religion in the Atlantic Age, 1550–1900* (Farnham, 2013), pp. 67–87.

Clark, Emily and Mary Laven (eds.), *Women and Religion in the Atlantic Age, 1550–1900* (Farnham, 2013).

Crabtree, Sarah, '"A Beautiful and Practical Lesson of Jurisprudence": The Transatlantic Quaker Ministry in an Age of Revolution', *Radical History Review*, vol. 99 (2007), pp. 51–79.

———*Holy Nation: The Transatlantic Quaker Ministry in an Age of Revolution* (Chicago, 2015).

Crawford, Patricia, 'Public Duty, Conscience, and Women in Early Modern England', in John Morrill, Paul Slack, and Daniel Woolf (eds.), *Public Duty and Private Conscience in Seventeenth-Century England* (Oxford, 1993), pp. 57–76.

———*Women and Religion in England 1500–1720* (London, 1993).

———'Women's Published Writings 1600–1700', in Mary Prior (ed.), *Women in English Society 1500–1800* (London, 1991), pp. 158–209.

Cressy, David, *Birth, Marriage, and Death: Ritual, Religion, and the Life-Cycle in Tudor and Stuart England* (Oxford, 1997).

———*Coming Over: Migration and Communication between England and New England in the Seventeenth Century* (Cambridge, 1987).

———'Conflict, Consensus, and the Willingness to Wink: The Erosion of Community in Charles I's England', *Huntington Library Quarterly*, vol. 61, no. 2 (1998), pp. 131–149.

Damrosch, Leo, *The Sorrows of the Quaker Jesus: James Nayler and the Puritan Crackdown on the Free Spirit* (Cambridge, MA, 1996).

Dandelion, Pink, 'Guarded Domesticity and Engagement with "the World": The Separate Spheres of Quaker Quietism', *Common Knowledge*, vol. 16, no. 1 (2010), pp. 95–109.

Davies, Adrian, *The Quakers in English Society, 1655–1725* (Oxford, 2000).

Daybell, James (ed.), *Early Modern Women's Letter Writing, 1450–1700* (Basingstoke, 2001).

De Beer, E. S., *The Correspondence of John Locke in Eight Volumes* (vol. 5, Oxford, 1979).

Derrida, Jacques, *The Politics of Friendship* (London, 1997).

Dinan, Susan E. and Debra Meyers (eds.), *Women and Religion in Old and New Worlds* (London, 2001).

Dixon, Simon, 'The Life and Times of Peter Briggins', *Quaker Studies*, vol. 10, no. 2 (2006), pp. 185–202.

Donegan, Jane B., *Women and Men Midwives: Medicine, Morality and Misogyny in Early America* (London, 1978).

Downs, Laura Lee, *Writing Gender History* (2nd edn, London, 2010).

Dunn, Mary Maples, 'Latest Light on Women of Light', in Elisabeth Potts Brown and Susan Mosher Stuard (eds.), *Witness for Change: Quaker Women over Three Centuries* (London, 1989), pp. 71–85.

———'Saints and Sisters: Congregational and Quaker Women in the Early Colonial Period', *American Quarterly*, vol. 30, no. 5, Special Issue: Women and Religion (1978), pp. 582–601.

Earle, Rebecca (ed.), *Epistolary Selves: Letters and Letter-Writers 1600–1945* (Aldershot, 1999).

Edwards, Irene L., 'The Women Friends of London: The Two-Weeks and Box Meetings', *Journal of the Friends' Historical Society*, vol. 47, no. 1 (1955), pp. 3–21.

Eger, Elizabeth, '"The Noblest Commerce of Mankind": Conversation and Community in the Bluestocking Circle', in Sarah Knott and Barbara Taylor (eds.), *Women, Gender and Enlightenment* (Basingstoke, 2005), pp. 288–305.

Elmer, '"Saints or Sorcerers": Quakerism, Demonology, and the Decline of Witchcraft in Seventeenth-Century England', in Brian P. Levack (ed.), *Demonology, Religion, and Witchcraft: New Perspectives on Witchcraft, Magic and Demonology* (6 vols., London, 2001), vol. 1, pp. 437–471.

Evenden, Doreen, *The Midwives of Seventeenth-Century London* (Cambridge, 2000).

Ezell, Margaret J. M., *The Patriarch's Wife: Literary Evidence and the History of the Family* (London, 1987).

Fincham, Kenneth (ed.), *Visitation Articles and Injunctions of the Early Stuart Church* (2 vols., Church of England Record Society, Woodbridge, 1994–1998).

Fletcher, Anthony, *Gender, Sex, and Subordination in England, 1500–1800* (New Haven, CT, 1995).

Forbes, Susan, 'Quaker Tribalism', in Michael Zuckerman (ed.), *Friends and Neighbours: Group Life in America's First Plural Society* (Philadelphia, 1982), pp. 145–173.

Foyster, Elizabeth A., *Manhood in Early Modern England: Honour, Sex and Marriage* (London, 1999).

Fox, Adam, *Oral and Literate Culture in England, 1500–1700* (Oxford, 2000).

Freeman, Thomas, '"The Good Ministrye of Godlye and Vertuouse Women": The Elizabethan Martyrologists and the Female Supporters of the Marian Martyrs', *Journal of British Studies*, vol. 39, no. 1 (2000), pp. 8–33.

Froide, Amy M., 'The Religious Lives of Singlewomen in the Anglo-Atlantic World: Quaker Missionaries, Protestant Nuns, and Covert Catholics', in Daniella Kostroun and Lisa Vollendorf (eds.), *Women, Religion, and the Atlantic World (1600–1800)* (Toronto, 2009), pp. 60–78.

Frost, J. William, *The Quaker Family in Colonial America: A Portrait of the Society of Friends* (New York, 1973).

Furey, Constance M., 'Bound by Likeness: Vives and Erasmus on Marriage and Friendship', in Daniel T. Lochman, Maritere López, and Lorna Hutson (eds.),

Discourses and Representations of Friendship in Early Modern Europe, 1500–1700 (Farnham, 1988), pp. 29–43.

Gaskill, Malcolm, *Between Two Worlds: How the English Became Americans* (Oxford, 2014).

Gill, Catie, '"Bad Catholics": Anti-Popery in *This Is a Short Relation* (Katherine Evans and Sarah Cheevers, 1662)', in Paul Salzman (ed.), *Expanding the Canon of Early Modern Women's Writing* (Cambridge, 2010), p. 234–247.

——*Women in the Seventeenth-Century Quaker Community: A Literary Study of Political Identities, 1650–1700* (Aldershot, 2005).

Gowing, Laura, 'The Politics of Women's Friendship in Early Modern England', in Laura Gowing, Michael Hunter, and Miri Rubin (eds.), *Love, Friendship and Faith in Europe, 1300–1800* (Basingstoke, 2005), pp. 131–149.

Gowing, Laura, Michael Hunter and Miri Rubin (eds.), *Love, Friendship and Faith in Europe, 1300–1800* (Basingstoke, 2005).

Graham, E., H. Hinds, E. Hobby and H. Wilcox (eds.), *Her Own Life: Autobiographical Writings by 17th Century Englishwomen* (London, 1989).

Greaves, Richard L., *God's Other Children: Protestant Nonconformists and the Emergence of Denominational Churches in Ireland, 1660–1700* (Stanford, CA, 1997).

Green, James N., 'The Book Trade in the Middle Colonies, 1680–1720', in Hugh Amory and David D. Hall (eds.), *The Colonial Book in the Atlantic World* (Chapel Hill, NC, 2007), pp. 199–223.

Greverz, Kaspar von, *Religion and Culture in Early Modern Europe, 1500–1800* (Oxford, 2008).

Gummere, Amelia Mott, *Friends in Burlington* (Philadelphia, 1884).

Hagglund, Betty, 'Changes in Roles and Relationships: Multiauthored Epistles from the Aberdeen Quaker Women's Meeting' in Carolyn D. Williams, Angela Escott, and Louise Duckling (eds.), *Woman to Woman: Female Negotiations during the Long Eighteenth Century* (Newark, DE, 2010), pp. 137–156.

Hamm, Thomas D., *The Quakers in America* (New York, 2003).

Harvey, Karen, *The Little Republic: Masculinity and Domestic Authority in Eighteenth-Century Britain* (Oxford, 2012).

Haydon, Colin, *Anti-Catholicism in Eighteenth-Century England, c. 1714–80: A Political and Social Study* (Manchester, 1993).

Heal, Felicity, *Hospitality in Early Modern England* (Oxford, 1990).

Heilke, Thomas, 'From Civic Friendship to Communities of Believers: Anabaptist Challenges to Lutheran and Calvinist Discourses', in Daniel T. Lochman, Maritere López, and Lorna Hutson (eds.), *Discourses and Representations of Friendship in Early Modern Europe, 1500–1700* (Farnham, 1988), pp. 225–238.

Herbert, Amanda E., 'Companions in Preaching and Suffering: Itinerant Female Quakers in the Seventeenth- and Eighteenth-Century British Atlantic World', *Early American Studies: An Interdisciplinary Journal*, vol. 9, no. 1 (2011), pp. 73–113.

——*Female Alliances: Gender, Identity, and Friendship in Early Modern Britain* (London, 2014).

Hess, Ann Giardina, 'Midwifery Practice among the Quakers in Southern Rural England in the Late Seventeenth Century', in Hilary Marland (ed.), *The Art of Midwifery: Early Modern Midwives in Europe* (London, 1993), pp. 49–76.

Higgins, Patricia, 'The Reactions of Women, with Special Reference to Women Petitioners', in Brian Manning (ed.), *Politics, Religion and the English Civil War* (London, 1973), pp. 179–224.

Hinds, Hilary, *God's Englishwomen: Seventeenth-Century Radical Sectarian Writing and Feminist Criticism* (Manchester, 1996).

Holton, Sandra Stanley, 'Kinship and Friendship: Quaker Women's Networks and the Women's Movement', *Women's Historical Review*, vol. 14, nos. 3 and 4 (2005), pp. 365–384.

———*Quaker Women: Personal Life, Memory and Radicalism in the Lives of Women Friends, 1780–1930* (London, 2007).

Horle, Craig W., *Quakers and the English Legal System, 1660–1688* (Philadelphia, 1988).

Houlbrooke, Ralph A., *The English Family 1450–1700* (London, 1984).

Hull, W., *Benjamin Furly and Quakerism in Rotterdam* (Swarthmore, PA, 1941).

Jaffary, Nora E. (ed.), *Gender, Race and Religion in the Colonization of the Americas* (Aldershot, 2007).

James, Carolyn and Bill Kent, 'Renaissance Friendships: Traditional Truths, New and Dissenting Voices', in Barbara Caine (ed.), *Friendship: A History* (London, 2009), pp. 111–164.

Jennings, Judith, *Gender, Religion, and Radicalism in the Long Eighteenth Century: The 'Ingenious Quaker' and Her Connections* (Aldershot, 2006).

Joint Committee of Hopewell Friends, *Hopewell Friends History, 1734–1934, Frederick County: Records of Hopewell Monthly Meetings and Meetings Reporting to Hopewell* (Baltimore, MD, 1936).

Jones, Rufus, *The Later Periods of Quakerism* (2 vols., London, 1921).

Keeble, N. H., *The Literary Culture of Nonconformity in Later Seventeenth-Century England* (Leicester, 1987).

Kent, Stephen A., 'Seven Thousand "Hand-Maids and Daughters of the Lord": Lincolnshire and Cheshire Quaker Women's Anti-Tithe Protests in Late Interregnum and Restoration England', in Sylvia Brown (ed.), *Women, Gender, and Radical Religion in Early Modern Europe* (Leiden, The Netherlands, 2007), pp. 65–96.

Kerber, Linda, 'Separate Spheres, Female Worlds, Woman's Place: The Rhetoric of Women's History', *Journal of American History*, vol. 75, no. 1 (1988), pp. 9–39.

Kilroy, Phil, 'Quaker Women in Ireland, 1660–1740', *Irish Journal of Feminist Studies*, vol. 2, no. 2 (1997), pp. 1–16.

Klein, Lawrence E., 'Gender, Conversation and the Public Sphere in Early Eighteenth-Century England', in Michael Worton and Judith Still (eds.), *Textuality and Sexuality: Reading Theories and Practices* (Manchester, 1993), pp. 100–115.

Knights, Mark, *The Devil in Disguise: Deception, Delusion, and Fanaticism in the Early English Enlightenment* (Oxford, 2011).

Knott, Sarah, *Sensibility and the American Revolution* (Chapel Hill, NC, 2009).

Kostroun, Daniella and Lisa Vollendorf (eds.), *Women, Religion, and the Atlantic World (1600–1800)* (Toronto, 2009).

Kunze, Bonnelyn Young, *Margaret Fell and the Rise of Quakerism* (London, 1994).

———'"Poore and in Necessity": Margaret Fell and Quaker Female Philanthropy in North-West England in the Late Seventeenth Century', *Albion*, vol. 21, no. 4 (1989), pp. 559–580.

Labouchere, Rachel, *Deborah Darby of Coalbrookdale, 1754–1810: Her Visits to America, Ireland, Scotland, Wales, England and the Channel Isles* (York, 1993).

Laing, Annette, 'Crossing Denominational Boundaries: Two Early American Women and Religion in the Atlantic World', in Emily Clark and Mary Laven (eds.), *Women and Religion in the Atlantic Age, 1550–1900* (Farnham, 2013), pp. 89–121.

Lake, Peter, 'Anti-Popery: The Structure of a Prejudice', in Richard Cust and Ann Hughes (eds.), *Conflict in Early Stuart England: Studies in Religion and Politics, 1603–1642* (London, 1989), pp. 72–106.

Landes, Jordan, *London Quakers in the Trans-Atlantic World: The Creation of an Early Modern Community* (Houndmills, 2015).

Larson, Rebecca, *Daughters of Light: Quaker Women Preaching and Prophesying in the Colonies and Abroad, 1700–1775* (New York, 1999).

Lawrence, Anna M., *One Family under God: Love, Belonging, and Authority in Early Transatlantic Methodism* (Philadelphia, 2011).

Levenduski, Cristine M., *Peculiar Power: A Quaker Woman Preacher in Eighteenth-Century America* (London, 1996).

Levy, Barry, 'The Birth of the "Modern Family" in Early America: Quaker and Anglican Families in the Delaware Valley, Pennsylvania, 1681–1750', in Michael Zuckerman (ed.), *Friends and Neighbours: Group Life in America's First Plural Society* (Philadelphia, 1982), pp. 26–64.

———*Quakers and the American Family: British Settlement in the Delaware Valley* (Oxford, 1988).

Lindman, Janet Moore, *Bodies of Belief: Baptist Community in Early America* (Philadelphia, 2008).

Lochman, Daniel T., Maritere López, and Lorna Hutson (eds.), *Discourses and Representations of Friendship in Early Modern Europe, 1500–1700* (Farnham, 1988)

Ludlow, Dorothy, 'Shaking Patriarchy's Foundations: Sectarian Women in England, 1641–1700', in Richard L. Greaves (ed.), *Triumph over Silence* (London, 1985), pp. 93–124.

Lyles, A. M., *Methodism Mocked: The Satiric Reaction to Methodism in the 18th Century* (London, 1960).

Mack, Phyllis, *Heart Religion in the British Enlightenment: Gender and Emotion in Early Methodism* (Cambridge, 2008).

———*Visionary Women: Ecstatic Prophecy in Seventeenth-Century England* (Berkeley, CA, 1994).

Major, Emma, *Madam Britannia: Women, Church, and Nation 1712–1812* (Oxford, 2011).

Malmgreen, Gail, 'Domestic Discords: Women and the Family in East Cheshire Methodism, 1750–1830', in Jim Obelkevich, Lyndal Roper, and Raphael Samuel (eds.), *Disciplines of Faith: Studies in Religion, Politics and Patriarchy* (London, 1987), pp. 50–70.

Marietta, Jack D., *The Reformation of American Quakerism, 1748–1783* (Philadelphia, 1984).

Marotti, Arthur F., *Religious Ideology and Cultural Fantasy: Catholic and Anti-Catholic Discourses in Early Modern England* (Notre Dame, IN, 2005).

Martin, Lucinda, 'Jacob Boehme and the Anthropology of German Pietism', in Ariel Hessayon and Sarah Apetrei (eds.), *An Introduction to Jacob Boehme* (Abingdon, 2014), pp. 120–143.

McEntee, Ann Marie, '"The [un] Civill-Sisterhood of Oranges and Lemons": Female Petitioners and Demonstrators, 1642–53', *Prose Studies: History, Theory, Criticism*, vol. 14, no. 3 (1991), pp. 92–111.

Mee, Jon, *Conversable Worlds: Literature, Contention and Community, 1762 to 1830* (Oxford, 2011).

Mendelson, Sara and Patricia Crawford, *Women in Early Modern England, 1550–1720* (Oxford, 1998).

Michaelson, Patricia Howell, 'Religious Bases of Eighteenth-Century Feminism: Mary Wollstonecraft and the Quakers', *Women's Studies*, vol. 22, no. 3 (1993), pp. 281–295.

Miller, John, '"A Suffering People": English Quakers and Their Neighbours c. 1650–c. 1700', *Past and Present*, 188 (2005), pp. 71–103.

Moore, Rosemary, *The Light in Their Consciences: Early Quakers in Britain, 1646–1666* (University Park, PA, 2000).

Morgan, Sue, 'Women, Religion and Feminism: Past, Present and Future Perspectives', in Sue Morgan (ed.), *Women, Religion and Feminism in Britain, 1750–1900* (Basingstoke, 2002), pp. 1–19.

Mount, Harry, 'Egbert van Heemskerck's Quaker Meetings Revisited', *Journal of the Warburg and Courtauld Institutes*, vol. 56 (1993), pp. 209–228.

Mullett, Michael, 'From Sect to Denomination? Social Developments in Eighteenth-Century English Quakerism', *Journal of Religious History*, vol. 13, no. 2 (1984), pp. 168–191.

Myers, Albert Cook, *Immigration of the Irish Quakers into Pennsylvania, 1682–1750* (Swarthmore, PA, 1902).

Ng, Su Fang, *Literature and the Politics of Family in Seventeenth-Century England* (Cambridge, 2007).

Niblett, Matthew, 'The Death of Puritanism? Protestant Dissent and the Problem of Luxury in Eighteenth-Century England', *Studies on Voltaire and the Eighteenth Century*, vol. 6 (2008), pp. 251–259.

Norton, Mary Beth, *Separated by Their Sex: Women in Public and Private in the Colonial Atlantic World* (London, 2011).

O'Brien, Karen, *Women and Enlightenment in Eighteenth-Century Britain* (Cambridge, 2009).

O'Day, Rosemary, *The Family and Family Relationships, 1500–1900* (Basingstoke, 1994).

——*Women's Agency in Early Modern Britain and the American Colonies: Patriarchy, Partnership and Patronage* (London, 2007).

Ozment, Stephen E., *When Fathers Ruled: Family Life in Reformation Europe* (London, 1983).

Pangle, Lorraine Smith, *Aristotle and the Philosophy of Friendship* (Cambridge, 2003).

Parish, Debra L., 'The Power of Female Pietism: Women as Spiritual Authorities and Religious Role Models in Seventeenth-Century England', *Journal of Religious History*, vol. 17, no. 1 (1992), pp. 33–46.

Pearsall, Sarah M., *Atlantic Families: Lives and Letters in the Later Eighteenth Century* (Oxford, 2008).

Perry, Ruth, 'Mary Astell and Enlightenment' in Sarah Knott and Barbara Taylor (eds.), *Women, Gender and Enlightenment* (Basingstoke, 2005), pp. 357–370.

Pestana, Carla Gardina, 'Between Religious Marketplace and Spiritual Wasteland: Religion in the British Atlantic World', *History Compass*, vol. 2 (2004), pp. 1–12.

————*Quakers and Baptists in Colonial Massachusetts* (Cambridge, 1991).

Peters, Christine, *Patterns of Piety: Women, Gender and Religion in Late Medieval and Reformation England* (Cambridge, 2003).

Peters, Kate, *Print Culture and the Early Quakers* (Cambridge, 2005).

Polder, Kristianna, *Matrimony in the True Church: The Seventeenth-Century Quaker Marriage Approbation Discipline* (London, 2015).

Pullin, Naomi, 'Providence, Punishment and Identity Formation in the Late-Stuart Quaker Community, c. 1650–1700', *The Seventeenth Century*, vol. 31, no. 4 (2016), pp. 471–494.

————'In Pursuit of Heavenly Guidance: The Religious Context of Catherine Exley's Life and Writings', in Rebecca Probert (ed.), *Catherine Exley's Diary: The Life and Times of an Army Wife in the Peninsular War* (Kenilworth, 2014), pp. 79–95.

————'"She Suffered for My Sake": Female Martyrs and Lay Activists in Transatlantic Quakerism, 1650–1710', in Catie Gill and Michele Lise Tarter (eds.), *New Critical Studies on Early Quaker Women, 1650–1800* (Oxford, 2018), pp. 110–127.

Raffe, Alasdair, 'Female Authority and Lay Activism in Scottish Presbyterianism, 1660–1740', in Sarah Apetrei and Hannah Smith (eds.), *Religion and Women in Britain, c. 1660–1760* (Farnham, 2015), pp. 61–78.

Raines, Robert, 'Notes on Egbert van Heemskerck and the English Taste for Genre', *Walpole Society*, vol. 53 (1987), pp. 119–141.

Rapley, Elizabeth, *The Dévotes: Women and Church in Seventeenth-Century France* (Montreal, 1990).

Raven, James, 'The Importation of Books in the Eighteenth Century', in Hugh Amory and David D. Hall (eds.), *The Colonial Book in the Atlantic World* (Chapel Hill, NC, 2007), pp. 183–198.

Reay, Barry, *The Quakers and the English Revolution* (London, 1985).

Reinke-Williams, Tim, *Women, Work and Sociability in Early Modern London* (Basingstoke, 2014).

Richey, Russell, *Early American Methodism* (Bloomington, IN, 1991).

Roberts, Penny, 'Peace, Ritual and Sexual Violence during the Religious Wars', in G. Murdock, P. Roberts, and A. Spicer (eds.), *Ritual and Violence: Natalie Zemon Davis and Early Modern France* (Oxford, 2012), pp. 75–99.

Roper, Lyndal, *The Holy Household: Women and Morals in Reformation Augsburg* (Oxford, 1989).

Rowlands, Marie B., 'Recusant Women 1560–1640' in Mary Prior (ed.), *Women in English Society, 1500–1800* (London, 1991), pp. 112–135.

Rowntree, S. J., *Quakerism Past and Present: Being an Inquiry into the Causes of Its Decline* (London, 1859).

Ryan, James Emmett, *Imaginary Friends: Representing Quakers in American Culture, 1650–1950* (London, 2009).

Scott, David, *Quakerism in York, 1650–1720* (York, 1991).

Searle, Alison, 'Women, Marriage and Agency in Restoration Dissent', in Sarah Apetrei and Hannah Smith (eds.), *Religion and Women in Britain, c. 1660–1760* (Farnham, 2015), pp. 23–40.

Shaw, Gareth, 'The Inferior Parts of the Body: The Development and Role of Women's Meetings in the Early Quaker Movement', *Quaker Studies*, vol. 9, no. 2 (2005), pp. 191–203.

Shepard, Alexandra, *Accounting for Oneself: Worth, Status, and the Social Order in Early Modern England* (Oxford, 2015).

————'Crediting Women in the Early Modern English Economy', *History Workshop Journal*, vol. 79, no. 1 (2015), pp. 1–24.

————*Meanings of Manhood in Early Modern England* (Oxford, 2003).

Shepard, Alexandra and Phil Withington (eds.), *Communities in Early Modern England: Networks, Place, Rhetoric* (Manchester, 2000).

Shields, David S., *Civil Tongues and Polite Letters in British America* (Chapel Hill, NC, 1997).

Shoemaker, *Gender in English Society, 1650–1850: The Emergence of Separate Spheres?* (London, 1998).

Skidmore, Gil (ed.), *Strength in Weakness: Writings of Eighteenth-Century Quaker Women* (Oxford, 2003).

Soderlund, Jean R., 'Women's Authority in Pennsylvania and New Jersey Quaker Meetings, 1680–1760', *William and Mary Quarterly*, vol. 44, no. 4 (1987), pp. 722–749.

Steele, Ian K., *The English Atlantic 1675–1740: An Exploration of Communication and Community* (New York, 1986).

Stevenson, Bill, 'The Social Integration of Post-Restoration Dissenters, 1660–1725', in Margaret Spufford (ed.), *The World of Rural Dissenters, 1520–1725* (Cambridge, 1995), pp. 360–387.

Tadmor, Naomi, *Family and Friends in Eighteenth-Century England: Household, Kinship, and Patronage* (Cambridge, 2001).

Tarbin, Stephanie and Susan Broomhall (eds.), *Women, Identities and Communities in Early Modern Europe* (Aldershot, 2008).

Tarter, Michele Lise, 'Quaking in the Light: The Politics of Quaker Women's Corporeal Prophecy in the Seventeenth-Century Transatlantic World', in Janet Moore Lindman and Michele Lise Tarter (eds.), *A Centre of Wonders: The Body in Early America* (New York, 2001), pp. 145–162.

Thomas, Keith V., *The Ends of Life: Roads to Fulfilment in Early Modern England* (Oxford, 2009).

————*Religion and the Decline of Magic: Studies in Popular Beliefs in Sixteenth- and Seventeenth-Century England* (Harmondsworth, 1991).

————'Women and the Civil War Sects', *Past and Present*, vol. 13 (1958), pp. 42–62.

Tolles, Frederick B., *Meeting House and Counting House: The Quaker Merchants of Colonial Philadelphia, 1682–1763* (New York, 1948).

————*Quakers and the Atlantic Culture* (New York, 1960).

Tomes, Nancy, 'The Quaker Connection: Visiting Patterns among Women in the Philadelphia Society of Friends, 1750–1800', in Michael Zuckerman (ed.), *Friends and Neighbours: Group Life in America's First Plural Society* (Philadelphia, 1982), pp. 174–195.

Trevett, Christine, *Quaker Women Prophets in England and Wales 1650–1700* (Lampeter, 2000).

————*Women and Quakerism in the 17th Century* (York, 1991).

Tual, Jacques, 'Sexual Equality and Conjugal Harmony: The Way to Celestial Bliss. A View of Early Quaker Matrimony', *Journal of the Friends' Historical Society*, vol. 55, no. 6 (1988), pp. 161–174.

Ulrich, Laurel Thatcher, *Good Wives: Image and Reality in the Lives of Women in Northern New England, 1650–1750* (Oxford, 1983).

Underdown, 'The Taming of the Scold: The Enforcement of Patriarchal Authority in Early Modern England', in Anthony Fletcher and John Stevenson (eds.), *Order and Disorder in Early Modern England* (Cambridge, 1985), pp. 116–136.

Valenze, Deborah, *The Social Life of Money in the English Past* (Cambridge, 2006).
Vann, Richard T., *The Social Development of English Quakerism 1655–1755* (Cambridge, MA, 1969).
Vann, Richard T. and David Eversley, *Friends in Life and Death: The British and Irish Quakers in the Demographic Transition, 1650–1900* (Cambridge, 1992).
Vickery, Amanda, *The Gentleman's Daughter: Women's Lives in Georgian England* (London, 1998).
———'Golden Age to Separate Spheres? A Review of the Categories and Chronology of English Women's History', *Historical Journal*, vol. 36, no. 2 (1993), pp. 383–414.
Walker, Claire, *Gender and Politics in Early Modern Europe: English Convents in France and the Low Countries* (Basingstoke, 2003).
———'"When God Shall Restore Them to Their Kingdoms": Nuns, Exiled Stuarts and English Catholic Identity, 1688–1745', in Sarah Apetrei and Hannah Smith (eds.), *Religion and Women in Britain, c. 1660–1760* (Farnham, 2015), pp. 79–97.
Walsh, John, 'Methodism and the Mob in the Eighteenth Century', in G. J. Cuming and Derek Baker (eds.), *Popular Belief and Practice* (Studies in Church History, 8, Cambridge, 1972), pp. 213–227.
Walsham, Alexandra, *Charitable Hatred: Tolerance and Intolerance in England, 1500–1700* (Manchester, 2006).
Warner, Michael, *The Letters of the Republic: Publication and the Public Sphere in Eighteenth-Century America* (London, 1990).
Weber, Max, *Max Weber: Essays in Sociology*, trans. H. H. Gerth and C. Wright Mills (London, 2013).
———*The Protestant Ethic and the Spirit of Capitalism*, trans. Talcott Parsons; with an introduction by Anthony Giddens (London, 2001).
———*The Sociology of Religion*, trans. Ephraim Fischoff (London, 1965).
Whitehouse, Tessa, 'Godly Dispositions and Textual Conditions: The Literary Sociology of International Religious Exchanges, c. 1722–1740', *History of European Ideas*, vol. 39, no. 3 (2013), pp. 394–408.
Whiting, Amanda Jane, *Women and Petitioning in the Seventeenth-Century English Revolution: Deference, Difference, and Dissent* (Turnhout, Belgium, 2015).
Whittle, Jane and Elizabeth Griffiths, *Consumption and Gender in the Early Seventeenth-Century Household: The World of Alice Le Strange* (Oxford, 2012).
Whyman, Susan E., *The Pen and the People: English Letter Writers, 1660–1800* (Oxford, 2009).
Wiesner, Merry, 'Nuns, Wives, and Mothers: Women and the Reformation in Germany', in Sherrin Marshall (ed.), *Women in Reformation and Counter-Reformation Europe: Public and Private Worlds* (Bloomington, IN, 1989), pp. 8–28.
Wilcox, Catherine M., *Theology and Women's Ministry in Seventeenth-Century English Quakerism* (Lampeter, 1961).
Willen, Diane, 'Women and Religion in Early Modern England', in Sherrin Marshall (ed.), *Women in Reformation and Counter-Reformation Europe: Public and Private Worlds* (Bloomington, IN, 1989), pp. 140–165.
Wiseman, Jacqueline P., 'Friendship: Bonds and Binds in a Voluntary Relationship', *Journal of Social and Personal Relations*, vol. 3 (1986), pp. 191–211.
Wright, Sheila, '"Every Good Woman Needs a Companion of Her Own Sex": Quaker Women and Spiritual Friendship, 1750–1850', in Sue Morgan (ed.), *Women, Religion and Feminism in Britain, 1750–1900* (Basingstoke, 2002), pp. 89–104.

——'Quakerism and Its Implications for Quaker Women: The Women Itinerant Ministers of York Meeting, 1780–1840', in W. J. Sheils and Diana Wood (eds.), *Women in the Church* (Studies in Church History, 27, Oxford, 1990), pp. 403–414.
——'"Truly Dear Hearts": Family and Spirituality in Quaker Women's Writings, 1680–1750', in Sylvia Brown (ed.), *Women, Gender and Radical Religion in Early Modern Europe* (Leiden, The Netherlands, 2007), pp. 97–113.
Wulf, Karin, *Not All Wives: Women of Colonial Philadelphia* (London, 2000).
——'Women and Families in Early (North) America and the Wider (Atlantic) World', *History Compass*, vol. 8, no. 3 (2010), pp. 238–247.
Zemon Davis, Natalie, *Women on the Margins: Three Seventeenth-Century Lives* (London, 1995).

UNPUBLISHED SOURCES AND PHD THESES

Alton, Edwin H., 'The Story of Marsden Meeting' (LRSF typescript, 1963).
Dixon, Simon, 'Quaker Communities in London, 1667–c. 1714', Royal Holloway, University of London (2005).
Plant, Helen, 'Gender and the Aristocracy of Dissent: A Comparative Study of the Beliefs, Status and Roles of Women in Quaker and Unitarian Communities, 1770–1830, with Particular Reference to Yorkshire', University of York (2000).
Ryan, Michele Denise, '"In My Hand for Lending": Quaker Women's Meetings in London, 1659–1700', University of California, Santa Cruz (2003). Consulted at Library of the Religious Society of Friends.

INDEX

Aberdeen Women's Meeting, 167–168
Affirmation Act, The (1695–96), 7
Akehurst, Mary, 38
Allestree, Richard, 84
American colonies, Quakerism in,
    48–49, 56, 89–91, 122, 130–132,
    138, 173–174, 176–177, 203,
    240–241, 257–258
  emigration to and growth of, 2,
    20–22, 39, 104, 107–108, 256–257
  enhanced authority of women,
    14–15, 102–103, 118–121
  organisation and structure of, 104–105
  preaching in, 10, 13, 60, 62, 73,
    190–191, 194–197, 235
  reformation of, 89–90, 255
  religious experimentalism, 244
American Indians, relations with, 20,
    203, 216–217, 233–234
American Revolution, 203, 255, 257–258
Andrews, Elizabeth (Farmer), 162, 227
Anglicanism. See Church of England
anti-Quaker writing and imagery, 6, 31, 39,
    51, 65, 204–22, 239, 247, 249–250
  against female preaching, 208–210,
    234, 236
  in the American colonies, 204–205,
    216–217
  links to other sectarian and dissenting
    movements, 214–215
  on Women's Meetings, 94, 114–115,
    220–222
  sexual slurs, 211–212, 218–219,
    221–222
  subversion of the family, 206, 212,
    218–219, 222
  witchcraft and demonic possession,
    213–214, 216
Aristotle, 156, 186n150, 188, 189
Articles of Visitation, 123
Ashbridge, Elizabeth (Sampson), 39, 191
Astell, Mary, 179, 245–246, 260
Athenian Mercury, The, 170
Audland, Anne (Camm), 5, 82, 167
Audland, John, 82, 188

Bacon, Francis, 45, 156, 186n150
Bacon, Margaret Hope, 9, 89, 102–103,
    120, 121
Ballitore Quaker School, Ireland,
    33–34, 228
Banks, John, 53
Baptists, 4, 168, 214, 244, 258
  history of, 16
  in North America, 16, 18, 99, 124
  women's authority and roles, 18, 70,
    91, 94, 99, 101, 124, 127
Barbados Women's Meeting,
    Caribbean, 1, 24
Barclay, Robert, 4, 48, 216
Barker, Mabel, 83–84
Barking Women's Meeting, London, 148
Barwick, Grace, 161–162
Bathurst, Ann, 17, 52
Bell, Deborah, 43, 192, 236
Bell, Mercy, 27–28, 134, 147, 163, 166, 173
Bellers, John, 231, 233
Besse, Joseph, 76, 229

Bevan, Barbara, 85
Bevan, John, 85
Bewley, George, 88
Bibliotheca Anti-Quakeriana, 206
Biddle, Esther, 162
Blaugdone, Barbara, 222
Boehm, Anthony William, 67, 248–249
Boles, Abigail. *See* Watson, Abigail
   (Boles)
Bosanquet, Mary. *See* Fletcher, Mary
   (Bosanquet)
Bourginon, Antoinette, 17, 208, 219
Bownas, Samuel, 42–43, 77, 188
Bowne, Hannah, 46, 51, 63–64
Bowne, John, 46, 51, 64
Bowne, Mary, 181
Box Meeting, London, 96, 116, 121,
   126–128, 135, 147, 167–168,
   193n182
Braithwaite, Elizabeth
   (Braytwhaite), 224
Bray, Alan, 48, 155–156, 171, 188, 194
Brissot de Warville, Jean Pierre, 21, 238,
   240–241
Bristol, 57, 66, 86, 94, 128,
   200–201, 231
Bristol Corporation of the Poor,
   231n124, 233
Bristol workhouse, 231–233
Brooksop, Joan, 58
Brown, Thomas, 219
Buckinghamshire, 179–181
Buckon, Rachel (Brecon), 241–243
Bunyan, John, 52, 80
Burlington Meeting, West Jersey,
   95, 150
   elders within, 134, 135, 142–143
   history of, 107–108
   partnership between Men's and
      Women's Meetings, 117
   tasks completed by Men's and
      Women's Meetings, 109–112,
      116–119, 129–131
Bush, Phyllis, 148

Callender, Hannah (Sansom), 140,
   173–175, 233, 244
Calvinism, 16–17, 164, 165, 198. *See
   also* Puritanism; Presbyterianism;
   and Pietism

Camm, Anne. *See* Audland,
   Anne (Camm)
Camm, John, 78, 188
Camm, Mabel, 78
Cannon, John, 200, 228, 229
Capp, Bernard, 37, 180–181
Caribbean. *See* Barbados Women's
   Meeting; Tortola Meeting
Catholicism
   anti-Catholic polemic, 207, 221
   hospitality, 195–197
   Quakerism compared to, 214
   women's authority and involvement
      in, 18, 98–99, 115, 127
celibacy, 52, 54–56, 71, 91, 188, 196,
   258. *See also* singleness
Chamber, Grace (Hall), 136
charity. *See* philanthropy
Charles II, King of Britain, 6, 8,
   38, 162
Cheevers, Sarah, 9, 19, 69, 183–185
Cheshire, 78, 144, 226
Chester Meeting, Pennsylvania, 95,
   102n38, 149–150
   elders within, 132–134, 140,
      142–143, 146
   history of, 107–108
   tasks completed by Men's and
      Women's Meetings, 48–49,
      109–115, 118, 119, 125,
      129–131, 137
children and youths, 14, 41, 144
   care of, 19, 50–52, 63–66,
      101–102
   See also education
Chubb, Sarah, 231–232. *See also* Bristol
   workhouse
Church of England, 123, 228
   marriage and courtship culture, 69,
      113, 115, 123
   women's authority within, 80, 84,
      125, 240
   See also Reformation, the
Cicero, 156, 248
Clarendon Code, The (1661–1665). *See*
   persecution of Quakers
Clarkson, Thomas, 15–16, 44, 87, 149,
   172, 245
Clayton, Anne, 162
Collier, Rebecca (Collins), 241–243

commerce and business, 66, 78, 124,
  230, 250
  women's involvement in, 79–81, 89,
    227–228
  See also Bristol workhouse; midwives
community, Quaker sense of, 5, 30–31,
  153–154, 160, 164–171, 173, 177–
  179, 197, 259. *See also* friendship;
  imagined community
Connaught, Ireland, 236
Connecticut. *See* New England
Conventicle Act, The (1664), 6, 75, 225
conversation, 157, 178
  epistolary, 93, 247–249
  for spiritual edification, 83, 152,
    166, 175
Cork, 39, 62, 93, 222
Cork Monthly Meeting, 107
Crawford, Patricia, 37, 71, 81, 84, 98,
  127, 159, 193, 203
Cross, Margaret, 180, 267–268
Cumbria. *See* Westmorland
Curwen, Alice, 44, 60, 71, 160–161

Dale, Elizabeth, 49–50
Danson, Thomas, 212
Darby, Abiah, 72
Darby, Deborah, 58
Davies, Richard, 46
De Crèvecoeur, J. Hector St John, 21,
  119–120, 176–177
De Montaigne, Michel, 45, 157
Dennis, Elizabeth, 53, 163
Dewsbury, William, 76
Dowell, Elizabeth, 86
Drinker, Elizabeth (Sandwith), 244
Drummond, May (Mary), 200–202,
  236–237, 239, 243, 245
Dublin Half-Year Meeting, 7, 93, 104,
  121, 138, 141, 238
Dublin Women's Meeting, 105n48,
  121, 141

Edinburgh, 191, 233, 236
Edmundson, Margaret, 76, 77
Edmundson, William, 76, 77, 79
education, 9, 84, 245
  female learning, 147, 179, 246
  of poor children, 231
  Quaker family, 41–43, 69–72, 83–90

Quaker schools and teachers, 42,
  228–229. *See also* Ballitore Quaker
  School, Ireland
  Quaker views on, 41–42, 91, 114,
    144, 254
Ellis, Alice, 81–82
Ellis, William, 81–82
endogamy. *See* marriage
England, Quakerism in, 104, 144, 202,
  231, 237
  population and growth of, 2, 21,
    106–107, 131
  preaching in, 57, 60, 73
  See also London, Quakerism in
English Civil Wars, 3, 16, 225, 226
Enlightenment, the, 242
  admiration of Quakerism, 21,
    240–249
  changing views on women, 12, 178,
    246, 248–250
Erasmus, Desiderius, 156
Evans, Katharine, 9, 19, 69–70,
  183–185
Exley, Catherine, 40

Fairfax Meeting, Virginia, 95,
  149, 150
  elders within, 141n176, 143, 145
  history of, 108
  tasks completed by Men's and
    Women's Meetings, 109–112, 117,
    119, 120, 126, 131–132
family, the. *See* household, the
Farmer, Priscilla, 27, 65, 163, 166, 173
Farmer, Ralph, 213
fatherhood, 19, 51, 87–88, 101–102.
  See also household, the
Fell, Margaret, 5, 9, 49, 56, 94, 116,
  160, 167
  founding of Meeting system, 7, 97
Fell, Sarah, 115n75, 135n152
Female Tatler, The, 220
Fenn, Jane. *See* Hoskins, Jane (Fenn)
Fifth Monarchists, 214–215, 225
Fisher, Mary, 6, 9
Fleming, Daniel, 227
Fletcher, Mary (Bosanquet), 54, 71,
  169, 196
Follows, Ruth, 51, 60, 65–66, 166,
  195n193

Forster, Mary
  These Several Papers (1659), 225–226
Fothergill, John, 87
Fothergill, Samuel, 168, 169, 193
Fothergill, Susanna, 193
Fox, George, 3–4, 5, 11, 29, 52, 53, 56,
  72, 223
  founding of Meeting system, 7,
    10, 20, 94, 96–97, 102. *See also*
    Quaker Meetings; Women's
    Meetings
  views on women, 84, 96, 97, 100,
    126–127
Friendly Association for Regaining and
  Preserving Peace with the Indians,
  217, 234
friendship
  colonial and British disparities,
    176–177
  definitions of, 153, 155–156,
    159–167
  distance, 31, 154, 155, 181,
    192–197, 199
  enemies and strangers, 160–163, 171,
    194–195
  gendered understandings of, 156–159,
    170–171, 187
  guidance on selecting a friend, 158, 190
  in classical texts, 156–157, 187–190
  in marriage and the family, 45,
    155–156
  inequality within, 189–190
  of Jonathan and David, 182,
    187, 188
  Quaker individualism and exclusivity,
    154, 162–164, 171, 174–175,
    180–182
  Quaker refutation of polite customs,
    154, 172–173, 176–177, 198
  reformulation of family bonds, 5,
    167–169, 254
  religious teachings on, 158–159, 161,
    171, 187, 194
  spiritual, 170–171, 182–189,
    193–194, 198
  universal, 160–163, 165–166, 201

Gentleman's Magazine, The, 200,
  245, 247
Gill, Catie, 11, 44, 59, 159n30, 185, 211

gossips, 179–181, 267–268. *See also*
  sociability
Gouge, William, 36, 37, 45, 47, 84, 87
Gowden, Grace, 176
Gratton, Anne, 61, 79
Gratton, John, 61, 79, 81
Greer, Mary, 86
Griffith, Alice, 137

Hall, Alice (Featherstone), 64–66, 210
Hallywell, Henry, 205
Hargreaves, Mary, 77
Harrison, James, 78
Haydock, Eleanor, 47
Hayes, Alice, 37–38, 234
Heemskerck, Egbert van, 209
Henshaw, Frances (Dodshon), 236, 237
Herbert, Amanda E., 158, 164, 185,
  186, 190, 191
Herbert, Ann More, 72
Higginson, Francis, 207
Hill, Richard, 48, 73
Hinds, Hilary, 8, 26, 58
Holme, Elizabeth, 56
Holme, Mary, 170
Hornor, Tabitha, 170, 194
Hoskins, Jane (Fenn), 133, 146, 183
hospitality, 194–197, 207, 235–236
  Quaker hosts, 185, 195–197
  women's involvement and authority
    in, 195–197, 259
household of faith, 24, 32, 92
household, the, 14, 15, 36
  and Atlantic history, 22, 24–25
  Quaker disruption to, 8, 19, 26,
    36–40, 52, 57–59, 61, 224
  Quaker women's authority within,
    14, 29–30, 34–35, 43–50, 68,
    79–91, 102, 245, 255
  and Quakerism, 29–30, 36,
    42, 52, 90
  as site of female empowerment, 18,
    41, 58–74, 245, 252, 254. *See also*
    Women's Meetings
  structure and ordering of, 36–38,
    40, 50–52
Hubberthorne, Richard, 160
Hudson, Elizabeth, 164, 187, 191
Hughes, Elizabeth, 78
Hume, David, 247–248

Hume, Sophia, 162, 230, 248
Hutchinson, Elizabeth, 41, 163

imagined community, 1, 5, 23–24, 31,
    151, 167, 193–194, 196, 252,
    257–258. *See also* friendship
integration of Quakers with non-
    Quakers, 39, 89–90, 202, 223–234,
    237–245, 247–249, 251, 254–255,
    259–260
  anxiety about, 122, 236–239
  See also toleration
Ireland, Quakerism in, 20, 33,
    75–76, 88
  Meeting and disciplinary structures,
    7, 104, 121, 125, 138
  Meetings as transatlantic hub, 107
  ministers, 13, 64, 70, 73, 195n193,
    210, 236, 263
  population, 21, 107, 131
  suffering, 39, 222
  See also Tipperary Meeting, Munster,
    Ireland

Jacob, Elizabeth, 50, 65
Johnson, Samuel, 165, 246–247

Keith, George, 163
Kendal Fund, 97. *See also* Fell,
    Margaret
Kendal Meeting, Westmorland, 72, 95,
    148, 149
  elders within, 136, 139, 143
  history of, 106–107
  lack of female authority in, 116, 121
  partnership between Men's and
    Women's Meetings, 117
  tasks completed by Men's and
    Women's Meetings, 109–116, 113,
    114, 115–116, 119, 123, 128,
    130, 144
Kent, Frances, 229
Knowles, Mary (Morris), 165–166,
    246–247

Lancashire, 77, 121, 128, 227, 236. *See
    also* Marsden Meeting, Lancashire
Lancaster Quarterly Meeting, 85, 115, 138
Lancaster, Lydia (Rawlinson), 144–145,
    168, 169

Langhorne, John, 218
Larson, Rebecca, 13, 24, 56, 64, 70,
    102, 202, 250
Lawrence, Anna M., 54, 71, 101, 103,
    168, 188, 206
Lead, Jane, 17, 55
Levy, Barry, 14, 22, 25, 35, 56, 83, 89,
    90, 102, 114, 137, 144, 240, 245
Lewis, Margaret, 57
Lincolnshire, 226
Lloyd, Elizabeth, 77
Lloyd, Grace, 132–134, 136, 146, 186
Lloyd, Mary, 65
Lloyd, Sarah, 168
Locke, John, 21, 241–243
Loddington, William, 100
Logan, Sarah, 85
London Women's Meeting, 1, 3, 10,
    19, 24, 56, 193, 233,
    252–253, 257
  elders of, 11, 28, 134, 147
  See also Box Meeting, London
London, Quakerism in, 1, 32n110, 42,
    79, 94, 107, 204, 230, 241
  Birth Notes, 179–181, 230,
    267–269
  ministers, 44–45, 61, 65, 72–73, 162,
    190, 241–244
  See also Yearly Meeting, London
Love, Christopher, 54, 80
Lovel, Edith, 62, 139
Lucas, Margaret, 39–40
Lupton, Donald, 208

Mack, Phyllis, 9, 11, 12, 47, 57, 66, 69,
    121, 153, 165, 171, 187, 208, 209,
    222, 258, 260
marriage
  between Quakers and non-Quakers,
    36–41, 49–50, 67–68, 86
  courtship, 46–49, 113–115
  domestic economy, 79–81
  female subjection within, 36–39,
    46–47, 207
  love, 43–49
  Quaker conception of, 33–34, 40–50,
    59, 63–66, 76–77, 113
  sexual passion, 48
  See also Quaker Meetings;
    household, the

Marsden Meeting, Lancashire, 77, 95, 130, 135n155, 149
  elders within, 139, 143, 144n182, 148
  history of, 106–107
  tasks completed by Men's and Women's Meetings, 109–112, 116, 119, 123, 124, 126–131, 137–138
Maryland Meeting, 193
masculinity, 19, 51–54, 61, 65–66, 126
  and Quaker friendship, 182–183, 188
Mather, Increase, 216
Mather, William, 94, 114
Meeting Houses, 15, 105–106, 116, 130, 151, 173
Metford, Jane, 228, 229
Methodism, 21, 214, 218, 240, 259
  anti-Methodist writing and imagery, 206, 210, 218, 221, 240
  friendship, 188–189
  in the American colonies, 103, 244
  marriage and the family, 40, 47, 54–55, 66, 168–169
  ministerial culture of, 54–56, 70–71, 91, 196, 197
  numbers of female converts and members, 18, 99, 244–245
  organisation of, 17, 100
  women's authority and involvement in, 17, 18, 52, 94, 99–101, 127, 151, 196
midwives, 181, 230, 267–269
Milton, John, 45
ministry, Quakers
  as a cause of domestic conflict, 37–39, 67–68
  balance with family life, 29–30, 34–35, 53–54, 62–64, 68–74, 81–83, 87–88, 183
  certificates for travel, 8, 11, 101
  dangers of travel, 19, 62, 69–70, 184–185, 191–192
  discipline of ministers, 236–237
  domestic support of, 64–66
  economic disruption caused by, 65–66, 79–81, 209–210
  enhanced domestic status of women, 69–70

female ministers, 8, 13–14, 19, 33, 34, 50–74, 144–146, 161–162, 182–192, 208–210, 234–239
  inter-generationalism, 72–73
  numbers of ministers, 13–14, 57n118, 263tA1.1
  reception from non-Quaker audiences, 200–201, 222, 234–239, 241–246, 251
  relationship with companions, 164, 182–192, 199
Mollineux, Mary, 152–153, 174–175, 177–178
More, Hannah, 173
Moravianism, 16, 52, 244
Morris, Anthony, 72, 87
Morris, Sarah, 135n152, 146, 166, 166n63
Morris, Susanna, 73, 185, 197
Mother in Israel, 36, 69–71, 86, 91, 100–102
motherhood, 70–71, 91–92, 168–169, 254
  grandmothers, 64–65
  influence on Quaker ministry, 42–43, 59–74
  Quaker conception of, 9, 14, 40–43, 83–90, 101, 102, 167–168
  See also household, the
Mucklow, William, 114

Nayler, James, 5–6, 211
New England, Quakerism in, 56, 124n106, 202, 235, 241
  Nantucket, 89, 120, 176–177
  opposition to, 216–217, 222–223
New Garden Meeting, Pennsylvania, 122, 139n172, 142
New Jersey. *See* Burlington Meeting, West Jersey
Niesen, Geertruyd Deriks, 83
nonconformity, 80, 164–165, 175, 203, 232, 249
non-itinerant Quaker women, 3, 22, 25, 29, 35, 91, 140, 203, 252, 254, 259
  admiration for, 86–87, 90, 197
  impact of suffering on, 80–83
  See also hospitality; Women's Meetings
Norris, Elizabeth, 146, 187
Norton, John, 216

oath swearing, 7, 78, 228–230, 255
Old Bailey presentments, 226–227
Owen, Frances, 174–175, 178
Oxfordshire
  Banbury, 78, 167

Payton, Catherine (Phillips), 55, 61,
  182–183, 186, 190, 191, 195, 235
Pearson, Jane, 61, 62
Peisley, Mary (Neale), 163, 183,
  186–187, 189, 191, 195, 235
Pemberton, Israel, 195, 217
Pemberton, Mary, 62, 185, 193,
  196–197
Pemberton, Phebe, 89, 181
Pemberton, Rachel, 86, 133, 175, 195
Penn, William, 20–22, 45, 46, 76,
  165, 178n110, 216, 242. *See also*
  Pennsylvania
Pennsylvania, 16, 18, 62, 204, 233–234,
  244, 252
  as a source of admiration, 240–241
  Delaware Valley, 114
  foundation of, 20
  'Holy Experiment', 20–22, 203,
    240–241
  Quaker population and settlement in,
    20, 107, 108
  Quakerism in, 22, 26–27, 73, 85, 89,
    120, 132–133, 146, 194, 203, 217,
    238. *See also* Chester Meeting,
    Pennsylvania
Pennsylvania Hospital, 233
persecution of Quakers, 5–8, 31, 121,
  160–161
  anti-Quaker legislation, 6, 68, 75
  during American Revolution,
    203, 255
  female suffering, 39, 74–79, 167,
    184–185, 201, 211, 222–223, 229
  impact on family, 60, 74–81, 91
  non-Quaker sympathy for sufferers,
    224–225, 250
  Quaker response to, 5–7, 96–97,
    128, 231
Philadelphia, 20, 86, 101–102, 133,
  138, 145–146, 163, 173–174, 194,
  195, 230, 233, 238
Philadelphia Almshouse, 233
Philadelphia workhouse, 233

Philadelphian Society, the, 16, 52,
  55, 244
philanthropy, 126–130, 147–148,
  231–234, 250. *See also* Kendal
  Fund; Bristol workhouse
Phillips, Catherine. *See* Payton,
  Catherine (Phillips)
Phillips, Katherine, 157
Pickworth, Henry, 220
Pietism, 16–17, 44, 91, 258, 259
  women's authority and involvement
    in, 52, 55, 151, 244
  See also Philadelphian Society, the;
    Moravianism
Pike, Elizabeth (Pim), 88
Pike, Joseph, 43
Pocock, Elizabeth, 79
Presbyterianism, 15, 54, 80. *See also*
  Savage, Sarah (Henry)
prophecy, 9, 17, 52, 187, 243
  decline in Quakerism, 11–12, 98, 253
  reactions to, 208, 212, 214, 222
  temporal balance, 29, 57, 62, 223
  See also ministry, Quakers
Protestant ethic, the, 232
Protestantism. *See* Church of England
providence, 67, 162–163, 182,
  189–192, 199
Public Friend. *See* ministry, Quakers
Puritanism, 85, 216, 259
  household order, 37, 40, 41,
    50, 87, 90
  marriage and courtship culture,
    45–47, 69, 113

Quaker Meetings, 22, 106–108, 246,
  256–258
  as extension of family, 101–102,
    144, 150
  discipline procedure, 117n80
  establishment and structure of, 7–8,
    10–11, 20, 97, 104–105
  for worship, 4, 14, 105, 175, 241–243
  marriage discipline procedure, 113–115
  roles within, 105, 134–140, 253–254
  writing culture of, 27, 28, 35,
    86, 219. *See also* transatlantic
    exchange
  written query process, 123–124
  See also Women's Meetings

Quakerism
  apparel and plainness testimonies,
    137–138, 172, 177, 219–220, 232,
    238, 250
  early radicalism, 5–6, 9, 98,
    210–212, 216
  growth of, 4, 256
  inner light, 4, 7, 34, 37, 41, 44, 48,
    54, 161, 201, 212, 242
  nomenclature, 5, 7, 153–154,
    160, 198
  peace testimony, 20, 203, 217, 255
  second and third generation. *See* sect
    to church transition
  theology, 3–5, 34, 40–41, 154,
    172–173, 175
Quakers Act, The (1695–96). *See*
  Affirmation Act, The (1695–96)
quietism/quietist, 9–10, 13, 83, 90, 162,
  198, 202, 223, 231. *See also* sect to
  church transition

Raper, Abigail, 134, 135n151
Reformation, the
  impact on women, 15, 36–37, 84,
    98–99, 245
  Marian martyrs, 74, 78
Restoration, the, 6, 41, 59, 68, 80, 96, 216
Rhode Island. *See* New England
Rievaulx, Aelred of, 161
Ryan, Sarah, 66, 71, 169, 188–189

Sacheverell, Henry, 161
Sansom, Samuel, 45, 115n74
Savage, Sarah (Henry), 164
Scotland, Quakerism in, 21, 67, 167,
  191–192, 233
Second Day Morning Meeting, 8, 11
sect to church transition, 2, 11, 95, 100,
  163, 216, 231, 251–253
  emphasis on the family, 35, 41, 71,
    87, 144, 260
  Quaker isolationism, 201, 223
  Quaker Meeting system, 10, 95,
    97, 253
sensibility, 17, 157–158. *See also*
  friendship; sociability
separation of spheres, 10, 12–13, 15,
  18, 98–99, 170, 254. *See also*
  household, the

Shackleton, Elizabeth (Carleton),
  23, 33–35, 136, 197, 228–229,
  247–248
Shackleton, Richard, 33–34, 88, 136,
  139, 163, 228
Shepard, Alexandra, 51, 80, 188
Shropshire, 162, 227
Simmonds, Martha, 9, 211
singleness, 49, 54–56, 58, 168–169, 189
  Quaker Meeting elders, 135,
    145–146
Smith, Joseph. *See Bibliotheca
  Anti-Quakeriana*
sociability, 152–154, 157–158, 172,
  188, 192. *See also* friendship
  as a distraction, 175–177
  social visiting, 173–174, 176–177,
    179–182, 238
  Women's Meetings as space for, 95,
    151, 153, 167–168, 173–175,
    178–179, 192–193, 257–259
Society of Friends. *See* Quakerism
sociology of deviance and deviant
    behaviour, 202, 249
Stirredge, Elizabeth, 8, 9, 19, 225
Story, Ann (Shippen), 59, 81, 88
Story, Bridget, 100–101
Story, Thomas, 59, 81, 88, 136,
  182–184, 191
Stout, William, 227
suffering, experience of. *See* persecution
  of Quakers

Tadmor, Naomi, 36, 155, 159–160
Taylor, Jeremy, 45, 156, 161, 170, 188
Taylor, Mary (Batt), 74–76
Taylor, Sarah, 166
Teresa of Avila, Saint, 98, 164, 245
Thomas Aquinas, Saint, 161
Thomas, Keith V., 37, 50, 186, 189, 192
Tipperary Meeting, Munster, Ireland,
  93, 95, 149
  elders within, 139, 143, 147–149
  history of, 107
  tasks completed by Men's and
    Women's Meetings, 109–112, 119,
    123, 125, 126, 129
tithes, 6, 60, 76, 77, 80–81, 128,
  225–226
toleration, 203, 254–255

in the American colonies, 122, 203,
204, 240
of Quakerism, 6–7, 31–32, 224–227
Quaker attempts to secure, 68,
97, 165
See also Toleration Act, The (1689);
Affirmation Act, The (1695–96)
Toleration Act, The (1689), 6, 32, 75, 83,
131, 201, 202, 204, 223, 225, 254
Tortola Meeting, Caribbean, 93, 118
Townsend, Theophila, 83
transatlantic exchange, 22–25, 32, 153,
192–193, 255–260
letters and epistles, 1–2, 30–31, 35,
41–42, 151, 192–193, 257
Quaker ministers, 19–20, 30, 73,
192–194, 196–197, 199
See also friendship; imagined
community
Trapnel, Hannah (Anna), 214–215
Travers, Rebecca, 11
Trevett, Christine, 9, 35, 56, 98

Underhill, Thomas, 212
United States. *See* American colonies,
Quakerism in
Upcott, Anne, 224

Venner, Thomas, 214–215
Verney, Edmund, 229
Virginia. *See* Fairfax Meeting, Virginia
Vokins, Joan, 27, 58–59, 69–71, 94,
172, 185, 190
Voltaire, François-Marie Arouet, 21,
237, 241

Wales, Quakerism in, 78, 85
Walker, William, 206–207
Wardell, Deborah, 101
Warder, Ann, 176, 233–234, 238
Watson, Abigail (Boles), 62, 72–73,
186, 190, 194
Waugh, Dorothy, 39
Webb, Elizabeth, 67, 248–249
Weber, Max, 2n4, 95, 141
Wesley, John, 54, 245. *See also* Methodism
Wesley, Susanna, 245
Westmorland, 80, 97, 106–107, 121,
128, 227. *See also* Kendal Meeting,
Westmorland

Weston, Daniel, 51, 194
Weston, Mary, 51, 60, 62–63, 133,
154, 185–187, 189, 190, 194, 196,
197, 235
Whitall, Ann, 89–90, 140
White, Mary, 214
Whitefield, George, 210, 218
Whitehead, George, 160
Whitton, Catharine, 144
Wigham, Mabel, 70
Wilkinson-Story schism, 94, 114, 121
Wilson, Rachel, 190
Wilson, Thomas, 53
Winstanley, William
Yea and Nay Almanac, 210, 211, 222
Women's Meetings, 1, 14, 19, 26, 30,
32, 85–86, 92, 173, 250
authority within, 102–103, 114–115,
117–118, 124–125, 131–132,
140–151
collaboration with Men's Meetings,
97, 125, 149
disparities between colonial and
British Meetings, 119–122, 150,
177, 255, 256
establishment of, 10–11, 94–98
impact on women's visibility within the
movement, 10–11, 30, 97, 98–101,
121, 127, 149–151, 252–253
opposition to, 94–95, 114–115,
220–222. *See also*
Wilkinson-Story schism
responsibilities of, 10, 108–132,
136–139, 264–266
roles within, 132–149. *See also*
Mother in Israel
structure and organisation of, 14–15,
104–108, 132
Woolley, Hannah, 158
Worrell, Sarah, 73
Wright, Anne, 38–39, 67–68
writing
account books, 103, 128, 227
almanacs, 62–63, 210
circulation and distribution of
printed materials, 26–27, 178,
204–205
diaries and diarists, 6, 26, 89, 140,
173–174, 176, 200, 228, 233,
238, 244

writing (*cont.*)
  letters, epistles and correspondence,
    1–2, 7, 26–28, 35, 62, 67, 82, 93,
    123, 133, 179, 192–194, 247–248,
    252, 257. *See also* transatlantic
    exchange
  memorials, 28, 53, 77–79, 86–87, 90,
    132–133, 136, 163
  poetry, 152–153, 173, 177–178
  Quaker literacy and numeracy, 134,
    135, 146, 147
  Quaker Meeting records, 26, 30, 93–94,
    105, 134, 142–144, 179, 230
  Quaker suffering literature, 74–76,
    222–225. *See also* persecution of
    Quakers, 229

spiritual autobiographies, journals
  and memoirs, 25–27, 33, 42–43,
  59–64, 71–72, 182–183, 191–192,
  235–236
Wynn, Deborah, 79, 224–225

Yarnall, Alice, 137
Yearly Meeting, London, 7, 13, 42, 61,
  84, 93, 105, 172
  establishment of Women's Meeting,
  105, 120–121
Yearly Meeting, Philadelphia, 105n47,
  107–108
  Women's Meeting, 120–121,
  133, 146
Yorkshire, 72, 79, 81–82, 196

CPSIA information can be obtained
at www.ICGtesting.com
Printed in the USA
LVHW052032131220
674083LV00008B/154

9 781316 649626